FOREST FUTURES

Science, Politics, and Policy for the Next Century

Edited by
Karen Arabas and Joe Bowersox

ROWMAN & LITTLEFIELD PUBLISHERS, INC.
Lanham • Boulder • New York • Toronto • Oxford

ROWMAN & LITTLEFIELD PUBLISHERS, INC.

Published in the United States of America
by Rowman & Littlefield Publishers, Inc.
A wholly owned subsidiary of The Rowman & Littlefield Publishing Group, Inc.
4501 Forbes Boulevard, Suite 200, Lanham, Maryland 20706
www.rowmanlittlefield.com

PO Box 317
Oxford
OX2 9RU, UK

British Library Cataloguing in Publication Information Available

Library of Congress Cataloging-in-Publication Data

Forest Futures: Science, Politics, and Policy for the Next Century /
edited by Karen Arabas and Joe Bowersox.
    p. cm.
Includes bibliographical references and index.
    ISBN 0-7425-3134-1 (hardcover : alk. paper)—ISBN 0-7425-3135-X
(pbk.: alk. paper)
    1. Forests and forestry—Northwest, Pacific. 2. Sustainable
forestry—Northwest, Pacific. 3. Forest policy—Northwest, Pacific. 4.
Forest management—Northwest, Pacific. I. Arabas, Karen, 1962– II.
Bowersox, Joe, 1963–
    SD144.A13F67 2003
    634.9'09795—dc22

                                                                                          2003015000

Printed in the United States of America

∞™ The paper used in this publication meets the minimum requirements of
American National Standard for Information Sciences—Permanence of Paper
for Printed Library Materials, ANSI/NISO Z39.48-1992.

For Julia and Corwin
and the forests in their future

Contents

Figures and Tables

Figures

Tables

Acronyms

ACS   Aquatic Conservation Strategy
AMA   Adaptive Management Areas
ATFS   American Tree Farmers System
AWA   Administratively Withdrawn Areas
BA   Biological Assessment
BiOp   Biological Opinion
BLM   Bureau of Land Management
CESU   Cooperative Ecosystem Studies Units
C.F.R.   Code of Federal Regulations
CIRES   Cooperative Institute for Research in the Environ-
          mental Sciences
CRCs   conservation rental contracts
CSA   Canadian Standards Association
EIS   Environmental Impact Statement
EMP   Effectiveness Monitoring Plan
EPA   Environmental Protection Agency
ESA   Endangered Species Act
FCR   Forest Community Research
FEMAT   Forest Ecosystem Management Assessment Team
FLPMA   Federal Land Policy and Management Act

FR	Federal Register
FS	Forest Service (same as USFS)
FSC	Forest Stewardship Council
FWS	Fish and Wildlife Service
GAO	General Accounting Office
GEA	Global Environmental Assessment
GPNF	Gifford Pinchot National Forest
GIS	geographic information system
GMOs	genetically modified organisms
ha	hectare
HFRA	Healthy Forests Restoration Act
ICBEMP	Interior Columbia Basin Ecosystem Management Plan
IPCC	Intergovernmental Panel on Climate Change
ISC	Interagency Scientific Committee
ISO	International Standards Organization
LEI	Lembaga Ekolabe Indonesia
LRMP	Land and Resource Management Plan
LS/OG	Late Successional/Old-Growth
LSRs	Late-Successional Reserves
MCPFE	Ministerial Conference for the Protection of Forests in Europe
MIS	management indicator species
MLA	Mineral Leasing Act
MTCC	Malaysian Timber Certification Council
MUSYA	Multiple-Use Sustained Yield Act
NAPA	National Academy of Public Administration
NEPA	National Environmental Policy Act
NFMA	National Forest Management Act
NFS	National Forest System
NMFS	National Marine Fisheries Service
NOAA	National Oceanic and Atmospheric Administration
NPS	National Park Service
NRC	National Research Council
NWFP	Northwest Forest Plan
NSO	northern spotted owl
NWI	National Wilderness Institute
OCSLA	Outer Continental Shelf Lands Act

ODF	Oregon Department of Forestry
OFRI	Oregon Forest Resources Institute
OG	old growth
ORS	Oregon Revised Statutes
PEAC	Pacific Environmental Advocacy Center
PEFC	Pan European Forest Certification
PNW	Pacific Northwest
RFF	Resources for the Future
ROD	Record of Decision
RR	Riparian Reserves
SB	Senate Bill
SAF	Society of American Foresters
SAT	Scientific Assessment Team
SEIS	Supplemental Environmental Impact Statement
SFI	Sustainable Forestry Initiative
U.N.	United Nations
U.S.C.	United States Code
USDA	United States Department of Agriculture
USDI	United States Department of the Interior
USFS	United States Forest Service
VRHS	variable retention harvest system
WG	Working Group
WGA	Western Governors' Association
WUI	wildland-urban interface

Legislation

Department of Interior and Related Agencies Appropriation Act of 2001. Public Law (P.L.) 106–291

Endangered Species Act of 1973, 16 U.S.C. 1531–1544 (1994)

Federal Land Policy and Management Act of 1976, 43 U.S.C. 1701 et seq.

Federal Water Pollution Control Act of 1972, 33 U.S.C. 1151 et seq.

Healthy Forests Restoration Act of 2003, H.R. (House Resolution) 1904–108th Congress

Marine Mammal Protection Act of 1972, 16 U.S.C. 1371 et seq.

McSweeny–McNary Act of 1928, 16 U.S.C. 581, 581a, 581b–581i

Mineral Leasing Act for Acquired Lands of 1947, 30 U.S.C. 351 et seq.

Multiple Use and Sustained Yield Act of 1960, 16 U.S.C. 528–531

National Environmental Policy Act of 1969, 42 U.S.C. 4321–4347d (1994 & Supp. III 1997)

National Forest Management Act of 1976, 16 U.S.C. 472a, 521b, 1600, 1611–1614 (1994 & Supp. III 1997)

Oregon Forest Practices Act, ORS 527.660

Oregon Forestland–Urban Interface Fire Protection Act of 1997, ORS 477.031

Organic Administration Act of 1897, 16 U.S.C. 475

Outer Continental Shelf Lands Act of 1953, 43 U.S.C. 1331–1356

Renewable Resources Planning Act of 1974, 16 U.S.C. 1600 et seq.

Wilderness Act of 1964, 16 U.S.C. 1131 et seq.

Foreword

The Northwest Forest Plan represents the most extensive change in forest management policy since passage of the Wilderness Act of 1964. The great difference, of course, is that while the Wilderness Act was implemented directly by the Congress, the Forest Plan was initiated by a federal judge in the form of an injunction that shut down logging operations on every national forest in the Pacific Northwest.

Judge Dwyer's injunction, handed down a year in advance of the 1992 presidential election, provided our incoming administration an unprecedented opportunity to demonstrate newly emerging concepts of forest ecosystem management and restoration. In April of 1993 the president launched our effort with a day-long town hall meeting in Portland, Oregon. We followed up with a crash planning effort and blitzed the media in every crossroads in the Cascades. In July, President Clinton signed the Forest Plan Directive.

The two distinctive features of the Plan were its geographic scale and the extent of species coverage. The Plan covered the entire Cascades ecosystem, more than 9.7 million hectares (24 million acres) of federal forest lands stretching from Puget

Sound clear down to San Francisco Bay. It was land-use planning on a scale without precedent.

The Plan also made a comprehensive assessment, not just of the spotted owl and the marbled murrelet but of several hundred other species—fungi, reptiles, amphibians, plants, fish, birds, and other mammals characteristic of the old-growth forest ecosystem. It was a monumental undertaking that in turn revolutionized administration of the Endangered Species Act, ensuring that henceforth habitat conservation plans would move away from single species toward habitat-based multispecies plans.

Today, with ten years of on-the-ground experience, it is time for a careful retrospective look at successes and failures, at lessons learned, and directions for the future. In the intervening ten years scientific studies have brought forth a great deal of new information, all contributing to a better understanding of the complexities of these forest ecosystems. Researchers have deepened our understanding of forests as dynamic, continually changing systems, constantly affected by both small and catastrophic events. We have learned a lot about the interaction between streams and their watersheds, embodied in a concept called watershed analysis. And the onset of a new cycle of catastrophic wildfire has taken us into contentious and unresolved issues of forest health.

In the beginning we knew there would have to be a sharp reduction in the amount of timber cut in order to preserve these forest systems. The appropriate level of reduction was in dispute then, and it continues to be to this day. The chapters in this volume examine all these issues, bringing to bear much of the knowledge and insights that have accumulated since 1993. As will be apparent to the reader, many of the controversies continue within the covers of this volume, proving once again that forest management is an inexact science that necessarily incorporates the changing needs and desires of the owners of these magnificent places—the American people.

Bruce Babbitt

Acknowledgments

We express our thanks to the following people, whose collaboration on this volume was essential to its completion: Allisa Jones and Laura Leete of the Willamette University Public Policy Research Center, and Chris Gramlich at Willamette University's Instructional Design Center for logistical and technical support; our students Jenny Andrews, Aaron Lien, and Kaitlin Marousis for research assistance; Tori Haring-Smith for her encouragement; Keith Hadley for his advice; our editor Brian Romer for his enthusiasm and belief in the project; The American Political Science Association Congressional Fellowship Program; The Dempsey Foundation and the Hewlett Foundation, without whose generous support this project would not have been possible.

And finally, we are most grateful to our families for their support and patience.

Introduction: Natural and Human History of Pacific Northwest Forests

Karen Arabas and Joe Bowersox

For the last ten years in federal forest policy, the management term of choice has been ecosystem management. Whether the area of concern is the forested regions of New England, the desert Southwest, the Sierra Nevadas, or the interior West, the concepts explicit and implicit in ecosystem management—landscape scale assessment and monitoring, adaptive management, holism, research/management partnerships—are now often addressed with this comprehensive management paradigm (Johnson et al. 1999a).

At its inception, ecosystem management suggested that multiple objectives (i.e., protection of biological diversity, improvement of critical habitat, commodity production, etc.) could be simultaneously achieved with scientifically rigorous and adaptive management, which supplemented existing management structures and guidelines with new organizational processes and standards. As the Clinton administration sought to address an ongoing political crisis in forest management in 1993 and 1994, scientists and policy makers seized the opportunity and launched the first large-scale effort of ecosystem management.

The result was the Northwest Forest Plan (NWFP), covering 9.7 million hectares (24 million acres) of federal forests in Washington, Oregon, and California. This book is an attempt to assess the accomplishments of the NWFP, and to evaluate its impact upon federal forest management more generally. To give this assessment some context, we begin by examining the ecological and social landscapes of the region the Plan encompasses.

Ecology of the Pacific Northwest Forests

When we ask our students to compile a list of terms describing the forests Euro-American settlers found when they reached the Pacific Northwest (PNW), they invariably include adjectives like *majestic, towering, huge, ancient,* and *stable.* And who, having viewed old photographs and settler's descriptions, would disagree? Within the context of the ecological development of PNW forests, however, two important points should be made. The first is the complexity in *pattern* of PNW forest vegetation. Prior to Euro-American settlement, the forested landscape was characterized by a mosaic of age classes, structures, and species rather than a sea of old-growth Douglas fir. Second, and key to understanding these patterns, are the *processes* that have shaped and continue to shape these forests. Far from being stable and self-perpetuating, PNW forests were wrought and continue to evolve in a dynamic, disturbance-ridden environment driven primarily by climate, vegetation, and fire interactions (see Whitlock et al. 2003). Furthermore, human action has significantly altered natural patterns and processes. As Whitlock and Knox (2002) note, "Logging, farming, grazing, mining, and fire elimination in the last century have altered vegetation and fire regimes on a regional scale more than any other event in the last 11,000 years" (224).

Historic Forest Patterns

One of the striking features of the PNW forest is its trademark conifers. These coniferous forests have a rather short (when compared to tropical forests) though fascinating evolutionary history that is, unfortunately, beyond the scope of this introduction (see Detling 1968, Wolfe 1968, Waring and Franklin 1979, Whitlock 1992). Suffice it to say that 65 to 13 million years ago, northerly and southerly regional geofloras (the Arcto Tertiary and Madro Tertiary) evolved into the modern vegetation types of the PNW (Detling 1968). The conifer forests we know today are adapted to climate conditions with wet, mild winters and hot, arid summers. Because photosynthesis is limited by lack of water, hardwoods are stressed during the growing season (summer). This gives a competitive advantage to conifers, which maintain their leaves (needles) year round and thus can grow in the winter months when water is available (Waring and Franklin 1979, Perry 1994). As a result, conifers dominate the PNW landscape.

Superimposed onto *large-scale* regional climatic patterns, the physical geography of the PNW provides a template for *smaller-scale* forest variation and diversity. Over a transect from west to east, both topographic and edaphic (soil) characteristics influence forest composition in the PNW.[1] Intercepting Pacific Ocean moisture, the forests of PNW coastal mountains have fairly well developed, moderately deep soils (Franklin and Dyrness 1988) and harbor the mixed-conifer forests that are the focus of the NWFP—Sitka spruce (*Picea sitchensis*), western hemlock (*Tsuga heterophylla*), and Douglas fir (*Pseudotsuga menziesii*), as well as a variety of hardwoods. The interior valleys lying in the lee of the Coast Range are the warmest and driest areas west of the crest of the Cascades (Franklin and Dyrness 1988). Though they contain a wide range of soils, the climate controls species composition: the valleys historically supported oak woodlands and prairie. Rising 5,000 feet from the east side of the valley floor, the Cascades wring out any remaining moisture. A variety of soil types—generally well developed and moderately deep—support mixed conifer forests—Douglas fir, western hemlock, and western red cedar (*Thuja plicata*), with Pacific silver fir (*Abies amabilis*) and noble fir (*Abies procera*) occurring at higher elevations. At cooler, wetter, and higher elevations are the subalpine forests—mountain hemlock (*Tsuga mertensiana*), subalpine fir (*Abies lasiocarpa*), and lodgepole pine (*Pinus contorta*). Air masses depleted of moisture warm as they descend the east flank of the Cascades, flow into the

Intermontane region, host to ponderosa pine (*Pinus ponderosa*) forests and juniper (*Juniperus occidentalis*) woodlands occupying the driest sites, with grand fir (*Abies grandis*) and Douglas-fir forests favoring more mesic (moist) sites (Franklin and Dyrness 1988). Though this description is necessarily broad and paints a somewhat homogeneous picture of PNW forests, variation and patchiness exist within each of these forest types as a result of topographic, edaphic, and climatic heterogeneity. (For more detail, see Franklin and Dyrness 1988, Loy et al. 2001.)

Processes

The mosaic of PNW forests shaped by these climatic, topographic, and edaphic patterns is made more dynamic by two critical processes: biotic interactions and disturbance. Biotic interactions refer to relationships of individual organisms, populations, and species to one another, and include population dynamics, competition, and mutualism. Disturbances are processes that affect forest composition, structure, and function. Natural agents of disturbance include fire, wind, pathogens, and insects. Human-induced disturbances include logging, mining, farming, and road building. Both disturbances and biotic interactions are implicated in forest succession in which forest community composition, structure, and function change over time.

The biotic interactions among organisms of PNW forests take place within the larger context of the other PNW ecosystems, the North American landscape, and the entire biosphere. Many of these interactions take place between two species: for instance, the mutualistic relationship between fungi and plant roots (mycorrhizae) expands the nutrient- and water-gathering ability of the plant while feeding the fungus; competition for light resources controls occurrence of Douglas fir and western hemlock; and predator-prey interactions create continual feedback regulating population levels. Beyond these typical examples is another set of complicated "higher-order interactions" (Perry 1994) that take place among more than two species. For example, keystone species are considered to have such a wide variety of interactions within an ecosystem that loss of a keystone may result in further disruptions and even extinctions throughout the ecosystem. This concept is known as a trophic cascade (MacDonald 2003), and it can be extended to groups of species (e.g., decomposers), habitats (e.g., dead wood), and abiotic processes (e.g., fire). The complexity that evolves from these ecosystem interactions creates a dynamic stability that can persist for centuries.

Disturbance patterns are also complex, but several important characteristics can be noted here. First, disturbances in a given forest ecosystem occur along a continuum of spatial and temporal scales ranging from large, infrequent disturbances (e.g., stand-replacing fires) to smaller, more frequent ones (e.g., single tree-gap creation). Second, the disturbance regime of a given forest ecosystem is complex, and may involve a variety of different disturbance agents acting across a range of spatial and temporal scales (e.g., drought may promote insect outbreak; windfall can trigger insect attack; and both increase fuel loads, resulting in stand-replacing fire). Third, disturbances result from interrelated factors occurring at each scale, and thus must be considered in their larger context. For example, disturbance affecting a forest stand will likely have a cause-and-effect relationship with adjacent stands. Finally, we tend to think of disturbances as processes that generate new patterns on the landscape (for example, stand-replacing fires that result in even-aged stands). However, we must also consider the potential for landscape patterns to influence disturbance processes (i.e., stands with low fuel loads may not burn; see Turner 1989, Perry 1994, Romme 1982).

PNW forests are subject to a variety of natural disturbances including wind, insects, pathogens, and fire. Central to an understanding of the region, however, is the role fire has played. Historically wildfire has been a major disturbance agent in PNW forests: its ecological role includes thinning stands, preparing seedbeds, reducing fuels, reducing competition, creating wildlife habitat, and influencing carbon, nutrient, and water cycling (Agee 1993, Barnes et al. 1998). The ecological impacts of fire vary depending on the fire regime, and fire regimes show spatial and temporal differences throughout PNW forests (Whitlock and

Knox 2002, Whitlock et al. 2003). Coastal and subalpine forests have longer intervals between fires (greater than 300 years), and when fire does occur, it is usually severe (Agee 1993). The mixed-conifer Coast Range fire regime is characterized by both high- and low-severity fires. Fahnestock and Agee (1983) estimate mean fire return intervals for the region at 230 years, noting extensive temporal and spatial variability. In drier portions of the western Cascades, Morrison and Swanson (1990) found higher fire frequencies (ca. 100 years). In the drier east-side forests, frequent light surface fires (1–25 years) characterized pre–Euro-American settlement (Agee 1993).

The response of forests to fire depends on fire frequency and severity. Regardless of severity, fires (like most disturbances) tend to interrupt the successional pathway a forest would take in the absence of disturbance. For example, in the absence of disturbance a stand of Douglas fir eventually will be replaced by the "steady-state" western hemlock because of hemlock's shade tolerance and ability to reproduce in the understory. When fire is introduced at 300- to 600-year intervals, light-tolerant Douglas fir will establish in fire-generated gaps, resulting in a patchy, mixed forest of western hemlock and Douglas fir. If fire frequency increases to 200–300 years, an open canopy will be maintained, favoring light-tolerant Douglas fir (Huff 1984).

On the east side of the Cascades, pre–Euro-American fire frequencies of 10–25 years were characterized by low-intensity fires that maintained open stands of ponderosa pine by killing competing vegetation and encouraging ponderosa pine regeneration (Agee 1993). Historical stands show clear spatial and temporal patterns: wide age ranges with clusters or patches of similar-aged trees across the landscape represent a variety of disturbance intervals (Morrow 1985).

The Forest Landscape of the Twenty-First Century

The forest landscape of the twenty-first century coevolved over millennia with the complex patterns and processes briefly outlined earlier. Although humans have been added to the scene only relatively recently, there is sufficient concern about the impacts of our use of forests. Within the past few decades research has demonstrated that our extractive activities may directly and indirectly affect forest ecosystem health (see Franklin and Forman 1987).

On the simplest level, timber extraction since Euro-American settlement has reduced the amount of old-growth forest in the PNW (see Perry, this volume). In the Oregon Coast Range, for example, old growth was estimated at 61 percent prior to the fires of the 1840s (Ripple 1994). Others (Teensma et al. 1991) estimate 40 percent old growth in 1850, dropping to 16 percent in 1890, with current coverage ranging from 5 to 16 percent (Bolsinger and Waddell 1993, Congalton et al. 1993). The regional landscape west of the Cascades is currently dominated by young stands of Douglas fir, a commercially valuable species.

More importantly, our extractive activities and associated land-use practices have altered the natural dynamics of these forests. Logging on short rotations (i.e., 40–70 years) arrests successional processes and can decrease forest health by depleting soil nutrients and promoting pathogens such as laminated root rot. Fire exclusion and suppression eliminate a natural disturbance from the landscape, causing increased competition and tree mortality, an increased probability of insect and pathogen outbreaks, and shifts in forest structure and composition. Decreases in what might potentially be keystone habitat may result in trophic cascading. Political schemes to manage the landscape impose a static organization on a landscape exemplified by dynamism. But to better understand how and why these ecological changes to the landscape have come about, one must examine the social, political, and economic context of Euro-American settlement.

Contributing Factors and Patterns of Human and Natural Resource Exploitation

The forests of the Pacific Northwest have long been subject to significant human impacts. Over the course of several thousand years of regional habitation, the Native Americans of the PNW developed rather sophisticated management techniques—most often utilizing fire—to alter the forest landscape to retain prairies, improve wildlife habitat, and encourage production of root and rhizome foodstuffs like camas. Some even suggest that such large-scale human disturbances may have been a factor in the establishment and maintenance of the ponderosa pine forests east of the Cascades. Nevertheless, these Native American impacts tended to be confined by natural ecological factors (Whitlock and Knox 2002).

With the advent of Euro-American settlement in the PNW in the early 1800s, several forces inhibited the more traditional Euro-American pattern of forest exploitation in which forests were transformed to agriculture (Williams 1992). These factors included the region's early geographic and economic isolation, the landscape and climate, and national politics. However, three things—gold, gasoline, and global war—eventually created the conditions for greater, more aggressive forest exploitation.

From the beginning, exploitation posed particular challenges previously not encountered in North America. In part this was due to the motivations of the earliest arrivals, mainly French Canadian, British, and American fur trappers. These trappers sought riches and economic gain not in the forests themselves, but in the beavers and other fur-bearing animals inhabiting them. Furthermore, as Williams (1992) notes, the nature of the forested landscape itself inhibited early ventures by more sedentary settlers in forest-related commerce. The trees were so large, the soils so poor, and the markets so distant that the traditional pattern of clearing the forest, selling the timber, burning the stumps (for marketable potash), and converting the land base to farmland simply made no economic sense. Hence, until the late 1840s, exploitation of the region's forests was essentially limited to subsistence uses of fuel wood and local construction.

Gold—and the San Francisco Market

The discovery of gold at Sutter's Mill in 1848 changed the dynamic, by creating both the capital and the market necessary to sustain commercial logging throughout the region. The overnight transformation of San Francisco from a sleepy pueblo to the bustling center of the California gold rush required a tremendous influx of raw materials to fuel the construction boom. However, the landscape again dictated the patterns and processes of exploitation, for the forested areas of Northern California, Oregon, and Washington were comprised of difficult terrain, rapid, shallow streams, and few natural ports. Such physical features made the transport of logs extremely difficult and cost intensive (Robbins 1988). Thus, in the early decades of commercial harvesting in the PNW, logging was primarily confined to the tidewater areas along the coast, in places like Coos Bay and Puget Sound. Raw logs or finished product were shipped by sea to the lumber-hungry gold fields of California and the burgeoning metropolis of San Francisco. Early operations were often vertically integrated, with the logging camps, mills, and ships all owned by the same entrepreneur. Many of these timber barons came to the West from the Northeast or the Midwest, lured by significant and sustainable profits in the San Francisco timber trade (Williams 1992, Robbins 1997, Robbins 1988). Given the geographic isolation of the PNW from the rest of the nation, San Francisco continued to dominate the regional timber market well into the twentieth century. Early secondary markets included Japan, New Zealand, and even Australia, since it was simply more cost effective to trade in the Western Pacific than in the rest of North America (Robbins 1997, Robbins 1988, Haynes 2003).

Unlike exploitation and ownership patterns in the rest of the continental United States, it was clear from the beginning in the Pacific Northwest that the federal government would play a major role in determining the nature and scale of forest utilization. This was largely because the federal government was the principal landowner: what lands the federal government did not cede to states, counties, municipal governments, railroads, or private individuals, it retained. This federal predominance, however, was only partly by design. Originally, Congress and its duly appointed land agents had planned to divest the federal government of most of its lands (Clawson 1983, Wilkinson 1992). Yet, despite the best efforts of the government land offices to legally (or even illegally) sell or give land to various parties, by the late 1800s the federal government found that for much of the land under its control there were no willing buyers, or even outright takers. To this day the federal government is the single largest landowner in Oregon, Washington, and California, holding title to 48 percent of those three states (Clawson 1983, NWI 1995).

Exploitation of the tidewater lands and other easily accessible areas throughout the region was so severe that by the late 1800s local and regional authorities were contributing to national arguments for the proper stewardship of the nation's forests (Pinchot 1947, Wilkinson 1992, Robbins 1988, Williams 1992). In 1891, Congress authorized creation of forest reserves from lands still in the public domain. In the next seven years, President Cleveland established over 16.2 million hectares (40 million acres) of forest reserves, administered by the Department of Interior's General Land Office. Many of these reserves were located in the Pacific Northwest. For instance, in 1893 Cleveland established the mammoth Cascade Forest Reserve, a thirty-mile-wide swath of forest along the crest of the Cascade Mountains, from the Columbia River to the California border. In 1897, Cleveland created similar (albeit smaller) reserves in the Cascades and Sierras of Washington and Northern California. President Theodore Roosevelt added extensively to these early reserves, and in response to evidence of mismanagement and graft, control was transferred to the newly created U.S. Forest Service within the U.S. Department of Agriculture in 1905 (Clawson 1983, Pinchot 1947, USFS n.d.).[2] Through the years additions and subtractions from these federal forest lands have occurred; today, federal forest lands in Oregon, Washington, and Northern California encompass 15.2 million hectares (37.6 million acres) on thirty-seven administrative units.[3]

Technological Innovations

Even as state and federal authorities sought means to safeguard and conserve forest lands for future use, the region's logging and lumber barons employed technology to press farther into the virgin forests, away from the cutover bays, estuaries, and riverbanks. Operators found it harder to get to where the trees were. Thus, they expended labor and capital to construct skid roads, dig canals, and build short-line railroads. Steam engines and steam donkeys replaced ox and horse teams for transporting logs and lumber to rivers and bay fronts (Robbins 1988, Robbins 1997, Yaffee 1994). But three twentieth-century logging innovations—the gas-powered chain saw, the bulldozer, and the log truck—were critical to expansion of the wood products industry in the region. Bulldozers could construct skid and logging roads on terrain previously inaccessible, while chain saws allowed two or three workers to harvest in a day what previously had taken a crew a week. Log trucks could negotiate temporary roads and inexpensively and rapidly deliver logs to mills and ports. These innovations made the PNW the single largest producer of forest products in the nation by the 1920s (Robbins 1988, Wilkinson 1992, Robbins 1997).

Though private industry was harvesting with abandon—prior to World War II, little harvesting occurred on federal forest lands in the PNW—federal forest management activities focused primarily on preventing and suppressing fires and on conserving timber resources for future exploitation. Indeed, political pressure kept federal harvest rates to a minimum, since volume off public lands would compete with and depress the price of private timber. Prior to 1930, total federal harvest rates never reached 2 billion board feet a year (see Yaffee 1994, Clawson 1983, Wilkinson 1992). But by the 1930s private timber operations were in dire straits: their forests were severely depleted, and with the onslaught of global depression many forest landowners simply abandoned their lands rather than pay delinquent taxes. Mill and logging operations throughout the region met a similar fate (Robbins 1988, Robbins 1997).[4]

World War II and Beyond

Thus, with the outbreak of war in 1941, the federal government was forced to fill the timber void. In fact, World War II signaled the beginning of the golden age of lumber in the region: the war effort required billions of board feet of timber for everything from training barracks to torpedo boats. By order of President Roosevelt, the federal government subsidized lucrative harvest contracts on federal lands in order to meet wartime demands. Throughout the region mills reopened after receiving assurances of long-term, noncompetitive federal purchase contracts. In effect, timber production was so important the government signaled it was willing to subsidize it without consideration of cost. The industry expanded accordingly (Robbins 1997, Wilkinson 1992, Hubbard 2000).

The importance of wood for the war effort also led to fire suppression policies that have had long-lasting economic and ecological consequences. During World War II, wildfire was considered a domestic enemy ready to sabotage a vital industry. Federal officials quickly developed a quasi-military, fire-fighting organization to which it devoted extensive personnel and resources. To this day, the gung-ho nature of the federal fire-fighting community is legendary, replete with "heli-tack" crews, air-tanker retardant bombers, smoke-jumper units, and traditional "ground-pounders" in hand-to-hand combat on the fire lines (Herron 2001). The mentality has been further reinforced by the repeated use of air and army National Guard units in suppression efforts. Fire suppression now can cost the federal government over $2.2 billion a year (USFS 2003a).

World War II initiated other dynamics that reshaped the industry and the region: the influx of workers to emerging industrial centers like Portland and Seattle, coupled with improved surface transportation, assured that market demand for the region's timber would no longer remain at the mercy of San Francisco. As the nation returned to a peacetime economy in the late 1940s, the federal government continued to expand its harvest rates on public lands to meet homebuilding and paper needs. This in turn fostered industry dependence on cheap federal timber, and public forest managers quickly learned that professional advancement depended on "getting the cut out." By the 1950s, Oregon, Washington, and Northern California accounted for over 50 percent of the forest products produced in the nation. By the 1980s, nearly 10 billion board feet of timber per year were coming off federal forest lands—6 billion board feet from Oregon and Washington alone (Warren 2002). Because of cheap federal timber and smaller stabilized private harvests, the Pacific Northwest would retain national market dominance until the spotted owl wars of the 1980s (Yaffee 1994, Wilkinson 1992, Hubbard 2000, Robbins 1997, Robbins 1988, Clawson 1983, see also Beuter, this volume; see figure I.1).

While the management mandates for federal forest managers were altered in the 1960s and 1970s to include other functions like recreation, wildlife management, and conservation of biological diversity,[5] emphasis remained on commodity production: though the official doctrine was "multiple use," timber was *primus inter pares* (Wilkinson 1992, Yaffee 1994). Given timber's dominant status, the geographic and economic primacy of federal lands became the focal point of controversy as endangered species issues emerged in the 1980s. The NWFP threatened to

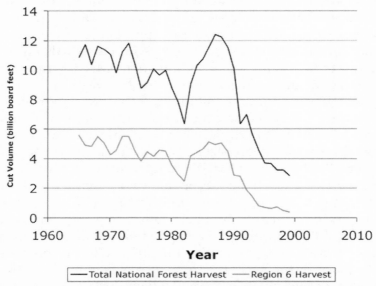

Figure I.1.   National Forest Timber Harvests for All National Forests and for Region 6 (Oregon and Washington), 1965–1999. Note low point in early 1980s due to recession followed by a period of accelerated harvests during the Reagan and Bush I administrations. (Sources: Warren 2002, Prestemon and Abt 2002.)

constrict the public timber pipeline—with consequent political, economic, and social effects on rural communities dependent upon cheap federal supplies. But the NWFP also purposefully privileged habitat protection on public lands to spare additional impacts on private holdings (Yaffee 1994). What many might call a Faustian bargain had been struck.

Understanding the Primacy of Politics

While it is easy to see the central role that politics has played in recent management decisions regarding our federal forests, it is important to recognize that all along, politics has been as ubiquitous a contemporary feature on the forest landscape as the trees themselves. This phenomenon is simply an artifact of 1848: the forests were seen as a storehouse for a valuable commodity that, with effort, could be transformed into individual and social wealth. As gatekeeper to this vast wealth, the federal government soon became the dominant political arena for forest politics. Early politics centered on utilizing forest land as an enticement for settlement and economic development, as the federal government issued land grants to individuals and corporations to foster creation of a population base and transportation infrastructure sufficient to secure the vast lands of the Oregon, Washington, and California territories to the nation. Whether these were 160-acre tracts granted to individual settlers under the original Homestead Act of 1862 or vast grants to railroads (like the 3.1 million hectare [7.7 million acres] ceded to the Northern Pacific Line in the Washington territory alone), such grants were a critical tool for economic and political integration, and the impetus for much graft and corruption (Clawson 1983, Ficken 1987). In turn, such policies ultimately transformed the region's political landscape, leading to political domination first by the railroads, then the timber industry, while also producing radical labor and political reform movements in the early twentieth century (Bowersox in press, Robbins 1988).

Beginning in the mid-twentieth century, a limited set of political actors controlled federal forest policy, with the federal land management agencies the center of attention, since in the postwar period the U.S. Forest Service (USFS) (and to a lesser extent the Bureau of Land Management [BLM]) was in an enviable position of controlling a coveted resource. A tightly organized "policy subsystem" comprised of regional members of Congress serving on committees with public forest jurisdiction, agency officials, and regional forest industry interests crafted public forest policies for mutual benefit: industry achieved access to cheap trees, agencies received bigger budgets and congressional and clientele support, and politicians claimed credit and were reelected (Burnett and Davis 2002, Clarke and McCool 1996). For at least two decades this subsystem stirred little conflict or controversy, satisfying the appetite of a wood-hungry nation—but at the price of fragmenting vital ecosystems. Though no longer as dominant and certainly no longer uncontroversial as it was in the 1950s and 1960s, the importance of this policy subsystem and the distributive benefits it provides can still be seen today. For instance, recent hazardous fuels reduction policies beneficial to industry exemplify the staying power of this collection of interests (see Bowersox, this volume).

By all accounts, the social, economic, and political legacy of this forest policy subsystem is enormous. Simply consider the importance of timber to the regional economy, which until the spotted owl wars of the 1980s employed over 135,000 personnel in Oregon and Washington alone (Warren 2002). But it would be incorrect to argue that timber provided stable communities. As Robbins (1988) notes, since the late 1800s the region's timber economy has seen repeating "boom" and "bust" cycles, as market demand fluctuated based upon larger national and international economic events. Furthermore, while forest-industry job losses have been routinely blamed upon the decline in federal timber supplies resulting from the NWFP, the real story is much more complicated. Much of the displacement stems from technological innovation, as mills and logging operations modernized in the 1970s and 1980s. For instance, between 1980 and 1989, total regional harvest levels actually *increased 23 percent,* though total forest-related employment *declined 6.25 percent* (Warren 2002, Robbins 1988).

As the 1990s dawned, Northwest forests became the setting for a national controversy: a small avian predator, the northern spotted owl (NSO) (*Strix occidentalis caurina*), was listed as threatened under the Endangered Species Act (ESA). The inability to either resolve or contain the conflict contributed to the electoral defeat of an incumbent president. Faced with additional evidence of declining forest health, including the listing of other forest-dependent species like the marbled murrelet (*Brachyramphus marmoratus*) and certain anadromous fish, a new administration acted quickly to address the political crisis. Ten years later, the pathbreaking management plan crafted to address forest health, endangered species, and economic concerns remains at the heart of national debates over forest management (see Mapes 2003). The chapters of this book—each independently assessing the NWFP from a different perspective—give testimony to the Plan's unique and problematic legacy.

Organization of This Volume

Forest Futures provides an opportunity to examine contemporary issues of forest policy and ecology in light of one of the most controversial developments in federal forest policy since fire suppression. Though "only" covering federal forest lands within the range of the northern spotted owl (essentially all national forests and BLM districts west of the Cascades in Northern California, Oregon, and Washington—9.7 million hectares [24 million acres] in all), the NWFP affects some of the most commercially productive forests in the continental United States. Furthermore, the Plan started from scratch regarding the organization and processes necessary for achieving multiple management objectives, including safeguarding biological resources, protecting ecosystem services, and addressing the economic needs of human communities. New land designations with specific standards and guidelines were created, and processes initiated to assure that managers, scientists, and stakeholders cooperated to achieve the Plan's goals. Additional supplementary programs (i.e., the Northwest Economic Adjustment Initiative) were created to assist communities and individuals in transition. At the time, policy makers and managers knew that they were embarking into new territory: no one was sure what the consequences would be. This book may be viewed as a partial and provisional assessment of the NWFP's strengths, weaknesses, and prospects for survival.

Forest Futures is organized around three basic themes relevant to the NWFP: sustainability, the role of science in policy making, and endangered species. In the first three parts, the reader will find chapters by experts with extensive experience in the subject matter, as well as a final commentary chapter, meant to reflect upon and to promote thoughtful debate about the issues raised in the chapters. The fourth part of the volume looks beyond the NWFP, asking the questions: What have we learned? and What next?

Part I, "What Is Sustainable Forestry?" addresses one of the fundamental if implicit goals of the NWFP. Policy makers sought a fragile balance between biological restoration of a fragmented ecosystem and the needs of human communities and individuals long dependent upon extraction of commodities from that ecosystem. The first four chapters of part I are authored by individuals intimately involved in the origins, creation, and evaluation of the Plan. Jack Ward Thomas was lead scientist on several of the early assessments of the northern spotted owl, and chaired the task force charged with constructing the NWFP—the Forest Ecosystem Management Assessment Team (FEMAT). Thomas also served as chief of the USFS from 1993 until 1996. In chapter 1, Thomas provides an account of the scientific objectives and political compromises of the NWFP, and he discusses ongoing issues regarding its implementation. Dave Perry, a prominent forest ecologist and expert on PNW forest ecosystems, has been a thoughtful scientific contributor to discussions regarding the NWFP's construction and implementation. In chapter 2, Perry shares his views regarding the scientific assumptions of the Plan's interpretation of adaptive ecosystem management. In 1991 and 1992, during the height of the "spotted owl wars," John Beuter was acting Assistant Secretary for Agriculture, U.S. Department of Agriculture, overseeing the

USFS in the Bush I administration. In chapter 3, Dr. Beuter judges the Plan's capacity to produce a sustainable and viable level of commodity production, and assesses the Plan's economic consequences for the region. Roger Sedjo is Senior Fellow with Resources for the Future and a member of the Committee of Scientists assigned the role of assessing the Plan in the late 1990s. In chapter 4, Sedjo provides insight regarding alternative means of certifying the environmental impact of forest products harvested from public or private lands. Finally, in chapter 5, Bob Pepperman Taylor provides a thoughtful and lively discussion of the ambiguity of terms like *sustainability*, and encourages us to pursue more fundamental deliberation over the normative values implicit in forest policy generally and the Pacific Northwest Forest Plan specifically.

Part II, "Science and Policy Making," investigates the increasingly fuzzy intersection between science, the practitioners of science, and management paradigms and practices. In part II, these four chapters are authored by individuals who have devoted much of their professional lives to examining the science–policy nexus both as academics and policy practitioners. In chapter 6, Ronald Mitchell, a political scientist with expertise in international environmental policy, and his coauthors investigate the ways in which science has been successfully incorporated into global environmental issues and asks to what extent this has occurred with the NWFP. In particular, they focus on cooperation among scientists, policy makers, managers, and stakeholders and the ability to bridge boundaries among them through the NWFP. In chapter 7, Fred Swanson examines the specific roles scientists have played in forest policy and management in the PNW. Drawing on his experience studying interactions of physical disturbance processes with forest and stream ecosystems, and his role in FEMAT, Dr. Swanson discusses how various worldviews of scientists, and the public's perception of those scientists, present challenges for integrating science and policy. In chapter 8, law professor and public interest lawyer Dan Rohlf, whose teaching, scholarship, and advocacy center on conservation of biological diversity, uses the NWFP as an example of how science may be used and misused in resource planning, management, and policy making. In chapter 9, Roger Pielke weaves themes from the three chapters into a thought-provoking chapter on the differences between "policy" (a decision) and "politics" (the process by which a decision is made). It is critical, he cautions, to distinguish between the two so that we may use science in its most appropriate context.

Part III, "Considering Threatened and Endangered Species," focuses on what has been one of the most contentious issues in PNW forest management, endangered species. Chapters 10 through 12 represent three disparate perspectives on endangered species management: biology, law, and economics. Chapter 10 provides a demographic overview of the most famous endangered resident of Pacific Northwest forests, the NSO. Dr. Steven H. Ackers, a wildlife biologist, details current population trends of the NSO in the Central Cascades of Oregon. He contends that scientific and political uncertainty may together bring about NSO extinction. In chapter 11, Susan Jane Brown, a lawyer representing various environmental groups that have sued under the NWFP, examines the importance of scale and scope in the biological assessments utilized to evaluate agency compliance with the ESA. Brown suggests that scale and scope issues fundamentally affect whether actions such as harvest activities or road building are perceived as causing harm to a listed species. Dr. Richard Stroup, an economist with the Center for Free Market Environmentalism, argues in chapter 12 that as seen in the battle over protection of the NSO, the ESA produces perverse incentives for public and private land managers. These perverse incentives may motivate destruction of habitat rather than its preservation. Stroup suggests market-based incentives, such as conservation easements, may do a better job of preserving species and protecting property rights. Finally, in chapter 13 we turn to philosopher Peter List to tie the chapters together, commenting on the values and attitudes underlying human relationships to forests and forest management.

Part IV, "Forest Futures and Present Challenges: Beyond the Northwest Forest Plan" examines the future of the NWFP under the Bush II administration and beyond. In chapter 14 former governor of Oregon John Kitzhaber draws on his experience with the Western Governors' Association, demonstrating successes in sustainable forestry management in the Blue Mountains of Oregon. Kitzhaber critiques the Bush II administration's shift in support of such management toward its own "Healthy Forests" strategy. In chapter 15, political scientist Joe Bowersox invokes ecological theory to examine the politics of wildfire in Congress and its impact upon regional and national forest policy. Chapter 16 is a retrospective look at the NWFP and future policy challenges, by Margaret Shannon. Shannon, a member of the Committee of Scientists and FEMAT, uses modernism and postmodernism as analogies to passive and adaptive management approaches, and in explaining why our modern institutional structures failed to properly implement FEMAT. Finally, Joe Bowersox and Karen Arabas discuss emergent issues in forest policy in the wake of the NWFP, and suggest some tentative steps for more fully realizing the goals of ecosystem management.

Notes

1. Soil characteristics important to vegetation include water retention and availability, nutrient availability, pH, and organic matter.

2. Federal forest lands in the Pacific Northwest also include tracts in Oregon and Washington managed by the Department of Interior Bureau of Land Management (BLM). Originally lands granted in the 1860s to railroad and toll road companies, these were reclaimed and reconveyed to the federal government in 1916 (Clawson 1983).

3. These consist of twenty-seven national forests in Oregon, Washington, and California, and ten Oregon and Washington BLM districts.

4. Sometimes these abandoned lands eventually found their way back to public ownership. Oregon's 146,000-hectare (364,000-acre) Tillamook State Forest is the result of abandoned private lands (see Wells 1999).

5. See especially, the Multiple Use Sustained Yield Act (1960), the National Environmental Policy Act (1969), the Endangered Species Act (1973), the National Forest Management Act (1976), and the Federal Land Policy and Management Act (1976).

I
WHAT IS
SUSTAINABLE FORESTRY?

1

Sustainability of the Northwest Forest Plan: Still to Be Tested

Jack Ward Thomas

Any discussion of "sustainability" related to the Northwest Forest Plan (NWFP) must begin with some understanding of the history related to the development and execution (or lack thereof) of the NWFP. The NWFP was driven by the need to meet the requirements of the Endangered Species Act (ESA) of 1973 and the "viability clause" of the Forest Service's (FS) regulations issued pursuant to the National Forest Management Act of 1976. The primary mention of "sustainability" of production of outputs from the national forests occurs in the Multiple-Use Sustained Yield Act (MUSYA) of 1960, which broadened the FS's mandate to include outdoor recreation, range, and wildlife in addition to the timber supply and watershed protection concerns expressed in the Organic Administration Act of 1897. "Sustained yield" was defined as "the achievement and maintenance in perpetuity of a high-level annual or regular output of the various natural resources of the National Forests without impairment of the productivity of the land." By the late 1980s, a series of federal court decisions had made it clear that compliance with these legal requirements of later-passed laws and regulations (specifically those of the ESA) overrode those directions.

The basic work underlying the NWFP was produced by the Forest Ecosystem Management Assessment Team (FEMAT) established by President Clinton through the auspices of the Forest Conference Executive Committee, composed of ten department and agency heads. In their direction to FEMAT, they quoted President Clinton's observations made at the conclusion of the Forest Summit held in Portland, Oregon, in the spring of 1993 to guide FEMAT's activities, and directed FEMAT to:

1. Consider human and economic dimensions of the problem solution;
2. Protect the long-term health of forests, wildlife, and waterways;
3. Put forth efforts that are scientifically sound, ecologically credible, and legally responsible;
4. Produce a predictable and sustainable level of timber sales and non-timber resources that will not degrade the environment; and
5. Employ and emphasize collaboration in management as opposed to confrontation. (FEMAT 1993)

In addition, FEMAT (1993) was instructed to minimize impacts on non-federal land, make suggestions for adaptive management; examine silvicultural management to achieve objectives; use an ecosystem management approach; and apply the "viability standard" from the FS's planning regulations (65 FR 67514) to Bureau of Land Management (BLM) lands.

More specific directives were given regarding the central goal of addressing biological diversity. FEMAT (1993) was instructed to maintain and restore habitat conditions for the northern spotted owl (NSO) (*Strix occidentalis caurina*) and the marbled murrelet (*Brachyramphus marmoratum*); maintain and restore habitat conditions to support viable populations, well distributed across current ranges, of all species known or reasonably expected to be associated with old-growth habitat conditions; maintain and/or restore spawning and rearing habitat to support recovery and maintenance of viable populations of anadromous fish species and other fish species considered "sensitive" or "at risk" on federal lands;

and maintain or create a connected, interactive, old-growth forest ecosystem on federal lands. No planning and assessment team dealing with forest management, before or since, has been handed a more complex and daunting series of tasks. In addition, this "mission impossible" was to be accomplished in sixty days (later expanded to ninety days).

In short, when dealing with the habitat of a threatened species designated by the U.S. Fish and Wildlife Service (FWS) or the National Marine Fisheries Service (NMFS), the paramount concern with sustainability focuses on those species, no matter what the odds of success. Other concerns, such as sustainability of timber production, moved to a subordinate position. As a result, a sustainable yield of wood products was but one desired outcome of the NWFP. But, if there were slippage in meeting projections of timber outputs, it would have to be accepted before the welfare of the threatened species was negatively affected, or other goals of effort left unmet. That is, any "slack" of mandated outputs that existed for FEMAT was in the form of timber yields. Consistent reluctance to come to grips with the realities of the ESA resulted in ongoing and dramatic declines in the anticipated timber yields as continued cutting of old-growth forests reduced management options due to the combination of habitat loss and coincidental fragmentation of remaining old-growth habitat.

My purpose in this chapter is to lay out the circumstances that led to the development of the NWFP. I then describe the circumstances that have resulted in the failure of the NWFP to meet expectations for the production of forecast timber volume. I conclude with recommendations for alterations in the current management approach.

Management History of the Pacific Northwest Forests

Tracing the management history of the federal forests in the Pacific Northwest (PNW), since 1973, is a painful, embarrassing, and agonizing story of reluctance of the government to comply with the ESA and the "viability clause." Consider the stated purpose of the ESA. "The purposes of this Act are to provide a means whereby the *ecosystems* (emphasis added) upon which endangered species and threatened species may be conserved, (and) to provide a program for the conservation of such endangered species and threatened species. . . ." Add to that the requirements of the "viability clause" of the FS's planning regulations (which have the force of law), which read, "Viable populations of all native, and desirable non-native vertebrates, will be maintained well-distributed within the planning area" (36 CRF ch. II; 7-1-91 Edition, 219.19). That requirement, which by order of President Clinton was applied to all federal lands within the purview of the NWFP, was even more constraining than the ESA. It was clear by the mid-1980s, at least to some, that the situation would come to crisis over the issue of old-growth forests.

By the mid-1980s, most of the old-growth forests on private land had been logged, and cutting of old growth had shifted to the federal lands and continued apace. The idea was to take up the slack in national timber supply and maintain the timber industry in the Pacific Northwest until timber again became available from the private land cut over prior to 1980 (see Beuter, this volume). On the surface this was a scheme that made absolute sense from the commercial forestry, economic, employment, and therefore, political point of view. However, almost totally unforeseen by land-management agency leadership and political operatives, concern over rapid diminution and fragmentation of old growth was rapidly growing in an environmental community that was exploding in numbers and influence. The beauty and venerable age of old-growth forests allowed for considerable hyperbole in debate (e.g., "old trees some of which were alive at the birth of Christ, etc."), and given its rapid diminution, it would have been difficult to find a better cause and a better poster child for the growing environmental legions.

By the late 1980s, evidence was building that the NSO was closely associated with old-growth forests and declining in numbers as old growth was inexorably cut and habitat coincidentally fragmented (Thomas et al. 1990). The handwriting was on the wall, and professionals in the FS and the FWS knew it. However, several efforts internal to the FS to address the looming problem were ordered terminated by agency officials when social, economic, and political costs were considered too great to face by politically appointed overseers. Oddly, anticipated costs at that time were to prove a tiny fraction of what would finally ensue. There is a lesson here. In matters of coming to grips with the requirements of the ESA it is likely to be much less costly to act quickly than to delay, because options rapidly disappear and make more draconian responses necessary in the end.

Interagency Scientific Committee

By 1989, it was clear that the northern spotted owl was to be listed as "threatened" and resistance to that inevitability was increasingly embarrassing and less legally tenable. The heads of the FS (Dale Robertson), FWS (John Turner), BLM (Cyrus Jamison), and the National Park Service (James Ridenour) named a select team of biologists, the Interagency Scientific Committee (ISC), to devise a management strategy for the northern spotted owl. Team members were Jack Ward Thomas (Chairman), Eric Forsman, Barry Noon, and Jared Verner of the FS, E. Charles Meslow of the FWS, and Joseph Lint of the BLM. The ISC warned that the old-growth ecosystem was the developing issue and not the survival of a subspecies of owl. To the ISC, focus on a single subspecies (though legally required) seemed shortsighted, yet their mandate did not change.

By instruction from the four agency heads, the ISC was to confine its prescriptions to public lands. This political decision was to carry through all successive proposals and plans. Adverse economic impacts were to be absorbed on public lands, and constraints on private lands were to be avoided. That decision may not have been the best ecological solution, but it was politically and economically astute. Private landowners got off cheap relative to what would have been an optimal ecological solution.

The ISC report (Thomas et al. 1990) established a baseline premise upon which all subsequent planning efforts were based. Clearly, any biologically viable and legally defensible plan to sustain old growth and northern spotted owls would have to begin with forests in old-growth condition and containing owls. This was made necessary by the simple fact that it can take hundreds of years for stands to reach the age and structural conditions typical of old growth. And, because old-growth stands would decline in amount over longer time frames due to stochastic stand-replacing events (e.g., fire, blowdown, etc.), it would be necessary to plan for replacement stands appropriately distributed over the landscape. It was also critical to consider amounts, sizing, and spacing of stands over very long time frames.

Almost simultaneously with the release of the ISC report, the northern spotted owl was listed as threatened. At first, all involved agencies accepted the ISC strategy. Then, BLM's director Cyrus Jamison, with the approval of Secretary of Interior Manual Lujan, withdrew BLM lands from the strategy in favor of another approach, which was promised but never definitively described. Legal challenges quickly followed, and U.S. District Court Judge William Dwyer issued an injunction against any further cutting of old growth on federal lands within the range of the northern spotted owl. What seemed an astute political maneuver by the BLM turned out to be an economic, legal, and political disaster. In his decision, Judge Dwyer instructed the government to answer two questions. First, would BLM's withdrawal render the ISC strategy unlikely to preserve the northern spotted owl? Second, what would be the effect on the viability of thirty-four other species ISC had noted as likely associated with old growth? (*Seattle Audubon Society v. Lyons*, 1994). The second question was prescient. Judge Dwyer obviously understood the purpose of the ESA relative to preserving ecosystems upon which threatened species depended.

Scientific Assessment Team

The Scientific Assessment Team (SAT), chaired by Dr. Jack Ward Thomas of the FS, was assigned to answer those questions (Thomas et al. 1993). The SAT believed that the number of species strongly associated with old growth greatly exceeded the thirty-four species so far identified and recommended an attempt to address Judge Dwyer's underlying question.

Agency administrators agreed (Thomas et al. 1993). The answer to the first question was that it was impossible to discern what the BLM alternative entailed. The answer to the second identified at least 312 plants, 149 invertebrates, 112 stocks of anadromous fish, 4 resident fish, and 90 terrestrial vertebrates likely associated with old growth (Thomas et al. 1993). In other words, the northern spotted owl was but the tip of the iceberg related to threatened species and old growth. It was a question of ecosystems and had been since enactment of the ESA in 1973, seventeen years before. It has now been thirty years, and some still do not have the message.

Enter the "God Squad"

Cyrus Jamison, BLM's director, with the support of the Secretary of Interior, Manual Lujan, hung tough and appealed to the Endangered Species Committee (the so-called God Squad) established by the ESA (16 U.S.C. 1536(e)–(h)) to determine if the economic, social, and political costs of preserving a threatened species were unbearable enough to accept extinction of the species or subspecies in question. In this case, the fate of forty-four timber sales in old-growth forests was pitted against survival of the northern spotted owl. The Endangered Species Committee is composed of the Secretary of the Interior (who is also chair), chairman of the Council of Economic Advisors, administrator of the Environmental Protection Agency, administrator of the National Oceanic and Atmospheric Administration, secretary of the army, and one representative from each affected state. The high-ranking political appointees who made up the God Squad flinched and, in a politically driven and humiliating "split the baby" decision, approved a handful of sales with the proviso that BLM would, thereafter, comply with the ISC strategy (Thomas et al. 1993). Reluctant to accept the strategy, the G. H. Bush administration deferred action until after the presidential election of 1992. In the meantime, the ISC and its report were put "on trial" internal to the administrative branch and subjected to several additional outside reviews. Both the ISC and its work survived unscathed, save for political pounding (Thomas et al. 1993).

The Gang of Four and the Presidential Election 1992

The House Agriculture Committee gave up on the Bush administration to facilitate and accept a solution and decided to attempt a legislative solution. Chairman Kika De La Garza of Texas named a four-person committee—pejoratively tagged "The Gang of Four" by a timber industry spokesman—to develop management options for federal forests within the range of the northern spotted owl for consideration by Congress. The Gang (which was enlarged to six to deal with fisheries issues) was charged with assessing the socioeconomic consequences of each alternative developed. Members included Drs. John Gordon of Yale, Jerry Franklin of the University of Washington, K. Norman Johnson of Oregon State University, and Jack Ward Thomas, James Sedell, and Gordon Reeves of the FS. The chairman of the Forestry Subcommittee of the House Committee on Agriculture, Harold Volkmer of Missouri, also warned the Gang not to let them "get surprised by some damned fish." The playing field was, once again, enlarged: the Gang delivered some forty options. In the end, the House Agriculture Committee deemed the issue "too hot to handle" and deferred it until after the presidential election.

The issue of the northern spotted owl and protection of old growth on public lands were issues in the 1992 presidential campaign. Candidates President George H. W. Bush and H. Ross Perot took a "jobs vs. owls" approach with a promise to revise the constraining laws following their election. Candidate Governor William Clinton took no clearly definable position but promised a solution to the impasse shortly after taking office. In the spring of 1993, President Clinton convened the Forest Summit in Portland, Oregon.

Forest Ecosystem Management Assessment Team (FEMAT)

At the close of the Forest Summit, President Clinton named yet another select team, this time including economists and social and political scientists along with the veterans of earlier efforts from the ranks of wildlife, fisheries, and conservation biologists. Foresters, geographic information system (GIS) specialists, cartographers, ecologists, botanists, entomologists, and other specialists were also included. The team was dubbed the Forest Ecosystem Management Assessment Team (FMAT), chaired by Jack Ward Thomas, and given sixty days (later expanded to ninety days) to deliver management alternatives, with full assessment of each, to the president for his consideration (see the introduction to this chapter for the specific tasks assigned). By this time, various runs of salmon (which brought the NMFS into the game) and the marbled murrelet (another vertebrate species associated with late-successional forests) had been declared to be "threatened" and had to be addressed in assessment and planning activities. The Agriculture Committee's admonition to the ISC team not to "let us get surprised by some damn fish" had proven prescient.

Analyses conducted by the FEMAT (1993) roughly mirrored the earlier efforts of the SAT (Thomas et al. 1993) in that over 1,000 species of plants and animals were suspected to be closely associated with late-successional forest conditions. Again, it was clear that it was the late-successional forest ecosystem that was threatened. The northern spotted owl, the marbled murrelet, and anadromous fish were but the tip of the threatened species iceberg. The FEMAT delivered ten options to the president. President Clinton selected Option 9, which can be described as a dynamic plan formulated around aggressive and active management. Elements of Option 9 included designation of Late-Successional Reserves (LSRs), streamside buffers, and Adaptive Management Areas (AMAs). Late-Successional Reserves, forty-five in number, were located across the landscape as allowed by the presence of significant amounts of old growth on federal lands. These reserves ranged from 3,200 to 85,000 hectares (8,000 to 136,000 acres) and averaged 26,700 hectares (66,000 acres) in size. The amounts of old growth included within reserves varied widely. The intent was to maintain existing old growth in the reserves and to manage younger stands to attain the tree size and stand structure resembling old growth. Most reserves were designed to ultimately contain at least twenty pairs of northern spotted owls (the number of pairs that were anticipated to persist long-term without immigration). Existing old-growth stands within reserves were to be preserved and younger stands managed (i.e., thinned) to speed development of larger, more widely spaced trees to emulate old-growth structure. A coarse filter approach (whereby old-growth stands were assumed to contain associated species) was employed. Old-growth stands occurring in the "matrix" between reserves were open to timber cutting, save for eighty-acre patches around existing northern spotted owl nests. These patches were intended to provide for nest sites once surrounding stands reached sixty to eighty years of age, and serve as sources to "inoculate" maturing stands with old-growth associated plants and animals. Reserves in fire-prone forests east of the Cascade crest and in southern Oregon and northern California were to be aggressively managed to reduce risk of stand-replacing fire. Old-growth forests with a stand-replacing fire return interval of centuries were reserved, in the short term, from active management. All reserves were given highest priority for suppression of wildfire (FEMAT 1993).

In addition to the LSRs, default streamside buffers (in keeping with the precautionary principle) were, on average, triple the expected width after adjustments following watershed assessments. These assessments and adjustments were to be quickly completed. The final buffers were subject to management to meet overall objectives (stream shading and bank stabilization—and possibly including timber production).

Ten AMAs were designated in various forest types to allow tests of alternative management approaches to retaining threatened species. These AMAs ranged from 34,000 to 162,000 hectares (83,900 to 399,500 acres) in size and totaled 528,660 hectares (1,306,300 acres).

The Northwest Forest Plan

After FEMAT reported and President Clinton selected Option 9, a second team prepared the required Environmental Impact Statement and the Record of Decision. The result was dubbed the Northwest Forest Plan. "Bells and whistles" were added that dramatically altered Option 9, particularly regarding future failure to meet projected timber yields and the dramatically increased costs of execution of proposed sales. These changes were made to increase the chances that the NWFP would pass legal muster. The foremost of these changes involved searching old-growth stands proposed for cutting to determine if "sensitive species" were present—the survey-and-manage approach (USDA/USDI 1994a). If so, adjustments were made in the cutting plan to provide protection. As time passed, it became clear that the expected timber yields from cutting any old growth were less likely and more expensive to even examine as a potential course of action.

The survey-and-manage protocols shifted the approach of the NWFP from a coarse filter (the occurrence of species is predicted by the occurrence of habitat) to a fine filter (based on actual site specific data). Species associated with old-growth conditions would, with certainty, occur in such stands. Ergo, most (if not all) timber sales proposed for old-growth stands would either be forgone or altered. Significant additional costs also were inevitable, thereby negatively affecting economic viability of such timber sales.

Yet, the projected timber sale quantity in Option 9 (1.2 billion board feet per year) declined by less than 1 percent in the NWFP. The accuracy of the new timber projections was challenged internally, led by FS Chief Jack Ward Thomas, when the team leaders who prepared the Record of Decision presented their draft report in Washington, D.C., to Chair of the Council on Environmental Quality Katie McGinty; Undersecretary of Agriculture James Lyons; FS Chief Jack Ward Thomas; Director of the BLM Michael Dombeck; and various staff. The timber projections, however, were not modified; and crucial modifications in Option 9 specifying additional process (e.g., survey-and-manage protocols) prior to harvest of old growth in the matrix between reserves were accepted by the administration.

The NWFP was immediately challenged in court by the wood products industry and the environmental community, but for very different reasons. Judge William Dwyer upheld the

NWFP against all challenges, but, as his written opinion made clear, just barely (*Seattle Audubon Society v. Lyons*, 1994). Some government attorneys believed that without the survey and manage provisos inserted in the final Record of Decision, the NWFP would have been rejected. That conjecture probably had great weight in making that alteration to Option 9.

Sustainability of the NWFP

The NFWP was then, simply, not faithfully followed—for whatever reasons. These failures combined to have dramatic effect on the timber produced. The probable sale quantity had been at 1.1 billion board feet. Timber offered for sale peaked, in 1997, at 880 million board feet and declined to 308 million board feet in 2001. Departures from the NWFP included the following.

1. Cutting in old-growth stands was far below projections due to resistance from the environmental community and the economic and technical consequences of survey-and-manage protocols. This resulted from the rather obvious conclusion (at least at this point) that any survey for old-growth-associated species in old-growth stands would almost certainly reveal the presence of such species. That would, in turn, require adjustment in the sale or its abandonment.
2. Adaptive Management Areas (AMAs) were, essentially, managed no differently than other areas covered by the NWFP. This was probably due to the reluctance of regulatory agencies to approve habitat modifications or departures from the overall plan as related to short-term impacts on threatened species.
3. Few "default" buffers of uncut forest along streamsides were reduced in width, nor were silvicultural activities carried out within the buffers. Watershed assessments were not completed in a timely fashion as disagreements between involved agencies and various technical specialists continued unresolved. Protocols were established that

far exceeded what was anticipated by FEMAT. Unadjusted buffers excluded road access to timber stands anticipated to be part of the timber harvest.

4. Active management within reserves to encourage rapid growth and appropriate structure in stands younger than eighty years was not vigorously, nor equally, pursued by national forests with LSRs. This was likely the result of costs of sale preparation, including attaining acquiescence of regulatory agencies relative to anticipated timber yields; that is, these were apt to be "deficient sales" with significant opposition.

5. Active management was only tentatively pursued in reserves in LSRs in fire-influenced landscapes due to cost-benefit ratios and opposition from segments of the environmental community. This left these reserves in worsening condition relative to stand-replacing fires, some of which occurred as predicted in 2002.

As a result, the NWFP did not produce the projected timber yields. Asking whether a plan not followed is "sustainable" is a non sequitur. Would the NWFP, if followed, be sustainable in relation to meeting the requirements of the ESA (and the viability clause of the FS's planning rule) and producing projected timber yields? Not likely. The projected timber yields were unrealistic given the predictable cost and impact of the survey-and-manage protocols. But, even then, other failures related to the Clinton administration's unwillingness to press ahead against protests from the environmental community (which in my opinion had more influence than those who were interested in producing a sustained flow of timber) may have been more responsible for the shortfalls. Those observations beg the question, would the NWFP have produced the outcomes predicted if the NWFP had been pursued as advertised? I have doubts, first expressed in 1994 at the meeting described earlier (presided over by the chair of the Council on Environmental Quality) that very little timber would come to market from old-growth stands in the matrix between LSRs due to the predictable consequences of the survey-and-manage protocols. But, who really knows without a test?

Even then, the question is not whether the NWFP is sustainable in the technical sense (which it may well be if executed without the requirement for survey and manage in old-growth stands in the matrix scheduled for timber harvest). But whether it is sustainable in the political, legal, and economic senses (which it has not been) is another question. In short, how can we discuss sustainability of outcomes for a plan that has never been executed (i.e., tested)? And, are social, political, and economic sustainability equally as important as sustainability of biological outputs? The Environmental Protection Agency (EPA) and court opinions answered that question, and the answer has been no.

It seems unlikely, due to hardening opinion and the specter of the ESA applied in the most conservative sense by the regulatory agencies and the courts, that any significant timber volume will be forthcoming from old growth on federal lands. That has nothing to do with questions related to "sustainability" or any other technical question. Concerns with sustainability were simply considered subordinate to meeting the requirements of the ESA.

The Northwest Forest Plan—Ten Years Later

Ten years have passed since commitment to the NWFP. Times have changed. Timber harvest from old-growth forests has become ever more unlikely due to the survey-and-manage provision and increasing political resistance. Declines in numbers of pairs of nesting northern spotted owls due to displacement by barred owls (*Strix varia*), an underappreciated factor in 1990, increases the value of remaining old growth to owl welfare—including that in the matrix between reserves (Ackers, this volume). However, it should be remembered that continued losses in numbers of northern spotted owls were anticipated to continue for several decades under the NWFP until numbers of surviving but displaced northern spotted owls came into balance with extant habitat (USDA/USDI, 1994b).

That may well gall technicians, but that matters little given the overriding demands of the ESA. For those who love old-growth forests, for reasons ranging from concern over associated plants and animals (or the ecosystems of which they are part), to the beauty and majesty of large old trees, there is no compromise. They have fought, and will fight mightily—and probably successfully—to save both old large trees and any remaining old-growth forest stands on national forests in the Pacific Northwest from being cut. Due to the ESA and consistent outcomes of related federal court decisions, they have the upper hand regarding national public opinion.

We technicians, and the lawyers who advise us, who are "left-brain dominated" technocrats, should have learned by now that it was not the northern spotted owl that was and is the question in the Northwest, nor was it marbled murrelets nor the myriad runs of anadromous fish at risk. It was not the many species—certainly hundreds of species—closely associated with old-growth forests. It was, technically and legally, the remnant old-growth ecosystem upon which threatened species depend that was, itself, threatened and endangered.

Or, is there even more to it than that, something more related to beauty, reverence, or other factors—"right-brained processes"— that foresters, wildlife biologists, other technicians, and lawyers are poorly prepared, reluctant, and even legally prohibited from considering? If so, this debate, and other raging debates about the future of the public's forests, are being argued and fought using surrogates for the real issues, the right-brained issues that are, perhaps, impossible to address in a technical approach. Perhaps consideration of sustainability should be expanded beyond the current application to goods and services to be inclusive of stand conditions determined to have value in and of themselves. Until then, arguments about sustainability are likely to mean little in the legal sense.

As a wildlife biologist/forester/ecologist, I now conclude that forest managers are faced with a paradox when it comes to carrying out the mandates of the ESA, and the FS's viability clause, related to old growth and associated species. No stand of trees, forest, or ecosystem, and the associated species of plants and animals, can be frozen in time; nor will it persist forever in an old-growth state. Ecosystems are dynamic and ever changing—vegetation sprouts, grows, and dies. The emergence of new life, and its growing and dying, are ongoing. Some trees die young and some live for centuries. Sometimes, death is sudden and widespread due to stand-replacing fire or dramatic blowdown or some other factor. Sustainability of old-growth forests and the species of plants and animals existing therein will, in the end, be dependent on forest managers and the societies that make the rules; on their understanding and operating with dynamic management approaches. LSRs are the beginning point—not the end of the matter. So, if a desired forest condition is to be maintained over the very long term, management must be dynamic and considerate of both short- and long-term risks. Minimization of short-term risks (the modus operandi of regulatory agencies and the federal courts) will come with a price tag related to significantly increased longer-term risks (the bane of land-management agencies) of failure to meet objectives over very long time frames.

However, any plan dealing with old-growth ecosystems must begin with remnant stands of old growth. Old growth may take centuries to develop, and it is doubtful whether facsimiles can be produced through innovative silviculture, though attempts to do so will be required if such forest conditions are to be maintained over the very long term. Even if the very long-term probability of maintaining old-growth stands of adequate amount, sizes, arrangement, and sufficient connection to sustain species associated with such conditions is slight, federal land managers are nonetheless required above all other objectives to achieve that end. To be absolutely crass, theirs is not to reason why, theirs is but to obey the law; and the overriding law is the ESA. And, they will execute, so long as they deem the instructions legal, in a manner prescribed by duly elected officials and their appointees; that is, the elected officials set policy, and the professionals execute those policies in compliance within boundaries of laws, regulations, and budget. When questions as to compliance with laws and regulations arise and reckoning is called for, the federal courts, not technical specialists and not interest groups, will judge when and whether they have performed adequately.

Clearly, the NWFP is the minimum (regarding the short-term protection of old-growth forests within the range of the northern spotted owl) that will currently pass muster with the federal courts. That is unlikely to change. However, the NWFP has not been diligently executed in other respects as well and, therefore, has not produced the predicted timber volumes (which I suspect is what we are really discussing when we consider "sustainability"). The NWFP can be evaluated at this point only based on how it has actually been executed. It is impossible to evaluate the results of the NWFP *if* executed as written.

Possible Futures

Even if the NWFP were followed, requirements for survey-and-manage, even after the number of "sensitive species" has been reduced, will preclude meeting the projected timber yields. If any timber is expected to be cut from old-growth stands on federal lands under the NWFP, it will be essential to do away with survey-and-manage requirements, or to drastically modify the approach to reduce costs and increase chances of cutting stands identified as open to such actions. Even then, legal and/or political resistance to any cutting of old-growth forests, including extreme varieties of civil disobedience by environmental extremists, seems highly likely.

Unless the administration in power is prepared to deal firmly and consistently with significant acts of civil disobedience, it would be well to adjust the NWFP to remove all old-growth forests on federal lands from consideration for cutting. Clearly, the Clinton administration did not take that approach and quickly backed away from such confrontation. Instead, it adjusted the NWFP without ever making it clear that it would, therefore, be impossible to meet the projected timber yields. Perhaps, the projected timber volumes should simply be adjusted to recognize that for ecological, legal, and political reasons, the cutting of old growth on national forests in the Pacific Northwest, and perhaps all federal lands, is simply at an end.

Then, if the adjusted NWFP is vigorously executed with full intent to follow adaptive management principles (i.e., it is adjusted appropriately and routinely as new knowledge and understanding evolves), the NWFP is, in my opinion, quite likely to be sustainable—both in technical and social, legal, and economic terms. At least, it is worth a try. In reality, it is likely the only game in town since there is simply, in the short term, no "wiggle room" left barring modifications in extant laws and regulations. No matter how many times the issue is revisited, under current laws and regulations, the same basic answers will emerge. And, it may be well to think over that old adage, "Doing the same thing over and over and expecting to get a different result is one definition of insanity."

As of late 2003, the Bush administration was moving forward with two thrusts in forest policy that could significantly alter the playing field related to the management of the federal forests in the Pacific Northwest. The first was the "Healthy Forest Initiative" mounted in response to the dramatic wildfire seasons of 1994, 2000, and 2002. Forest conditions that evolved over nearly a century of vigorous application of fire suppression policies are increasingly vulnerable to widespread stand-replacing wildfire. Exacerbating the associated political problems is the ongoing encroachment of human habitation (i.e., structures) into forested areas and, specifically, into the interface between public and private lands (see Bowersox and Arabas, this volume).

The suggested management response is increasingly centered on the thinning of forests, with particular spatial emphasis on wildland-urban interface areas. The management purpose is to reduce the danger of crown fires along with coincident reduction of ground-level fuels and introduction of frequently applied controlled burns to maintain those conditions. Alterations in the enabling bureaucratic process—including assessment of environmental effect, public involvement, and appeals—are being proposed by the administration in order to speed actions while reducing associated costs (see Bowersox and Arabas, this volume).

Some, perhaps most, environmentalists are keenly suspicious of this thrust as a subterfuge to more easily extract merchantable trees from public lands that would otherwise not be available. Proponents note the current high costs of such actions and propose removal of some merchantable trees to offset those costs and, simultaneously, provide raw materials to mills with associated jobs and offset imports of wood from Canada and other foreign suppliers. The outcome of this initiative could have significant influence on the sustainability of the NWFP and the likelihood that LSRs, particularly those in fire-influenced forest communities, will be spared from stand-replacing wildfire.

At the same time, the administration ordered the FS to proceed with significant revisions in the regulations issued pursuant to the National Forest Management Act that govern forest planning and management. As proposed, these new regulations would significantly streamline planning, public participation, and appeals processes, and thereby significantly reduce the time, costs, and uncertainties related to achievement of management activities. In fact, some of the current regulations (i.e., the "viability clause") are impossible to meet in their strictest interpretation—both technically and fiscally. Yet, critics maintain that these changes are a ploy to reduce environmental safeguards and enhance opportunities for extraction of timber and creation of associated infrastructure (e.g., roads, landings, etc.).

How this hassle will evolve is unclear. The environmentalists were quick off the starting blocks and showed their dramatic public relations skills in influencing a large number of newspapers, within a very short time span of one another, to editorialize against the proposal. The editorialists made very similar points in very similar language. Such political pressures have essentially thwarted all past efforts to revise these regulations as power shifted in each of the elections that delayed the adoption. This time around, though the adoption of new regulations was, once again, delayed until after national elections, there may be a different outcome. This time, for the first time, the party in power gained seats in both the House and Senate and, in the process, garnered no debts to environmental activists. This time, sustained efforts related to the processes associated with the management of the federal forests may actually come to fruition (see Bowersox, this volume).

Regardless of how such an outcome is evaluated in the political arena, such change would enhance chances of sustainable management related to execution of the NWFP by reducing costs and increasing the likelihood that management actions would be executed in a more timely, lower-cost fashion.

Only time will tell.

Note

This chapter is based on a talk given at the Forest Futures Conference at Willamette University in Salem, Oregon, on September 25, 2002.

2

Ecological Realities of the Northwest Forest Plan

David A. Perry

In 1994 David Wilcove, at that time a scientist with the Environmental Defense Fund, wrote:

> From an ecologist's perspective, the battle over the northern spotted owl and its old-growth forests is especially noteworthy for two reasons. First, in contrast to previous efforts to save a particular place or a particular species, this controversy has centered around an entire ecosystem (the Pacific Northwest old-growth forests). . . . Second, more than any other natural resource controversy in recent years, this one has been shaped by scientific research. (Wilcove 1994)

The Forest Ecosystem Management Assessment Team (FEMAT) was formed at the behest of the Clinton administration in response to the crisis over threatened biological diversity and management of federal lands in the Pacific Northwest (PNW) (see Thomas, this volume). Comprising more than one hundred scientists and support personnel, FEMAT was charged with developing an array of management options for federal lands in the range of the northern spotted owl (NSO), including "alternatives that range from a medium to a very high probability of ensuring the viability of species." The Clinton administration chose one of these—Option 9—and that became, with some relatively minor modification, the Northwest Forest Plan (NWFP).

What follows is my assessment of the ecological realities of the NWFP. The first two sections of the chapter deal with the condition of forest ecosystems in the Pacific Northwest by the early 1990s (the raw material with which FEMAT had to work) and the ecological basis of the NWFP. I conclude with some comments addressing the larger contextual realities of conservation in today's world: economic, social, and the "certain uncertainties" that flow from a complex, poorly understood, and highly perturbed biosphere. I have drawn on current scientific knowledge, and my experience as a member of one of a number of expert panels convened to critique and rate the various options, and my experience as a member of the Marbled Murrelet Recovery Team, which was crafting a recovery plan at the same time FEMAT was developing its set of options. The assessments and opinions are strictly my own unless otherwise noted.

You Can't Make a Silk Purse Out of a Sow's Ear . . .

> The legacies of land-use activities continue to influence ecosystem structure and function for decades or centuries—or even longer—after those activities have ceased. (Foster et al. 2003)

The Burden of History

Any conservation strategy must deal with the legacies of past land use. The regional landscape inherited by FEMAT was heavily logged over, and significant amounts of the remaining old-growth[1] forest were fragmented and isolated within a sea of younger forests. It's impossible to say precisely how much old-growth forest there was in the Pacific Northwest prior to the arrival of Euro-Americans. The earliest thorough survey was carried out in the 1930s, one of a number done by the United States Forest Service (USFS) at that time, under a mandate from the U.S. Congress to document the nation's forest resources (the

McSweeny-McNary Forest Research Act of 1928). According to the authors of the report on the Douglas-fir (*Pseudotsuga menziesii*) region of western Oregon and Washington, the commonly held belief at that time was that old-growth (OG) Douglas fir once covered about 3.5 million hectares (8.6 million acres) (Andrews and Cowlin 1940). If one assumes (probably correctly) that all cutovers and deforested burns in the 1930s had been Douglas-fir forests, the survey documented a little less than 5 million hectares (12.3 million acres) of existing or former Douglas-fir forests (of all ages), which would put the historical proportion of OG Douglas-fir at about 70 percent of the region's total forested area. By 1936, a combination of logging and wildfire had reduced that by half. By the early 1990s, estimates put the proportion of OG at 14 to 18 percent of all coniferous forest types in western Oregon, western Washington, and northwest California (NRC 2000). If northwest California is excluded, the number is closer to 13 percent. Loss of OG in the ponderosa pine region of eastern Oregon and Washington has been even more dramatic, from an original cover estimated at nearly 90 percent to less than 10 percent today (NRC 2000).

Whatever the exact numbers may be, there is no doubt that by far the majority of OG forests in Oregon and Washington have either been logged or burned in wildfires over the past 150 years. But loss of OG does not tell the whole story from a conservation standpoint. Three other factors come into play to reduce the habitat value of the OG that does remain, and to create other conservation problems as well: fragmentation of remaining OG into small blocks, the "foreign" nature of the cutover landscape arising from the fact that clear-cuts and traditionally managed plantations are poor mimics of the ecosystems that result from natural disturbances, and permeation of the forested landscape by an intensive road network. The impacts of these and other factors are wide ranging and are addressed in the following sections.

Fragmentation

Forests on federal lands in the PNW became highly fragmented because of an approach to logging called "staggered setting." In staggered settings, cutting units are laid out as patches within the matrix of uncut forests, something like taking scattered bites out of the middle of a pancake instead of eating from the edge. One of the rationales behind this approach was to enhance diversity, reflecting common thought in the 1950s and 1960s that creating edges was a good thing biologically (which it is for some species; see Yoakum and Dasmann 1971). In a landmark paper, Franklin and Forman (1987) pointed out that the end result of the staggered setting approach was increasing fragmentation of uncut forests into small blocks, which is precisely what has happened in the Pacific Northwest. In the Olympic National Forest, for example, "more than 87 percent of the old growth in 1940 was in patches larger than 4,000 hectares [10,000 acres]. In 1988, only one patch larger than 4,000 hectares remained, and 60 percent of what remained of the old growth was in patches smaller than 40 hectares [100 acres]" (Noss and Cooperrider 1994, citing work by Morrison 1990). (See figure 2.1).

The resulting fragmentation (particularly of older forests) in the west is problematic, but difficult to demonstrate with scientific rigor. One obvious issue is that, while 2,000 hectares (5,000 acres) of contiguous OG, for example, is likely to provide quality habitat for deep-forest vertebrates such as spotted owls (*Strix occidentalis caurina*) or American martens (*Martes americana*), 2,000 hectares of OG distributed in 20-hectare (50-acre) blocks within an intensively managed matrix is unlikely to do so. In an intensively managed landscape, even mature forest islands large enough to provide suitable habitat for OG dependents are isolated within a matrix that may be inhospitable to their movement, effectively isolating blocks from one another with consequences for gene flow and viability of regional populations (see Thomas et al. 1990).

In their study of fragmentation effects on vertebrates in northern California, Rosenberg and Raphael (1986) found that, while bird and amphibian species richness were higher in more fragmented landscapes, some species, including northern spotted owls and fishers (*Martes pennanti*), were negatively affected by fragmentation. Rosenberg and Raphael illustrate a larger point that sometimes gets lost in policy discussions. Trends in

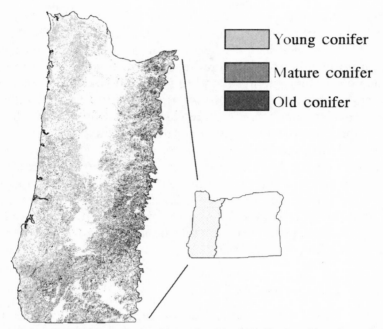

Young conifer

Mature conifer

Old conifer

Figure 2.1.   1988 Western Oregon Vegetation Map: Conifer Age. Map shows the relative ages of closed conifer forests in the study area of Western Oregon. The data are from the 1988 Western Oregon Vegetation Mapping Project, which uses 1988 Thematic Mapper data and ground reference data. Note younger age of Coast Range conifers (left side of map) relative to Cascade Range (right side of map). The oak woodland–dominated Willamette Valley is in the center of the map. (See Arabas and Bowersox, this volume.) After Cohen 1998.

overall biological diversity do not necessarily reflect what is going on with particular species or species guilds. As was shown in California, overall diversity may be increased while species requiring special habitats are reduced in number. Total biological diversity without reference to the composition of that diversity is a target so general as to be virtually worthless from the standpoint of conservation ecology.

Among other problems, a highly fragmented landscape offers limited options for placing large blocks of threatened habitat in reserves. Conservation biologists once debated the value of many small versus a few large reserves; however, that issue was put to rest nearly twenty years ago, and today a basic tenet of reserve design is that bigger is better (Noss and Cooperrider 1994, Terborgh and Soule 1999, Lindenmayer and Franklin 2002). As the size of OG patches declines below some critical level, species that reside within them and overall ecosystem integrity become increasingly vulnerable in several respects. The likelihood of weed invasion is greater compared to large intact blocks, and interior forest species may become more susceptible to predators. In the PNW there is speculation that northern spotted owls are more vulnerable to predation by great horned owls (*Bubo virginianus*) and competition from barred owls (*Strix varia*) in fragmented than in intact landscapes (Thomas et al. 1990). The poor nesting success of marbled murrelets (*Brachyramphus marmoratus*) is thought to be due in large part to nest predation by corvids (crows, ravens, jays) that probably benefit from landscape fragmentation (Miller et al. 1997).

Natural Disturbances

Problems arising from reduction and fragmentation of OG habitat are compounded by the characteristics of young forests dominating the matrix. Aside from the fact that trees are killed, clear-cutting bears little resemblance to natural disturbances, which leave a plethora of structural legacies such as deadwood and residual living trees. Additionally, natural disturbances such as fire and windthrow usually have a frequency distribution characterized by many small and a few large events, and hence leave a more variable patch mosaic than does intensive forestry (Perry 1998).

Although the focus of conservation in the PNW has been OG forests, another limiting habitat for many species in a landscape dominated by commercial forests may be the structurally complex successional stages following natural disturbances. Recent studies indicate that plant community structure during recovery from disturbance also differs significantly between managed forests and the historic natural disturbance regime. Studies in the western Cascades, Oregon Coast Range, and Oregon Siskiyous show that OG forests, once thought to be even-aged, are actually mosaics of age classes (Franklin et al. 1981, Tappeiner et al. 1997a, Poage 2001, Sensenig 2002). These studies suggest that for decades following a major disturbance, many forest stands were characterized by widely spaced conifer regeneration with scattered residual legacy trees, abundant shrubs and hardwood trees, and without doubt large amounts of deadwood. Such stands probably provided suitable habitat for at least some species that are now associated primarily with OG (Hansen et al. 1991). For example, hardwoods are critically important refugia for OG-associated lichens following disturbance (Neitlich and McCune 1997). Fourteen species of birds and three mammal species found in the Oregon Coast Range are closely associated with hardwood trees and shrubs (Hayes and Hagar 2002). Hardwoods, grasses, and forbs have been found to support 90 percent of the *Lepidopteran* species (moths and butterflies) in Oregon conifer forests (Hammond and Miller 1998).

Deadwood

Another critical habitat (and structural feature) that is sharply reduced in managed landscapes is large deadwood. In natural landscapes two distinct processes produced large deadwood: major disturbances such as crown fires and windstorms killed trees, just as logging does. The major difference, however, is that the boles of large trees killed by natural disturbances stayed in the ecosystem, pulsing from 100 to 1,000 Mg/hectare of deadwood into functional pathways quite distinct from those of living trees. Decades later, as forests matured into the old-growth stage, large deadwood was input to the system as individual old trees died from senescence and the biotic agents that often accompany senescence (fungi, insects). Grove (2002, 2) states: "Large-diameter, over-mature, senescent, moribund, decadent, or veteran trees . . . form the centerpiece of the mature timber habitat concept." Nowhere is this truer than in the mesic old-growth forests of the Pacific Northwest, which average from ten to greater than twenty times more biomass in large snags and logs than eastern deciduous forests or conifer forests in drier regions of the West (Harmon et al. 1986).

Large deadwood is used by a diverse community of vertebrates, invertebrates, and microbes (Harmon et al. 1986). According to Harris (1984), forty-five species of terrestrial vertebrates found in the Cascade Mountains do not occur in young forests without snags and logs. Cavities for nesting are especially important for year-round resident birds (Harmon et al. 1986). Large logs in streams play a major role in creating pools, which in turn increase habitat complexity and the diversity of fish (FEMAT 1993). Insects that depend on dead or dying wood for at least some part of their life cycle, along with the food web they support, are termed *saproxylic*. Deyrup (1976) recorded more than 300 species of saproxylic insects from Douglas fir in Washington. Large deadwood is also used by a rich variety of fungi, lichens, and bacteria (Amaranthus et al. 1994, Waters et al. 1997, Goodman and Trofymow 1998, Smith et al. 2000, Molina et al. 2001). The various bacterial types colonizing decaying wood include actinorhizal nitrogen-fixing bacteria (i.e., symbiotic with alders, ceanothus species, and several other angiosperm species) and free-living, nitrogen-fixing bacteria, which are introduced into the logs by bark beetles (Griffiths et al. 1993, Li et al. 1997, Crawford and Li 1997).

Diversity

Loss of the complex ecosystems that characterized both early and late-successional stages has affected habitat for a large number of species, including many that are endangered, threatened, or species of concern (Hayes and Hagar 2002). FEMAT listed 104 species of lichens and bryophytes, 234 species of fungi, and 4 functional groups of invertebrates as being "of management concern" (FEMAT 1993). Our knowledge base is so poor for many of these species that implications for their continued viability are unclear, and probably differ from one species to another depending on life-history characteristics, adaptability, and other ecological factors. Microbes, invertebrates, and many small vertebrates don't have the large area requirements of vertebrates high on the food chain (e.g., spotted owls, martens, fishers). The "umbrella species" concept hypothesizes that, if those needing large areas are protected, those with similar habitat requirements but smaller area needs will be protected as well (Noss and Cooperrider 1994). However, when species with very different dispersal abilities are included under the umbrella, issues related to biological connectivity among reserves must be considered. Species who find the managed matrix an unfriendly environment risk isolation, genetic deterioration, and ultimate extinction when suitable habitat is spread too widely. For these organisms, questions arise about the suitability of a reserve system based on the dispersal capabilities of a bird. In theory, the dense network of riparian reserves created by the NWFP provide connectivity, a point to which I'll return.

Homogeneity

Significant alteration of landscape patterns affects processes that may affect habitat and overall system health. As landscapes become increasingly dominated by younger forests, large crown fires become more likely (Franklin and Forman 1987, Perry 1988). In some areas, greater amounts of forest edge lead to more windthrow, and the size of residual patches is eroded with every large windstorm. The homogeneity of managed as compared to natural landscapes sets the stage for pest problems (Manion 1981, Perry 1988), and in fact probably accounts for the current epidemic of Swiss needle cast in the coastal fog belts of Oregon and Washington (Filip et al. 2000). Despite the name, Swiss needle cast, a foliar disease of Douglas fir, is native to the Pacific Northwest, and apparently caused little or no problems prior to the advent of intensive Douglas-fir culture (Filip et al. 2000).

Hydrology and Sedimentation

Hydrology also has been significantly affected by logging in the Pacific Northwest. Studies in western Oregon show that clear-cuts and roads act synergistically to alter hydrology, resulting in more early spring runoff (higher peak stream flows), lower summer flows, and increased sedimentation (Jones and Grant 1996, Swanson et al. 1989), severely affecting instream habitat. By the time of FEMAT, salmon stocks in the Pacific Northwest were in serious decline. A 1991 study by the American Fisheries Society concluded that more than 106 stocks of anadromous salmonids had become extinct in Oregon, Washington, Idaho, and California; and of the remaining stocks, 160 were judged to be at serious risk (cited from NRC 2000). Numerous factors have contributed to these declines, including dams, changing ocean conditions, sedimentation from logging roads, and loss of pool habitat due to removal of large woody debris from streams. Studies of cutthroat trout in the Alsea Basin of the Oregon Coast Range show that logging alone can lead to significant declines (NRC 2000).

Sedimentation can have impacts that reach beyond streams to estuaries and near-shore ecosystems. As Quileute tribal councilman Chris Morganroth notes of his fifty-two years on the Olympic Peninsula:

> The last kelp beds I observed outside the mouth of the Quillayute River were during the 1950s and early 1960s. The coastal floor to a mile or so out is now covered with silt that once nourished the forests. Kelp and all other seaweeds need clean rock to grow on. Those rocks are buried under mud and silt. . . . It used to be that after a storm the kelp tore loose from their "holdfast" and washed ashore in huge entangled masses . . . [that] served as part of a food chain for a myriad of shorebirds. Now the shorebirds have diminished nearly to nothing. When the kelp beds were intact, it was a haven for a variety of sea life. . . . [In the past] the resources . . . on this coast were in such abundance that the aboriginal people could take what they needed at their leisure. For the past 10 to 20 years the gathering of seafood on the Pacific Coast has been very limited for anyone.

Functional Diversity and Ecosystem Health

In discussing ecological reality it is important to distinguish between taxonomic extinction and functional extinction: a species may persist in reserves, while any unique ecological role it might play is lost to the larger landscape. Unfortunately this complex issue is characterized by large uncertainties in the knowledge base, experimental difficulty, and—the inevitable result of the foregoing—scientific controversy. Discussing the topic in any depth is beyond the scope of this chapter (see Schulze and

Mooney 1994, Loreau et al. 2001, Kinzig et al. 2001). But the issue is of central importance to sustainability, and a consideration of ecological implications of any land-use strategy would not be complete without touching on some of its essential aspects.

Since every species within an ecosystem acts on something else, it is a simple fact that all species play some functional role. Some species play a "keystone" role, which is to say they have a disproportionate effect on critical ecosystem functions and therefore on the persistence of other species (Bond 1994). Some examples in Pacific Northwest forests are the various species of nitrogen-fixing plants (e.g., *Alnus* sp., *Ceanothus* sp.); the beaver (a "builder" that creates ponds and wetlands); and the ubiquitous millipede, *Harpaphe haydeniana*, which consumes most of the conifer needles that fall to the forest floor and in so doing plays an essential role in the decomposition process (Moldenke and Lattin 1990, Perry 1994). Structures can also play a keystone role, large deadwood being a classic example.

It seems likely that most species are not keystones, although sometimes it can be difficult to say with certainty whether a species is or is not (Perry 1994). From a general conceptual view, most ecologists probably subscribe to what is termed the "rivet-popper hypothesis" (Ehrlich 1994). Ehrlich and Erhlich (1981, XII) describe it this way:

> Ecosystems, like well-made airplanes, tend to have redundant subsystems and other "design" features that permit them to continue functioning after absorbing a certain amount of abuse. A dozen rivets, or a dozen species, might never be missed. On the other hand, a thirteenth rivet popped from a wing flap, or the extinction of a key species involved in the cycling of nitrogen, could lead to a serious accident.

It doesn't necessarily take the extinction of a key species to destabilize an ecosystem. Systems may also lose resilience through the erosion of redundancy (death by a thousand cuts), or through changes in spatial patterns that alter relationships (Holling 1988, Perry 1994, Kareiva and Wennergren 1995). Vulnerabilities may not become apparent until the system is stressed in some way—a weakened airplane may do fine in good weather but come apart in a storm (Perry 1988, 1994). Moreover, a great deal of empirical evidence, as well as models, show that changes in the system state may be rapid and, once started, difficult or impossible to reverse (Perry et al. 1989, Kareiva and Wennergren 1995, Perry 1995).

What implications might the foregoing have for the forests of the Pacific Northwest? Several impacts of simplified or otherwise altered landscapes (e.g., roading) have already been seen: increased erosion, altered hydrology, and the current epidemic of Swiss needle cast. A century of excluding fire—a keystone process—has greatly altered dry forest types throughout the West, increasing vulnerability to catastrophic crown fires (Agee 1993). Though we often think of greater biodiversity translating to greater ecosystem stability, in dry forest types quite the opposite occurred: the greater species and structural diversity that resulted from fire exclusion was a destabilizing rather than a stabilizing force (a useful caution about the dangers of overgeneralizing in ecology). Younger stands in more mesic portions of the region are probably also more vulnerable to fire now than historically. But, in contrast to the dry forests, in mesic forests increased vulnerability does come from loss of diversity (Perry 1988). Foresters have long been aware that some hardwoods are "fire retarders," including maples, alders, madrone, tanoak, and some *Ceanothus* sp. (Perry 1988, Weatherspoon and Skinner 1995), from which it follows that the mixed conifer–hardwood communities that characterized many natural successions in the western Cascades, Coast Ranges, and Siskiyou Mountains are likely to have been more fire resistant than densely stocked young conifer stands.

These and other concerns regarding impacts of the modern landscape on functional integrity of regional ecosystems are likely to be answered only through experience gained in the course of time. Returning to the wing-rivet metaphor, the change in climate associated with global warming may be the storm that tells us the condition of our airplane. So to summarize, by the time FEMAT was formed, both terrestrial and aquatic habitats in Pacific Northwest forests had been severely affected, and ecologic processes significantly altered. As is most often the case in human dealings with the environment, we had overshot the mark and were playing catch-up.

. . . But You Might Be Able to Make a Pretty Good Leather One

Management of biodiversity through ecosystem management creates a very broad, challenging, uncharted decision space for managers. (Thomas et al. 1993)

Any conservation strategy in a nation with significant amounts of private property is constrained by patterns of land ownership. In this regard, with its high proportion of forest lands in federal ownership, the PNW has a significant advantage. FEMAT was handed a highly altered regional landscape, but the key elements needed for protection and restoration were largely within its jurisdictional scope. (This was not universally true, however, especially in the case of the marbled murrelet, where key areas in northwest Oregon and southwest Washington are in private or state ownership.) Moreover, never before has so much ecological brainpower been assembled in such an intense setting. The result was a remarkable piece of work, incorporating much current thinking regarding landscape ecology, ecosystem dynamics, reserve design, and conservation strategies encompassing whole landscapes rather than the traditional approach of putting all the conservation eggs in the basket of reserves. From the standpoint of process, FEMAT was widely recognized as setting a standard for how to incorporate science in building conservation policy.

This is not to say FEMAT was perfect and without critics. For some, the reserve design employed by FEMAT was a laudable example of the use of metapopulation theory (which focuses on fragmented populations) in conservation (Hedrick et al. 1996), while others saw the real issue being absolute habitat loss, with fragmentation being a secondary concern (Boyce 2002). In fact, the latter position was clearly reflected by FEMAT scientists, who explicitly stated that overall habitat loss was the central issue (FEMAT 1993).

Some scientists (including myself) thought approaches in the matrix were not included that should have been, though there is no way to tell how they would have fared in the evaluation and rating process employed by FEMAT. One example of an alternative approach is the Central Cascades Adaptive Management Area (AMA), which developed a strategy based on historic disturbance patterns, including some areas of long rotation. Their approach is projected to produce additional older forest and greater landscape continuity over time than would be produced by the Plan in the same area.[2] Another example of an alternative approach is the conservation plan for the Klamath-Siskiyou ecoregion developed by the Conservation Biology Institute (Strittholt et al. 1999), which included significantly more protected area than the NWFP. "Our proposed . . . reserve network," stated Strittholt et al. (1999), "meets conservation objectives . . . much better than the NWFP and other conservation measures currently in place by offering improved protection to a number of important natural features."

On-the-ground design of any conservation plan can be boiled down to three key elements: size and location of protected areas (reserves), pathways of interconnection among reserves, and management approaches in unreserved lands (the matrix). When the habitat in question has a finite lifetime, such as forests in areas susceptible to stand-replacing disturbances, there must be provision for replacement habitat (see reserved or potentially reserved younger forests). Finally, there must be a workable plan for monitoring success and changing course when objectives are not being met (adaptive management).

Reserves and Interconnections

Most conservation scientists would probably agree that reserves and their interconnections are foundational, though by themselves are unlikely to be sufficient (Franklin 1993, Noss et al. 1999, Terborgh and Soule 1999, Groom et al. 1999, Lindenmayer and Franklin 2002). Some managers and scientists have argued that reserves are a bad conservation investment, and that the whole landscape should be managed (see Oliver et al. 1997). That view was firmly rejected by panels of both the Ecological Society of America and the National Research Council, primarily because it is untested, risky, and the downside—extinction—is irreversible (Aber et al. 2000, NRC 2000; also see Noss et al. 1999).

Some of the controversy over the importance of reserves stems from different conceptions of what can or cannot be done within them (Noss et al. 1999). Opponents of reserves have generally viewed them as areas where any management is off limits, while many proponents have taken a more liberal view. For example, an influential group of conservation biologists discusses reserves as having two components: core areas, where management is limited to activities aimed at improving and maintaining ecosystem health, and buffer areas, in which management for commodities is permissible so long as critical habitats are not compromised (Terborgh and Soule 1999 and chapters therein).

How does the NWFP stack up with levels of protection recommended in general by conservation biologists? Soule and Sanjayan (1998) argue that 35 to 75 percent of the land surface in some form of protection is required to prevent significant loss of diversity. Fahrig (1999) suggests that if habitat falls below 20 to 30 percent, species survival will be affected. Strittholt et al. (1999) cite literature showing recommendations generally fall in the range 25 to 75 percent, and average about 50 percent of the lands at issue.

Models by Lande (1988) predicted the northern spotted owl could not persist if less than 20 percent of the area within the owl's range is in suitable habitat, a threshold that has already been crossed. The data pulled together by FEMAT and preceding analyses showed that current habitat was already only 13 percent of the total land area within the owl's range (FEMAT 1993).

Considering those areas that qualify as core reserves, which include Late-Successional Reserves (LSR), Riparian Reserves (RR), and Administratively Withdrawn Areas (AWA), the NWFP protects 47 percent of the total federal lands within its jurisdiction (USDA/USDI 1994a). Northern spotted owl habitat within national parks adds about 2 percent. When all forestland ownerships (public, private, state) within the former range of the owl are included, the proportion protected in core reserves falls to around 20 percent. Taken by itself, this is barely adequate; though it is a considerably higher level of protection than is found in many other regions. As I mentioned earlier, however, the efficacy of a core reserve system cannot be evaluated without reference to what is done on surrounding lands. In the NWFP this means federal lands outside the core reserves (known as the "matrix"), to which we will return after discussing some additional points about the core reserves.

It is important to note two things about the core reserves established by FEMAT. First, not all forests within reserves provide suitable mature or old-growth habitat, though all are intended to at some point in the future. Second, some management is allowed within reserves. Most of the area protected by the NWFP is in LSRs, which include significant amounts of young forests (approximately 58 percent; FEMAT 1993), and within which some harvest of younger trees is allowed. There were both practical and ecological reasons for including young forests in LSRs. To understand the practical reason it is first necessary to understand the basic strategy of reserve design employed by FEMAT. Two basic principles were to: (1) make reserves large enough for each to (eventually) support a number of northern spotted owls, thus buffering against inevitable losses of individuals; and (2) locate reserves no further apart than known dispersal distances of juvenile northern spotted owls. The only way those objectives could be met was to incorporate young stands, in the hopes they would eventually mature to make suitable habitat.

Though the ecological reasoning on the latter point is sound, it is also problematic for at least two reasons. First, with growing evidence that today's young forests have little resemblance to the current OG in its youth, the question arises as to whether they will ever mature to provide the same structure and processes as today's OG. Second, densely stocked young forests tend to be more susceptible than older forests to some disturbances, such as crown fire and snowdown (where heavy snow loads topple trees). Thinning in reserves (strongly encouraged by the panel of ecosystem scientists convened to rate options) was allowed as a way to encourage development of at least some OG characteristics (big trees, multiple canopy layers) and to lower risk of catastrophic disturbances.

Management in the Matrix

Individual animals must be able to move among reserves in order to maintain integrity of the gene pool and replace losses that cannot be replaced from within a given reserve. Protected movement corridors are the most common approach in conservation science, though there is a great deal of uncertainty about how well these work. Hence a strategy that also allows for movement through the matrix is ecologically preferable to one that does not, and the more movement allowed through the matrix the less important corridors become (Lindenmayer and Franklin 2002). FEMAT relied heavily on riparian buffers to provide corridors, an approach used by Harris (1984) in his strategy for conserving forest diversity in the Douglas-fir region. Given the high density of streams in most of the range of the spotted owl, riparian buffers alone provide a great deal of connectivity. However, comparisons of bird, mammal, and amphibian diversity between riparian zones and upslope areas of mature, unmanaged forests in the Oregon Coast Range show that a significant number of species use only upslope areas, raising doubts about the efficacy of riparian-only connectance (McGarigal and McComb 1992, McComb et al. 1993). Thus, a major implication is that the matrix will play a key role in the sufficiency of both total habitat and connectance among core reserves.

Standards and guidelines for implementing the NWFP go into some detail about management in the matrix (USDA/USDI 1994a). Basically, there are four primary elements: (1) requirements for maintaining certain levels of snags, coarse woody debris, and large, green trees; (2) requirements to minimize soil and litter disturbance during harvest; (3) provisions for buffer areas around occupied marbled murrelet sites and northern spotted owl activity centers (these buffers are designated "unmapped LSRs," hence function as small core reserves); and (4) retention of old-growth fragments in watersheds where little remains. Other requirements focus on localized conditions or species. In addition, survey-and-management provisions apply on all land allocations and cover 244 species of fungi, 104 species of lichens and bryophytes, 43 species of mollusks, 4 functional guilds of arthropods (each containing many species), 17 species of vascular plants, 5 amphibian species, and one mammal (the red tree vole) (*Arborimus longicaudus longicaudus*). The exact requirements of survey-and-manage vary with species, but the intent is to locate rare or sensitive species and modify management to protect them, though managers are left with considerable discretion about what is or is not done in areas where these species are found.

Of the management guidelines given in the NWFP for the matrix, the most pervasive and long-lasting influence will result from retaining large trees, an approach termed variable retention harvest system—VRHS (Franklin et al. 1997, Lindenmayer and Franklin 2002). The NWFP directs managers to retain trees on at least 15 percent of the area of any harvest unit, with at least 70 percent of that (10.5 percent of the harvest unit) in aggregates of the oldest live trees (USDA/USDI 1994a). The primary objectives of VRHS are to maintain a degree of structural complexity and provide a future source of large deadwood within the harvested landscape, both of which are critical for maintaining animal diversity and certain ecological processes (Franklin 1994, Perry 1994, Marcot 1997, Carey et al. 1999, Hayes and Hagar 2002, Lindenmayer and Franklin 2002). The standards and guidelines specify that patches of retained trees are to be left indefinitely, a necessary requirement if the trees within patches are to eventually function as large deadwood.

VRHS is necessary to create a diversity of native habitats within the matrix, but by itself is unlikely to be sufficient (Carey et al. 1999). If standard fiber-intensive practices are followed, managers will aim for rapid crown closure by commercial species within young stands, a logical approach when the objective is efficient wood production. However, closed conifer stands, while preferred by some animal species, are the least diverse developmental stage in Pacific Northwest forests (Carey et al. 1999, Hayes and Hagar 2002). However, either thinning or selection harvests can be used to create and maintain species and structural diversity in young stands (DeBell et al. 1997, Hayes et al. 1997, Tappeiner et al. 1997b, Carey et al. 1999, Emmingham 2002, Hayes and Hagar 2002).

Thinning is a standard practice in commercial forestry, and enhances understory growth for a time. However, creating stands with abundant angiosperms, conifer regeneration, and diverse canopy layers requires a different approach than normally used for timber production alone (Tappeiner et al. 1997). Trees grow and fill space rapidly on the productive sites that typify much of the Coast Range and western Cascades, therefore keeping overstory canopies open for relatively long time periods (decades) requires either heavier thinning or more frequent commercial thinning entries than is the norm.

Long rotations are often mentioned as an option in the matrix, especially in conjunction with thinning (Curtis and Marshall 1993, Curtis 1997, Carey et al. 1999, Lindenmayer and Franklin 2002). Rotation length influences the structure of both stands and landscapes. At the stand level, long rotations "provide the potential to grow larger trees, accumulate more organic matter, and develop other structural features associated with more advanced successional conditions" (Lindenmayer and Franklin 2002, 192). At the scale of landscapes, long rotations translate into a lower proportion of recent harvests and a higher proportion of older stands, which in turn influence not only the array of habitats, but susceptibility to weed invasion (greater in newly harvested stands), and processes such as erosion and nutrient loss (Curtis 1997, Carey et al. 1999, Lindenmayer and Franklin 2002). Contrary to long-held beliefs, recent data show that stand productivity remains high well past 100 years of age, especially when coupled with periodic commercial thinning (Curtis 1997).

Selection harvesting, either of single trees or small groups of trees, coupled with VRHS has the potential to produce a great deal of structural diversity at a small-patch scale. But if not done carefully, selection harvesting can result in stands converting to shade-tolerant species such as western hemlock (*Tsuga heterophylla*), which from a diversity standpoint is good for some portions of the landscape but not good for large portions. Successful selection silviculture demands a great deal of on-the-ground expertise in both forestry and ecology. The costs associated with those demands, along with a long-held (and incorrect) belief that selection systems cannot work with Douglas fir, probably account for a reluctance to use it more widely (Emmingham 2002).

Any silvicultural approach for which creating diversity is an objective must recognize the importance of horizontal diversity (patchiness at a variety of scales) as well as vertical diversity (canopy layers), which translates into a need for diverse approaches. As Hayes and Hagar (2002, 116) put it, "no single management prescription should be applied over vast stretches of land." The reason is straightforward: different species have different needs. For example, in studies summarized by Hayes and Hagar (2002), some bird species responded positively to thinning and others negatively. That kind of response is typical, and from an ecological standpoint not surprising. Excessive horizontal uniformity results when selection systems are applied widely, when any one thinning regime is applied widely, or when nothing is done with extensive stands of dense young trees. Carey et al. (1999) suggest variable-density thinnings as an approach to creating horizontal diversity in young stands. Mixtures of variable-density thinning and selection harvesting would further diversify landscapes.

In summary, the NWFP incorporates an extensive and well-designed system of core reserves, and provides for continuity of some essential habitats within the matrix (large deadwood). The structural complexity of the matrix, hence the diversity it supports, would benefit from additional silvicultural measures such as variable-density thinning and long rotations on at least a portion of the landscape.

Ecology Writ Large

The new conservation science is much bigger than biology. And other parts . . . have more to do with the law, economics, politics, world trade, and the whole sustainability agenda, than with conservation biology as such. (John Lawton, in *Society for Conservation Biology Newsletter*, November 2002)

The real world to which Lawton refers, with its dizzying multitude of intricate, sometimes unfathomable ecological–social–economic–political interactions, and the often unpredictable consequences that flow from those interactions, is ecology writ large. As Lawton implies, no conservation strategy with a chance of working can ignore it. As the subtitle of the FEMAT report indicates ("An Ecological, Social, and Economic Assessment") the NWFP did not ignore it. President Clinton had stated "we must never ignore the human and economic dimensions of these problems" (Shannon and Johnson 1994, 6), and Option 9—which was projected to provide 116,000 jobs—was selected as the best option to balance the competing needs and wants of society.

The ecological cost of choosing Option 9 was that one-third of remaining mature and old-growth forests were left unprotected and eligible to be logged (with significant constraints discussed in the previous section) hence greater risk to OG-dependent species than a strategy that protected all. Thomas (1994, 19) summed up the position of FEMAT biologists: "timber harvests from federal forests of the owl region in the near future will come at the cost of increasing the risk to species dependent on these forests."

As it turns out, harvest levels promised under Option 9 have never been achieved (see Beuter and Thomas, this volume); but nevertheless, the economy of the Pacific Northwest remained exceptionally strong (Niemi et al. 1999). We now have the situation in which the economic part of the equation has shifted (the region is much less dependent on logging than it was ten years ago) but with approximately 700,000 hectares (1.7 million acres) of late-successional and old-growth forests still unprotected, the conservation part has not been altered accordingly. A recent National Research Council report concluded (NRC 2000, 201):

> Forest Management in the Pacific Northwest should include the conservation and protection of most or all of the remaining late-successional and old-growth forests. . . . The remaining late-successional and old-growth forests could form the cores of regional forests managed for truly and indefinitely sustainable production of timber, fish, clean water, recreation, and numerous other amenities of forested ecosystems.

In summary, the process leading to the NWFP occurred in two stages. The first was strictly scientific: derivation of options based on the best available biological information. The second was political (and did not involve FEMAT scientists): the selection of the option judged to have the best chance of balancing competing needs.

The Unknown, the Unknowable, and the Irreversible

> Long-term predictions about the destiny of any species are likely to remain academic exercises because the predictions generally assume that the environment remains unchanged— which we know is not going to happen—and because our models will rarely be good enough to make accurate predictions anyway. (Hanski 2002)

Conservation science is fraught with uncertainties that can be roughly divided into two types: those that, in theory at least, will eventually be resolved, and those that are for all practical purposes beyond the reach of prediction, hence will always be uncertain. In the first category are things such as the efficacy of modified silvicultural practices (e.g., green tree retention) in providing habitat for species associated with structurally diverse natural forests, or how well corridors of a certain design work. These things will be learned through experience, so long as we have the commitment and funding to monitor the results of our efforts. Hopefully, if the medicine is not working, we will find that out before all the patients have died.

The second category results from living in an Earth system that comprises multitudes of nested complex systems, and more nested complex systems within those, and so on. The capacity for surprise is enormous. As Pascal put it, "Imagination tires before nature." The potential for novel and unpredictable outcomes goes up when a system is heavily perturbed, as our planet has been with human activity. The obvious example is climate change, which is certain to happen; but the degree of change, timing, and implications for both conservation and economics are highly uncertain. Similarly, wildfires will happen, and some will affect either present or future late-successional and old-growth habitat, but there is no way to predict how much. Fires have already taken a toll. The Biscuit Fire, which burned in southwest Oregon during the late summer of 2002, is estimated to have destroyed about 20,000 hectares (50,000 acres) of spotted owl nesting habitat and another 12,000 hectares (30,000 acres) of foraging habitat (Lee Webb, personal communication). In 1995, the Warner Creek fire (arson) burnt most of an LSR in the Central Cascades of Oregon.

Yet probably the worst threat to the northern spotted owl is its close cousin, the barred owl (*Strix varia*). Forty years ago the barred owl, slightly larger and more of a habitat generalist than the spotted owl, was not found west of the crest of the Rocky Mountains. At some point, for reasons that so far are unclear, the barred owl began to spread west across southern British Columbia and down into the Pacific Northwest. In the early 1990s barred owls were rare in Olympic National Park; now they are found as far south as northern California. Barred owls attack spotted owls, drive them from their territory, crossbreed with them, and sometimes kill them. It isn't obvious how any conservation strategy that starts with a highly altered landscape could protect the spotted owl from the barred owl, and the same may be said about the unknown number of native species that either are or will be threatened by the spread of exotic organisms and the stresses associated with climate change.

Conservation science is built largely around carving out sanctuaries and their interconnections, using the tools of science to make judgments about how much and where. That strategy is necessary, but by itself unlikely to be sufficient in today's world, where many threats to endangered species do not respect boundaries. Changing climate, wildfire, altered predation and competitive relationships due to various environmental and ecological changes, the spread of exotic weeds, pathogens, and viruses must be dealt with on a national and global basis. The challenges are daunting. Moreover, nature has great momentum, and many ecological changes are for all practical purposes irreversible once set in motion. While mitigation may be possible, the idea that we can "control" nature is illusory, and a strategy of reaction rather than proaction carries significant risk of failure.

A truly heroic effort has been, and is still being, made to save OG-dependent species in the Pacific Northwest, and still the outcome is in doubt (see Ackers, this volume). There is a message here for conservation efforts in areas of the tropics and boreal forests, where there may still be options to be proactive: don't wait until species needing protection are already pushed to an edge. Once that happens and options are foreclosed, the chances for successful win-win solutions go down, and the chances for lose-lose outcomes go up.

In Summary

The objective of FEMAT was to produce a set of options for management and rate the probabilities of each for conserving old-growth ecosystems and the species that depend on them. The resulting process was probably the greatest scientific effort ever brought to bear on a conservation issue. Unfortunately, the array of possible conservation strategies was limited by a highly altered regional landscape and species already pushed to an edge. Though most public attention has focused on the northern spotted owl and the marbled murrelet, large numbers of other species have also lost significant amounts of habitat. FEMAT's approach to stabilize and restore diversity was groundbreaking, drawing on the most current thinking in ecology and conservation science.

The Clinton administration's selection of one option (Option 9) from the ten produced by FEMAT scientists was an attempt to maintain a certain level of logging (about 1 billion board feet/year) while at the same time protecting species dependent on old growth. This meant leaving about one-third of remaining old-growth and mature forests open to logging, further reducing habitat that, from an ecological standpoint, was already deficient. To date, survey-and-manage requirements in the NWFP have provided considerable de facto protection to critical habitat in the matrix, though a shift in policy at the federal level could change that. Over the past several years, thousands of hectares of old-growth habitat have been lost to wildfire, while an unknown but almost certainly large amount of northern spotted owl habitat has been degraded by or outright lost to barred owls. It seems almost certain that habitat is being lost or degraded significantly faster than it is being created by maturing forests—we are literally losing ground. From an ecological standpoint, ensuring protection of remaining mature and old-growth forests is even more critical now than at the time the NWFP was formulated. Measures to protect diversity will also benefit from a wider array of silvicultural options in the matrix, including variable-density thinning and long rotations. From an ecological standpoint, the greatest threats to the success of the NWFP are uncertainties—in basic biological and ecological knowledge, in where the Earth as a system is headed—both of which emerge from the complex and poorly understood workings of nature.

Notes

This chapter is based on a talk given at the Forest Futures Conference, held at Willamette University in Salem, Oregon, on September 25, 2002.

1. Old growth refers to forests with dominant trees generally over 180–200 years old. Mature forests are those in the stage preceding old growth, but beginning to develop old-growth structure. Depending on conditions, forests enter maturity at around eighty years of age. FEMAT used the term *late successional,* or at times LS/OG (late-successional/ old growth) to denote either mature, old growth, or both.
2. For a description of this model, see www.fsl.orst.edu/ccem.

3

Sustained Yield: Goals, Policies, Promises

John H. Beuter

Sustained yield has been a basic tenet of "good forestry" in the United States for well over 100 years. It was conceived in Europe upon concerns for the well-being of future generations in response to forest exploitation and destruction. Traditionally, the focus of sustained yield has been on sustainable timber production, thus making sustained yield a pejorative in the spin of modern environmentalist factions opposed to harvesting trees. Yet, the concept of sustainability thrives, as in sustainable forests, sustainable ecosystems, and sustainable development. So, what's wrong with sustainable timber production?

Despite strong participation of numerous interdisciplinary scientists in developing the Northwest Forest Plan (NWFP; see USDA/USDI 1994a and 1994b), timber harvesting remains at the core of controversy about the management of federal forests in the Northwest. Attempts to meet timber harvest levels envisioned under the NWFP have been thwarted by numerous appeals and litigation, even for timber sales aimed at improving forest health and alleviating the risk of catastrophic wildfires. Endless second-guessing of good-faith efforts to implement the NWFP has made some federal forest managers hesitant to even propose projects that involve timber harvesting.

Public opinion favors strong protection for federal forests. Timber harvesting is often portrayed in the media as a threat to the health and sustainability of forests. Ironically, professional foresters see responsible harvesting as an essential component of maintaining forest health and productivity. Early foresters conceived of sustainable timber yields as the key to forest sustainability. After all, you can't sustain a regular flow of timber without sustaining the forest.

Because of the sustained yield's focus on timber harvesting as the guiding measure of sustainability, some believe it is incompatible with concepts of sustainable forestry that focus on maintaining standards of ecosystem composition, structure, and function over time. Sustained yield forestry has guided federal forest management in the United States for most of the past century. The NWFP changes the focus of forest planning from potential outputs (forest uses) to maintaining attributes and interactions within the forest. Ostensibly, both approaches sustain forests and benefit society. Considering aggregate costs and benefits, the discussion that follows suggests we could do a lot worse than sustained yield forestry in meeting multiple forest objectives, and that it is not clear that the NWFP is much of an improvement.

Sustained Yield

As envisioned by early foresters, sustained yield would be assured by achieving a balance of desirable tree species and forest characteristics across the landscape, with tree ages ranging from seedlings to mature trees that might be harvested to provide wood products. This was called a regulated, or normal, forest. Tree maturity was defined by a rotation age, the age at which it was believed the trees should be harvested because of diminished growth rate (physical or financial), or imminent tree mortality (Society of American Foresters 1958).

Sustained yield harvesting generally involves intermediate harvesting (thinning) to maintain stand vigor and enhance the growth of high-quality wood. Final harvest at rotation age was intended to provide income needed to sustain both the forest owner and the forest. Harvested trees provide growing space for the next generation of trees. It is in the forest owner's best interest to apply silvicultural and related forest practices to assure prompt regeneration of harvested areas.[1]

The long-run ideal for sustained yield forestry is a regular, predictable periodic harvest equal to the periodic growth of the forest. For the regulated forest with a balance of age classes from regeneration to rotation age, annual harvest would equal annual growth and the distribution of growing stock would remain constant over time. Each year, the oldest age class would be harvested and the harvested ground would be regenerated, thus becoming the youngest age class. During the year, all other age classes move up one year and the balance of age classes, from regeneration to rotation age, is maintained.

A regulated forest rarely exists in a single ownership, but can exist de facto across a landscape of multiple owners operating independently such that they harvest at different times and end up with differing age components in their forests. If the aggregate of owners approaches a balance of age classes, their forests might function as a regulated, sustained yield forest whereby periodic harvest approximates periodic growth. It will be seen later in this chapter that this situation appears to exist in Oregon.

Harvest Controls

While sustained yield forestry is neat and tidy as a concept, it is not easy to implement. Balancing species and age classes over time requires not only careful control of forest composition and harvest rates but also contending with risks of catastrophic losses that might affect sustainability, such as weather, insects, disease, wildfire, and even, in modern times, the possibility of new regulatory constraints imposed on forest owners to protect imperiled species or provide for other public benefits.

Prior to the 1960s, harvest was controlled by simple formulas, with periodic harvest a function of periodic growth and the need or desire to build up growing stock (as in the depleted forests of Europe and the eastern United States) or draw down growing stock (as in the "overabundant" forests of the Pacific Northwest). Whatever the starting condition of the forest, the long-run goal was for periodic harvest to equal periodic growth, sustainable indefinitely. In the era of simple formulas foresters took for granted nontimber objectives, figuring that they had provided for ecosystem sustainability just by maintaining a balance of age classes and forest structure across the landscape (Beuter 1974).

With the advent of computers in the 1960s, simple sustained yield formulas gave way to more complex simulation and optimization models, making it possible to control not only the level of harvest, but also the transition to a sustainable forest with harvest equal to growth indefinitely. It became possible to introduce constraints to protect nontimber forest values, such as modifying silvicultural systems and harvesting rules to protect wildlife habitat, viewsheds, and stream zones. Essentially, the models were structured to calculate the maximum sustainable harvest level, subject to desired levels of protection for the forest and environment. The output charted timber harvest potential in the transition to the long-term, steady-state forest condition.

Goal, Policy, or Promise: A Contrast

Over time, the concept of sustained yield has been viewed as a goal, a policy, and a promise. As a goal, sustained yield is an end in itself, oriented primarily toward the structure of the forest—that is, achieving a balance of tree age classes across the landscape. Timber and other forest outputs, while not primary objectives, would be derived from achieving the desired forest structure. As a policy, sustained yield becomes a means to the achievement of goals such as maximum sustainable harvest levels and related economic and social benefits. As a promise, sustained yield provides confidence for investments in forest-based enterprises that may be important components of the economic base of some communities and regions. With all other things remaining constant, sustained yield promised community stability for forest-dependent economies.

Some have suggested sustained yield is an ideal having questionable practical value. Maybe so, but that doesn't make it useless. Carl Schurz, Secretary of the Interior under President Rutherford B. Hayes, has been quoted as saying: "Ideals are like the stars. We may never reach them, but we need them to guide our way."

Under the NWFP, today's federal foresters are challenged to explicitly account for a variety of ecosystem impacts that might occur when timber is harvested. The desired outcome for the NWFP remains sustainable forests and sustainable outputs from the forest, including harvest levels, but the means for achieving those objectives is harder to comprehend than with the sustained yield forestry model. As a goal, it is not clear what the NWFP is supposed to accomplish beyond a vague notion of forest protection. As a policy, it is not clear what the costs and benefits of the NWFP are, and whether it is the best policy for accomplishing whatever is to be accomplished. As a promise, the NWFP offers little beyond devotion to ecosystem management, which Freeman (2002) describes as an "undefined concept that the agency [U.S. Forest Service] could shape in the context of political debates . . . the agency's attempt to mollify [popular and scientific interests] with the promise of using science to meet its political demands."

Timber harvesting and economic and community benefits clearly are secondary considerations of the NWFP, with little assurance of what outcomes might be expected. Under the sustained yield model, periodic timber harvesting is integral to the plan to maintain the structure of the forest. Timber harvesting is precluded on much of federal forest and land—seemingly, a matter of indifference even on parts of the forest where it might be allowed.

The sustained yield model looks outward from the forest to sustainably meet the needs of people, subject to constraints to protect the forest and related environment. The NWFP looks inward to meet perceived needs of the forest, with little apparent consideration for meeting the needs of people beyond a universal desire to protect forests. Both approaches are concerned about forest sustainability, and it's not certain they need to be markedly incompatible with regard to ecosystem values. The main point of departure between the two approaches is timber harvest potential.

Timber Harvest Potential

Timber harvest potential is determined by the inherent capability of the land to grow trees valued as timber; the intensity of management (labor and capital) applied toward growing timber; and external constraints imposed by markets, competition, and social institutions that might limit timber harvest potential or affect confidence to invest in timber production. Private forest owners have incentive to seek highest and best use to maximize the market value of their land. Forest land converted to higher-valued nonforest uses has little or no potential to produce timber. The same is true for federal forest land on which timber harvesting is precluded or restricted to provide public benefits deemed higher and better than timber production.

For forest land having physical and biological capability to grow timber, and that is economically and technically suitable for timber production and not reserved or dedicated to another use, the main determinants of harvest potential are (Beuter et al. 1976):

- Inherent timber-growing productivity (site capability),
- Characteristics of the existing timber inventory (species, size, quality, location, etc.),
- Type and intensity of timber management,
- Constraints on timber management practices and harvesting,
- Time horizon and conditions that define sustainability.[2]

Federal Forests

Timber harvest on federal forests has been shrinking mainly because of constraints on management practices and harvesting that have put large areas of forest off limits for timber production and limited options on other land that might still be eligible for harvesting. It should be emphasized that harvest potential is not limited by land capability, existing timber inventory, or past management practices, but rather by policy decisions that favor non-timber objectives. The timber inventory that still might be available for harvest has shifted toward younger, premature age classes, with harvesting for the foreseeable future mostly limited to thinning. Even where timber management is allowed, management intensity options have been limited by policy decisions, such as restrictions on clear-cutting and the use of chemical herbicides to control undesirable vegetation (such as blackberries and Scotch broom) that competes with desirable trees.

Under the NWFP, sustainable harvest on federal lands has been limited mainly by internal policy decisions believed to increase public benefits by favoring nontimber forest objectives. What timber harvest might be feasible under the NWFP has been further constrained by administrative appeals and litigation by outside interests aimed at further reducing timber harvesting from federal lands.

Even before the NWFP, federal forest plans in the Northwest were being rewritten to provide additional protection to stream habitat and old-growth stands believed to be strategically important for the recovery of spotted owls (*Strix occidentalis caurina*) and marbled murrelets (*Brachyramphus marmoratus*). An analysis by Oregon State University, taking into account protection then envisioned as needed to threatened and endangered species, projected a sustainable harvest of 3.8 billion board feet per year from federal forests in Oregon (Sessions et al. 1991). Under the NWFP and constraints proposed for eastern Oregon harvest under the Interior Columbia Basin Ecosystem Management Plan (ICBEMP—pertaining to federal forests in eastern Oregon), the sustainable harvest for federal forests in Oregon dropped from 3.8 to 1.3 billion board feet (Beuter 1998a). The actual federal harvest in Oregon for the last five years (1997–2001) averaged about 400 million board feet per year, 70 percent below the planned sustainable harvest for federal lands (ODF 1977–2001).

Nonfederal Forests

Steep harvest reductions on federal forests have increased interest in the potential for sustainable timber harvesting on nonfederal forests (state and private ownerships). Timber always has been a mainstay of Oregon's economic base, particularly for the nonmetropolitan areas of the state. As recently as 1994, timber and wood products industries comprised about one-fourth of Oregon's economic base, and as much as one-third of the economic base for rural Oregon (Beuter 1998a).

Nonfederal forests are subject to rules and regulations under Oregon's forest practices and protection laws (OFRI 2002). Oregon's forest laws are among the strictest in the nation. In addition, Oregon's comprehensive land-use planning laws and regulations restrict most private forest land to forest use only. This means that the market value of private forest land is almost solely dependent on its potential to produce crops of marketable timber. For personal reasons or protection of environmental values, individuals and organizations have been known to pay as much or more for forest land as its market value for timber production, but that is the exception. Professional market value appraisals of forest land in Oregon for transactions and IRS estate valuations are based primarily on the market value of standing timber and timber production potential for bare forest land.

Oregon has about 11.3 million hectares (28 million acres) of forest land—58 percent federal, 42 percent nonfederal. Despite the disparity of acreage, the sustainable harvest potential of 3.7 billion board feet per year for nonfederal forests is about the same as the aforementioned 3.8 billion board feet for federal forests before the NWFP (Sessions et al. 1991). Most areas of nonfederal forest land are capable and suitable for timber management and, in contrast to federal forests, are assumed to be available for harvesting. Nonfederal forests are managed more intensively for timber production than federal forests, which accounts in part for greater sustainable harvest potential relative to area of nonfederal forest land.

Empirical Evidence

But is the timber productivity on nonfederal forests sustainable? Timber harvesting in Oregon over the past seventy-seven years may provide some clues about sustainability (figure 3.1).

The wild swings of harvest over time in figure 3.1 belie sustainability. To some extent that is accurate. Consider nonfederal

Figure 3.1. Oregon Timber Harvest, 1925–2001, with Reference to Projected Sustainability. [Sources: Nonfederal and federal timber harvest: 1925–1949, Wall 1972; 1950–1976, USDA Forest Service; 1977–2001, Oregon Department of Forestry, federal and nonfederal sustainable harvest, Sessions et al. 1991; NW Forest Plan+ (accounts for the impacts of both the Northwest Forest Plan in western Oregon and the Interior Columbia Basin Ecosystem Management Plan (ICBEMP) for federal forests in eastern Oregon), Johnson et al. 1993, and assumption drawn by author for the ICBEMP impact (Beuter, 1998a)]

harvesting prior to the 1960s (dark line). Except for a major dip during the Great Depression of the 1930s, harvesting from nonfederal (mostly private) land increased steeply through the 1950s, the result of a lot of factors coming together during the same time period:

- An abundance of mature, old-growth timber on both federal and nonfederal forests, but little interest in federal timber sales
- The development of technology, such as steam donkeys, railroad logging, chain saws, better forest roads, and bigger trucks and tractors, making logging in the Pacific Northwest more efficient
- Extraordinary market demand for wood products during the post-depression era, World War II, and the postwar building boom
- Diminished supplies of timber in other parts of the United States because of earlier exploitation

Oregon's nonfederal harvest peaked in 1952, also the peak year for total harvest in the state (10.8 billion board feet). As nonfederal old-growth inventories diminished, harvest plummeted and the wood products industry increased pressure for more timber sales on federal forests.

Prior to the 1930s, there wasn't much of a federal timber sale program. Sales were considered upon application by prospective purchasers. In some cases, the U.S. Forest Service made large timber offerings to induce economic development in isolated rural areas, for example, the 1923 Bear Valley Sale on the Malheur National Forest in which almost a billion board feet of timber was offered with the requirement that the purchaser build a sawmill and eighty miles of common carrier railroad (Wiener 1982).

Both the U.S. Forest Service and Bureau of Land Management got serious about selling timber by the 1940s—as can be seen by the federal timber harvest, which rose steeply until the 1960s (figure 3.1, gray line). Federal harvest bounced around between four and five billion board feet per year during the 1960s and 1970s and then began a steady decline as scientists and others raised environmental and sustainability issues. The increase in federal harvest during the latter half of the 1980s is not because of increased timber selling during that period. The increase was largely due to the harvest of timber sales made during the 1970s which were not harvested during the severe recession in the early 1980s (note the steep drop in harvest in the early 1980s—figure 3.1). The decline became precipitous in the 1990s with the emergence of endangered species issues followed by the NWFP and ICBEMP, and the subsequent flurry of appeals and litigation for many projects involving timber harvesting. So much for sustainability!

But wait. Remember that the study by Sessions et al. (1991) projected sustainable harvest levels of 3.8 and 3.7 billion board feet per year for federal and nonfederal forests, respectively (figure 3.1). The federal sustainable harvest under the NWFP and ICBEMP is projected at only 1.3 billion board feet per year (NW Forest Plan+ in figure 3.1). But, federal harvest since 1994 has been significantly below even this reduced level of sustainability, plunging to 173 million board feet in 2001—less than half the volume harvested from federal forests in 1932, in the depths of the Great Depression. As pointed out earlier, the federal harvest reductions are mainly because of policy decisions, not exploitation or devastation of the federal forests.

The real story of sustainability is on the nonfederal forests. Following the exploitive harvesting of old-growth timber that came to an end by the 1960s, nonfederal harvest settled in the range of 3.0 to 4.5 billion board feet per year (figure 3.1). Declining inventories of timber and the advent of Oregon's Forest Practices Act (OFRI 2002) brought the harvest below four billion board feet in 1976. Since 1975, nonfederal harvest has remained between three and four billion board feet with an average of 3.6 billion board feet per year, about the same as what Sessions et al. (1991) projected as a sustainable level. This is remarkable considering that nonfederal forests are owned by state and local governments and thousands of individuals and companies who make autonomous decisions about if, when, where, and how much timber to harvest, without any central direction or control. Oregon's Forest Practices Act (OFRI 2002) regulates only harvesting practices for safety and protection of environmental values, and enforces the legal requirement to reforest following a harvest operation.

Achieving Sustained Outcome

How is it that these many owners, operating largely on their own, have in aggregate harvested over the past twenty-five years at a level that apparently is sustainable indefinitely? This yield is especially impressive considering that much of these owners' forestland was heavily exploited and devastated (by today's standards) in the first half of the twentieth century by logging practices that are mostly illegal today.

The answers lie in the natural resilience of Oregon's forests, the enlightenment of forest owners through research and education, improved fire protection, some degree of regulation through Oregon's forest practices rules and land-use laws, and some degree of market influence.

Natural Resilience

About 80 percent of the volume harvested from nonfederal lands in recent years has come from trees 50 to 70 years old (Lettman 1995). It is a truism that a 70-year-old tree harvested today was a seedling 70 years ago (1932). But enforced reforestation didn't exist 70 years ago, and voluntary efforts to plant after harvesting were rare in those days. The same was true in 1952, the highest harvest year in Oregon's history and the year that today's 50-year-old trees were born. So, much of today's harvest was possible because of the natural regeneration of forests following harvesting in the period from 1932 to 1952.

Forest Owner Enlightenment and Improved Fire Protection

Intensive reforestation efforts by forest owners and improved fire protection were spurred by the devastating Tillamook fires of the 1930s and 1940s, but it was the 1960s before reliable reforestation practices began to be developed by researchers. In the 1960s, it was estimated that half the seedlings planted were dead or doomed when they were planted because of poor handling and planting practices. Seedlings that did survive were threatened further by competing vegetation and animal damage because of poor site preparation and lack of monitoring. Gradually, through research and education efforts, forest owners learned about the need for site preparation, care of seedlings, and follow-up control of competing vegetation and animal damage. Regeneration failures are rare these days.[3]

Today's forest owners are also much more aware of the need to consider wildlife habitat and protection of streams for clean water and fish. Oregon's forest practices rules set a threshold of reasonable protection; but many landowners choose to do more, including offering their forests for third-party certification of sustainable practices (see Sedjo, this volume).

Nonfederal owners pay special levies to support forest fire prevention and suppression efforts for the forests in their fire prevention district. Devastating fires on nonfederal forests are relatively rare because most forest properties are well roaded and easily accessible for fire suppression. Intensive management practices, such as pre-commercial and commercial thinning, tend to reduce the risk of fire spread. And, finally, nonfederal owners tend to monitor their forests on a regular basis because of ongoing activity and realization of the value of their investment in the forest. Forest workers are apt to have continuous interaction with the forest, enhancing site-specific knowledge about the forest and its productive potential. In contrast, many federal forest officials these days are not schooled in forestry, have limited field experience, and are subject to frequent transfers, all of which limit their ability to gain intimate knowledge about the forests they manage.

Forest Practices Rules and Land-Use Zoning

Public debates about forest practices rules have made forest owners aware of societal expectations for environmental protection and other public benefits from forests. Arguments tend not to be about desired outcomes, but rather how to get from here to there. There is no question that forest practices rules and regulations in Oregon have enhanced protection and sustainability of a wide range of forest values.

Oregon's comprehensive land-use planning is easy to overlook as an incentive for forest owners to practice sustainable forestry (ORS 197.075). It is obvious that zoning forest land for exclusive forest use will keep it in forest. What may not be obvious is the incentive forest owners have to manage their forests to enhance market value. Folks do not generally buy forest land in Oregon hoping to make a killing with some higher and better use. When someone buys forest land, they are generally interested in forest management because most of the land value derives from how the forest is managed. And, most of the market value of forest land derives from timber production. So, it can be said that Oregon has legislated timber management into its future, a powerful incentive for forest owners to practice sustained yield forestry.

Market Influence

The market provides an important incentive for sustained yield forestry on nonfederal forests in Oregon. As noted earlier, timber provides most of the market value for forest land zoned for exclusive forest use. Forestry investments are long-term investments, with start-up costs often carried twenty or more years before offsetting revenues can be expected. Faith in the availability of markets is essential for investing in forest land.

Unfortunately, the turmoil surrounding the management of federal forests has already shaken confidence in markets for Pacific Northwest wood products and enhanced investors' confidence in competitive timber-producing regions, such as the U.S. South, Canada, and even New Zealand. Many wood products mills have closed in recent years because of federal harvest reductions, lessening competition for timber and making it more difficult to sell nonfederal timber. Ironically, some timber market niches in the Pacific Northwest deprived of federal timber are now being served by imports from as far away as Mexico, South America, and New Zealand.

Some have noted that curtailment of federal harvests has increased the value of nonfederal timber (Sohngen and Haynes 1994). That may have been true in the short run, but it is questionable for the long run. Timber from federal lands tends toward larger diameters than that supplied from nonfederal lands. Now, with large-log mills closing due to a lack of federal timber, nonfederal owners are finding their larger timber devalued by a lack of markets. It follows that the incentive to grow large timber is also evaporating, driving nonfederal owners toward short-rotation plantation forestry in order to preserve the value of their land. This is certainly an unintended consequence of the federal land policies aimed at preserving larger timber.

The Influence of Rotation Age on Sustainable Harvest

The emergence of the old-growth issue on federal forests in the Northwest has brought into question the ages at which timber should be harvested. It should be understood that tree age may be less relevant than forest structure for providing values associated with old-growth forests. On good productivity sites, large trees can be grown much faster than on poorer sites.

Whether large trees should be harvested on the federal lands is more a public policy issue than a forestry issue. A good part of the harvest reduction on federal forests is due to policies restricting the harvest of older large trees. In effect, reserved old-growth is set aside from timber management—the trees and the land are removed from the determination of sustainable harvest levels and should not be an issue for criticizing federal timber sales.

Yet, the harvesting of large trees remains an issue, even when it comes to thinning forests to reduce fire risk. Again, this is a policy call; however, it might be useful to provide the forester's perspective on rotation (harvest) ages and how they affect the productivity and economics of timber production.

A tree or a stand of trees has a life cycle, the same as most other organisms. There is a shaky beginning when survival may hang in the balance, followed by prolific growth and eventual decline in vigor (figure 3.2).

At what age should the forest owner harvest older trees and start a new generation of forest? It depends on the owner's objectives. With reference to figure 3.2, if an owner were seeking a high return on investment, it is likely she'd choose a rotation age somewhere between age 30 and 70 (at the age where the timber value growth rate drops below her discount rate). If an owner wanted to grow as much timber volume as possible over time, he'd choose a rotation of 75 years (the maximum average annual growth). And, if an owner was not concerned about maximizing financial returns or volume, he or she might grow the stand to old-growth status and harvest trees when they stop growing or die. And finally, if the owner's objective extends beyond old growth to the ecological benefits of deteriorating, dying, and dead trees, the owner might never harvest, allowing the stand to achieve its own destiny. The latter seems close to what the NWFP intends for much of the federal forest in Oregon.

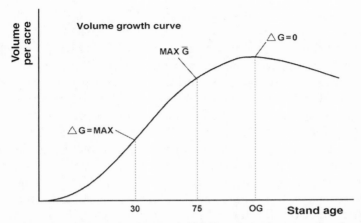

Figure 3.2. Life Cycle of a Stand of Timber. Ages shown are for discussion purposes only. Actual ages differ depending on species, site productivity, and a host of environmental factors. The marginal (e.g., annual) growth rate of a stand of timber begins to decline at, for example, age 30 (ΔG = MAX). Average growth rate of the stand (volume/age) eventually begins to decline at age 75 (MAX Ḡ). Net growth ceases altogether at some indeterminate age, typically when trees reach old-growth status (ΔG = 0), at which point the volume of timber in the stand may begin to decline.

The example is simplistic. Timber production–oriented forest owners tend to adjust constantly to market changes and circumstances dealt by nature. At the other end of the spectrum (benign neglect of old-growth reserves), the situation may not be as dismal as it sounds—witness revered old-growth stands that have been around for hundreds of years, with prospects for being around indefinitely, perhaps for hundreds of years more—or maybe not. Time will tell.

The lesson to be drawn is that forest owners have differing objectives, and in working to achieve those objectives, provide differing public benefits, from high-quality, reasonably priced building materials to old-growth habitat, in addition to the public benefits common to all forests (water, scenery, recreation, hunting, fishing, etc.).

"Saving the Forests"

Folks sometimes (usually with good intentions, but not always) try to impose requirements or restrictions that are insensitive to the objectives of forest owners and the impacts on public benefits. One example is Oregon Ballot Measure 64 (Beuter 1998b), which would have prohibited harvesting large trees on private land and restricted forest management options, and at the same time forced owners to longer rotation ages on portions of their land. If it had passed, the result would have been immediate devaluation of many forest properties, and disruption of timber supplies from private forests at the same time that harvests from federal forests were plummeting (Beuter 1998b). In the long run, sustainable annual timber harvest from nonfederal forests in Oregon would have dropped by about the same proportion as the federal reduction caused by the NWFP, from 3.8 to 1.3 billion board feet. The initiative was defeated soundly by Oregon voters.

Supporters of the initiative believed it was needed to preserve biological diversity (ecological integrity) and the sustainability of nonfederal forests. So far, this chapter has addressed only the sustainability of timber harvest on nonfederal lands, which under the sustained yield model would speak also for the sustainability of the forest. But, what about biological diversity and ecological integrity?

Recent studies offer hope that the mosaic of nonfederal forests across the landscape is producing not only sustainable timber harvest, but sustainable biological diversity and ecological integrity. A recent study examined the trade-offs between timber production and biodiversity on 526,000 hectares (1.3 million acres) in Oregon's Coast Range consisting of diverse forest ownership and management (Spies et al. 2002a). The metrics of the study were species diversity, ecosystem diversity, and ecosystem dynamics (forest health and vitality). The study found that trade-offs do exist, but the magnitude is "apparently small." With diverse ownership, impacts are always occurring but in different ways at different places at different times. Individual management impacts are relatively small in the context of the larger landscape, such that, as the study found, "relatively small differences in management approaches applied to portions of ownerships may not result in major changes to our aggregate measure of ecological integrity within a 100-year time frame." The authors caution that quantitative measures of biological diversity and ecological integrity are in the early stages of development and may change as new information becomes available.

Another study examined land ownership (including federal lands) and landscape structure in a spatial analysis of sixty-six Coast Range watersheds in Oregon (Stanfield et al. 2002). Among the findings of this study was that "forest cover diversity increased with land ownership diversity." The implications of this finding are that in the long run, biodiversity may be at least as well, if not better, preserved by the atomistic ownership of thousands of nonfederal owners as it might be by centrally planned management of large expanses of federal forest land, as was done with the NWFP.

Sustainability Redux

The concept of sustained yield forestry has been around for a long time. The theory is to manage forests to achieve sustainable timber harvests compatible with the forest owner's objectives for the forest. The key is to maintain a balance of tree age classes across the landscape. A profit-maximizing forest owner will tend to have less species diversity, a younger spread of tree ages, and more rapid turnover of the timber inventory. An owner less concerned with financial return who wishes to maximize timber volume or nontimber values of the forest will tend to have a wider spread of tree ages and less frequent turnover of the timber inventory. Any of these scenarios perpetuate the forest—sustainable forests are a necessary precondition for sustainable timber harvest. They differ in the potential levels of sustainable harvest and the sustainable structure of the forest (which is related to biological diversity and ecological integrity).

Nonfederal lands in Oregon have, in aggregate, demonstrated harvest sustainability over the past twenty-five years at close to long-run sustainable levels determined by scientific analysis of the productivity of the land, existing condition of the forests, and management practices. In addition, recent studies suggest that diverse ownership is associated with forest diversity, and ecological integrity seems to be sustainable across a broad landscape of diverse owners because individual management activities occur somewhat randomly on only portions of an ownership and have relatively little impact on the aggregate forest structure across the landscape.

Most nonfederal owners explicitly or implicitly manage with concepts of sustainable timber harvest, subject to forest protection laws and their own desires for profit and forest structure. They work to maintain the value of their land in an ever-changing world. This requires looking forward and outward from the forest to develop the confidence and commitment to justify their investment in forest land.

In contrast, the NWFP looks inward, focusing mainly on the biological and physical interactions within the forest. It is analogous to basic research in an ivory-tower laboratory, digging deeper and deeper to explore the mystery of how things work, with only the vaguest notion of ultimate value. Values are determined by people, and in a sense, the NWFP does represent people's values derived through the political process, not the marketplace. But it can be argued that the political process was characterized by less than perfect, if not distorted, knowledge about the state of our forests, their potential for sustainable outputs in conjunction with forest and ecosystem sustainability, and the economic and social costs of the plan.

Consideration of empirical evidence for nonfederal forests in Oregon suggests we could do a lot worse than sustained yield forestry. In aggregate, nonfederal owners are contributing sustainable forests and sustainable harvest, which in turn supports economic activity vital for sustenance of many rural communities in Oregon.

In contrast, the harvest reductions of the NWFP have devastated segments of Oregon's wood products–based economy, and the lack of commitment and follow-through on even the reduced timber harvest allowable under the plan has exacerbated the problem by discouraging upkeep of forest-industry infrastructure and new investment. The NWFP is not off to a good start, and only time will tell whether it is an improvement over the sustained yield concepts that guided federal forest management for most of the twentieth century. Don't bet on it.

Notes

This chapter is based on a talk given at the Forest Futures Conference at Willamette University in Salem, Oregon, on September 25, 2002.

1. In Oregon (as well as other states), regeneration of desirable species to appropriate stocking levels after harvesting is required by law (ORS 527.710). This applies to all types of harvest methods, from single tree selection to clear-cutting. Regeneration may be accomplished by natural seeding from the residual forest (usually most appropriate for selection harvesting) or planting of nursery-grown seedlings (usually a must for clear-cutting).

2. Timber harvest scheduling and projection models determine an allowable harvest level for a given year or period, subject to the solution being sustainable over a specified time horizon, say 400 years, with an ending condition that defines the forest structure at the end of the time horizon; for example, harvest must equal growth (implying a regulated forest), or all harvest in the last period of the projection has to come from timber above a certain age class (implying a regulated forest with rotation age at the youngest age class eligible for harvest in the last period of the projection). The latter test ensures that harvest at any time during the time horizon does not jeopardize the potential for continuing sustainable harvesting beyond the time horizon.

3. The Oregon Department of Forestry issues an annual Reforestation Accomplishment Report. The report for 1999, issued in 2001, reported that of 115,436 acres requiring reforestation (following harvesting), 99.6 percent were reforested. Of 106,393 acres required to meet the "free-to-grow" standard that defines successful regeneration within three years of harvest, 99.7 percent of the acres met the standard (Oregon Department of Forestry 2001). Accomplishment reports for past years showed similar levels of success.

4

Challenges to Sustainable Forestry: Management and Economics

Roger A. Sedjo

A number of years ago when I was working on my book *Sustainability of Temperate Forests* (Sedjo et al. 1998), I had a conversation with a French forester who said in essence, "This whole inquiry is silly. The French had forests 1,000 years ago and we still have forests today. Therefore, they must be sustainable." I must admit I found some wisdom in this observation. Even advocates of forest certification have recently acknowledged that "scientific data do not yet support a single consensus on the definition of biological sustainability, especially given regional variations in ecology; the same is true for socioeconomic sustainability" (Heaton and Donovan 1997, 55). Another critic, Flasche (1997), was probably correct when he characterized today's sustainable forestry as more of a philosophy of how forests should be cared for than a definable condition of the forests or a set of acceptable management practices. One of the tasks for those interested in sustainable forestry is to translate the philosophy into operational concepts.

As just demonstrated, the concept of sustainable forestry is an elusive one. Most foresters are familiar with the concept of "sustainable yield forestry," which simply calls for future timber yields to be equal to or greater than earlier yields. In that context it was never quite clear whether maintaining yields was truly sustainable yield management if the application of outside inputs, such as fertilizer, were required. However, as practiced, the Forest Service's "allowable cut" concept allowed larger harvest rates if it could be demonstrated that growth could be increased through management, including additional inputs (see Beuter in this volume). Sustainable forestry as the term is now being used, however, appears to be quite a different concept. My interpretation is that sustainable forestry today refers to forest ecosystem sustainability, which involves a wide range of considerations beyond timber production. Certification is a process whereby the forest management practices of an organization, and thus the wood from its harvests, is "certified" as meeting a standard of forest management judged to be acceptable, established by an organization such as the Forest Stewardship Council (FSC) or the Sustainable Forestry Initiative (SFI). After briefly examining paradigm shifts in the field of forest ecology and the implications for managing for sustainability, I explore the origins of forest certification from international and domestic concern over the health of the world's forests. I then discuss some of the ecological and economic obstacles encountered by certification regimes generally and particularly in North America. I conclude by suggesting that certification may have a positive, albeit limited, effect on improving forest practices.

What Forest Ecology Tells Us about Sustainability

Forest ecology as a scientific field is undergoing some fundamental changes. A question this discipline must resolve is, "what is the most useful construct for understanding the behavior of forests through time?" For years, foresters used the model of natural forest systems moving systematically through a number of well-defined states toward a unique and final "climax" forest. The climax forest state would persist in equilibrium with the surrounding environment until substantially disturbed, as with a fire. Following disturbance, it would return to an earlier state and again progress toward its climax state. Thus, to understand a particular forest system was to understand the unique path from forest regeneration to its forest climax, and the various states in route. However, this concept presents problems for certification. For example, Botkin (1990) points out that Kirtland's warblers (*Dendroica kirtlandii*) require a 6- to 21-year-old jack pine (*Pinus banksiana*) forest for nesting. So, if the forest is maintained at too young an age, the warbler population will go to zero. If the forest is allowed to become much older, the warbler population will also go to zero. Does loss of this one species suggest the forest ecosystem is not sustainable? Not at all. But it does demonstrate that if the goal is the conservation of the warbler, then a specific disturbance regime is required to meet that goal.

More generally, as the preceding case suggests, one would expect to find different species in old forests than in young forests, even along the same successional pathway. If the maintenance of all species existing on a site is used as a criterion of sustainability, as it is in many certification audits, then young forests would never be allowed to grow old. Obviously, if a broader landscape approach were taken, then one would manage to maintain certain portions of the landscape in the various successional stages. However, this is not possible on individual stands, or small- to medium-sized forest ownerships. Thus, the certification of sustainability at less than the landscape level becomes extremely problematical.

An example of this problem is found in the viability regulation in the National Forest Management Act of 1976 (NFMA). The provision calls for maintaining viable self-sustaining populations that are well distributed throughout the species' range. However, as Botkin (1990) has shown, a changing forest involves a changing mix and population of species. Under this circumstance the species' range could change. Thus, to be consistent with the nature of the forest, the viability regulation would need to be interpreted to allow specific provisions for this change. The regulation can easily be interpreted as envisaging what is essentially a static forest rather than one that is dynamic.

In fact, the problem may be even more complex than this (Botkin and Sobel 1975). In an important book, *Discordant Harmonies* (1990), Botkin summarizes challenges to the traditional concept of a well-behaved forest system moving toward a unique climax condition. The result is a substantially revised concept of ecosystem sustainability. By this new more complex view, the forest is no longer seen as moving through a narrow set of given stages until it reaches maturity or a climax state, at which point it continues until it is disturbed and sent back to an earlier or beginning state, only to move again through the progressions. Rather, Botkin suggests that we now understand a forest ecosystem as a set of states. For each state, there is a set of variables that characterize that state. As the values of the variables change within their potential ranges, the forest too will change. Thus, there is no longer a necessary, unique path. Rather, there are a large number of potential paths. For example, a disturbed oak forest could be replaced by a new oak forest, but it might also be replaced by a pine forest. As natural perturbations occur or management is carried out, the trajectory of the system will change. Note that there need not be any climax state and the forest need not repeat an earlier cycle, although it may. The various states may or may not recur. Through time, species may be gained or lost within the context of this much more complex ecosystem; for example, different species are likely to inhabit an oak forest than a pine forest. An implication is that some species may be present in some states, but not others. And the absence of species through time may suggest a new state has been reached but need not imply the loss of broad ecosystem sustainability (Botkin 1990, 155–56).

How should a forest certifier deal with this complexity? Some forest ecologists believe that although certifiers say they no longer accept the concept of a climax forest, in fact the certification procedures, as commonly applied, are tied very tightly to the now-obsolete concept of a climax forest. Even more distressingly, they often appear to be tied to the concept of a static forest. Thus, one could argue that certification, rather than ensuring ecological sustainability through its relevant range, may inhibit it.

Why Certification?

Having raised these limitations, there nevertheless appear to be some important reasons why certification has developed the momentum that it has. Although concern among foresters and conservationists about forest sustainability has a long history, recent concerns about the plight of the world's forests were triggered in the late 1970s as wild "guesstimates" of the rate of deforestation, particularly tropical deforestation, were made by some environmental authors. Although these early estimates turned out to be excessively high, these concerns precipitated more comprehensive estimates made by the United Nations. The UN estimates, which still indicated fairly rapid rates of tropical deforestation, also revealed that the nontropical forests of the world were experiencing net afforestation. However, it took until the mid-1990s before this fact became well recognized, even by the experts.

Additionally, the 1992 UN Conference on Environmental and Development at Rio de Janeiro, also known as the Earth Summit, generated some important forest initiatives. A forestry objective identified as a priority in Rio and on the ascendancy since then has been that of sustainably managed forestry. At the intergovernmental level, it has been manifest in a number of international understandings and declarations. At the private level, it is manifest in the emergence of a relatively large number of "sustainable forest management" auditing and certifying groups; the relatively large number of forests that are involved in these activities; and the development of eco-labeled products, made from "certified" wood. Most of the certification activity is occurring in the industrial temperate countries, where forest management is practiced and institutions exist that allow for relatively easy monitoring.

The concern of the environmental community over the conditions of the world's forests appears to be shared to a substantial extent by much of the public. Even when forests are logged for wood for products, much of the public would like this to be done in a sustainable way. Some major retailers of wood products have started to market eco-labeled products drawn from sustainable or well-managed forests. We see retailers like Home Depot wrestling with the idea of carrying eco-labeled wood products or of carrying *only* eco-labeled wood products. The problem is not limited to solidwood products. A senior manager of a major newspaper, who was concerned that the wood used for his paper's newsprint came from sustainable forests, told me that when he asked his daughter why she would not read the newspaper she said, "your newspaper is killing my trees." The senior manager recognized that it was in his newspaper's interest that people not think of newspapers as killers of trees.

It is clear that much of the public wants to believe that our forests are well managed, even though they often appear to be unwilling to pay a significantly higher price for wood from certified forests or for eco-labeled products that are processed from wood from certified forests. As shall be noted later, it remains unclear whether certification provides profitability. Yet it is also unclear just what certification requires.

Forest Auditing for Sustainability Certification

The idea of financial auditing, as I understand it, is to capture the financial situation of a company at a point in time. Financial auditing is driven by the concept of profitability. This concept is tied to understanding the relationship of revenues to costs, both today and for the future. Appropriate financial auditing should provide information as to the recent and current profitability of the firm, as well as provide information on liabilities that are likely to affect future profitability. Auditing procedures are subject to numerous debates as to how certain items ought to be treated. However, there are generally accepted accounting principles, although these may differ across countries. Furthermore, auditing evolves as new products raise new challenges, a situation that is currently under way in the financial community.

Forest auditing for certification, however, is fundamentally different from financial auditing. While forest auditing is still in its infancy, it is pretty clear that there is substantially less clarity in what is being measured compared to financial accounting. This is particularly true when certification is addressing social issues as well as forest management issues. Broadly interpreted, forest auditing objectives also include many social ends as well as ecological and economic ends. This raises some questions. Should labor-intensive forest management be supported for social objectives even if it requires continued external subsidies? More generally, is financial sustainability part of forest sustainability? If so, who will guarantee it? Can we justify subsidizing sustainable forest management on forests that are not now—and may never—turn a profit?

The Forest Stewardship Council (FSC) was an early advocate and practitioner of forest certification. With its roots in the environmental community, the FSC moved to gain support from industry internationally and to establish a system of forest certification with a stable of forest auditors. The FSC has been successful in establishing itself in a host of countries and regions around the world and is truly international in its coverage. The Sustainable Forestry Initiative (SFI) is a more recent certification organization and is found entirely in North America, primarily in the United States. Created largely as a response to the FSC, the SFI has board members representing both the forest industry and the environmental community. Table 4.1 indicates a host of other certifying groups, largely regional, including the Canadian Standards Association, the Pan European Forest Certification organization, and the Malaysian Timber Certification Council.

Table 4.1.   Forest Areas Certified Worldwide, with Available Certification Regimes

Country	Million Acres	Percent	FSC	SFI	CSA	ATFS	PEFC	MTCC	LEI
Canada	43	15	x	x	x				
United States	74	25	x	x		x			
Europe	155	53	x				x		
Other industrialized country	2	1	x						
Developing countries (excludes ISO)	18	6	x					x	x
TOTAL	292	100							

Certification systems:
ATFS—American Tree Farmers System
CSA—Canadian Standards Association
FSC—Forest Stewardship Council
ISO—International Standards Organization
LEI—Lembaga Ekolabe Indonesia

MTCC—Malaysian Timber Certification Council
PEFC—Pan European Forest Certification
SFI—Sustainable Forestry Initiative

Source: Certification Watch 2002.

The certification systems differ in their relative emphasis on ecological, social, and economic aspects. For example, in a recent field-based comparison of the two major certification systems in North America, the FSC generally rates higher on socioeconomic issues in certification, while the SFI rates higher on applicability of standards to the local context (Mater et al. 2002). The results of a comparative assessment on a large number of features by the Meridian Institute are presented in table 4.2.

However, even when certification focuses solely on forest management, a lack of clarity sometimes emerges. In a recent visit to a forest in northern Wisconsin that has received the FSC's certification, my discussions with managers suggested that the focus of audits tends to change from period to period depending upon the technical expertise of the certifiers. Additionally, the FSC standards were sometimes viewed as vague. For example, certifiers wanted the managers to leave more standing trees per acre after a harvest. How many should they leave? the managers asked. A specific answer was not given. It was simply conveyed that more standing trees were preferred to fewer. Nevertheless, the forest was certified. There is a saying that "to manage one must be able to measure." What measurements are required to determine when the forest is being managed sustainably and when it is not? Often, this is not clear. It should also be noted that this same forest had not generated profits for many years. Profitability can clearly be measured. Is a forest sustainable in a social sense if it cannot cover its costs?

Even within a particular standards-setting organization, major differences occur. Perhaps this is not surprising. FSC recognized that a single standard was not sensible for all of the many regions around the world, and so it has created local teams to develop regionally specific standards. However, the standards finally chosen seem to have a great deal to do with the makeup of the various groups. For example, FSC established a different certification standards in the Canadian Maritime Provinces from that established in the New England states—two separate but ecologically similar regions. The resulting standards were so different that JD Irving, a forestry firm with forest lands in both regions, withdrew from its earlier agreement to meet FSC certification standards on its Maritime lands, believing that the new standards were too onerous,

Table 4.2. Meridian Institute Comparison of SFI and FSC Certification Standards

Addressed by Both SFI and FSC, Same Approach	Addressed by Both, Different Approach	Addressed by One, or by Each with a Very Different Approach
Water Quality Both require site-specific riparian protection planning, implementation, and evaluation	**Unique Forest Areas** SFI: identify and appropriately manage FSC: protect and monitor	**Forest Plantations** SFI: no explicit reference FSC: prohibits conversion of natural forests; plantations can be certified if conditions met
Soil Protection Both recognize soil as the fundamental foundation of forest productivity and require written soil protection policies	**Sustained Yield** Both require harvests consistent with growth and yield models, and modification based on new information. FSC requires ten-year average	**Socioeconomic Impacts** SFI: not required FSC: requires periodic assessment
Fire, Disease Protection Both require protections from fire, pathogens, and disease	**Clearcutting and Even-aged Management** SFI: 120-acre clear-cut limit; permits even-aged management if compatible with habitat diversity FSC: 40-acre clearcut limit; green-tree retention and mimicking of natural disturbance path size	**Use of GMOs** SFI: comply with existing regulations and protocols FSC: total prohibition
Monitoring and Adaptive Management Both monitor, measure, report, and revise plans. FSC requires annual public audits	**Roads** SFI: requires road construction best management practices, no limit on extent of network FSC: explicit requirements and minimization of network	**Biological Conservation** SFI: "contribute to conservation of biological diversity," including funding research FSC: detailed list of requirements to conserve

Table 4.2. (*continued*)

Protection of Cultural/ Historic Sites	Visual Impact	Maintenance of Ecological Function
Both require protection; FSC requires consultation with indigenous peoples	SFI: requires aesthetic consideration in all activities FSC: interim standards employed by certifying bodies	SFI: no explicit requirement FSC: detailed requirements and stand characteristics
Public Access Required when consistent with forest management. FSC accommodates traditional and customary use	**Financial Viability** SFI: no explicit requirement, but requires practices that are economically responsible FSC: requires assessment of viability	**Environmental Impact Assessment** SFI: no explicit requirement but partially implicit in comprehensive management planning requirement FSC: required
Efficiency of Resources Use Both minimize waste associated with harvesting and processing	**Staff Competency** SFI: requires training FSC: requires assessment of competency	**Public Consultation** SFI: report to association; consult with state regulators FSC: consult/report to all parties and stakeholders
	Management Planning Framework SFI: requires plans where appropriate FSC: requires detailed plan and public availability	**Employee Health and Safety** SFI: compliance with state and federal laws FSC: requires compensation to regional norms, right to organize, opportunity to participate in management decisions
	Use of Chemicals SFI: prudent use, reduce, and use integrated pest management FSC: minimize use	**Legal Compliance** SFI: performance measures require compliance with federal laws and regulations FSC: mandates

(*continued*)

Table 4.2. (*continued*)

		compliance with all laws, regulations, and international agreements
		Indigenous People's Rights SFI: not addressed FSC: explicitly recognized

Source: Meridian Institute 2001.

while at the same time agreeing to meet the presumably less oner-ous FSC certification standards on its New England lands. The factors leading to the very different certification standards on similar forestlands are documented in a study from the Canadian-American Center at the University of Maine (Cashore and Lawson, in press). The differences have much to do with the history of earlier relationships between industry and environmentalists. My point here is simply that there is as yet no broadly accepted common understanding as to what the standards should be—even for similar lands within a given standards organization. In fairness, however, one might argue that the problem is simply that forest auditing, now in its infancy, will require a period of time before the various issues are resolved and a common and consistent cross-regional standard emerges.

Price Premium Incentives

Another economic issue concerns incentives for certification. Financial incentives would involve changes in costs and certified-wood product prices. As long as certification is voluntary, a forest firm will weigh the advantages of certification against those remaining uncertified. Forest certification is going to involve some costs in essentially all cases. In a 1997 study of private U.S. forests, Abt and Murray (1998, personal communication) estimated that about 50 percent of the harvest could meet FSC certification standards at a cost increase of 10 percent or less. However, the remaining 50 percent would require a cost increase above 10 percent. In addition, if raw wood from sustainable forests is going to be converted to eco-labeled products, additional costs are incurred to maintain the chain of custody to processing facilities.

Given these costs, a major incentive for certification has been the notion that the wood market was willing to pay a premium for wood certified as sustainably produced. Conceptually, forests that are certified as sustainably managed are eligible to provide wood for eco-labeled products. Eco-labeled products, bearing some identification, would be viewed as more desirable at least by some subset of consumers, and thus could bring a price premium in the market. The price premium would give owners a direct financial incentive to incur the additional costs associated with certifiable management.

However, on the product price side, the question is one of consumer willingness to incur the higher price premium to purchase certified (eco-labeled) products. So far the experience is not encouraging. A number of studies have suggested that the consumer's willingness to pay higher prices is limited, especially when lower-priced, noncertified substitutes are available. However, many firms and organizations appear to be willing to assume the higher cost of certification for public image purposes. In the United States, for example, the American Forest & Paper Association requires all of its industry members to agree to work toward a concept of sustainable forestry, even if not formally certified. Although the price premium rarely occurs (Sedjo and Swallow 2002), producers may still participate for either altruistic reasons and/or to generate public good will.

The Situation in the United States

In the United States the dominant forest issue both before and after Rio was a continuation of an earlier policy debate that focused largely on the questions of appropriate management, timber harvests, and other outputs of the nation's publicly owned forestlands. The conflict was particularly strident in the Pacific Northwest, with its large areas of old-growth forests and a population of the threatened northern spotted owl (*Strix occidentalis caurina*). Most of those forests are in the public domain, which raises a different set of management and harvest issues.

The creation of the forest reserves in the United States in the latter part of the nineteenth century envisioned a sustainable forest system, albeit a system that would generate timber while providing water protection. Over the roughly 100 years of the Forest Service's existence, it has gone through a number of alternative management modes for the nation's forests. Clawson (1983) characterized the early period, roughly the pre–World War II period, as one of benign neglect. This may have been generally true, with the exception that fire in the forest has been actively suppressed since the early part of the twentieth century. Our nation is now seriously reassessing that policy, since its results have changed the character of natural disturbance regimes.

The period after 1960 has been referred to as one of sustained yield forestry and multiple use. These objectives were codified in the Multiple-Use Sustained Yield Act (MUSYA) of 1960 and again in the 1976 NFMA. The uses of the forest—timber, water protection, recreation, wildlife, and forage—were clearly delineated in those statutes, and other provisions were made for the creation of separate wilderness reserves. Although the relative and absolute magnitudes of the outputs were determined by congressional budget processes and oversight, the budget is influenced by annual battles involving various interest groups. In the 1990s, ecosystem management was introduced. It was never quite clear whether ecosystem management was an alternative form of multiple use, or a new management system that involved new goals and objectives (see Thomas, this volume). Analysts have interpreted ecosystem management both ways. Many of us believed it was the latter, although lacking a legal mandate; the identification of new objectives was often presented as a simple updating of the multiple-use charter.

In any event, the objectives of management clearly have changed as timber harvests from the entire National Forest System (NFS) fell from some 12 billion board feet in the late 1980s to about 2 billion board feet currently. In fact, one chief of the Forest Service has argued that the de facto objective of Forest Service management in the mid-1990s was species preservation (Thomas 2000).

For U.S. private forests, the response to the post-Rio move toward certification was initial resistance, based partly on the argument that the widespread ownership of fairly small forest areas would make auditing costs prohibitive. However, the American Tree Farmers System (ATFS) has had certification inspection for many years. Gradually, the forest industry is coming to accept the general notion of sustainable forestry. Working with conservation organizations, it has developed a certifying and auditing system. The SFI, originally the creation of the U.S. timber industry, is now an independent entity.

Although certification now involves a substantial portion of the world's forests in some regions (table 4.1), important unresolved issues persist. For example, forest certification initially was designed to relate to management practices on forests that are being or are expected to be harvested. The applicability of certification to forests not intended for harvest appears limited. Hence, the relation between the movement to forest certification and the Northwest Forest Plan, for example, is still unclear. While worldwide, certification has been given to both private and public lands (e.g., the FSC certified the public forests of Poland), these forests are generally intended for harvest. And, the certification of some Canadian forests on Crown (government) lands is contemplated. Early in the process there was a question of whether certification was appropriate for the U.S. NFS. However, significant elements of the U.S. environmental community appeared to oppose forest certification of public forests, since it implies both management and logging. Many of these groups do not want any harvesting from the NFS and so might oppose certifying these lands. In any event, thus far there have been few calls for certification of the NFS.

The Future of Forest Sustainability and Certification

What then is the future of forest sustainability and/or certification? Although on the basis of some of the previous observations it may appear bleak, I view the move to forest certification positively and generally consistent with some form of sustainability. Certification may not necessarily bring sustainability, and sustainability may not require certification, but certification will probably bring generally more favorable forest practices. Additionally, certification that recognizes a role for periodic harvests need not get hung up on understanding the full range of forest states.

Furthermore, I believe the public wants sustainability, and some type of certification will provide them with assurance. However, the public generally doesn't want to get involved in the details. Certification, even if highly flawed, is providing an imprimatur whereby many environmentalists now find timber harvesting an acceptable activity. This is a great improvement over the situation when many environmentalists rejected any and all logging. Second, I might note that most certifying organizations are now referring to certification of "well-managed forests," rather than "sustainably managed forests," which was the previous terminology. It is reassuring that certifiers now recognize that they are not sure what sustainability really means. While this doesn't resolve all of the thorny ecological issues, at least it is less presumptuous. And, despite the lack of clarity regarding sustainability, foresters do believe they know something about best management practices. Third, there now exists a lively competition among certifying organizations. Thus, the threat of a single certifier having a monopoly, with all the problems and dislocations that might involve, has probably been avoided. I anticipate the development of a market in which both certified and noncertified wood will be traded, with at most a modest price differential between them. Some markets, such as in wealthy countries, may carry almost exclusively certified wood.

Will the world's forests be better for certification? Perhaps slightly, but not as much as some might have believed (Cote 1999). Much of the tropics, where management is often a real problem, have resisted and will probably continue to resist certification. In the tropics deforestation is driven as much by land conversion, largely due to agriculture, as by any other single factor. This trend is unlikely to be very responsive to certification. Furthermore, as we have seen in certification efforts thus far, the forests that can be easily certified are doing so. Where the costs are substantial, forests are tending to resist certification. Since there will almost surely be markets available for both certified and noncertified wood, harvests will continue on noncertified forests. Finally, certification will provide a stream of steady employment for foresters and environmentalists alike. Surely, this will be viewed as desirable by these groups.

Note

This chapter is based on a talk given at the Forest Futures Conference at Willamette University in Salem, Oregon, on September 25, 2002.

5

Sustainability and Public Values

Bob Pepperman Taylor

The chapters in this part make two points clear: first, there is no general agreement about what it would mean for forestry to be sustainable; second, *sustainability* is a term that can obscure as much as it clarifies in debates about the future of forests. Regarding the first point, there is no agreement among the authors about how to define sustainability. Beuter wants to restrict the meaning to sustained timber yield; Sedjo's comments make us think that the phrase "well-managed forests," while equally ambiguous, might be more honest than the word *sustainability*, which seems to imply a greater level of scientific and nonnormative precision; Perry concludes that "from an ecological standpoint" there remain tremendous uncertainties about how to achieve sustainability within "the complex and poorly understood workings of nature"; and Thomas clearly shows the impossibility of simultaneously achieving sustainability in all good things we might desire, from timber yields to broader ecological goods to economic, political, recreational, and aesthetic values. This leads to the second point: it is certainly tempting to take Thomas's lead and throw up our hands and suggest that *sustainability* has often become a term of art, rhetorically designed to claim the moral high ground in an argument rather than clarify or honestly declare one's true intentions in debates such as those surrounding the Northwest Forest Plan (NWFP).

In this chapter, I will try to frame these two points within a broader historical and political context. To do this, I will take a brief detour from the NWFP to discuss our conservation tradition as it has grown out of the American progressivism of the early twentieth century. These comments will suggest that the ambiguity in the idea of sustainability reflects a deeper set of historic tensions in the conservation movement. I will also argue that it is best to admit and clarify these tensions, even while acknowledging the impossibility of any conservation policy, such as the NWFP, fully satisfying all the conservation values a democratic society generates.

Left-Brain, Right-Brain Values

Thomas's frustration is worth a closer look. He writes about the incommensurability of the views of "technicians" like himself ("left-brain dominated" folks), and those who value old trees and old-growth stands intrinsically, aesthetically, or romantically ("right-brain dominated" folks). He suggests that the idea of sustainability is just a surrogate for the real issues at stake in these fights, and this might very well be true. What is certainly true is that appealing to sustainability will not settle the issues between the two groups, for the simple reason that they mean different things by the term; each seeks to protect and conserve different things.

Although this incompatibility of values is disconcerting to Thomas, it represents a historically rich fight and a legitimate one. Americans have never been squeamish about "subduing the wilderness," exploiting our natural resources, working to build ever-increasing wealth without end, shaping the environment to suit our freely chosen ends. The progressives who invented and promoted conservation in the early twentieth century were very clear in their insistence that nature be mastered for the ever-increasing benefit of American citizens. This was not only a crude desire for riches—although riches were necessary if we were to fulfill the democratic mission of abolishing poverty. Walter Weyl wrote that it is "the increasing wealth of America, not the growing poverty of any class, upon which the hope of a full democracy must be based" (Weyl 1912, 191). Even more importantly, scientific mastery of the natural world (and the social world as well, but that's another story) was the precondition for freedom, for only such mastery allowed a free people to sculpt and shape their environment to reflect their free will. Walter Lippmann said this as powerfully as any member of the progressive generation: "The scientific spirit is the discipline of democracy, the escape from drift, the outlook of free man. Its direction is to distinguish fact from fancy; its 'enthusiasm is for the possible'; its promise is the shaping of fact to a chastened and honest dream" (Lippmann 1985, 151). Conservation (and our modern language of sustainability) was just one obvious tool that the progressives developed to fulfill this dream, a dream of wealth and power and self-assertion that reaches from our earliest historical memory to the present. This is our left-brain tradition of practical, responsible, capable, and productive men and women.

A counterpoint to this tradition, however, is a romantic appreciation of the beauty, awe, majesty, terror, and inspiration that can be found in the natural world. The landscape has always provided the context for American introspection, moral aspiration, and moral criticism—as in the writings of the transcendentalists Emerson and Thoreau; in much of our greatest literature, from Hawthorne to Faulkner to such contemporaries as Cormac McCarthy; and within such popular arts as music (think of "America the Beautiful") and film (for better or worse, what would our image of heroism be without that most American of movie genres, the Western?). Our greatest of all progressive conservationists, Theodore Roosevelt, hoped not only that we would find utility in nature, but that we would learn beauty too, as when he approvingly wrote that "Men began to appreciate the need of preserving wildlife, not only because it was useful, but also because it was beautiful"

(Roosevelt 1926, 425). Even Roosevelt, as pugnacious and practical and worldly as an American could be, found the inspiration to promote a right-brain appreciation of our natural world.

The fight between our masterful and romantic impulses toward nature has become acute in our own time because the resources available to both sets of needs have become increasingly scarce. Our mastery has become so extensive, our society so large and developed, our industry so pervasive, that the romantic need for a wild, untamed, masterless nature is simply not to be satisfied by contemporary generations with the ease it once was. The struggle between the utilitarians and the romantics is more zero-sum than it was when the landscape still provided huge unmanaged, uncontrolled expanses of forest, and when "management" itself was a much more modest endeavor, due to less-developed technology.

The first point to make about the tension between our left-brain and right-brain understandings of our forests is simply that they both make legitimate demands upon us. The struggle between them, well described by Thomas, is the source of great frustration to both camps, generating compromises that seem to satisfy neither group to any great extent. But the political contest between the two is actually essential to our true inheritance. This is not a fight in which only one side controls the moral high ground, as some would have us believe—such as those who argue that advocates of old-growth forests are misanthropes or elitists, or those who argue that those who advocate sustainable timber yield are just greedy capitalists. There is no choice but to recognize the legitimacy of both sets of demands, that people need both timber and some wild and ancient forests (or the best we can provide on this count at this time in history), that we would suffer if we lost either, and that this requires that we make messy, unhappy compromises between the two. Like law and sausage, it is not pretty to watch the making of public policy such as that which controls the Northwestern forests. It would be worse, however, if either the technicians or the romantics alone controlled the process.

Nature and America's Moral Character

There is another way of looking at these matters, however, which Thomas's dichotomy misses. Romantics are often great individualists, who view nature as a source of personal inspiration, even salvation—as in Emerson's call for each of us to be inspired by nature to "Build, therefore, your own world" (Emerson 1983, 48). Early conservationists, however, viewed nature as a democratic and public space and object. Walter Lippmann speaks to this point too: "One of the great promises of the conservation movement is the evidence it gave of a passionate attachment to public possessions" (Lippmann 1985, 130). For the progressives, in both their utilitarian or nonutilitarian incarnations, the conservation and appreciation of nature is less about personal insight and salvation than about public things, about democratic values and our public character.

Perhaps the greatest representative of this progressive impulse is Aldo Leopold, himself a child of the progressive conservationists. Leopold's critical eye is focused sharply on the "economists," those who would view nature as nothing other than resources for promoting what they took to be progress, that is, the production of ever-greater wealth. He writes that "Only economists mistake physical opulence for riches" (Leopold 1966, 177). He contends, to the contrary, that what we need is a "little healthy contempt for a plethora of material blessings" (xix) if we are to learn to resist the "modern dogma" of "comfort at any cost" (76). The conservationism Leopold promotes in *Sand County Almanac* and other essays is aimed to teach not only sustainability, as it were, but something much deeper and more important. What he mourns the most is the changing of American character in a direction he thinks represents a turn for the worst. As we become more technically adept at mastering nature, we find a "corresponding shrinkage in cultural values, especially split-rail [i.e., pioneer] values and ethical restraints" (216). In short, Leopold believes that our promotion of utilitarian progress has become lopsided and ethically suspect. We have stopped thinking about who we should be and instead think only about what we want ("To build a road is so much simpler than to think of what the country really needs" [107]). We have become rich but morally unrestrained, no longer guided by the modest "split-rail" values of an earlier America. We have lost our ability to feel humbled and awestruck before something greater than our own desires and pleasures. The result is not only harm to the natural world, but harm to the moral character of American society.

The point is that for Leopold, and the progressive conservation tradition he represents, arguing about caring for the land and natural resources is a political fight in the deepest sense, a fight about the very character of our society, about who we are collectively, what we stand for, and what we will become. Leopold worried deeply that we were losing the kind of ethical restraints which guided previous generations of Americans, and he made his case for conservation in part on the need for retrieval of such restraints. Any argument we might have with Leopold is not merely a technical argument about the science of conservation. It is, instead, a broader political argument about the values that must inform our public policy.

The Need for Normative Deliberation

As the authors in this part make abundantly clear, the public policy toward any complex environmental issue, such as maintaining the sustainability of Northwestern forests, makes for a lot of confusion. Inspired by Perry, we may want to say that science will someday give us the answers we need to guide our public policy. Or, like Beuter, we might argue that if we pursue one particular set of values (sustainable yields on privately owned land), that all other values will be satisfied as well. But there is no reason to think that either of these views would be satisfactory in meeting the full challenge we face. Although we need good science to guide our understanding of what is possible, no science can answer the normative questions about the mediation of conflicting values (say, between economic and aesthetic values, or between "ecological" values as understood apart from human communities and "ecological" values including these communities). And Beuter's comment that fire control is more successful on private lands because they have more and better roads only underscores the degree to which his vision cannot begin to satisfy those for whom a forest with fewer roads is a greater, more valuable forest. The conservation legacy teaches us to be skeptical about the temptation to think that either the development of natural science, or the pursuit of one set of public values (say, economic utility), will produce all desirable outcomes. There is no avoiding the broader political and ethical debates, or the compromises that need to be found between conflicting public values.

If I am right about these lessons from our conservation tradition, there are three conclusions that recommend themselves to us as we think about public policies such as the NWFP:

1. Thomas's frustration with the degree to which sustainability has become a surrogate for broader ethical and political concerns is right on target. These broader concerns, however, are absolutely legitimate, but there is also much to be said in favor of honesty and integrity in advertising. Although there are often political and legal temptations to not be forthright about one's purposes and intentions, these temptations lead more to short-term than long-term victories. My suspicion is that over the long haul a more direct and honest advocacy is the best policy. Any group that appeals to sustainability, or any other values, in a way that muddies rather than clarifies our values is ultimately helping to discredit the view being advocated.

2. To suggest, as I have, that we need to view policy fights like those over the NWFP as broader political debates (not just economic or scientific debates) does not, by any means, automatically recommend one set of outcomes over another. What would one who learns from Aldo Leopold think about the harvesting of old-growth timber? Frankly, I don't know, in any definitive sense, even though many environmentalists think they do. We shouldn't forget that those rural communities that survive

by cutting timber are precisely the types of communities Leopold might cherish as counterweights to the urban consumer society he feared. He also feared, however, our temptation to view all natural resources as mere economic commodities to be managed. The point isn't that Leopold's theory gives us the answer to our difficult policy debates today. It is rather that we need to be honest and clear about precisely what values we are promoting via our proposed policies, and the fact that the choices we advocate have implications for our political and social character beyond the health or sustainability of the Northwestern forests themselves.

3. For all the confusion and difficulty such an approach to conservation policy creates, it beats the alternatives. Democratic public policy will always be less than fully consistent or coherent; the confusion of policy values and goals that Thomas so powerfully presents is to be expected in democratic societies with lots of conflicting values and interests, combined with the freedom to vigorously pursue these values and interests through the courts, through lobbying, and through extra-political pressure such as demonstrations and civil disobedience. Without this free and pluralist (and often downright ornery) democratic society, it would be much easier to organize conservation policy around one dominant principle or idea. Doing so, however, would never allow for the (ever so imperfect) representation of the broad array of legitimate public values that democratic compromise requires. While the politics may look like the problem to those inside the policy system who are advocating one perspective or trying to devise a program of implementation, from the perspective of citizens at large the politics look more like the best solution available.

II

SCIENCE AND
POLICY MAKING

6

Science, Scientists, and the Policy Process: Lessons from Global Environmental Assessments for the Northwest Forest Plan

Ronald B. Mitchell, William C. Clark, David W. Cash, and Frank Alcock

Scientific assessments related to forest management in the Pacific Northwest (PNW) share several characteristics with the many recent "global environmental assessments" that have sought to bring scientific information to bear on global environmental problems. Like most global environmental problems, managing Pacific Northwest forests engages questions of considerable ecological uncertainty and complexity. Although policy makers seek out scientists to help them make decisions, scientific understanding of the state of the ecological system, its trends, and the underlying causal relationships that drive it remains incomplete. As with climate change, acid rain, and biodiversity, successful forest management requires understanding the science and also addressing the competing interests of the multiple policy actors affected by any policy responses that may stem from an assessment. Also like many global environmental problems, ecological and economic forces at the national, state, and local levels influence the health of Northwest forests, the value and viability of different management strategies, and the variety of actors who must be involved in any management effort. Although many of the specifics surely differ, this chapter offers some lessons for

Northwest forest management derived from the successes and failures of global assessments in contributing to the resolution of global environmental problems.

This chapter reports findings from a five-year research project that examined assessments of climate change, biotechnology, acid rain, persistent organic pollutants, fisheries, and water management in an attempt to explain why some assessments had significant influence while others had almost no influence. For example, the most influential of several assessments of acid rain in Poland and Bulgaria were those that involved consultation with a range of stakeholders, including various ministries, sulfur-emitting power plants, and environmental advocacy groups. Similarly, advice based on climate forecasts regarding the planting of drought-resistant plants in Zimbabwe was followed more consistently by those commercial farmers involved in developing that advice than by subsistence farmers who were simply handed planting advice by agricultural extension service agents. Qualitative comparisons both within and across ten such qualitative case studies have led to four main conclusions that are described in the first section. The second section then demonstrates how an assessment's influence depends on the extent to which different audiences judge the assessment as salient, credible, and legitimate. How assessment institutions respond to the many obstacles to assessment influence is covered in the third section. The final section examines scientific assessments of Pacific Northwest forests in light of our framework and suggests that careful, consistent institutional design may increase the chances of science contributing to government policy making and legal decision making.

A Framework for Understanding Assessment Influence

How does scientific information influence global environmental management, and what distinguishes influential assessments from those that "sink without a trace?" We summarize here several major findings.

1. *Influential assessments are rare. An assessment is more likely to have influence if multiple audiences perceive it as salient, credible, and legitimate.* Assessment influence is usually indirect, altering an issue's development by identifying and defining a problem, mobilizing certain actors, and altering the goals, alternatives, and knowledge actors consider germane to that problem. Significant influence depends on three "attributions" multiple audiences make about an assessment, "attributions" that are not objective characteristics of an assessment but that reflect actor-specific criteria and standards:
   - *Salience*: Is the assessment relevant for me either because it can inform my behavioral choices or because others who find it relevant to their choices are likely to use it?
   - *Credibility*: Is the assessment reliable in the sense of meeting my standards of scientific plausibility and technical adequacy better than other available sources of information on current and future states of the world, causal relationships, and likely outcomes from decisions?
   - *Legitimacy*: Is the assessment respectful and unbiased in addressing the values, concerns, and questions of myself and others I believe it should address?
2. *Assessments frequently lack influence due to barriers and boundaries that separate information "producers" from information "users" and that separate users from each other. Boundaries between science and policy, different countries, competing interests and ideologies, and actors operating at different scales inhibit use of an assessment's information.* Producing any assessment requires bridging a wide variety of barriers. Producing an influential assessment requires being attentive to multiple audiences, each of which evaluates assessments using a different set of social, cultural, political, economic, and scientific criteria.
3. *Assessment processes gain influence by recognizing the tensions and trade-offs among salience, credibility, and legitimacy.* Making an assessment salient enough, credible enough,

and legitimate enough to convince even a single audience to change its beliefs and actions is challenging since choices that increase salience often reduce credibility and legitimacy, and vice versa. And choices that increase salience (or credibility or legitimacy) with one audience often reduce its salience (or credibility or legitimacy) with one or more other audiences.

4. *Assessment institutions' formal and informal rules regarding participation, scope, content, process, and framing determine which audiences find an assessment salient, credible, and legitimate. The difficulty of making assessments influential makes procedures for institutional learning particularly important.* Our research highlights that no single institutional design consistently produces influential assessments. Influence derives from addressing questions, employing evidence and expertise, and following processes that reflect the multiple, intersecting, and competing interests and abilities of potential users of that particular assessment. Assessments have been made influential by involving relevant stakeholders, by regulating the assessment's scope and content, and by their framing of certain facts, beliefs, and options (and not others) as central to resolving a problem. Provisions for institutional learning and self-reflection are essential given the many obstacles to producing effective assessments.

These findings are drawn from some cases in which assessments produced direct and immediate changes in policies and behaviors. Policy makers may request an assessment and incorporate its findings into current debates or follow its recommendations. Likewise, assessments sometimes provide local economic and social decision makers with new information that clarifies their interests and the impact of their behaviors in ways that lead them to change those behaviors. Yet, our project has found such short causal chains between assessments and policy or behavior change are the exception; the influence of most assessments is less direct or immediate. Assessments often alter the policy realm in ways that take time before their effects are evident in shifts in the policy debate or changes in the choices of policy makers and economic and social actors.

One major, indeed often intended influence of an assessment is to make "problems" out of policies and behaviors whose environmental impacts were previously ignored or considered benign. To alter policy and behavior, an assessment must convince policy makers that a problem exists. Thus, the several American and international assessments of carbon dioxide and global warming undertaken during the late 1970s and early 1980s failed to produce any significant political action on climate change. Indeed, the scientific conclusions of the 1985 "Villach" climate change assessment (produced under the auspices of the International Council of Scientific Unions, the World Meteorological Organization, and the United Nations Environment Programme) were almost identical to those of previous assessments. Unlike earlier assessments, this assessment convinced influential political actors of the need for action because the same science was now more salient to policy makers. This was due to more careful framing by the assessment's authors and heightened global environmental concern in response to negotiations of the first ozone depletion agreement (Torrance in press). Assessments can also alter political debates because their nominally descriptive claims about the causes of an environmental problem become politically charged allocations of blame for the problem and responsibility for its resolution.

Putting an issue on the policy agenda or raising its visibility can lead many actors—and may require policy makers—to discuss the issue. Assessments increase the attention, concern, resources, and strategies that already engaged political and economic actors bring to an environmental issue. Those already active on an issue may publicize elements of an assessment to mobilize those with coincident interests without mobilizing their opponents (Litfin 1994). Media coverage of an assessment also leads some actors to mobilize (and others to demobilize) and makes some arguments easier (and others harder) to make.

Assessments also alter what goals and options are considered politically viable. Even if an assessment does not alter an actor's core values and preferences, by drawing attention to an issue an assessment can lead actors to increase the priority given to certain goals and decrease that given to others. Identifying the environmental consequences of a policy can introduce environmental goals into decisions previously viewed as economic or national security concerns. Assessments also introduce new options, alter perceived costs and benefits of existing options, and increase the costs of doing nothing.

Audience Attributions as Conditions for Assessment Influence

Our research was motivated by the recognition that, as the climate change example suggests, some assessments have considerable influence while others have little, if any. We have found the best explanation of this variation in the differences in judgments or attributions made by different audiences of an assessment's salience, credibility, and legitimacy. Each audience uses its own values and standards in making such judgments which, in turn, determine their responsiveness to an assessment.

Salience

An assessment's influence begins with salience; that is, actors must be both aware of the assessment and deem it relevant to their behavior. An assessment can be salient because an audience considers the information directly important to its choices or because so many other actors are thinking about, talking about, and acting on the information that it cannot be ignored. Assessments often lack salience because producers of an assessment focus on scientifically important rather than policy-relevant questions. Similarly, they may address relevant questions too late, after decisions they might inform have been made. Yet, they also can arrive too "soon," as evident in the early climate change assessments that lacked influence because policy makers were not yet receptive to scientific calls for action on this global environmental problem (Torrance in press). Assessments also lose salience when their solutions are not tailored to the scale, scope, or context needed by users (Cash in press, Moser in press, Patt in press).

Credibility

Assessments must also be credible. Audiences must see the assessment's facts, theories, causal beliefs, and options either as "true" or as better than competing information. Scientific assessments are useful precisely when complexity and uncertainty preclude most people from independently evaluating scientific information on a topic (Haas 1992). Thus, policy makers and other audiences must evaluate an assessment's credibility "by proxy" based on credentials and process. Usually credibility is based on expertise and trustworthiness. Audiences judge expertise by whether experts from requisite disciplines were involved and whether appropriate data and models were used (Andonova in press). Audiences judge trustworthiness based on an evaluation of whether assessment processes generally protected the biases and policy preferences of assessment producers from unduly influencing the knowledge creation and dissemination processes. Thus, credibility comes more readily for assessments that are consistent with existing knowledge or face few alternative sources of information. Credibility with many audiences can be undermined if "outside" scientists question an assessment's perspectives, assumptions, data, and models. Independent Canadian scientists undermined government fish stock assessments by criticizing their data sources and statistical methods (Alcock in press). American climate change "skeptics" have highlighted uncertainties about both the extent and causes of climate change (Franz 1998). Indian scientists have reduced the influence of Intergovernmental Panel on Climate Change (IPCC) reports by arguing that climate change is not caused primarily by the "normal, legitimate" activities of all countries but by the "aberrant, luxury" activities of a relatively few industrialized countries (Biermann in press).

Legitimacy

Lastly, assessment influence depends on attributions of legitimacy. Audiences want to know an assessment process was "fair" and considered appropriate values, concerns, and perspectives. Concerns regarding who participated and who did not, the processes for making those choices, and how information is produced, vetted, and disseminated play important roles here. Legitimacy often requires either involving relevant stakeholders or taking their concerns, perspectives, and interests into account. Central to legitimacy is the notion that if scientific assessments are going to influence policy, then the interests of those affected by those policies should be considered in the assessment process. Actors contest the legitimacy of assessments supporting policies that disproportionately harm their interests. Thus, in biosafety negotiations, developing country governments have challenged assessments that promote a narrow definition of genetically modified organisms (GMOs) out of fear they will not be able to manage the flood of imports (and associated risks) that would result if only a limited list of GMOs are regulated (Gupta in press). Processes can be as important to legitimacy as outputs. Indeed, an actor may reject even those recommendations in an assessment that coincide with their interests if they believe the assessment process was controlled by those opposed to their interests.

How Institutions Foster Assessment Influence

Producing an assessment that is influential with multiple audiences requires managing boundaries that divide science and policy, diverse disciplines, and local, national, and even international jurisdictions. Strategies, mechanisms, and conditions that promote one attribution with one audience often undermine other attributions with other audiences. For instance, institutional efforts to enhance an assessment's credibility by involving the "most qualified" scientists may undermine salience and legitimacy with those who believe their perspectives and concerns would be ignored by an economically and politically nonrepresentative set of scientific elites. On the other hand, including nonscientists or poorly qualified scientists to enhance legitimacy or salience can undermine credibility with other audiences. Similarly, an assessment that limits itself to "the science" may have little salience for policy makers, and an assessment too attentive to policy debates may lack credibility with scientists. Institutions and entities conducting assessments therefore face a difficult task of managing the many boundaries that impede assessment influence (Cash 2001, Guston et al. 2000).

Managing these boundaries effectively to minimize trade-offs and tensions among salience, credibility, and legitimacy involves choices regarding participation, scope, content, processes, and framing. Although assessment "institutions" sometimes consist simply of an ad hoc group of scientists who produce a single "state of the science" report on a given issue, many assessments result from the work of ongoing social institutions consisting of regular meetings and formalized procedures, as evident in the annual stock assessments common to much international fisheries management. The complexity of managing multiple attributions across multiple audiences dictates that assessment institutions (whether ad hoc or ongoing) usually succeed only by learning from, and improving on, either their own experience or that of other institutions.

Participation

Since most audiences' evaluations of salience, credibility, and legitimacy involve asking "Who wrote this assessment?" increasing an assessment's influence requires institutional designs that either involve members of an audience directly in an assessment or establish processes that ensure their knowledge, ideas, and concerns are incorporated in the assessment. For example, power plant operators, farmers, and fishermen have been far more supportive of and responsive to recommendations in those assessments of acid rain, drought forecasting, and fish stocks in which they have been involved (Andonova in press, Patt in press, Alcock in press). These strategies make it more likely that audiences on various sides of science–policy, national, scale, and interdisciplinary divides understand the concerns and perspectives of those on other sides of those divides. Participation influences salience by addressing an audience's questions and concerns, incorporating information they have on a problem, and providing information and recommendations sensitive to the decisions they face and the context in which they face them. Participation influences credibility by determining which audiences view assessors as having the necessary expertise and trustworthiness. Participation influences legitimacy by bringing relevant stakeholders' values and perspectives into the assessment and providing evidence that this occurred, thereby increasing the likelihood that findings and recommendations "make sense" to those the assessment seeks to influence. Participants also help communicate an assessment's results in ways that make it more salient, credible, and legitimate to their constituencies (Eckley in press).

Scope, Content, and Process

What an assessment does and does not assess also matters. Attributions of credibility depend on specific, not generic, notions of what expertise is relevant to a given problem. Legitimacy also declines when audiences view an assessment's scope as exceeding the expertise of those involved. Some institutions balance salience and credibility by involving nonscientific stakeholders in scoping an assessment and framing the final report while having scientific experts manage the analysis. The use of scientific findings by coastal zone managers in Hawai'i and Maine and water districts in the American Midwest has depended critically on ongoing discussions among government officials, local decision makers, and stakeholders to ensure relevant questions are asked and answered in a timely manner (Moser in press, Cash in press). At times, making an assessment salient to decision makers requires engaging social scientists as well as natural scientists and having the assessment directly address policy-relevant questions. Managing these tensions sometimes requires building rather than bridging boundaries: the IPCC enhanced its Third Assessment Report's credibility by relying on separate working groups to address aspects of climate change requiring different types of expertise (WG-1 on climate change science, WG-2 on impacts, adaptation, and vulnerability, and WG-3 on mitigation) but maintained its salience by producing a "Summary for Policymakers" explicitly designed to provide "policy-relevant, but not policy-prescriptive," answers to the questions of climate change negotiators (Watson and the Core Writing Team 2001, 1).

Framing

How an assessment defines and discusses a problem and potential solutions also conditions its influence. Framing—how included information is worded, shaped, and contextualized—reflects both the self-conscious scientific and policy goals of assessors and their often less self-conscious interests, biases, and blind spots. Careful framing can increase the chances that an assessment disrupts an existing equilibrium of goals, options, and knowledge by convincing various audiences that current policies and behaviors are no longer the best ways to achieve their goals. "Marketing" assessments requires framing them in ways that audiences can understand and incorporate. An assessment in Maine made the far-off risks of climate change more salient to policy makers by noting that current decisions about shoreline developments would increase the state's vulnerability to sea-level rise by limiting the state's ability to respond to it (Moser in press). Salience depends on communicating assessment content to resonate with an audience's current goals and concerns, definition of a problem, and preferred solutions. Those who conduct an assessment can influence but not control its framing since industry, nongovernmental organizations, and the media usually are central to the introduction of assessments into the policy debate. Beyond framing issues, increasing the chances that an assessment will alter behavior can require helping audiences develop the capacity to understand findings in an assessment (Gupta in press, Biermann in press). Many poor Zimbabwean farmers did not plant drought-resistant crops in response to climate forecasts because agriculture extension services did not devote resources to helping those farmers understand the forecasts (Patt in press).

Learning and Self-Reflection

Assessments perform these complex tasks better when they institutionalize critical self-reflection and evaluation (Gunderson et al. 1995, Social Learning Group 2001a, Social Learning Group 2001b). Scientific assessments are social communication processes intended to manage the boundaries between experts and decision makers. Some institutions assemble an assessment group, produce a single report, and disband; others produce sequences of assessments on different problems; and yet others dedicate considerable resources to ongoing assessments, for example, of fish stocks, acid rain, and climate change (Alcock in press, VanDeveer in press). These different designs pose different challenges to learning. Relatively transient assessments can tailor participant lists and processes to match particular problems and audiences but may also reinvent networks of participants, recommit obvious blunders, and leave behind few lessons for others (Eckley in press). More permanent assessment organizations, like those addressing water management in the American Midwest, capture lessons from prior assessments in personnel and procedures and develop networks of assessment producers and users who, over time, learn to work with and understand one another (Guston 1996, Guston 1999, Cash in press). But risk aversion, reluctance to admit error, reliance on a fixed set of participants, and other problems common to more permanent bureaucracies may also impede learning.

Environmental Assessments and Management of Pacific Northwest Forests

What lessons can global environmental assessments offer us regarding scientific assessments of Pacific Northwest forests? Examining over a dozen regional assessments of these forests described by Haynes and Perez (2001), Johnson (1997), and Yaffee (1994) confirms that they have faced pitfalls similar to those encountered by global assessments and have succeeded when using similar strategies. Most, though not all, have had little influence on forest management (Johnson 1997, 407–8). In part, this reflects inherent obstacles to the influence of science in a highly contested policy context. Forest science is already salient for many audiences in the Northwest and the nation, but the underlying conflict between economic and ecological perspectives on forest management has regularly led multiple audiences to reject scientific inputs as illegitimate and to call into question their credibility.

Participation rules help explain why some assessments have been more influential than others. The 1993 Forest Ecosystem Management Assessment Team (FEMAT) report had considerable influence on the policy debate, but its participation rules produced implementation difficulties. The decision to involve political appointees from the Clinton administration while excluding federal forest managers undercut FEMAT's scientific credibility. It also led to legal challenges and undermined the legitimacy and salience of FEMAT's findings with the very people charged with implementing its complex management procedures (Johnson 1997, 406–7). By contrast, the 1994 Northwest Forest Plan (NWFP) that emerged from the FEMAT process required creation of adaptive management groups to facilitate the use of science in forest management. The NWFP's promotion of interactions between scientists and managers has led "to research with greater policy relevance, altered the way in which some scientists selected and pursued research agendas, and altered notions of the process to ensure science quality." Additionally, it has helped managers devise "scientifically sound, new approaches to managing ecosystems," tested their efficacy in managing ecosystems for multiple uses, and demonstrated the relevance of research to ongoing forest management (Haynes and Perez 2001, 98–99, 101).

Even participation in basic data gathering can improve both the science being done and the acceptance of subsequent scientific findings. Although forest ecosystems do not hew to private/public distinctions, most assessments have analyzed data regarding forests on federal land because data for private forestlands are usually not available (Johnson 1997, 403). If they could be engaged in the assessment process, private landowners could offer scientists otherwise-unavailable data that would improve scientific research by providing both a more complete picture of Northwest ecosystems and more information about different strategies of forest management. Over time, an ongoing dialogue of private landowners and loggers with scientists and managers could facilitate mutual understanding that would make scientific findings more credible, especially if those findings reflected data provided by landowners. It may also ease implementation difficulties, as landowners come to see their concerns reflected in forest management decisions. This type of positive dynamic between stakeholders, scientists, and managers was particularly evident in one of our case studies: although eastern European power companies had good reason to resist costly power plant regulations designed to meet European Union environmental standards, involving them in assessments of how to meet those standards produced more credible science. Corporate data was far more accurate than government data, and corporate involvement produced regulations that these companies were more willing to accept, since they saw their concerns addressed and treated with respect (Andonova in press).

A major obstacle to the influence of forest assessments stems from the deep conflict in the values, interests, and biases of loggers, environmentalists, and other audiences involved in the forest policy debate. Yet, the assessment process itself may help reduce these conflicts. Deeply held views do not change overnight, nor are they particularly susceptible to the influence of scientific information. But involving nonscientists (both stakeholders and managers) in ongoing and joint assessment processes to foster the short-term goal of increasing the incorporation of scientific insights into economic and political decisions can, over the long term, also foster deeper understanding among competing stakeholders. If scientists and forest managers can channel the shared interest of timber companies, woodland owners, and environmental groups in improved scientific understanding of forests into joint exercises in data collection, model building, and environmental monitoring, those joint assessment exercises can build trust and facilitate understanding among those with initially opposing views. In the best of circumstances (which, admittedly, are difficult to create), the focus of such efforts on "the science" rather than "the politics" can foster mutual understanding and even grudging respect, which in turn can be the foundation for subsequent consensus building on larger issues. Assessments will be taken more seriously by competing sides in the forest debate if those representatives of each side who are involved in the assessment can show how the questions asked make it salient, the process of conducting the science makes it credible, and the process for balancing interests and concerns makes it legitimate.

The NWFP already has elements that reflect the need for assessment processes to self-consciously learn from its experiences. Ideally, the Adaptive Management approach entails "learning partnerships" in which researchers, managers, and stakeholders can participate together in developing alternative management techniques, identifying their ecological and economic impacts, and discussing the valuation of those consequences (Haynes and Perez 2001). This produces a more coherent and integrated form of management in which assessments are long-term processes with experts and users "co-producing" a shared body of usable knowledge. The NWFP also has developed a "multiple pathways" approach of random allocation of two or more management treatments to similar areas to compare their impacts. This approach has obvious analytic benefits in providing "controlled case comparisons," but has also required stakeholders (who often have "little tolerance" of other stakeholders' values) to "temporarily suspend their opposition to alternative views to allow the comparison" (Haynes and Perez 2001, 41–42). Although the temporary suspension of opposition is accepted by stakeholders for scientific reasons, it starts a process of collaboration and mutual respect that can have important social consequences (Haynes and Perez 2001, 42).

President George W. Bush's Healthy Forest Initiative of 2002 runs some risk of altering these positive trends (Bush 2002). Although the Initiative calls for a renewed commitment to the NWFP's conservation strategy of balancing timber and environmental interests, it also calls for "long-term stewardship contracts with the private sector, non-profit organizations, and local communities" (Bush 2002, 3). If those contracts provide those who receive them exclusive authority in forest management, they are likely to undo recent gains in forest management made by having timber companies and loggers work with scientists, forest managers, and other interested stakeholders. If, instead, those contracts include provisions that require or foster such cooperation, they may allow continuing progress in incorporating improved science regarding what makes a "healthy" forest into improved practices that actually make our forests healthier.

Institutional design plays a crucial role in how much scientific information influences contentious policy debates, such as the debate over the future of the Northwest forests. Ensuring that environmental assessments foster effective environmental policy requires ongoing cooperation among scientists, policy makers, resource managers, and stakeholders. But fostering such cooperation requires bridging the many boundaries between these different actors in the policy process. For forest science to contribute to sustainable ecosystem management, multiple audiences must simultaneously view the science as salient, credible, and legitimate. The current NWFP has already taken important steps away from the traditional conception of assessments as "a one-way transfer of information from scientists to managers" and stakeholders (Haynes and Perez 2001, 42). Rather, it pays attention to manager and stakeholder interests and perspectives and thus increases the contribution science makes to policy by asking salient questions and taking account of legitimate social, political, and economic concerns. The NWFP's ultimate success, however, will require going yet further to bridge the numerous boundaries that separate scientists, policy makers, managers, and stakeholders.

Notes

This chapter summarizes the findings reported in William C. Clark, Ronald B. Mitchell, David W. Cash, and Frank Alcock, *Information as Influence: How Institutions Mediate the Impact of Scientific Assessments on Global Environmental Affairs* (Cambridge, Mass.: Kennedy School of Government, Harvard University, Faculty Research Working Paper RWP02–044, 2002) and in Ronald B. Mitchell, William C. Clark, David W. Cash, and Frank Alcock, eds., *Global Environmental Assessments: Information, Institutions, and Influence* (in press). These ideas were developed over five years of collaborative research, working closely with fellows and faculty engaged in the Global Environmental Assessments project. For more information on the Global Environmental Assessments project, please visit www.ksg.harvard.edu/gea/. We wish to thank all the fellows and faculty involved in that project for their helpful insights throughout the project. The ideas in this chapter were influenced, in particular, by work with Robert O. Keohane and Barbara Connolly, to whom we are deeply indebted. The Global Environmental Assessment (GEA) project has been supported by a core grant from the National Science Foundation (Award

No. SBR–9521910) for the "Global Environmental Assessment Team." Supplemental support to the GEA Team has been provided by the National Oceanic and Atmospheric Administration, the Department of Energy, the National Aeronautics and Space Administration, the National Science Foundation, and the National Institute for Global Environmental Change. Additional support has been provided by the Department of Energy (Award No. DE–FG02–95ER62122) for the project, "Assessment Strategies for Global Environmental Change," the National Institute for Global Environmental Change (Awards No. 901214–HAR, LWT 62–123–06518) for the project "Towards Useful Integrated Assessments," the Center for Integrated Study of the Human Dimensions of Global Integrated Assessment at Carnegie Mellon University (NSF Award No. SBR–9521914) for the project "The Use of Global Environmental Assessments," the Belfer Center for Science and International Affairs at Harvard University's Kennedy School of Government, the International Human Dimensions Programme on Global Environmental Change, Harvard's Weatherhead Center for International Affairs, Harvard's Environmental Information Center, the International Institute for Applied Systems Analysis, the German Academic Exchange Service, the Heinrich Böll Foundation in Germany, the Massachusetts Institute of Technology's Center for Environmental Initiatives, the Heinz Family Foundation, the Heinz Center for Science, Economics and the Environment, and the National Center for Environmental Decision-making Research. Generous additional support has been provided to Ronald B. Mitchell through a Sabbatical Fellowship in the Humanities and Social Sciences from the American Philosophical Society and a 2002 Summer Research Award from the University of Oregon.

This chapter is based on a talk given by Ron Mitchell at the Forest Futures Conference at Willamette University in Salem, Oregon, on September 25, 2002.

7

Roles of Scientists in Forestry Policy and Management: Views from the Pacific Northwest

Frederick J. Swanson

The Pacific Northwest (PNW) of the United States has been a hotbed of forest policy conflict. Old-growth forests and northern spotted owls (*Strix occidentalis caurina*) have become icons in a struggle to decide the future of federally managed forest lands. Science and scientists have played many roles on behalf of the many interests involved in the fray, so this is a rich environment to examine general perspectives on roles of scientists in natural resource issues. In this chapter, I examine many of the venues for science engagement with policy and management; review the spectrum of roles of scientists in decision making and how those roles are perceived by different groups; and consider the different worldviews that scientists bring to policy-relevant issues. While this account is largely descriptive, I close with personal concerns about progress in formulating viable forest policy.

These representations and interpretations are based on my experience as a scientist participating in the Pacific Northwest events, and not as a scholar with experience in the sociology and history of science. This contributes to a narrowness of view, especially the focus on scientists and not the many other important players in forest policy and management. My view is shaped by the good fortune of working three decades in the research-management partnership centered on the H. J. Andrews Experimental Forest in the Oregon Cascades, involving the Pacific Northwest Research Station and Willamette National Forest of the United States Department of Agriculture (USDA) Forest Service and Oregon State University. Work within this partnership spans basic science sponsored by the National Science Foundation to applied studies to forestry and watershed management applications. Such partnerships are rare, despite periodic encouragement and applause from the leadership of partner institutions. Participants in the partnership centered on the H. J. Andrews Forest have been involved to some degree in nearly all of the roles discussed in this chapter.

Despite this chapter's focus on the Pacific Northwest, the issue of scientists' roles in natural resource issues generally is significant (Lubchenco 1998) and thoughtfully considered elsewhere (see Jasanoff 1990, Mills and Clark 2001). Dramatic changes in natural resource management are occurring around the globe and, in a longer-term perspective, Holling (1995) has argued that natural resource management and policy may undergo cycles of abrupt overthrow of dominant management paradigms. Gunderson et al. (1995) argue that the nature of science in service to natural resource policy and management must undergo fundamental change from experimental, deterministic approaches to more holistic science. Furthermore, they argue that science should be part of institutions with good learning capability through adaptive management to reduce social convulsions and improve management.

Realms of Science Input to Forestry Policy and Management

The course of forest management and policy in the Pacific Northwest seems to match well the pattern of periodic convulsions outlined by Holling (1995), in which decades of extractive management of a natural resource, such as fisheries and forests, lead up to a crisis triggered by natural or social forces. We can trace scientists' roles in relation to a period of crisis schematically through figure 7.1, in which the shaded central line from left to right represents resource management and policy over time, passing from a period of relative stability through a period of crisis and ultimately to a new period of stability. This depiction of Pacific Northwest federal forestry issues stretches from the post–World War II inception of the extraction forestry period, through the intense old-growth and spotted owl conflicts of the 1990s, to the last decade's efforts to implement the Northwest Forest Plan (NWFP), which was intended to guide the postcrisis period of forest management.

Underpinning and influencing gradual and convulsive change in natural resource policy and management are the general context of governance, developments in basic science, and sustained research-management partnerships (bottom of figure 7.1). *Governance* in the federal case, which is central to Pacific Northwest issues, involves consideration of the political party in control of Congress and the White House, and the role of the judiciary and legislative branches of government. For example, in

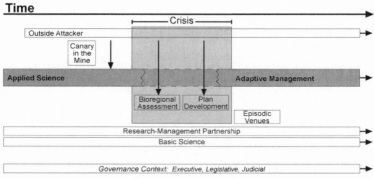

Figure 7.1.   Nine Venues of Direct Science Engagement to Policy and Management. Schematic representation over time of venues of direct science engagement to policy and management, shown in the context of one approach to engaging science (applied science) leading to crisis followed by another approach (adaptive management). Note that the nine venues of engagement are set within a broader governance context that includes executive, legislative, and judicial subcontexts.

the case of the NWFP, the judiciary played a significant role early in the period of change; litigation filled the void created by an absence of legislative solutions to political and social gridlock, as court injunctions stopped logging. These circumstances may have frozen the central issue somewhat on the initial species focus rather than let it broaden to give more balanced treatment of the broad spectrum of relevant social and ecological issues. Congress did convene several venues for science input on relevant issues through use of expert panels (Franklin 1995). This set the stage for involvement by President Clinton (see Thomas, this volume).

Scientists are important, though perhaps indirect players in policy matters through continued conduct of *basic science* (figure 7.1) in fields such as ecology and fisheries sciences. These fields contribute to change in general public perception, language, and technical knowledge about the ecosystems from which natural resources are extracted. The governance context of this science may be important in that support of basic environmental sciences can wax and wane as various political interests see advantage in the types and intensity of science conducted. Interestingly, basic science of old-growth forests in the Pacific Northwest was supported at the H. J. Andrews Forest in the 1970s by the National Science Foundation with no expectation or motivation of its relevance. As ecosystem science has developed over time, forests have come to be viewed more as ecosystems than as tree farms.

Research-management partnerships, such as that centered on the H. J. Andrews Forest, may also be sustained over many decades and through major changes in management and policy (figure 7.1). Work in such partnerships can be distinguished from *basic science*, which lacks near-term expectation of relevance, and *applied science*, which focuses on near-term relevance and minor modification of existing management paradigms, rather than aggressive attention to testing new, more radical, science-based approaches to management that may have relevance in the future. Given the common multidecade lags between inception of ideas and general adoption of new practices, these partnership activities necessarily persist through periodic changes in policy. Examples include the research at the H. J. Andrews Forest on old growth and management of wood in streams beginning in the

1970s. Current work on landscape management based in part on historic wildfire regimes (Cissel et al. 1999) may find broader application in coming decades if policy shifts from a species focus to better balance with an ecosystem focus.

In the period between management and policy crises a large cadre of scientists conduct *applied science* with the intent to improve efficiency of the management paradigm of the day. In the case of development of intensive plantation forestry, this work included improving seedling culture and planting technology, tree genetics, and methods for suppression of competing vegetation, all with the objective of enhancing wood production. Scientist-to-manager communications in this context has been referred to as "technology transfer," which reflects the role of science in supporting current policy. Scientists who draw research support from this work, managers whose work is resource extraction, and local communities supported by the work are all tightly linked to continuation of the existing policy and management approach. However, as ecosystems or social systems (e.g., communities) become stressed, scientists may take on the role of giving warning of impending problems, acting as the "canary in the mine" (figure 7.1). This role may take the form initially of dissent internal to management and research organizations involved in executing established policy. Scientists outside these management and research organizations may take on the role of *outside attackers* of the management paradigm of the day through public statements, participation in lawsuits, and other means (figure 7.1). Some scientists are always attacking from the inside or outside, but their numbers may increase as conflict builds.

When policies and management paradigms collapse in crises or "train wrecks" (Holling 1995), groups of scientists, such as blue ribbon panels, may help define the current situation by participating in development of a *bioregional assessment* (Johnson et al. 1999a). Bioregional assessments commonly provide objective information about the state and capability of the natural resource and social systems to provide goods and services expected by society. In the past two decades these assessments have covered vast tracts of the United States, from south Florida to the Northern Forest Lands of Maine to the Columbia River Basin (Johnson et al. 1999a). Building from information provided by a bioregional assessment, scientists involved in the assessments or other scientists may help chart the future course of policy and management set forth in a *management plan*. Scientists' tasks in preparation of management plans may include formulation of alternative plans and evaluation of their consequences. In figure 7.1 bioregional assessments and subsequent development of management plans occur during the crisis and influence the path of management after the crisis.

In the Pacific Northwest these steps culminated in the Forest Ecosystem Management Assessment Team report (FEMAT) and the NWFP (FEMAT 1993, USDA/USDI 1994a, Franklin 1995, Johnson et al. 1999b). The roles of science and scientists in these efforts have been thoroughly critiqued (see Johnson and Shannon 1994, Johnson et al. 1999b). While the NWFP is criticized by some as overemphasizing environmental protection, others point out that strong emphasis on species protection reflects the context set by the spotted owl litigation. Other scientists played the role of outside attackers of the assessment and the NWFP, charging that important science views and management alternatives were granted meager attention or ignored altogether. A high level of controversy seems to come with operating in the realm of high-profile political issues, even for scientists.

As with other natural resource crises (Gunderson et al. 1995), the NWFP was intended to conclude a policy crisis with a new action plan and the future use of *adaptive management* to test assumptions in the plan and develop new management approaches. Since adaptive management involves designing and conducting management actions to test hypotheses about the functioning of large, natural resource systems, scientists must play central roles in this continuing learning process. To encourage the adaptive management process, the NWFP designated Adaptive Management Areas (AMA), where scientists and land managers work together to develop and test new approaches to management. While in the precrisis period in the Northwest (1950s–1980s), and generally across the Forest Service, the phrase "technology transfer" connoted support of the current management paradigm, the currently vogue "adaptive management" language implies a sustained commitment to learning that may lead to profound change in the management approach. Surprisingly, scientists now have potentially deeper involvement in management through the adaptive management process, for adaptive management is intended to guide *incremental* change in management and prevent the *convulsive* change hypothesized by Holling (1995) and earlier experienced by the Pacific Northwest in the spotted owl and old-growth wars.

Scientists also take part in *episodic venues* that involve them in policy and management issues for periods of months to years. This contrasts with the multidecade time scale of adaptive management programs dealing with long-term processes, such as forest landscape management. Examples of episodic venues include serving on blue ribbon panels to advise policy makers, conducting research studies of effects of alternative management approaches (see Spies et al. 2002b), and consulting on technical matters related to lawsuits concerning development and implementation of management plans. These sorts of activities may occur at any time, but may be more common during and near crisis periods.

Scientists may play several of these roles simultaneously or in sequence. The social context of issues may influence a scientist's choice of roles. In an area with sparse science talent, for example, scientists may be more inclined to move to the role of canary in the mine than in an environment such as the Pacific Northwest, where forestry issues are very mature and all major interests have strong science talent.

Roles of Scientists in Natural Resource Policy Decisions

What is the appropriate role of scientists in making decisions about policy and management? Several Oregon State University social scientists have addressed this question for Pacific Northwest federal forestlands. Steel et al. (2001) and Lach et al. (2003) sampled the views of four different categories of actors: research scientists, land managers, members of interest groups and organizations (including environmental and forest products industry), and members of the "attentive public." In a study of fifty interviews and more than 600 written surveys, Lach et al. (2003) had respondents rank the appropriate conduct for H. J. Andrews Forest scientists in Pacific Northwest forestry issues across five stages of a gradient of engagement in decision making:

- *Report* scientific results that others use in making decisions on natural resource management issues.
- Report and *interpret* results for others who are involved in natural resource management decisions.
- Working closely with managers and others, *integrate* scientific results into management decisions.
- Actively *advocate* for specific and preferred natural resource management decisions.
- *Make decisions* about natural resource management and policy.

Steel et al. (2001) found widespread support across all groups of respondents for the "integrate" role of scientists—80 percent of respondents agreed with the "integrate" role and 63 percent the "interpret" role, the second most favored. However, some important differences were registered by the various groups. For example, some members of interest groups wanted scientists to play the "advocate" role, which raises the question of "who is the scientist?" and "whose science is it?" People with Ph.D.-level science training work for research, education, land management, environmental, and industrial organizations. Each of these organizations has distinct expectations and reward systems for their scientists. Despite diverse personal values and senses of appropriate levels of advocacy amongst scientists overall, scientists rated "make the decision" lowest of the four groups (Lach et al. 2003), in part because of concern about loss of credibility if their engagement reaches the "advocate" and "make the decision" levels. Scientists feared their research could be viewed as lacking objectivity and possibly slanted to influence decisions. Even without that potential loss of credibility, scientists were concerned that increased engagement in policy and management distracts from the science work. Another indication of scientists' tendency to stick within the science community mind-set was their emphasis on measuring individual credibility by their reputation in their field and the quality of the publications and data they generate. In contrast, nonscientists associated scientists' credibility with their ability to communicate with the public, elected officials, and media (Lach et al. 2003).

In contrast, a broader sampling of the Pacific Northwest of the United States and British Columbia using the same questions revealed greater acceptance by Canadians of scientists taking on deeper levels of engagement. Canadians recorded 49 and 20 percent agreement with the "advocate" and "make the decision" roles, respectively, compared with 32 and 14 percent for the U.S. respondents (Steel et al. 2001). In summary, these results indicate that some areas of strong agreement exist among the different groups of respondents, but some significant differences of opinion distinguish groups in the Oregon sample from other domestic and international contexts.

Alternative Worldviews of Forest Resource Management: A Challenge for Integration

Approaches to management of forest landscapes align with management objectives and the worldview of scientists. By *worldview* I mean the dominant ecosystem or resource management objective held by an individual or a group, which influences their starting point for discussion of future management and management approaches for meeting objectives (figure 7.2). An anthropocentric worldview, for example, may see forests as foremost for human consumption and would therefore support an agricultural management approach carried out through intensive plantation forestry. A biocentric view may consider species protection paramount and support management based on a conservation biology approach using reserves and matrix prescriptions to accommodate particular species. An alternative worldview emphasizing ecosystem dynamics may favor sustaining the range of historic conditions as a management approach for balancing commodity and species objectives. Thus, each of these worldviews represents a dominant management objective and one or more associated management approaches used to achieve that objective (figure 7.2). Each worldview can say "we have science on our side": decades of research and development of intensive plantation forestry anchors the agricultural worldview; conservation biology for sustaining species rests on island biogeographic theory and species-focused science; and ecosystem dynamics perspectives are founded in disturbance ecology. The level of development varies greatly among these management approaches: plantation forestry has been half a century in development, conservation biology is a few decades old, and landscape management based on concepts of ecosystem dynamics is in its infancy.

In the Pacific Northwest we can trace proposed and actual policy and management regimes over the past several decades as

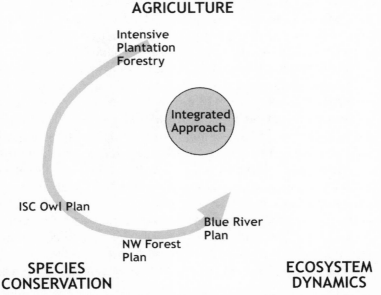

Figure 7.2. Schematic Representation of Contrasting Worldviews and Approaches to Forest Management. The arrow traces a possible path of integration from the intensive plantation forestry approach to a single-species-focused, conservation biology management system (e.g., Spotted Owl Plan of the Interagency Scientific Committee; Thomas et al. 1990) to ecosystem dynamics approaches, such as the Blue River Landscape Plan, which include consideration of historical disturbances regimes.

shifting from the agricultural approach of intensive plantation forestry to a conservation biology plan, the never-implemented spotted owl protection plan of the Interagency Scientific Committee (ISC) (Thomas et al. 1990) to the NWFP, which contains some recognition of fire and stream-flow regimes as important elements of ecosystem dynamics (figure 7.2). Over the course of events from the ISC to the NWFP there is progressive ramping up of components of the ecosystem considered—from a single species, to many species, to whole watersheds, to the bioregion as a whole. Franklin (1995) and Johnson et al. (1999b) trace this evolution of these and other science responses to policy and judicial considerations (see also Thomas, this volume). To extend the temporal perspective we may add a final point of comparison, the Blue River Landscape Plan, which strongly reflects an ecosystem dynamics component based in part on historic fire regimes (Cissel et al. 1999), is in early stages of development and testing in the Central Cascades Adaptive Management Area. This exploratory landscape plan and study considers the past 500 years of ecosystem change and uses that to plan management for the next 200 years.

This evolution of changing forest and landscape management approaches, represented schematically by the bold arrow in figure 7.2, may foreshadow a blending of the three approaches in a way that uses the best of each to meet local management objectives. Ultimately we probably need such a blending of these and other worldviews, including indigenous knowledge, to arrive at sustainable policy. The multiplicity of societal objectives—sustain species, ecosystems, ecological services (see Daily 1997)—calls for a multiplicity of approaches. We need to identify the strengths and weakness of each view and learn how to blend them to best meet local social and biophysical objectives, opportunities, and constraints. It is counterproductive to have competition among these worldviews and management approaches in either science or policy arenas.

Toward an Integrative Approach

I have briefly sketched three dimensions of involvement of scientists in natural resource policy and management—the diverse settings in which scientists play roles, their types and depths of engagement in decision making, and the worldviews they bring to issues. It is useful to reflect on each of these in terms relevant to scientists and to users of their information, and then examine the aggregate impact of these considerations on policy.

There is striking diversity of roles for scientists in natural resource policy and management. This diversity itself gives important checks and balances to the involvement of science, and thus, is an essential aspect of arriving at effective, sustainable policy, especially given the long time scales and uncertainties in management of forests and watersheds. An individual scientist may gain appreciation of the importance of this diversity of roles as his or her own roles change as a career matures, issues develop, the governance context changes, and institutions restructure.

Appropriate engagement of scientists in decision making has been heatedly debated, commonly under the theme of "What is acceptable advocacy?" In a provocative paper title, social scientists assert, "Science Advocacy Is Inevitable: Deal with It" (Shannon et al. 1996). Even advocating the use of science in management and policy decisions can be a bold act (Swanson and Greene 1999). For the scientist it is important to recognize their intended depth of engagement, being careful to not let "role creep" occur—for example, moving to deeper levels of advocacy than intended because of passion for a particular outcome on a particular issue. For those who may call on scientists for information, a scientist's record of past conduct, even a single digression into deeper-than-intended engagement may influence their credibility and effectiveness in substantive or perceptual terms. A scientist may wish to separate her roles as scientist and as citizen, but this distinction is very difficult for both the scientist and others to maintain.

Unrecognized differences of worldview commonly underlie frustrating debates among scientists about natural resource policy and management. Institutional, language, and conceptual barriers greatly impede communication among worldviews considered here. Compartmentalization of the science community arises in part from the fundamental divisions of ecological science, such as distictions among species/population, community, and ecosystem levels. Scientists separate into groups of similar worldview—academic departments, work units within government research labs, and scientific societies. Policy issues that call for integrated approaches can become battlegrounds for supremacy of worldviews even within science circles—in FEMAT, for example, one could hear "my endangered species trumps your fuzzy ecosystem dynamics concept" by implication, and that seems to be the way court rulings are playing out (*Pacific Coast Federation of Fishermen's Association v. National Marine Fisheries Servic* 1999).

An integrated approach to natural resource policy and management is essential to meeting society's complex objectives, yet integration across disciplines and worldviews remains a major challenge. Fragmentation within the science community is paralleled by piecemeal natural resource policy, developed in part in the context of a succession of high-profile issues. In the Pacific Northwest, for example, we have shifted from emphasis on efficiency of timber extraction and silvicultural practice to species protection, followed by heightened concern for watershed issues triggered by the 1996 floods. Water issues were quickly supplanted on the front pages of newspapers by fire hazard issues in the big fire years of 2000 and 2002. The issues have progressed, yet the NWFP retains a species protection focus because it was developed in response to litigation with that emphasis, in part because federal policies then had (and still have) a strong focus on species protection.

More integrated natural resource policy can be crafted in various contexts, such as in debate concerning specific policy issues, among scientists with differing worldviews, or in the research-management partnerships. The policy arena, where integration is much needed, is often too hot politically and too focused on the ultimate decision to foster thoughtful discourse. I feel that the science community has a social responsibility to integrate across worldviews outside the contentious policy arena before testing those ideas in the heat of policy conflict—a form of social-process adaptive management. The objective would be to identify the strengths and weaknesses of different management approaches and examine how they can be best mixed and matched to achieve local management objectives. Such an effort could critique a small set of case studies and develop alternative, more integrative, longer-term methods blending diverse approaches. The work of Gunderson et al. (1995) and Johnson et al. (1999a) takes the first step, but stops short of developing more integrative alternatives to the plans adopted. The National Science Foundation–sponsored National Center for Ecological Analysis and Synthesis in Santa Barbara, California, could provide a forum to bring together the perspectives of scientists, managers, and policy makers to begin work on this matter. However, this rather academic approach to integration across worldviews has the serious drawback of lacking the reality check of implementing real policy through real management.

Long-term work within a research-management partnership can be an important venue for integrating worldviews and management approaches though real-world adaptive management. A close, sustained working relationship of land managers and scientists with continuing public scrutiny and input can lead to a blending of worldviews and give scientists a context for very effectively playing the "integrate" role in a succession of decisions by line officers in the management organization. FEMAT and the NWFP assigned the adaptive management task to ten specific land areas (AMAs) and their line officers in an effort to increase the potential for success. However, developing and sustaining support and conduct of adaptive management has proven very difficult (Stankey et al. 2003). The land allocation for AMAs remains, but support of the learning process there is now left to individual national forests, whose budgets are severely constrained by continued reductions. It is distressing to note that the institutional commitment to adaptive management has faltered significantly—the Pacific Northwest Research Station eliminated support of AMAs in 1998, and the Regional Office of the National Forest System did so in 2003, before the NWFP was a decade old. Failure to have a strong and effective commitment to adaptive management increases the potential for convulsive rather than thoughtful, incremental change in management approaches (Holling 1995). The AMA network was a critical component of the overall adaptive management approach of the NWFP; if the adaptive management scheme set out in the plan is not workable, another should be developed. In short, adaptive management is an important investment in the future: absence of adaptive management diminishes the possibility of producing well-tested management schemes with both science and management credibility (the "right stuff") ready for implementation when a policy window allowing or requiring innovation opens.

An abundance of science relevant to regional policy issues, a strong commitment to having science-based policy and management, and keen public attention to forestry issues are hallmarks of the Pacific Northwest in recent decades. However, the region has been unable to mesh this incredible human resource, including scientific knowledge, with its even more impressive natural resources to arrive at workable future policy. Current struggles, for example, concern whether or not to thin forests for fuel reduction and enhancement of old-growth forest attributes in plantations, and whether short-term environmental damage from improvement of culverts on forest roads outweighs long-term watershed restoration. Science can help inform the trade-off considerations, but competing social worldviews of cut vs. no-cut have created stalemate. While frustrating, perhaps this should come as no surprise, since it is simply an extension of conflict extending back well into the nineteenth century (Wilkinson 1992). Contemporary biological, social, and physical sciences can contribute to framing issues and defining capabilities of ecosystems and social systems, but resolution of the issue remains largely a matter of social and political leadership.

Note

This chapter is based on a talk given at the Forest Futures Conference at Willamette University in Salem, Oregon, on September 25, 2002. These views have been developed over many years of work in the H. J. Andrews Experimental Forest and the Long-Term Ecological Research Program, Cascade Center for Ecosystem Management, and Central Cascades Adaptive Management Area centered there. I thank many colleagues and friends for discussions of the science-management-policy interface and K. Arabas, J. Bowersox, J. Cissel, J. Jones, J. Laurence, B. Shindler, and T. Spies for reviews of the manuscript. The opinions expressed are my own. For more information about the Andrews Forest program, see www.fsl.orst.edu/lter.

8

Science, Law, and Policy in Managing Natural Resources: Toward a Sound Mix Rather than a Sound Bite

Daniel J. Rohlf

Few natural resource management issues have generated more controversy than decisions involving how to manage "westside" old-growth forests of the Pacific Northwest (PNW), home of the famous (or infamous, depending on one's perspective) northern spotted owl (NSO) (*Strix occidentalis caurina*). Yet through years of often acrimonious debate, environmental advocates, timber industry supporters, and government officials have consistently agreed on one principle: federal agencies and other owners of forestlands should base their management decisions on "sound science."

Upon initial reflection, asserting that forest management decisions should rest on sound science is somewhat akin to supporting motherhood and apple pie. Would anyone suggest with a straight face that managers employ *poor* science? Probing this issue somewhat deeper, however, raises several important and difficult questions. If all interests support "science-based" forest management, why has it been so difficult to design and implement a strategy that enjoys broad agreement? What exactly does it mean to base management decisions on "science"? How does such a management approach also integrate legal requirements for forest management and protection of threatened and endangered species?

The Clinton administration's answers to these questions for federally owned land are embodied by the Northwest Forest Plan (NWFP), which sets forth a comprehensive forest management strategy for the entire range of northern spotted owls. To its proponents, the NWFP's key strengths include its foundation in science and its provisions for adaptive management. Many authors have pointed to the NWFP as a prime example of how modern "ecosystem management" can solve highly contentious environmental controversies (Houck 1997, Rule 2000).

Reality is something altogether different, however. Far from a biological tour de force, the NWFP actually incorporates a last-minute political compromise sold to the public as science. Its implementation over the past decade has revealed significant shortcomings in both the NWFP's ability to protect old-growth-dependent species and its capacity to deliver promised levels of timber harvest. This is due in part to inherent weaknesses in the NWFP itself, as well as failures on the part of the Forest Service, Bureau of Land Management (BLM), and Fish and Wildlife Service (FWS)—the federal agencies charged with implementing the NWFP—to carry out the NWFP's fundamental requirements. To make things appear as though the NWFP was working despite these shortcomings, the Clinton administration invented new and ostensibly scientific methodologies to justify the status quo, as well as blamed what officials labeled as meddlesome environmental appeals and lawsuits. On the other hand, the Bush administration subsequently signaled its intent to increase commodity production from Northwest forests by simply modifying or eliminating provisions of the NWFP that limit or slow timber harvest and similar activities (67 FR 64,601).

Though it may not have succeeded in its ambitious goals, the NWFP is at least a good example of the problems inherent in integrating science, law, and public policy. There are three essential ingredients to using scientific information to make public policy decisions about the natural world: well-defined standards established through a public forum; a consistent and transparent science process for determining compliance with these standards; and consistent implementation. With these three criteria as a framework, this chapter uses experiences with the NWFP as a vehicle with which to examine the futility of a quest for natural resources management driven purely by sound science. The succeeding sections demonstrate that truly successful management strategies must rest on a foundation of transparent policy decisions informed—but not determined—by a clear science process, as well as on a firm commitment to implementation.

Standards for Forest Management and Species Protection

In order to make decisions about how to manage a given resource, a manager obviously must have standards for defining a successful outcome. In other words, a manager needs a clear description of the goals she is expected to achieve in order to direct her decisions and actions. This in turn raises other important questions: Who gets to define the goals that direct management of a resource? What factors influence the nature of these goals? The NWFP's treatment of species security provides an excellent illustration of this standards problem.

Controversies over forest management in the Northwest came to a head in the late 1980s and early 1990s as a result of scientific studies showing that logging old-growth forests had caused a severe decline in the population of northern spotted owls (*Northern Spotted Owl v. Hodel* 1988, *Seattle Audubon Society v. Evans* 1991). This drop in the owls' population had far-reaching consequences for forest management due to two federal laws. First, regulations implementing the National Forest Management Act (NFMA) require that the Forest Service maintain "viable populations" of native vertebrates within national forests (36 C.F.R. § 219.19). (In 2002, however, the Bush administration proposed to amend the regulations to largely eliminate this requirement). Additionally, FWS listed spotted owls as "threatened" under the Endangered Species Act (ESA); this statute prohibits all federal agencies from taking actions that "jeopardize the continued existence of" listed species. As a result of lawsuits by environmental organizations, a federal judge ruled that the Forest Service had failed to develop a forest management strategy to meet these legal standards, and he issued a sweeping injunction on timber harvest within the owls' range until the agency did so (*Seattle Audubon Society v. Evans* 1991).

It is important to note that the court's decision did not specify what a "viable" population of spotted owls would be, or what was needed to avoid "jeopardy" to owls; the court merely held that the Forest Service had failed to adopt a plan for achieving these standards, whatever they require. Accordingly, in formulating the NWFP, the Forest Service and BLM had to grapple with a fundamental question—what level of protection for owls do these standards require?

Initially, most people think that defining a viable population of spotted owls or any other species, or describing what constitutes jeopardy to a species, involves a purely scientific determination (Houck 1997). This is not true. *Viable* and *jeopardy*—and similar terms such as *recovered, healthy, secure,* and even *endangered*—do not have a definitive biological meaning. Many people find this statement difficult to accept because they have been conditioned to separate science from policy rather than integrate these concepts. In fact, science has the tools to *describe* a term such as *viability*, but does not have the ability to *define* it. In other words, scientists can apply methodologies such as population viability analysis to assess viability, but such analysis merely generates a risk curve over time that depends on population size, metapopulation structure, and similar factors. However, such an analysis cannot identify the minimum point along that risk curve that all interested parties agree defines a "viable" population. Accordingly, for a term such as "viability" to have any usefulness in management, someone must provide a more specific definition of this concept, that is, identify the minimum point along a risk continuum at which the decision maker is comfortable that the risk to a population is within acceptable limits. Without such specificity, differences in opinion over a seemingly scientific concept are virtually inevitable. For example, many environmentalists will likely believe that spotted owls are not viable given their present population numbers and trend, whereas loggers may reach an entirely different conclusion given the same data. However, until some decision maker devises a clear definition of what constitutes a viable population of owls, it is impossible to say who is correct—as well as impossible to say how old-growth forests should be managed.

The key to creating such a definition lies in recognizing that such an exercise requires a blend of both science and policy. Most biologists describe the security of a population by specifying a magnitude of risk to the population's existence over a given time period. While any definition of species security must be couched in these or similar terms to have biological relevance, it is crucial to recognize that the level of risk a decision maker is willing to accept and what time frame she employs for describing a secure population—the minimum point along the biological risk curve at which a species is defined as viable—depends on a *policy* decision, not a biological determination. The decision involved in buying a life insurance policy illustrates this concept. A person might decide to purchase a policy that pays her beneficiary $50,000 in case of her death, or she might buy a much bigger policy that pays $1 million in case of her untimely demise. While objective factors such as the insured person's age and number of dependents obviously play a role in the decision of how much insurance to buy, the choice ultimately comes down to one that is completely *subjective,* namely, the individual's particular aversion to risk. It is usually possible to gain greater security from risk—that is, buy a more lucrative policy—but this security always comes at a cost; bigger insurance policies are more expensive. Hence, there is no "right" answer in deciding how much insurance to buy. Ultimately, the decision boils down to balancing how much risk one is willing to take and how much one is willing (or able) to spend to protect against risk. A noted conservation biologist has employed a similar analogy to illustrate the subjective nature of defining a viable population (Shaffer 1981).

The question of what constitutes a "secure" or "viable" population of spotted owls requires a similar policy choice. Science can inform this choice, but science cannot make it. While it is vital to know as much as possible about key biological parameters such as how much habitat each owl pair requires, the level of security afforded to owls ultimately depends on how much value (in economic, aesthetic, or even moral terms) society places on these birds. Moreover, this choice of security level for owls in turn has major implications for forest management: while a larger owl population faces a lower risk of extinction over a given time period, more owls require more protected habitat. Therefore, increased security comes at a cost to other potential uses (and users) of forest resources—in particular by resulting in less timber harvest. Like buying insurance, balancing the level of security for owls and the costs of this protection involves a subjective policy choice. A biologist thus cannot identify a socially desirable level of spotted owl security any more than an insurance agent can pick out the "right" policy for an individual.

While an individual obviously makes her own decision about how much insurance to buy, who decides how much society values owls? In other words, with high stakes for both the environment and the economy riding on the answer, who makes the policy call inherent in supplying a concise definition of species security? Law generally supplies the answer to this question, either explicitly or implicitly. As the body that writes federal laws, Congress obviously had the authority to decree a specific level of security when it passed the NFMA and ESA. However, by defining the standards for species security in these statutes in only vague terms, lawmakers essentially declined to exercise this power. [See 16 U.S.C. § 1604(g)(3)(B) ("provide for diversity of plant and animal communities); 16 U.S.C. § 1536(a)(2) (insure that federal action "is not likely to jeopardize the continued existence" of a listed species)]. In effect, therefore, Congress left to federal bureaucrats in the Forest Service and FWS the policy decision of how much protection to afford to forest species.

In formulating the NWFP, the Forest Service and BLM decided to manage old-growth forests so that spotted owls and other old-growth-dependent species have an 80 percent chance of remaining widespread across federal land for 100 years (USDA/USDI 1994a). This standard is significant for three reasons.

First, the NWFP's definition of security for old-growth species is unique in that it is one of only a handful of biologically explicit species management standards at the federal level. Many other standards, such as the Marine Mammal Protection Act's "optimum sustainable population" goal and the ESA's "threatened" and "endangered" categories carry such biologically general definitions as to provide managers virtually no concrete guidance for assessing compliance with these legal requirements. In contrast, the NWFP gives federal officials a specific guidepost for devising, implementing, and assessing a biologically based management strategy. While perhaps many may disagree with the standard's substance (i.e., its choice of an 80 percent level of certainty and a 100-year time period) the NWFP at least provides specificity for both of these parameters. As such, the NWFP is an important example of the sort of biologically explicit standard needed for all species management plans.

Second, it is instructive to examine how federal agencies devised the substance of the NWFP's standard. In short, a group of agency bureaucrats, agency scientists, and political appointees simply made it up—behind closed doors—in an atmosphere of heated political controversy (Yaffee 1994). As noted earlier, the standard of security for old-growth-dependent species should reflect the value society places on these species on federal land. Tellingly, however, the federal personnel who made this decision had virtually no process for seeking the public's views on this issue—or those of interest groups, industries, or anyone else. Said another way, a few people working for federal agencies devised, without input from anyone else, the management standard that supposedly represents the value that society as a whole places on old-growth-dependent species. While not atypical for federal management of biological resources, this sort of "black box" decision making is a poor way to make crucial public policy choices.

Finally, federal agencies staunchly defend the NWFP by routinely referring to it as based on the best science applicable to forest management. As discussed in this section, however, choosing a standard for species security involves a policy choice, not a scientific calculus. But by portraying the NWFP's management standard as based on science instead of policy, federal agencies need not defend their choice of how much value to place on old-growth species and their habitat. Rather, federal agencies can simply claim to have devised the "correct" management choice based on application of their biological expertise, and then dismiss criticisms from the public or other interested groups as inconsistent with science. The agencies have employed a similar argument in defending the NWFP in court, maintaining (successfully) that courts should defer to the agencies' biological expertise—when in fact the NWFP's driving standard resulted from a behind-the-scenes political compromise (*Gifford Pinchot Task Force v. U.S. Fish and Wildlife Service* 2002).

In sum, it is important to note how little the NWFP's standard of security for spotted owls and other old-growth-dependent species turns on science. Though informed by scientific information such as how much habitat a pair of owls require, the actual management standard for owls and other species resulted from a policy choice made unilaterally by federal bureaucrats. Federal agencies, however, have been quite successful at shielding their choice from public or judicial scrutiny by calling it "science," thus implying that judges and others must defer to the agencies' "expert" decision (*Inland Empire Public Lands Council v. U.S. Forest Service* 1996).

"Science Process" for Assessing Consistency with NWFP Standards

One of the traditional hallmarks of sound science is the idea that reliable information results only from a reliable process for gathering and analyzing data, generating conclusions, and validating those conclusions. The scientific community generally looks to the peer review and publication process to ensure that scientific findings have their foundation in sound methodology. At least in theory, review of a scientist's methods and analysis by her peers prior to publication will identify errors in technique or reasoning that could affect the validity of an investigator's conclusions (Meffe et al. 1998). Additionally, publication of peer-reviewed papers in professional journals creates a "transparent" process that allows scientists an opportunity to replicate, refine, or even refute the finding of their colleagues, thus gradually building a comprehensive body of reliable knowledge. Peer review also serves as a de facto mechanism for resolution of scientific disputes; scientists whose ideas lack support of their peers generally cannot publish their work and are not seen as credible in scientific circles, and their work is generally not admissible in court (*Daubert v. Merril Dow Pharmaceuticals* 1993).

Implementation of standards for species and ecosystem protection similarly demands a reliable and transparent process. In the case of forest management in the Pacific Northwest, the NWFP, as discussed earlier, specifies explicit standards for management. However, it is important to examine the NWFP, as well as agency implementation of the NWFP, to assess whether the relevant agencies and managers have devised a process for reliably assessing whether management actions are meeting the NWFP's standards.

Interestingly, the law contains little guidance for dealing with this crucial issue. Current regulations implementing the NFMA require that Forest Service officials monitor populations of "management indicator species," (MIS) species chosen by the agency as representative of a particular ecosystem or type of species. However, the regulations provide no guidance as to the details of the required monitoring. Consequently, the Forest Service has no standard agency-wide monitoring protocols, which has resulted in widely varying monitoring programs and methodologies across the many individual national forests throughout the country. Legal disputes over the type of monitoring required of the Forest Service have also produced mixed results because of the law's vagueness. In a case arising out of the Northwest, the Ninth Circuit Court of Appeals upheld as lawful a monitoring program that did not even attempt to census individuals of the designated MIS (*Inland Empire* 1996). Instead, managers had merely identified the type of habitat thought to be suitable for the species and assumed that the species was meeting the regulations' viability standard if the agency's management plan called for protection of a sufficient quantity of this habitat. On the other hand, a different federal appellate court held that a monitoring program must involve an actual count of individual members of MIS (*Sierra Club v. Martin* 1999).

The ESA contains the only other requirement related to the "science process" required of federal land managers. The ESA requires that agencies employ "the best scientific . . . information available" in ensuring that federal actions do not jeopardize threatened and endangered species. However, like the NFMA's monitoring requirement, this standard is very broad, and provides little real guidance to federal managers. Court decisions have done little to flesh out this "best science" mandate.

In the absence of clear direction in statutes and regulations, individual administrative units and federal managers have the authority and responsibility to create a process for implementing and assessing management strategies in light of applicable standards. Unfortunately, as experiences to date with the NWFP demonstrate, these administrative "science processes" often leave much to be desired.

In addition to a standard for species security, the NWFP contains an "Aquatic Conservation Strategy" (ACS). The ACS sets forth nine standards for protecting components of the ecosystem's watersheds, most of which require managers to "maintain and re-store" important aquatic features such as water quality, habitat structure, and similar characteristics (USDA/USDI 1994a). The National Marine Fisheries Service (NMFS) linked these standards to the ESA's jeopardy standard, determining that actions consis-tent with the ACS standards would also be consistent with the ESA's jeopardy standard (NMFS 1998, *Pacific Coast Federation of Fishermen's Associations v. National Marine Fisheries Service* 2001). The key "science process" question thus is as follows: How do federal managers determine whether proposed agency actions, in-cluding potentially disruptive actions such as timber sales, meet the standards for watershed protection set forth in the ACS?

Since neither legal requirements nor the NWFP specify a process for determining consistency with ACS standards, the Forest Service, BLM, and NMFS created their own. The agen-cies' process established extremely broad spatial and time scales for measuring consistency with these standards, designating "watersheds" of between 5,200 and 92,000 hectares (12,800 and 228,000 acres) as the appropriate area over which to measure individual proposals' impacts, and ten to twenty years as the relevant time frame (*Pacific Coast Federation of Fishermen's Asso-*

ciations 2001). Accordingly, when assessing whether or not a given timber sale would lead to violations of the ACS's mandates to "maintain and restore" key aquatic functions, the agencies assumed that a project would *not* have such impacts unless it led to negative impacts across an entire watershed that persisted more than at least a decade or more. This process resulted in determinations that virtually all proposed timber sales met ACS standards and would not jeopardize listed salmon present in streams affected by the sales.

Was this method of analyzing whether proposed actions were consistent with the NWFP's standards based on sound science? Arguably, it was not. By manipulating the spatial and temporal parameters of their analyses, federal managers were able to mask, and thus avoid considering, potentially serious environmental impacts on localized areas that can persist for up to a decade or more (see also Brown, this volume). However, the mechanisms employed by the scientific community to guard against this sort of behavior are largely informal and not reflected in the laws and regulations that govern resource management decisions of federal agencies. NMFS did not conduct any sort of peer review process of its method for determining ACS consistency, nor attempt to publish it in a scientific journal. Further, unlike science as practiced in a more academic setting, federal managers did not attempt to explain their rationale for designing the methodology they employed—they simply announced it. This situation is not atypical of other environmental and natural resource management decisions made by federal agencies; there is very often little legal or even institutional guidance to ensure that agencies design a "science process" in accord with sound scientific principles.

On occasion, however, judicial review approximates the peer review process's function as a scientific dispute resolution mechanism. Courts typically are very deferential to federal managers, and as a rule are reluctant to question the scientific validity of agencies' analytical methods (interestingly, this is not true in civil disputes between private parties; in such cases the U.S. Supreme Court directed federal judges to be scientific "gatekeepers," carefully scrutinizing scientific evidence for reliability before it can be admitted as evidence; see *Daubert v. Merrill Dow Pharmaceuticals* 1993). In egregious cases, though, courts may reject what they determine to be flawed science processes (*Idaho Sporting Congress v. Rittenhouse* 2002, *Seattle Audubon Society v. Evans* 1991).

Ultimately, this is what occurred in the case of ACS review under the NWFP. Environmental groups and fishing interests filed a lawsuit challenging this process. Both the lower court and appellate court recognized that the four- to five-year life cycle of threatened and endangered salmon makes them vulnerable to changes in the aquatic environment that persist for ten to twenty years; the courts also observed that the huge spatial scale of review employed by federal managers masked localized impacts to fish populations. As a result of these findings, the courts overturned the methodology chosen by the agencies to assess compliance with ACS standards as inconsistent with the ESA (*Pacific Coast Federation of Fishermen's Associations* 2001). In essence, the court determined that managers may not choose a science process that overlooks local and "short-term" impacts on forest resources, at least when management actions affect species facing extinction.

Overall, this example shows that the "science process" managers employ to assess consistency with a given management standard question often determines what the answer will be. Unfortunately, unlike the rigorous—albeit informal—process of peer review and publication that governs academic science, law and internal agency direction often contains no such safeguards to ensure that the results of agencies' consistency findings are scientifically accurate rather than influenced by a desire to reach a politically expedient answer.

NWFP Implementation

The final component for successfully integrating science and law in managing forests and other ecosystems is the most obvious, yet often the most difficult. Once officials have designed a management scheme or plan that establishes clear management standards, and have developed transparent methodologies for reliably determining whether management actions are meeting the standards, the responsible agencies and officials must fully implement the plan. It is hardly an earth-shattering revelation to assert that a plan must be implemented to be successful. However, there are many examples, including the NWFP, of implementation failures undermining management plans. These failures often result from lack of resources for implementation, lack of political or institutional will to carry out commitments in a management scheme, or sometimes from weaknesses in the design of the plan itself.

The NWFP's provisions for managing species dependent on old-growth forests other than northern spotted owls provide a good example of all of these types of implementation failure. The NWFP's survey-and-manage provisions require the Forest Service and BLM to survey areas of mature and old-growth forest for scores of rare or sensitive species prior to ground-disturbing activities. These provisions were included in the NWFP due to concern by the authors that many of these species were still at risk or little understood, making additional information gathering prior to timber harvest or similar activities an important element of avoiding ecologically crucial areas or designing mitigation measures in order to ultimately ensure the viability of these species over time.

From the outset of management under the NWFP, the Forest Service and BLM had a spotty record of implementing the survey-and-manage requirements. The prescribed surveys are both costly and time consuming, making them tempting to overlook by agencies constantly strapped for cash and pressured to meet commodity targets on a timely basis. After only a few years of management under the NWFP, it became clear that the Forest Service and BLM had simply failed to implement survey-and-management actions.

Of the three key aspects of integrating science and law in resource management, it is probably the easiest for law to influence plan implementation. Courts often have difficulty understanding the interaction of law and science in setting standards and are reluctant to review the scientific validity of agencies' science process, but judges are quite accustomed to enforcing implementation of provisions in a written plan. In the case of the NWFP's survey-and-manage requirements, a federal court responded to environmentalists' implementation challenge by enjoining timber sales across much of the Northwest pending full compliance by BLM and the Forest Service with these provisions (*Oregon Natural Resources Council Action v. Forest Service* 1999).

While the Clinton administration stepped up efforts to implement survey-and-manage requirements as a result of the suit and injunction, the Bush II administration took a different approach. Rather than improving implementation of these aspects of the NWFP, the Forest Service and BLM under Bush proposed to simply eliminate these requirements altogether (67 FR 64,601). While excising the survey-and-manage provisions would obviously solve the agencies' implementation problem, the Bush proposal did not offer a satisfactory explanation for how this action is consistent with meeting the NWFP's standards. Since implementation of a plan's components is the key to achieving a plan's goals—at least in the absence of a clear explanation for why certain plan requirements are unnecessary—simply eliminating problematic requirements is not a scientifically or legally sound means for resolving implementation difficulties.

Finally, widespread implementation problems with many different resource management plans suggests that agencies give too little thought to their ability to implement a plan during the process of formulating the plan itself. At best, this indicates that managers do not adequately consider the ability of agencies to implement management plans, including agencies' ability to fund the plans, as an integral part of drawing up plans. At worst, systematic implementation failures indicate that managers cynically create plans that appear sound—and that pass legal muster—while knowing that agencies will not be able to actually carry out all of the plans' requirements.

Science, Policy, Law, and Beyond

Like many sound bites, calls for resource management decisions based on science provide only a distorted and partial description of the challenges inherent in such management decisions. As exemplified well by federal efforts to manage old-growth forests in the Pacific Northwest under the NWFP, science plays an important, albeit limited, role in resource planning decisions. Policy makers must have scientific information to assist them in understanding the on-the-ground consequences of their decisions, but science provides no automatic answers to questions of acceptable degrees of risk and certainty. Accordingly, decisions such as choosing a standard for species security in Northwest forests represent a value judgment informed rather than determined by science. Congress did not make such a value judgment itself in legislation governing federal forest and species management, thus leaving these choices to agency decision makers. Agency personnel also must design sound "science processes" to assess whether management actions are complying with these chosen standards, and then actually implement all the elements of a management plan.

Unfortunately, experiences to date with the NWFP also provide good examples of a poor interaction between science and policy. Federal managers made key policy decisions underlying management standards behind closed doors, then portrayed these decisions as "scientific" and thus within the exclusive expertise of agency officials. Managers also have designed science processes with an eye toward justifying desired agency actions such as timber harvest rather than accurately assessing compliance with the NWFP's standards. Finally, in many cases implementation of clear provisions of the NWFP has been spotty, culminating in proposals to simply discard provisions of the NWFP that have slowed its commodity production goals.

Law influences the interactions between science and policy. Congress effectively determines who makes key decisions about standards, though in the context of forest management and species management lawmakers have effectively passed this authority to agency officials, who in turn have wielded it with little or no public input. Law can sometimes serve as a kind of scientific dispute resolution process, as when federal courts struck down agency attempts to hide the impacts of timber sales through use of huge scales of impact analysis. However, judicial willingness to carefully scrutinize agency science process decisions is usually limited only to the most egregious cases. On the other hand, as illustrated by the "survey and manage" injunction, courts are often more willing to require implementation of a management scheme's clear requirements.

Science, policy, and law are indispensable components of successful resource management. Just as important, however, are lawmakers, managers, and a public that understands the proper roles of each. Agencies and interest groups that justify their actions and goals by invoking science are often simply expressing a policy preference masked as science. Similarly, agencies have often devised processes to assess compliance with management standards that provide them with answers they want to hear, not true and impartial measurements. Finally, a management process only works to the extent that it is actually carried out. A leap in the effectiveness of resource management will occur when these concepts are more widely understood.

Note

This chapter is based on a talk given at the Forest Futures Conference at Willamette University in Salem, Oregon, on September 25, 2002.

9

Forests, Tornadoes, and Abortion: Thinking about Science, Politics, and Policy

Roger A. Pielke Jr.

Observers of science in policy and politics are of different minds about the potential of science to foster improved decision making. Forest policy is no different. On the one hand, optimists suggest that the mechanisms of science offer the potential for reducing political conflict:

> If scientists and forest managers can channel the shared interests of timber companies, woodland owners, and environmental groups in improved scientific understanding of forests into joint exercises in data collection, model building, and environmental monitoring, those joint assessment exercises can build trust and facilitate understanding among those with initially opposing views. In the best of circumstances (which, admittedly, are difficult to create), the focus of such efforts on "the science" rather than "the politics" can foster mutual understanding and even grudging respect, which in turn, can be the foundation for subsequent consensus building on larger issues. (Mitchell et al., this volume)

Such optimists find that the Northwest Forest Plan (NWFP) exemplifies many of the qualities of adaptive ecosystem management, and see potential for "continuing progress in incorporating

143

improved science regarding what makes a 'healthy' forest into improved practices that actually make our forests healthier" (Mitchell et al., this volume).

This view stands in stark contrast to that of Rohlf (this volume), who asserts that:

> many authors have pointed to the NWFP as a prime example of how modern "ecosystem management" can solve highly contentious environmental controversies. . . . Reality is something altogether different, however. Far from a biological tour de force, the NWFP actually incorporates a last-minute political compromise sold to the public as science.

Far from seeing science as a means to reduce political conflict, Rohlf sees science as just another battlefield for politics as usual: "Agencies and interest groups that justify their actions and goals by invoking science are often simply expressing a policy preference masked as science." Not only do the perspectives of the authors differ on the NWFP, they also represent profoundly contrasting views of science, politics, and policy.

In order to judge whether or not science offers a remedy for the pitfalls of politics, or whether science is just politics by another name, conceptual clarity would seem to offer an advantage. This chapter seeks such clarity through an extended "thought experiment"—an exercise in the imagination. Thought experiments allow the thinker to create carefully constructed scenarios in order to highlight aspects of the real world that are typically difficult to see or are somehow obscured. Politics and policy are concepts that are often conflated and hard to distinguish, making it difficult to understand the role of science in decision making. The thought experiment introduced in this chapter uses two scenarios to highlight the importance of the context of decision making as a critical factor that shapes the interconnections of science, politics, and policy.

It may be useful to begin with a few simple definitions of terms commonly used in this chapter. *Science* refers to the systematic pursuit of knowledge. *Policy* is synonymous with decision, and refers to a commitment to a particular course of action. *Politics* refers to the process of bargaining, negotiation, and compromise in pursuit of a desired goal. Distinguishing policy from politics is one objective of introducing the following "thought experiment."

Imagine that you are in an auditorium with about fifty other people. Perhaps you've gone to hear a lecture, or you are at a neighborhood meeting. As you entered the auditorium you noticed a thunderstorm approaching, but you paid it little attention. Suddenly, someone bursts into the room and exclaims that a tornado is fast approaching, and everyone must quickly proceed to the basement. Whatever formal event was going on is quickly transformed into several dozen hurried conversations, some expressing doubt, and the excited packing of purses and briefcases. As the milling about continues, someone shouts loudly to all in the room, "We must decide what to do!"

How might such a decision be made? For the purposes of this thought experiment, it is not unreasonable to assume that the people threatened by the tornado have a shared common interest in preserving their own lives.[1] Thus, to reach a consensus to commit to a course of action—say, stay in the auditorium and continue the meeting or go down to the basement—they would need to know if the tornado is indeed quickly coming this way. To collect this knowledge they might turn on the radio, hoping to hear a weather report, or just look out the window. If the tornado is indeed approaching the building, then it is easy to imagine that the group would quickly decide to move to the basement. The essential point of this example is that for the group in the auditorium, under these circumstances a commitment to a specific course of action can be resolved primarily through the systematic pursuit of knowledge, that is, science.

Let's call the process of bargaining, negotiation, and compromise in such situations tornado politics. Information plays such a critical role in tornado politics because participants in the decision-making process share a common objective—in this case, the goal of preserving one's life—and the scope of choice is highly restricted—stay or go. We will return to tornado politics shortly; but first, consider a very different sort of politics.

Imagine that you are in the same auditorium with the same group of fifty people; but in this case, instead of deciding whether or not to evacuate, the group is discussing whether or not to allow abortion to be practiced in the community. For simplicity's sake, let's just consider abortion generally, yes or no, and not in cases of medical necessity, or other special circumstances.[2] One person recognized to speak stands up and exclaims, "The practice of abortion violates my religious beliefs and therefore must be banned in our community!" The next speaker states with equal passion, "The community has no right to dictate what can or cannot occur inside a woman's body. The practice of abortion must remain legal!" As a murmur of dozens of conversations grows louder, someone shouts loudly to all in the room, "We must decide what to do!"

How might such a decision be made? For the group in the auditorium to commit to a course of action—to ban or allow abortion in the community—they might follow some sort of established procedure, such as a vote. They might form two groups (pro-life and pro-choice) and assign representatives to negotiate an outcome. If negotiations turn bad, they might even take up arms against one another to settle the matter by force, or they may even cease attempts to live together as one community. There are clearly many ways that such a decision might be made. However, one strategy that is extremely unlikely to lead to a resolution on this issue is to systematically pursue knowledge about abortion in the same manner that was proposed in the case of the approaching tornado. Why? On this issue among the group, there is no shared commitment to a specific goal; to the contrary, there are conflicting commitments based on differing values. And while information matters in this situation, arguably no amount or type of *scientific* information about abortion can reconcile those different values. Even so, perhaps the community's commitment to live under shared governance might lead to a desire to work together to achieve a legitimate outcome where all agree to live under the decision, once made. In such situations, let's call the process of bargaining, negotiation, and compromise "abortion politics."

The idealized examples of tornado politics or abortion politics help create a language that will allow us to investigate the complexities and the challenges of making decisions with and about science.

The following lists contrast the different roles and characteristics of information in decision making in tornado and abortion politics.

Tornado Politics	Abortion Politics
Evaluation	Rationalization
Used to help assess	Used to help justify decision
Decision alternatives	Commitments
Comprehensive	Selective
Rational	Emotional
Logical	Narrative
Enlightenment	Power
Technocracy	Pluralism

On the one hand, in tornado politics, scientific information is critical for decision makers to evaluate and compare decision alternatives. The information that is needed to make an effective decision lies outside of the room, hence the methods and perspectives of science are strengths in obtaining useful knowledge. This is very much the logic that underlies calls for scientific assessments designed to provide information to policy makers. A fundamental assumption in such cases is that once everyone obtains a shared level of understanding, a preferred course of action will become obvious and noncontroversial. In the case of a rapidly approaching tornado, this is undoubtedly true.

On the other hand, in abortion politics information certainly plays a role; but the relevant information is not scientific information about abortion. Information that might be shared in this case might be experiential in the form of narratives or anecdotes, or even information about how others view the issue. Information matters in this scenario, but plays a very different role in decision making than in the case of tornado politics. A decision in this case will result from the exercise of power in a decision-making system, and information will be used in an attempt to convince those sharing in the exercise of power to align with particular perspectives.

The roles and characteristics in the *Tornado Politics* column are similar to how we might describe scientific information, whereas those in the *Abortion Politics* column are quite contrary to conventional descriptions of scientific information. Because our society highly values scientific information, its characteristics are often portrayed in a positive light, and information with nonscientific characteristics is portrayed in a corresponding negative light. For example, no scientist wants to see his or her work described as "emotional" or "selective." But, comprehensive, logical, and rational are positive attributes, whether the information being described is scientific or not. This is one reason why advocates of different political views agree on the need for policy to be based on "sound science."

But a fundamental lesson of the thought experiments is that neither tornado politics nor abortion politics presents a "better" means of decision making, simply that the different types of politics arise from the context of decision making. Similarly, the role of information in one scenario versus another cannot be judged to be a "better" strategy, because each is appropriate for the context. This perspective is well understood by many advocates whose job it is to promote a particular political position. For example, in March 2003 the *New York Times* reported on a memo prepared by a Republican Party strategist discussing the party's approach to the environment (Lee 2003). The memo offered the following advice, as presented in the article:

- The term "climate change" should be used instead of "global warming" because "while global warming has catastrophic connotations attached to it, climate change sounds more controllable and less emotional challenge."
- "Conservationist" conveys a "moderate, reasoned, common sense position" while "environmentalist" has the "connotation of extremism."
- "Be even more active in recruiting experts who are sympathetic to your view and much more active in making them part of your message" because "people are more willing to trust scientists than politicians."

Kim Haddow of the Sierra Club, a group with positions usually at odds with the Republican Party, said that the memo's "advice is right. It's very smart—confounding, troubling, but smart." It is "smart" because the guidance in the memo for the presentation of environmental information is appropriate for the context—in this case, abortion politics.

A real-world example of a situation that evolved from tornado politics to abortion politics is the contested 2000 U.S. presidential election (see Sarewitz 2000). Selection of the president on Election Day is typically a very straightforward process: Vote. Count the votes. The candidate with the most electoral votes wins the election. This is clearly a case of tornado politics, where the relevant information is the number of votes cast for each candidate, collected comprehensively and rationally. But in 2000, with the electoral votes just about equal in forty-nine states, in Florida the election was so close that it was unclear who had received more votes. Whoever won Florida would win the presidency. The candidates quickly proposed alternative means for resolving the uncertainty. Count only these votes. No, count these. Finish by Friday. Take as long as is needed. Count the hanging chads. Revote. The systematic pursuit of information mattered less and less. Ultimately the election was decided by the Supreme Court.

Sarewitz (2000) asks, "Suppose we had asked a team of scientists—rather than the U.S. Supreme Court—to determine the winner of the Florida presidential election. . . . Could such an approach have worked?" His answer is no,

> because uncertainty does not cause conflicting values. As a political matter, the direction of causation is quite the opposite: uncertainties emerge because the value conflict—an election, an environmental controversy—remains politically unresolved. Conversely, once a value conflict is settled through political means, the underlying uncertainties effectively disappear. The Supreme Court is a legitimate means for achieving this end; a team of scientists is not.

In the case of the 2000 election, thank goodness for abortion politics; not because of the outcome, but because there was a legitimate outcome at all. An approach based on tornado politics (i.e., trying to precisely count the votes) may have led to greater uncertainties in who received more votes (e.g., what counts as a vote anyway?), proving incapable (just as in the case of abortion) in resolving a dispute over values. Often, wars and conflict result where the mechanisms of abortion politics are not considered as legitimate as decisions rendered by the U.S. Supreme Court.

Now let's take the thought experiment a step further. Imagine if, in the tornado example, the group decided to adopt abortion politics as the means for making a decision. That is, instead of seeking to assess the location and path of the tornado, they instead decided not to gather information and instead held a vote. This is almost so absurd as to be nonsensical. To disconnect the decision from the circumstances of the tornado is to invite a tragic outcome, or at best a good outcome determined only by chance.

Conversely, imagine if in the abortion example that the group were to adopt tornado politics as the means for making a decision. Here as well, one's thought experiment capabilities are pushed to the limit by trying to imagine what scientific study could conceivably lend any useful information to this decision process.[3] But this dissonance illustrates a central point of the thought experiment: In the idealized tornado case, scientific information matters. In fact, in the very simple example presented here, the information determines the decision. In the abortion case, scientific information matters not at all, and its pursuit would represent a distraction from the task of reconciling different value commitments through bargaining, negotiation, and compromise. As Sarewitz (1999) writes, "not only is there nothing wrong with the consequent messiness [of democratic politics], but all historical indications suggest that there is no viable alternative in a society that values freedom and justice and seeks to balance individual rights with the collective good."

Since there are so very few real-world decision contexts that set themselves up nicely as carefully constructed thought experiments, a natural question raised by these examples is how these issues manifest themselves in the real world of decision making with and about science. In reality, decisions, particularly those involving environmental issues, take on characteristics of tornado and abortion politics simultaneously. In such situations the following circumstances often apply. Alternative courses of action materially affect outcomes. To some degree, scientific information matters for understanding both the motivation for the decision and the consequences of alternative courses of action. At the same time, different perspectives and values shape commitments to alternative courses of action. There may be fundamental, irreducible uncertainty about the problem and policy options. Knowledge itself may be contested. And there may be lack of shared values on both ends and means. In such contexts it is important to accurately assess what science can and cannot do as a contribution to the democratic process.

So how might these thought experiments help us to reconcile the contrasting perspectives of Mitchell et al. (this volume) and Rohlf (this volume), introduced at the beginning of this chapter? One answer is that perhaps Mitchell et al. are largely viewing forest policy through a lens of tornado politics, while Rohlf views forest policy through a lens of abortion politics.

We see this in how each characterizes the other perspective. Mitchell et al. note the "deep conflict in the values, interests, and biases of loggers, environmentalists, and other audiences involved in the forest policy debate." Even so, they retain considerable optimism that scientific assessment "may help to reduce these conflicts." Such optimism is warranted only if one accepts certain assumptions about the role of information in forest policy. By contrast, Rohlf has a less sanguine view about the role of science: "policy makers must have information to assist them in understanding the on-the-ground consequences of their decisions, but science provides no automatic answers." Similarly, this warning about the limitations of science is also grounded in a particular view of the political context. Swanson (this volume) recognizes that forest policy encompasses both perspectives:

> An abundance of science relevant to regional policy issues, a strong commitment to having science-based policy and management, and keen public attention to forestry issues are hallmarks of the Pacific Northwest in recent decades. However, the region has been unable to mesh this incredible human resource, scientific knowledge, with its more impressive natural resources to arrive at workable future policy. . . . Science can help to inform the trade-off considerations, but competing social world views of cut vs. no-cut have created stalemate.

From this perspective, it would appear that a critical question to ask in any specific decision context is, what constructive role—if any—might scientists (including social scientists, humanists, and others who systematically pursue knowledge) hope to contribute to forest policy and politics?

While this question is more suitable for an introduction than a conclusion, the thought experiments introduced in this chapter highlight the point that any answer lies in first understanding the context of decision making, including the perspectives of the various stakeholders in the decision process. In the language of this chapter, the role of science in decision making will vary considerably to the extent that a particular decision context exhibits characteristics of tornado politics and abortion politics. In many situations, and forest policy is no different, elements of tornado politics and abortion politics will occur simultaneously. A danger for both science and democracy occurs when roles are mixed and science becomes politicized in the context of abortion politics, or when politics becomes scientized in the context of tornado politics (Pielke 2002). In such complex political, social, and scientific situations it is critical to differentiate policy from politics and to ensure that the role of science is appropriate to the needs of both.

Notes

1. By contrast, when a tornado appeared over Boulder, Colorado, in 1996 while I worked at the National Center for Atmospheric Research, most of my colleagues headed to the roof rather than the basement!

2. Also for the purposes of this thought experiment, please consider those individuals whose abortion views are a function of the viability of a fetus as accepting abortion under certain conditions.

3. Consider what scientific information would make you change your own views on abortion, whatever those views happen to be.

III

CONSIDERING THREATENED AND ENDANGERED SPECIES

10

Long-Term Population Monitoring of Northern Spotted Owls: Recent Results and Implications for the Northwest Forest Plan

Steven H. Ackers

Most of the other chapters in this book discuss the broad changes in forest management, economics, and public perceptions of the values and uses of Pacific Northwest (PNW) forests that have occurred over the past ten years. Here, I narrow the focus considerably to an important player in the events of the past decade, the northern spotted owl (NSO) (*Strix occidentalis caurina*). In addition to presenting a review of past research and an update of the present state of knowledge of this species, I also discuss the prospects for recovery and long-term persistence of this species under the Northwest Forest Plan (NWFP). Most importantly, I hope the reader comes away from this chapter reflecting upon some of the central questions surrounding the management of threatened and endangered species: What are the public's expectations and values that led to the creation of the Endangered Species Act (ESA) and the NWFP? Have these expectations and values changed with the hard lessons learned as a result of the spotted owl controversy? Is there a better way to proactively preserve our biological heritage than to respond to a rapidly accumulating list of species that are jeopardized by our actions? Admittedly, none of these questions will be definitively answered here. Indeed, these and related questions may not have definitive answers. But the questions themselves provide the impetus to reflect upon how we view our place in the world.

In many respects, the northern spotted owl has been a kind of "poster child" for the inevitable conflict between resource extraction by an ever-increasing human population and the requirements of plants and animals that occupy the habitats containing these resources. The lessons we have learned, and are continuing to learn, are broadly applicable to many situations in which meeting the demands of society alters the structure and function of ecosystems. The species that are found in one or a few unique habitats generally are the most vulnerable to the impacts of human activities (see Ruggiero et al. 1988, Lehmkuhl and Ruggiero 1991). These species developed their particular specializations and varying degrees of habitat dependence over many centuries while human technology developed the capability of permanently altering or destroying habitats over the course of a few decades.

The conflict surrounding the northern spotted owl and timber harvest illustrates this point quite well. In less than half a century, we developed the technology to quickly remove centuries-old timber from seemingly inaccessible locations. Recognition of the association between the northern spotted owl and late successional forests in the context of an accelerating rate of harvest resulted in the listing of the owl as a threatened species and subsequently severely affected the timber industry. This in turn created the need for a comprehensive management plan that crossed land ownership boundaries and considered many different species found in the forests of the Pacific Northwest. The NWFP was created in response to this need. Whether the NWFP becomes a model for addressing conflicts between resource use and habitat values in other systems or is eventually replaced by a plan with a different focus remains to be seen. In either case, the spotted owl controversy has presented an opportunity for adaptive management at a scale rarely, if ever, seen before.

Background

Research on the natural history of the northern spotted owl began in the central Oregon Cascade Mountains in the early 1970s (summarized in Forsman et al. 1984). Several literature reviews of the basic biology of spotted owls have been published elsewhere (see Gutiérrez 1985, Gutiérrez 1996), so I will not go into great detail here. Several life-history characteristics of spotted owls are relevant to their response to timber harvest, including their long life span, age at first breeding, and fecundity. Northern spotted owls can live fifteen to twenty years but generally do not reproduce every year. They typically produce only one or two (occasionally three) young and usually do not breed for the first time until after their second year of life. As a result of spreading out their reproductive effort over many years, fluctuations in density and population responses to environmental change may show a substantial time lag. The obvious implication for land managers is that the results of changes in management policy may not be apparent for many years.

The results of the initial studies of northern spotted owls also suggested that the subspecies was closely linked to the older stands of forest that provided much of the timber harvested from federal lands (reviewed in Gutiérrez and Carey 1985). Further research into habitat selection by spotted owls provided evidence that the harvest of old-growth forests negatively affected their populations (reviewed in Thomas et al. 1990). In response to these findings, several agencies and private organizations initiated demographic studies of northern spotted owl populations in the mid-1980s. A review of the evidence available as of 1990 led the Interagency Scientific Committee (ISC) to conclude that continued loss of habitat would put the spotted owl in jeopardy of extinction (Thomas et al. 1990). After the northern spotted owl was listed as a threatened species under the ESA in 1990 (USDI 1990) and the passage of the NWFP in 1994 (USDA/USDI 1994a), eight demographic study areas were identified to provide long-term data on spotted owl population trends (Lint et al. 1999). Each study area was intended to represent different physiographic provinces within the range of the northern spotted owl (defined in USDI 1992). In the sections that follow, I discuss the results of demographic research conducted from the H. J. Andrews Experimental Forest in the western Cascades province of Oregon.

The Demographic Studies

This research is fundamental to fulfillment of federal obligations under the ESA. The ESA requires that a recovery plan be developed for all species that are listed as threatened or endangered. The ultimate goal of the recovery plan for the northern spotted owl is to remove the subspecies from the list of threatened species when sufficient evidence is presented that indicates that northern spotted owls no longer require the protections provided under the ESA (USDI 1992). The evidence must consist of scientifically credible information that demonstrates a stable or increasing population across the range of this subspecies. The primary objective of the spotted owl demography studies is to estimate survivorship, fecundity, and the population rate of change as mandated by the recovery plan and the Effectiveness Monitoring Plan (EMP) (Lint et al. 1999). These parameters represent the vital rates of populations and as such are essential for accurately monitoring the status of spotted owl populations both among physiographic provinces and throughout their range.

An additional requirement of the recovery plan for the northern spotted owl is that land management agencies and landowners must make long-term commitments to provide the necessary habitat for spotted owls. A system of habitat reserves was initially proposed by the ISC to address the habitat needs of the northern spotted owl, but it was recognized early in the planning process that some of the reserves would contain a substantial amount of habitat in earlier seral stages than the owl typically uses (Thomas et al. 1990). These Late-Successional Reserves (LSRs) were expected to develop late-successional characteristics over time and provide additional habitat at a rate comparable to the rate of habitat loss through timber harvesting in the matrix lands. Additional small LSRs also were established to maintain connectivity between

LSRs (Thomas et al. 1990; see also Perry, this volume). Since 1990, the plan evolved to include other species associated with late-successional forests (USDA/USDI 1994a). The current system of LSRs specified in the NWFP are the result of this iterative process and are intended to provide the habitat base for the recovery of the northern spotted owl. The underlying principle is that the reserves should contain a sufficient number of spotted owls to produce enough offspring to replenish locally extirpated populations and sustain the populations within the LSRs (USDA/USDI 1994a).

An ancillary objective of the demography studies at the province level is to provide site-specific information to U.S. Forest Service (USFS) biologists about spotted owls in areas potentially affected by proposed management activities. In 1987, we monitored 52 activity centers in the H. J. Andrews study area. We increased the number of activity centers to 162, as new pairs were located and the scope of the project broadened to address the growing need for demographic information on spotted owls. Ideally, activity centers were to be based on the locations of historic nest trees, although locations of adults with young, pairs without young, or territorial single owls also were used as the basis of defining many activity centers. Continued monitoring since 1994 has shown that most activity centers correspond reasonably well to spotted owl territories, although many were established based on locations of nonterritorial owls or represent territories that are presently unoccupied. Because our focus is on annually locating and assessing the status of individually marked spotted owls, we are able to provide comprehensive information about the occupancy and productivity associated with each activity center. Our data allow USFS biologists to better assess the potential effects of proposed activities on spotted owl populations within the study area than if monitoring is restricted to only a few years prior to implementing a project.

Study Design

General Approach

Early attempts to assess the status of spotted owl populations focused on nocturnal calling surveys to obtain an index of population density based on response locations. However, it became apparent that density studies could provide only a rough assessment of population status. For example, nonterritorial owls (i.e., "floaters") generally are less responsive to calling surveys and are underrepresented as a result. Nonterritorial owls serve as a pool of individuals ready to replace the territorial breeding owls as they die. Unless individuals are distinguished, replacement of breeding owls by floaters or owls immigrating from outside of the study area cannot be detected. As a result, our ability to detect a population decline was hindered because a decrease in the number of breeding individuals is obscured by replacement of these individuals by the nonbreeding segment of the population (Franklin 1992).

Given the difficulties involved in obtaining an accurate estimate of population density, federal agencies began employing a mark-recapture approach in 1985 in which the survivorship and reproductive output of known individuals were used to estimate the rate of population change (see Franklin et al. 1996 for a more comprehensive review of the techniques involved). Spotted owls were captured and fitted with colored leg bands to facilitate identification of individuals during future breeding seasons. To determine the rate of change of the population, we focused on the breeding females in particular because this segment of the population drives the population growth rate. If the breeding females are not replaced through sufficient reproduction and subsequent recruitment into the breeding population, the population will be in decline (Anderson and Burnham 1992). By uniquely marking individual owls, we can account for the loss of a particular breeding female even if she is immediately replaced the following spring.

Population Parameters

Three parameters are central in assessing population trends in each of the long-term monitoring areas as well as throughout the range of the northern spotted owl. Fecundity, defined as the average number of female offspring fledged per non-juvenile female, is the parameter used to measure the amount of reproduction in the population. Next, age-specific survival probabilities are estimated for juveniles, 1-year olds, 2-year olds, and adults (i.e., individuals 3 years old or older) using methods developed for mark-recapture studies (see Franklin et al. 1996 for a review). Because emigration from the study area is indistinguishable from mortality, the actual parameter that is estimated is *apparent* survival, defined as the probability that an individual marked in a given year is still alive *and present on the study area* during the following year (Forsman et al. 1996). Fecundity and the age-specific survival probability for females are used to calculate the third parameter: the finite population rate of change, or lambda (λ). This parameter represents a quantitative assessment of the status of a population over a specified time interval. Confidence intervals of λ that include 1.0 indicate that a population is stable, while intervals above or below 1.0 indicate an increasing or decreasing population, respectively. Fecundity is calculated annually while the survivorship and population rate of change are calculated during periodic meta-analysis workshops in which all of the researchers meet to pool the results from all of the long-term monitoring areas to evaluate long-term, large-scale trends (Anderson and Burnham 1992, Burnham et al. 1994, Forsman et al. 1996, Franklin et al. 1999).

Study Area

Located in the central portion of the Willamette National Forest, the H. J. Andrews spotted owl demography study area encompasses over 152,000 hectares (377,000 acres) of land managed by the USFS (figure 10.1). Elevations range from approximately 400 m to just over 1,500 m. The predominant forest type is Douglas fir (*Pseudotsuga menziesii*)–western hemlock (*Tsuga heterophylla*), with stands of Pacific silver fir (*Abies amabilis*) and mountain hemlock (*Tsuga mertensiana*) at high elevations. Over half of the study area is either nonforest or has been harvested (Miller et al. 1996). Of the remaining forested habitat, approximately 60 to 65 percent is considered suitable habitat for spotted owls (L. Lyon, personal communication).

With the passage of the NWFP, the land within the study area was classified into several land-use allocations that allow for different levels and types of timber harvest near spotted owl

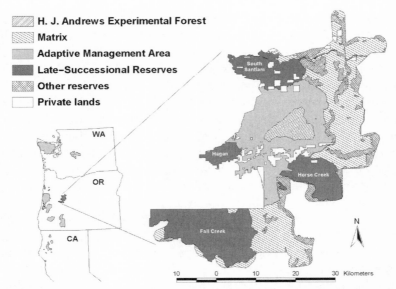

Figure 10.1.   The H. J. Andrews Study Area for the Central Cascades Northern Spotted Owl Demography Project. The lower left portion shows the relative positions of the
long-term monitoring areas. The right side shows the approximate boundary of the
H. J. Andrews study area and the various land-use allocations under the Northwest
Forest Plan. The H. J. Andrews Experimental Forest is located roughly in the center of
the study area.

territories. To date, there has been little implementation of the
timber harvest allowed under the plan. Therefore, the results
discussed in the next section can be thought of as a "snapshot"
of the current conditions that potentially could be affected by
full implementation of the NWFP.

Approximately 32 percent of the land within the study area has
been designated as matrix and will be available for harvest pending full implementation of the NWFP. Spotted owl management
within the matrix allocation consists of protecting 40-hectare (100-
acre) parcels surrounding activity centers together with riparian
reserves that provide connectivity among the activity centers. We
monitored forty-three spotted owl activity centers within the matrix allocation, accounting for approximately 24 percent of the total
number of activity centers on the study area.

The Adaptive Management Areas (AMA) represent a second
land-use allocation that will be subject to a variety of timber har-

vest practices. AMAs are intended for developing and testing alternative means of managing forests for multiple uses. Each AMA has a unique focus, making generalizations about the potential effects of AMAs on spotted owls difficult. The Central Cascades AMA represents 27 percent of the H. J. Andrews study area, which is substantially more than the 6 percent of the land area allocated to AMAs encompassed by the NWFP. The focus of much of the Central Cascades AMA is landscape-level management based on natural disturbance regimes (Cissel et al. 1999). The H. J. Andrews Experimental Forest is contained within this AMA. Between 43 and 47 spotted owl activity centers have been monitored in the AMA—some of which have been monitored since the earliest days of spotted owl research.

There are four LSRs within the H. J. Andrews study area that vary considerably in size and in the quantity of late-successional habitat, and have differing spotted owl occupancy and reproduction rates, suggesting that they are not at present equally valuable as spotted owl habitat. A key element in the potential for the LSRs to provide for the habitat requirements of spotted owls is the likelihood that reserves containing large proportions of early-successional habitat will remain undisturbed long enough for late-successional characteristics to develop. Large-scale disturbances such as stand-replacing fires, windthrow, or pathogen outbreaks could easily set back succession and delay the development of late-successional characteristics for several decades. This calls into question the likely effectiveness of the NWFP in bringing about the recovery of the northern spotted owl and forces us to reexamine our priorities and expectations regarding forest management.

These four LSRs account for 34 percent of the H. J. Andrews study area and 30 percent of the area affected by the NWFP. The largest amount of low-elevation, late-successional habitat is found in the Fall Creek LSR while the Horse Creek LSR contains a large proportion of high-elevation, late-successional habitat. The Hagan and South Santiam LSRs represent earlier seral stages at low and high elevations, respectively. The owl activity centers in the three LSRs included in the study prior to 1998 (Hagan, Horse Creek, and South Santiam) had considerably lower rates of occupancy and fecundity than the activity centers within the matrix and AMA allocations (see "Results and Discussion"). We began adding the activity centers in the Fall Creek LSR in 1998 when it became apparent that the other three LSRs were not providing an adequate sample to evaluate the effectiveness of these reserves. By 2000, we were monitoring all known activity centers in Fall Creek. Among all of the LSRs, we currently monitor 75 activity centers.

The remaining 12 percent of the study area consists of congressional and administrative reserves, which is considerably less than the 36 percent allocated range-wide by the NWFP. These reserves include wilderness areas, wild and scenic river corridors, research natural areas, and other areas previously excluded from timber harvest for reasons unrelated to spotted owl management. Only six spotted owl activity centers in the H. J. Andrews study area are located within these reserves, and much of the habitat is unsuitable for spotted owls. The importance of these types of areas to spotted owl conservation is a topic of considerable debate, but because they are underrepresented in the H. J. Andrews study area, the following discussion focuses on the matrix, AMA, and LSR allocations.

Results and Discussion

Activity Center Monitoring

The proportion of activity centers occupied by pairs increased sharply during the initial two years of the study, as the field crews learned the locations of nests and favored roosts. Since 1989, pair occupancy has shown a steady decline over time (figure 10.2). This is a cause for concern especially in light of the results of the 1998 meta-analysis that indicated a decline in the overall population of female spotted owls (Franklin et al. 1999). Most previous analyses have implicated habitat loss as the cause of this decline (see Bart and Forsman 1992). That the decline would continue beyond the near-cessation of timber harvest on public lands in the early 1990s is not unexpected, given the long life span of spotted owls. Pairs of owls may very well be capable

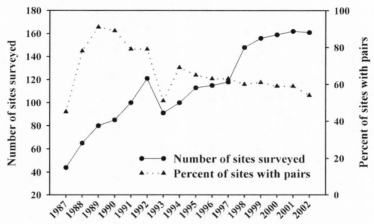

Figure 10.2. Pair Occupancy of Spotted Owl Activity Centers, 1987–2002. The number of spotted owl activity centers ("sites") surveyed in the H. J. Andrews study area from the beginning of the demography project to the present is shown by the solid line with circular symbols. The percentage of activity centers occupied by pairs is shown by the dotted line with triangles. Despite the increase in survey effort over time, the percentage of activity centers occupied by pairs of spotted owls has declined over time. (Source: Oregon Cooperative Fish and Wildlife Research Unit 2002.)

of surviving and reproducing even when a portion of the habitat within their home ranges has been removed. But if the young that are produced do not survive to eventually enter the breeding segment of the population, then the population will continue to decline as the older owls die.

The level of reproduction in the population is assessed annually in three ways: fecundity, previously defined as the average number of female offspring produced per female; the percentage of pairs that attempt to nest; and the percentage of nesting pairs that successfully fledge at least one young. Fecundity includes variation in the number of females that are paired, the number of paired females that nest, and the number of pairs that successfully fledge at least one young. This measure of productivity, along with female survivorship, is required to estimate the population rate of change, but offers few clues as to the underlying sources of variation. The percentage of pairs that attempt to nest shows considerable annual variation (figure 10.3). This may be due to fluctuations in prey availability and/or the severity of winter weather conditions. The percentage of nesting pairs that successfully fledge at least one young does not follow the same pattern and has shown a gradual increase since 1998 (figure 10.3). The cause(s) of this pattern are not yet known, but increased nest success and a possible dampening of the annual variation in nest attempts are encouraging. Whether these results will produce a stabilizing effect on the population growth rate will depend upon increased survivorship of the breeding females. The decline in pair occupancy mentioned earlier is not consistent with increased levels of survivorship, however. Updated survivorship and the population rate of change estimates will be calculated during the next meta-analysis workshop, expected to occur in the winter of 2003.

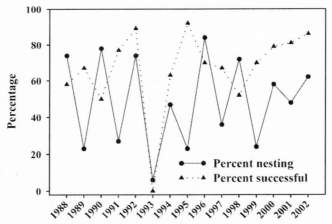

Figure 10.3. Spotted Owl Nesting and Fledging, 1989–2002. The percentage of spotted owl pairs that attempted to nest and the percentage of nesting pairs that successfully fledge at least one young in the H. J. Andrews study area have varied considerably from year to year. The rate of nesting attempts shows a strong biannual cycle; the amplitude of this cycle may be decreasing in recent years. The rate of nesting success does not seem to follow the same pattern and has risen steadily since 1998. (Source: Oregon Cooperative Fish and Wildlife Research Unit 2002.)

Meta-Analyses

The most recent meta-analysis conducted in 1998 included the eight long-term monitoring areas as well as seven studies of shorter duration (Franklin et al. 1999). Survivorship was modeled for all fifteen study areas and combined with the corresponding fecundity estimates to estimate the population rate of change for all of the study areas as well as across the range of the subspecies. Both the analysis of the H. J. Andrews study area and the meta-analysis across all study areas indicated that spotted owl populations were declining during the period included in the data. Within the H. J. Andrews study, the spotted owl population declined at an estimated average annual rate of 7.5 percent (95 percent confidence interval: 4.7–10.3 percent); the meta-analysis of all fifteen study areas indicated an average range-wide annual decline of 3.9 percent per year (95 percent confidence interval: 0.5–7.3 percent). It is important to note that the rate of decline across all study areas included a correction for juvenile emigration based upon radio telemetry data, while the rate for the H. J. Andrews study area did not. This suggests that the actual rate of decline for the H. J. Andrews study area was probably closer to the range-wide estimate. An additional consideration in interpreting the H. J. Andrews results is that these rates are point estimates (an average over the years of the studies). This implies that survivorship and fecundity have remained constant during the years of the study, which is not consistent with the results from several of the study areas that showed considerable variation in the vital rates over time.

Although the exact rate of decline is difficult to ascertain, these results provide a strong argument that spotted owl populations declined and are in agreement with the results from previous meta-analyses (Anderson and Burnham 1992, Forsman et al. 1996). Whether the decline will continue toward extinction, stabilize at a lower population density corresponding to the remaining amount of habitat, or is part of a long-term population cycle remains to be seen (Thomas et al. 1990). Unfortunately, differences in demographic parameters among land-use allocations cannot be inferred from the results of the 1998 meta-analysis because land-use allocations were not included as covariates.

Possible Effects of NWFP Land-Use Allocations

Since the 1998 meta-analysis, the H. J. Andrews study has begun to evaluate the potential effect of the NWFP land-use allocations on the demography of spotted owls. Because the number of years represented by these data is too small to effectively analyze the mark-recapture data, the following discussion is restricted to comparisons of pair occupancy and fecundity among land-use allocations since 2000.

The land area encompassed by the study is divided nearly equally among the matrix, AMA, and LSR allocations (figure 10.4). The number of activity centers monitored in each allocation has varied somewhat from year to year as more effort was invested in the Fall Creek area. Pair occupancy, defined as the percentage of activity centers occupied by pairs, is similar between the matrix and AMA allocations but lower among the activity centers in LSRs (figure 10.4). The low rate of pair occupancy in the LSRs is strongly affected by very low numbers of pairs in the

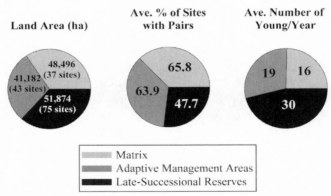

Figure 10.4. Northern Spotted Owl Demographics by Land Use in H. J. Andrews Study Area. The relative amounts of land in matrix, Adaptive Management Areas (AMA), and late-successional reserve (LSR) land-use allocations are roughly equal in the H. J. Andrews study area. A larger proportion of activity centers are located in LSRs, although lower rates of pair occupancy have been observed in LSRs from 2000 through 2002. Over half the average numbers of young produced annually during this period are from matrix and AMA lands that may be subject to timber harvest should the NWFP be fully implemented.

Hagan, Horse Creek, and South Santiam LSRs. At the same time, the total contribution of young is highest in the LSRs, largely as a result of high reproductive rates in Fall Creek.

The four LSRs vary considerably with respect to the amount of old growth and mid- to late-successional habitat (as defined in USDA/USDI 1998). Although spotted owls use mid- to late-successional habitat for roosting, foraging, and dispersal, the majority of nest and roost locations in the H. J. Andrews study area are in old-growth stands (i.e., stands greater than 200 years old). The Horse Creek LSR contains the highest proportion of old growth, but much of this is at or above 1,500 m, which is near the upper elevation limit for spotted owls in the western Cascades province. The South Santiam LSR also includes a large proportion of high-elevation habitat, most of which is too young to support many nesting pairs of spotted owls. Extensive stand-replacing fires occurred in the Hagan LSR approximately 100 and 150 years ago (Klopsch 1985) that left little old growth except in narrow, linear patches along the major streams. The Fall Creek LSR is as large as the other three LSRs combined and contains the best habitat for spotted owls because of the large amount of low-elevation old growth.

The overall contribution to the population of spotted owls in the H. J. Andrews study area is considerably greater from the Fall Creek LSR than from the other LSRs (figure 10.5). The average number of pairs and young found each year in Fall Creek is nearly three times that found in the other LSRs. This represents a 50 percent greater contribution to the population than would be expected based on relative size alone. Although the number of years that Fall Creek has been intensively monitored is inadequate to estimate survivorship and population rate of change, the high levels of pair occupancy and fecundity suggest that Fall Creek is much more likely to serve as an effective reserve for spotted owls.

Broader Implications

Two central issues affect the probability of recovery of the northern spotted owl under the NWFP. The first is whether the habitat in the LSRs is adequate to support a sufficient number of

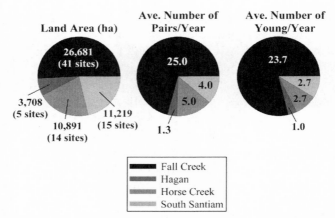

Figure 10.5. *Northern Spotted Owl Demographics in the Fall Creek Late-Successional Reserve (LSR). Within the lands allocated as LSRs, approximately half of the land area and over half of the activity centers are located in the Fall Creek LSR. The average number of pairs and the average production of young have been disproportionately higher in the Fall Creek reserve from 2000 through 2002.*

spotted owls and a sufficiently high level of reproduction to carry the populations through the period required for younger stands to develop suitable habitat characteristics. The second, closely related, issue is whether the impact on the population of lost reproduction and displaced pairs in the matrix and AMA allocations will be balanced by spotted owl reproduction in the LSRs, should timber harvest be fully implemented. Both will depend to a large extent on the time frame involved.

Prior to the increase in harvest rates in the 1940s and 1950s, it is likely that habitat quality varied among physiographic provinces over periods of many decades. Spotted owl populations in some provinces may have experienced moderate to severe declines in response to natural disturbances, while other provinces may have produced surplus numbers of offspring. This balance probably shifted across the landscape as large-scale disturbances affected the habitat within a particular province (F. Swanson, personal communication). The current conservation strategy for the northern spotted owl is based on a similar principle with regard to timber harvest and the development of late-successional characteristics in the LSRs. In the case of the NWFP, disturbances (i.e., timber-harvesting operations) are planned in the matrix land allocations, and the LSRs will be relied upon to provide the habitat for stable or increasing owl populations. If the rate of harvest exceeds the rate of habitat recovery in LSRs that currently lack sufficient amounts of suitable spotted owl habitat, then it is unlikely that spotted owls will persist. Current silvicultural research into possible ways to accelerate the development of late-successional characteristics is promising, but the success or failure of these experimental treatments will not be fully apparent for several years. Given that the development of late-successional characteristics is affected by the rate of natural disturbances, the rate of harvest may easily exceed the recruitment of habitat for spotted owls should a large-scale disturbance—such as a stand-replacing fire—set back succession in an LSR. Therefore, it may not be realistic to expect the rate of harvest to match the rate of habitat recovery; such a rate may be so slow that harvest on public lands would be economically negligible.

Because the results to date do not tell us anything about the extinction threshold for spotted owls, we are faced with choices based on relative levels of risk rather than empirical information. The risk of local extinction in portions of the owl's range with large areas of matrix already in harvest rotation and little high-quality owl habitat in LSRs may be higher than in regions with more old-growth forest encompassed by LSRs. Given that strong evidence has been presented that spotted owl populations are in decline (Franklin et al. 1999) and that the pair occupancy rate is declining (at least in the H. J. Andrews study area), the risk of extinction is likely to increase through time even without further habitat loss. Recently observed high levels of reproduction in the H. J. Andrews study area are encouraging; but it is impossible to predict if these levels will be maintained, or if fecundity has been high enough to halt or reverse the overall decline. We are essentially faced with a gamble based on observations of past patterns. Unfortunately, these patterns are contingent upon conditions remaining the same through time. This is highly unlikely given the complexity of forest ecosystems and the stochastic nature of the factors affecting them.

Furthermore, not all activity centers represent spotted owl territories, and not all owl territories contribute equally to the overall population. Intensive, long-term monitoring of individual activity centers is required to fully assess the contribution of these areas to the spotted owl population. Areas with a history of pair occupation and successful reproduction for more than five years should receive greater protection than activity centers that do not correspond as well to spotted owl territories. Many of the most highly productive owl pairs happen to be located in matrix and AMA land allocations. Conversely, many of the least-productive territories are located in LSRs. As noted earlier, the reason that some LSRs contain few spotted owls is that habitat quality and/or land area is inadequate to support more than a handful of pairs. LSRs that contain relatively few pairs of owls or pairs that seldom reproduce may not contain enough habitat to accommodate owls displaced during timber harvest in adjacent matrix and AMA lands.

Finally, it is worth noting that data from one physiographic province cannot be used to infer potential outcomes in other provinces or at a range-wide scale. Differences in past levels of timber harvest have had an effect on both the amount of remaining habitat and on the placement of LSRs within different study areas. In addition, forest ecology varies considerably throughout the range of the northern spotted owl, and this variation is reflected in the natural history of the owl. Differences in spotted owl biology and forest ecology have been overlooked or obfuscated in recent initiatives to increase the rate of timber harvest on public lands. For forest managers to successfully conserve our native forests and bring about the recovery of the northern spotted owl, public perception of forest ecology must be accurate so that society can make responsible decisions based on the best available science. Forest management policies that change with each new administration are unlikely to be successful or to teach us anything about how we might meet the needs of society while maintaining healthy and productive ecosystems.

Note

This chapter is based on a talk given at the Forest Futures Conference at Willamette University in Salem, Oregon, on September 25, 2002. I wish to express my sincerest gratitude to the many field biologists who have been involved in collecting the data presented here. In particular, I want to thank Rita Claremont, Tim Fox, Gila Fox, Dave Giessler, Jeff LaVoie, Adam Nelson, Jason Schilling, Stephanie Schroeder, Nicole Seaman, Devin Simmons, and Sheila Turner-Hane for their tireless efforts in the field since my arrival in 2000. Gary Miller, Keith Swindle, and Jim Thrailkill served as the project leaders before me, and I greatly appreciate the first-rate data and research infrastructure that I inherited from them. Robert Anthony, Karen Arabas, Joe Bowersox, Eric Forsman, Pete Loschl, Janice Reid, and Sheila Turner-Hane provided many valuable comments as I prepared to present the contents of this chapter at the Forest Futures Conference. Special thanks go to Sheila Turner-Hane for her last-minute edits to the final draft of this manuscript. The personnel at the H. J. Andrews Experimental Forest and the Willamette National Forest provided the housing, office space, communications, maps, and moral support that made this research possible. The demography research at the H. J. Andrews study area was conducted under the auspices of the Oregon Cooperative Fish and Wildlife Unit with funding from the USDA Forest Service, contract number NFS 02-JV-1060000-119.

11

Vicious Cycle: Programmatic Consultation on Northern Spotted Owls in the Pacific Northwest

Susan Jane Brown

In early July 2002, treesitters in the Berry Patch timber sale on the Willamette National Forest made a startling discovery: in the midst of the felling of ancient Douglas fir (*Pseudotsuga menziesii*) trees hundreds of years old, a family of northern spotted owls (NSOs) (*Strix occidentalis caurina*) was trying to survive. A few yards from active logging, two adult owls were attempting to coach their fledging owlet away from the nest tree to a stand of younger forest further away from the destruction. As captured on video, it is unclear whether the Berry Patch owls and their progeny made it to the relative safety of the adjacent tree plantation.

This is not the story of spotted owls that "fell through the cracks" of legal protection afforded to the species under the Endangered Species Act (ESA) and the Northwest Forest Plan (NWFP). When outraged citizens brought the video and logging to the attention of the Fish and Wildlife Service (FWS) and the United States Forest Service (USFS), both stated that clear-cutting adjacent to the nest tree was authorized under a programmatic Biological Opinion (BiOp), and incidental take statement issued by the FWS, as mandated under Section 7 of the ESA.

The NWFP, created in 1994 after years of controversy surrounding the management of old-growth forests on public lands in the Pacific Northwest (PNW), was designed to provide a sustainable supply of timber to the economy, protect endangered species, and restore degraded watersheds. While the legal impetus for the NWFP was the National Forest Management Act (NFMA), the ESA played a critical role in the development of the NWFP, and continues to play a major role in permitting ongoing timber harvest: in order for timber harvest to occur on federal public lands, the USFS and Bureau of Land Management (BLM) must undergo "Section 7 consultation" with the FWS. This process involves a request from the USFS or the BLM to engage in timber harvest that may ultimately affect a listed species such as the spotted owl and, usually, corresponding permission from the FWS to move ahead with the harvest activity. The document that chronicles the Section 7 consultation process is called a "Biological Opinion," and details the FWS's opinion regarding the biological and ecological effects to listed species as a result of timber harvest.

Since 1994, the FWS has largely chosen to satisfy its ESA Section 7 obligation within the Oregon range of the northern spotted owl by consulting on a programmatic basis: that is, FWS prepares a single document that assesses the effects on the species from all timber harvest within a geographical province for multiple years. These programmatic documents do not indicate how much or where the timber harvest will occur, only that it will not result in "jeopardy"—extinction—of the species. In turn, National Environmental Policy Act (NEPA) documentation for site-specific timber sales relies on these programmatic BiOps for their effects analysis for spotted owls. The result is a vicious cycle: the actual effects to the species are never identified or assessed, and the population of the Pacific Northwest's most famous resident continues to decline toward extinction (Oregon Cooperative Fish and Wildlife Research Unit 2000a, see also Krauss 2000, and Oregon Cooperative Fish and Wildlife Research Unit 2002b).

This chapter discusses programmatic consultation under the ESA and whether this method of meeting the obligations of Section 7 of the ESA are commensurate with preventing the extinction and promoting the recovery of the northern spotted owl. The chapter first outlines the current method of consultation in western Oregon, includes the problems of scale in these consultations, and then moves on to a short discussion of relevant case law on programmatic consultation under the ESA. Next, analogies are highlighted between programmatic ESA consultation and other laws, such as the NEPA. Finally, the chapter concludes that given existing case law and the mandates of the ESA, programmatic consultation as undertaken by the USFS, BLM, and FWS fails to meet the requirements of the ESA.

Background

Much has been said about the procedural hurdles created by the ESA, and some have lamented that similar to the process required by the NEPA, conservationists use the ESA's consultation process as a means to achieve a larger, "zero cut" objective. These critics allege that incremental decisions made by federal agencies are attacked at every level, and that broad, programmatic decisions fare little better in the courts. A "tyranny of small decisions" (Cooper 1993) has been declared, but scant consideration has been given to a "tyranny of large decisions" that seems to be developing in the Pacific Northwest, especially in the forests of western Oregon (Cooper 1993).

The USFS and BLM have historically fulfilled the consultation mandate of the ESA for northern spotted owls by consulting with the FWS on a site-specific basis, and they continue to use this method for timber sales in Washington and eastern Oregon. For example, when the USFS prepares a proposal to harvest 120 hectares (297 acres) of mature and old-growth habitat on the Gifford Pinchot National Forest in southwest Washington in the Goose Egg timber sale, it requests permission from the FWS to engage in this activity—and only this activity. In turn, FWS issues a BiOp for the Goose Egg timber sale that discusses how the timber sale will affect spotted owls and their habitat.

Conversely, the USFS and BLM in western Oregon consult with FWS on timber harvest on a provincial or "programmatic" basis, rather than a site-specific basis. "Programmatic" consultation "simply refers to broad-scale assessments tied to a variety of functions" (Cooper 1993, 94). Practically speaking, this means that the

FWS analyzes the effects of logging for at least two years on the spotted owl across several national forests and BLM Districts in a single BiOp. When consultation occurs over a scale of several million acres and affects a species that is still on the brink of extinction (Oregon Cooperative Fish and Wildlife Research Unit 2000a), the question arises, "in a broad-based assessment, how precisely do the affected environment and the resulting impacts need to be described?" (Cooper 1993, 95). I allege that the use of programmatic BiOps for northern spotted owls has resulted in the lack of any meaningful analysis of the impacts from logging on the species.

The Consultation Obligation of the Endangered Species Act

Section 7 of the ESA requires federal agencies, "in consultation with and with the assistance of the Secretary [of Interior] [to] utilize their authorities . . . to insure that any action authorized, funded, or carried out by such agency . . . is not likely to jeopardize the continued existence of any endangered or threatened species" (see USFS 2002a). The consultation process applies to both the FWS—which is responsible for terrestrial and non-anadromous fish species—and the National Marine Fisheries Service (NMFS), which is responsible for aquatic and anadromous fish species. This consultation obligation has been further refined by regulations implementing the ESA, which establishes the following process for consultation (figures 11.1 and 11.2).

In response to a proposed logging activity, the USFS (called an "action agency" because it is the agency undertaking the activity) asks FWS (called a "consulting agency" because it is asked for its opinion by the action agency) for a "species list," which is a list of listed species and their critical habitat that might exist in the planning area (50 C.F.R. § 402.12(c)). Thus starts the informal consultation process; the BLM must undergo the same process as an action agency, but because the USFS conducts most of the logging on public lands in Oregon, only it will be discussed. FWS has thirty days to provide this information (50 C.F.R. § 402.12(d)) and the USFS then has ninety days after the receipt of the species list to start preparing a Biological Assessment (BA) for the project (50 C.F.R. § 402.12(e)). The BA consists of the action agency's understanding of

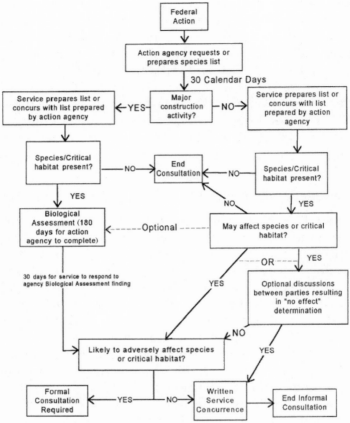

Figure 11.1. Flowchart of the Informal Consultation Process as Required of Federal Agencies by Section 7 of the Endangered Species Act. After USFWS/NMFS 1998.

the impacts of its action on listed species and any critical habitat in the planning area. The USFS has 180 days after it begins preparing the BA to finish preparation and submit it to FWS/NMFS for concurrence on the effects of the proposed action; see figure 11.1 (50 C.F.R. § 402.12(i)).

After receiving the BA, FWS has thirty days to decide whether it concurs with the action agency's findings in the biological assessment (50 C.F.R. § 402.12(j)). If there are no listed species present, or there is a "not likely to adversely affect" finding and

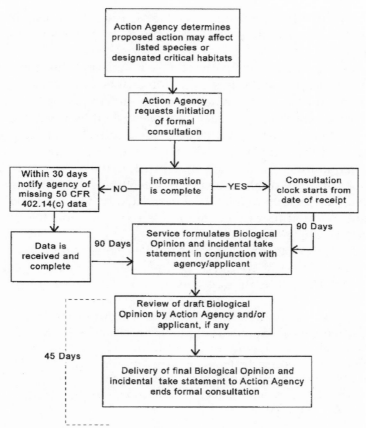

Figure 11.2. Flowchart of the Formal Consultation Process as Required of Federal Agencies by Section 7 of the Endangered Species Act. After USFWS/NMFS 1998.

concurrence by FWS, consultation is complete at this stage (50 C.F.R. § 402.12(k)). However, if the finding in the BA is "likely to adversely affect" or "may affect" a listed species and/or its habitat, formal consultation is required (50 C.F.R. § 402.14(a)). If formal consultation is required, the USFS forwards all of the information it used to compile the BA to FWS for use in FWS's preparation of a BiOp (50 C.F.R. § 402.14(c)). The consulting agency has ninety days from the receipt of this information to undergo consultation, and an additional forty-five days after the conclusion of consultation to issue a formal BiOp; see figure 11.2 (50 C.F.R. § 402.14(e)). If all of the preceding deadlines are met without delay, consultation can take a total of 465 days.

Among other things, the BiOp issued by the consulting agency must include a determination of whether or not the proposed action will result in jeopardy to the species and an "incidental take statement," which discloses whether a listed species will be "taken" or harmed as an indirect effect of an otherwise lawful activity (50 C.F.R. § 402.02). The extent of the incidental take is quantified in the take statement, usually reported as the number of individuals of a species affected. If the action agency exceeds the incidental take level permitted by the incidental take permit, reinitiation of consultation is required, and the process must start anew (50 C.F.R. § 402.16).

In addition to the duty to reinitiate consultation based on new information or changed circumstances, the duty to consult is a continuing obligation. As Jason Patlis (1994) has noted:

> To look at only discrete moments at which to consult under Section 7—such as initial adoption, amendments, revisions, or renewals of plans—does not satisfy the requirements of Section 7. These discrete moments may serve as triggers for reinitiation of consultation, but other triggers exist as well. Furthermore, these triggers do not address the scope of the analysis required. (66)

Patlis goes on to explain that

> In terms of the mechanics of consulting on programmatic action, one problem is that often the effects to be analyzed at the programmatic level are too remote temporally and too speculative scientifically. This does not negate the requirement to consider all direct and indirect effects of the programmatic action, however, nor does it allow for deferral of an analysis of the effects to the site-specific level. (67)

The scope of the required analysis and continued deferral of a jeopardy analysis is the crux of the issue in spotted owl consultation in western Oregon.

The Northwest Forest Plan Biological Opinion

In response to the "spotted owl wars" of the early 1990s, in 1994 the Clinton administration created a scientifically defensible land management plan for all federal lands located within the range of the northern spotted owl (see Thomas, also Rohlf, this volume). The NWFP purported to balance ecosystem protection for the owl with a sustainable supply of timber for the timber industry and local communities that had been dependent on logging (see Thomas, also Perry, this volume). In conjunction with the Environmental Impact Statement (EIS) prepared for the NWFP, FWS prepared a BiOp for the preferred alternative in the EIS, Option 9. The USFS and BLM selected Option 9 as the preferred alternative, and it became known as the Northwest Forest Plan upon implementation.

While the Option 9 BiOp declared that the *selection* of Option 9 would not result in jeopardy to the species, it specifically did not make a determination regarding whether *implementation* of site-specific actions under Option 9 (which subsequently became the basis for the NWFP) leaving such determinations of jeopardy to later BiOps for those actions (USDI 1994). This decision explicitly established the NWFP BiOp as a programmatic consultation document:

> Although programmatic actions generally do not involve ground-disturbing actions, and thus may not directly result in the taking of a listed species, they may indirectly result in takings through their continuing approval and implementation at the site-specific level. . . . While [direct, indirect, and cumulative] impacts may also be identified to a greater extent at the site-specific level, they may also be identified at the programmatic level, and some are exclusively identified at the programmatic level. (Patlis 1994, 68)

Given the explicit acknowledgment that the 1994 NWFP BiOp was a programmatic document, it was reasonable to assume that later, BiOps for timber harvest would be written to assess site-specific impacts of the implementation of the NWFP. However, at least in Oregon, site-specific analysis of the implementation of the NWFP has yet to occur in a meaningful way.

The 2000 Willamette Province BiOp

In 1998, several national forests and BLM Districts in the Willamette River Valley in central Oregon west of the Cascade Crest agreed to engage in programmatic Section 7 consultation for timber harvest activity for fiscal year 2000, which is hereinafter referred to as the 2000 Willamette BiOp (USDI 2000). Covering approximately 1.2 million hectares (3 million acres) of federal land (figure 11.3), the geopolitical scope of the consultation includes all of the Willamette and Mt. Hood National Forests, the Willamette Province portions of the Eugene and Salem BLM Districts, and the Willamette and Deschutes Province portions of the Columbia River Gorge National Scenic Area (USDI 2000, 13). The types of timber harvest activity covered by the 2000 Willamette BiOp include regeneration harvest, light to heavy thinning, down salvage removal, and individual tree removal, all of which "degrade, downgrade, or remove northern spotted owl habitat" (USDI 2000, 3, 5). In sum, 4,000 hectares (9,860 acres) of northern spotted owl habitat would be affected by the fiscal year 2000 timber harvest program within the consultation area (USDI 2000, 7).

In assessing the impacts of the proposed activities on the spotted owl, the FWS recognized that data were of limited and questionable quality in the corresponding BA, making an affects determination in the 2000 Willamette BiOp difficult (USDI 2000, 4). Consequently, the FWS *estimated* impacts to owls and their critical habitat, stating that "this opinion covers the expected impacts of activities, some of which have not been fully planned" (USDI 2000, 5). Given the lack of concrete information about the nature of the timber sales approved in the 2000 Willamette BiOp, the FWS concluded that there would be "an unquantified number of spotted owl pairs or resident singles" incidentally taken as a result of the activities permitted in the BiOp (USDI 2000, 30). As a result, "disturbance" activities (those that do not remove habitat) such as road construction would result in an "unquantifiable" amount of incidental take of spotted owls. In addition, because the exact nature of the consulted-on activities were unknown at the time of consultation—including location and

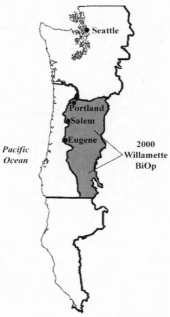

Figure 11.3. Area Covered by the Williamette BiOp. This area (shaded) includes terrestrial phys-iographic Provinces 5 and 8, as identified by the Northern Spotted Owl Recovery Team. Provinces are based on vegetation, soils, ge-ological history, and climate. After USDA 1994a.

acreage of timber sales, and which known owls would be affected—the FWS urged the action agencies to track "actual" impacts during the year (USDI 2000, 3).

Although the FWS urged the USFS and BLM to update the environmental baseline (the "starting point" of the analysis, before the effects of the proposed action have been added in) for the spotted owl as timber sales were implemented, there is no evidence that the action agencies have in fact updated the baseline for fiscal year 2000 (or later) projects; and certainly the agencies have not prepared timber-sale-specific BiOps to assess the effects of localized timber harvest. The lack of data upon which to base its fiscal year 2000 BiOp appeared to concern FWS, especially because the scientific knowledge about the behavior of owls in the Willamette Province seemed to be changing. For example, conventional wisdom taught that owlets fledged by July 1 of every year; however, Willamette National Forest and FWS biologists are reexamining this information and may eventually recommend extending the critical breeding season to July 15 (USDI 2000, 27). Indeed, the fact that the owlet in the Berry Patch timber sale could not easily escape the logging in the stand adjacent to its nest tree lends credence to this later date.

Changing scientific information and on-the-ground realities should be assessed in site-specific BiOps, which are flexible enough to take into consideration local circumstances, new information as it is developed, and the effects of previous timber harvest. In turn, these circumstances should be reflected in future management decisions. Aside from the practical usefulness of site-specific BiOps, there is substantial legal support for such analysis.

Case Law Interpreting the Obligations of Programmatic Consultation

The USFS, BLM, FWS, and NMFS have engaged in programmatic consultation for a variety of projects with varying degrees of legal success. In response to impending listings of anadromous fish, the USFS and NMFS in the 1990s agreed that "short-term jeopardy concerns would be addressed by consulting on individual projects," rather than reinitiating consultation on the land and resource management plans controlling timber harvest in eastern Oregon (Smith 1994, 263). The Ninth Circuit, however, disagreed with this approach, holding in *Pacific Rivers Council v. Thomas* (1994) that the ESA required the USFS and NMFS to consult not only on site-specific timber sales but also on the larger management plan that directed where the site-specific actions would be allowed to occur. The rationale for this decision was that the Land and Resource Management Plan (LRMP) was an ongoing action as defined by NEPA, and as the salmon listings altered the management requirements under the LRMP, reinitiation on the LRMP was required.

Similarly, in *Connor v. Burford* (1988), the Ninth Circuit held that "incremental consultation" on oil and gas leases was unlawful, because it deferred consultation to later stages in development of the resource and therefore obscured the cumulative impacts to listed species. The court explained that

> The biological opinions of the FWS, which concluded that leasing itself was not likely to jeopardize the protected species, did not assess the potential impact that post-leasing oil and gas activities might have on protected species. Rather, the FWS opinions relied on "incremental-step consultation," contemplating that additional biological evaluations would be prepared prior to all subsequent activities and that lessees' development proposal would be modified to protect species. (*Connor v. Burford* 1988, 1452)

As it did in *Pacific Rivers*, the Ninth Circuit required the FWS to prepare a comprehensive BiOp not only on the USFS's oil and gas leasing program but also on subsequent leases themselves. The court also addressed this issue in *North Slope Borough v. Andrus* (1980). There the D.C. court distinguished the Outer Continental Shelf Lands Act (OCSLA)—which specifically allows for segmentation of projects by statute—from the Mineral Leasing Act (MLA), at issue in *North Slope*. The court explained that the OCSLA was not incompatible with the ESA, because the statute provided for "checks and balances," which were absent in the MLA statute. The court was clear that the ESA will allow incremental consultation only when provided as such by the authorizing statute; in the absence of such allowance, consultations at the programmatic and site-specific level are required.

In *Lane County Audubon Society v. Jamison* (1992), the Ninth Circuit confronted a similar issue to that in *Pacific Rivers*. In *Lane County*, the BLM failed to consult with FWS on the Jamison Strategy, which set aside some old-growth habitat but allowed much of the remaining habitat to be logged, and instead consulted on individual timber sales implemented pursuant to the strategy.

The court opined that "the impact of each individual sale on owl habitat cannot be measured without reference to the management criteria established" at programmatic levels (*Lane County Audubon Society v. Jamison* 1992, 316). Moreover,

> Certainly a full accounting for impacts must be *cumulative as well as project specific* and in particular circumstances . . . that assessment may not be made with confidence. It is also true that decisions made at the planning level may have significant effects if implemented over time, a good reason for requiring consultation at this stage. However, no automatic judgment can be made that individual projects will undermine typically general and long run planning options. Where there is a reasonable basis for concluding that individual and cumulative impacts of a project are unlikely to prejudice a species of concern, significant programmatic error is remote. (*Lane County Audubon Society v. Jamison* 1992, 317)

The District Court for the Western District of Washington squarely addressed the scope of analysis issue in *Pacific Coast Federation of Fishermen's Associations v. National Marine Fisheries Service* (1999). In that case—the second of three eventual challenges to twenty-four timber sale BiOps—the court struck down NMFS' attempt to offset the short-term, site-specific impacts of old-growth logging by claiming that the impacts would be nonexistent at the larger, fifth field watershed scale (even if very evident at the site and adverse effects at the smaller, sixth field watershed scale were certain to occur), and that "passive restoration," the regrowth of trees in the same vicinity of the timber sale, would minimize any adverse effects from timber harvest. Specifically, the agency argued that timber harvest was consistent with the Aquatic Conservation Strategy (ACS) of the NWFP, and that because the ACS was designed to protect listed fish species pursuant to the ESA, compliance with the NWFP was compliance with the ESA (*Pacific Coast Federation of Fishermen's Associations v. National Marine Fisheries Service* 1999, 1068).

The court accepted NMFS's contention that compliance with the NWFP equaled compliance with the ESA, but subsequently held that the agency had not complied with the ACS in permitting the degradation of water quality and fish habitat at the stream level. The court agreed with the plaintiffs' contention that "focusing on so large a landscape [in consultation] masks each sales' impacts . . . by focusing on the watershed level, NMFS has ensured that few if any projects will create sufficient degradation at the watershed level to be deemed inconsistent with the ACS" (*Pacific Coast Federation of Fishermen's Associations v. National Marine Fisheries Service* 1999, 1069.) The court further explained that the scientific underpinning of the NWFP required ACS compliance at all spatial and temporal scales: regional, province, watershed, and site.

These cases all suggest that the approach utilized by the FWS in consulting on timber harvest in western Oregon is unlawful. First, *Pacific Rivers* counsels that consultation must occur not only on programmatic documents but also on projects implemented pursuant to that programmatic assessment. *Lane County* also indicates that federal agencies cannot ignore the cumulative impacts of piecemeal consultation: an assessment of site-specific projects *as well as* broad, landscape-level management plans must occur. Finally, *Pacific Coast Federation of Fishermen's Associations* weaves these two holdings together, asserting that the federal government can ensure consistency with the ESA only if it meets the requirements of a regional land management plan (the NWFP) that requires ESA consistency at the project level. Unfortunately, the 2000 Willamette BiOp fails to heed the teachings of these cases.

Analogies to Statutes That Compel Programmatic and Site-Specific ESA Consultation

National Environmental Policy Act

The courts have recognized the similarities between the NEPA and the ESA (*Thomas v. Peterson* 1985), an analysis that is especially applicable to programmatic consultation under the ESA. In exploring these similarities, it is important to remember that "programmatic actions of a federal agency are programs, plans, guidelines, or frameworks established primarily for the purpose of guiding subsequent, discrete, individual actions undertaken by the agency. *They themselves generally do not involve any ground-disturbing physical activity"* (Patlis 1994, 64; emphasis added; citing *City of Tenakee Springs v. Block* 1985). As opposed to traditional programmatic documentation, the 2000 Willamette BiOp permits ground-disturbing activity, even though the nature and location of that activity is not described in either the NWFP BiOp or the 2000 Willamette BiOp. In turn, the agency may "tier" site-specific analysis to the programmatic analysis: "following the preparation of a broad EIS, an agency may then prepare a subsequent EIS for site-specific actions within the scope of the original EIS. The subsequent EIS need only summarize and incorporate by reference discussions from the broader EIS" (*Conservation Law Fnd. et al. v. Federal Hwy. Admin. et al.* 1993). Furthermore, "where there are large-scale plans for regional development, NEPA requires both a programmatic and a site-specific EIS" (*Conservation Law Fnd. et al. v. Federal Hwy. Admin. et al.* 1993, 1407)[1] and simply preparing a programmatic EIS does not eliminate the need to prepare site-specific environmental documentation (Cooper 1993).

In programmatically consulting on timber harvest in the Willamette province for multiple years, FWS and the action agencies have foregone both site-specific NEPA and ESA analysis of timber harvest activities. Site-specific activities—timber sales—trigger the section 7 requirement on the part of the action agencies to prepare a biological assessment, which then may trigger the preparation of a biological opinion by FWS. In this case, however, the USFS and BLM acknowledge that the biological assessment prepared by the agencies to comply with section 7 of the ESA does not contain detailed descriptions of the locations and prescriptions of the timber sales that would form the basis of FWS's BiOp for those activities: the site-specific design of the timber sales would come later, *after* FWS rendered the BiOp. At this point, then, there is no true NEPA trigger, which would ordinarily result in the commencement of the formal consultation process. If there is no NEPA trigger, there can be no meaningful consultation.

The question then becomes, on exactly what type of activity is the FWS being asked to consult in this programmatic

BiOp? The answer seems to be "some logging in an area the size of New Jersey," but without any specifics. Consequently, there is no substantial assessment of whether the spotted owl's conservation and recovery will be ensured despite the logging permitted in the BiOp. Given the lack of concrete information about the activities that formed the basis of the BiOp, it can be argued that the entire process—from project formulation (a NEPA trigger leading to ESA consultation) to formal ESA Section 7 consultation—is fatally vague and therefore unlawful.

Delaying a site-specific ESA analysis of timber harvest impacts until some indefinite point in the future is the same type of avoidance of the ESA Section 7 jeopardy question evident in the NWFP BiOp. That consultation indicated that later, site-specific projects would necessitate consultation where the jeopardy question would be addressed; and the 2000 Willamette BiOp—touted as that site-specific analysis—similarly fails to describe project effects on a species that continues to decline precipitously. In commenting on the early days of the formulation of the NWFP, Cooper (1993) notes that

> While an agency has broad discretion in the choices of the scope of an EIS . . . it must be mindful of the political process. For example, the Forest Service had a clear choice in deciding between alternatives for spotted owl management and the broader question of the management of old growth timber. It chose the latter, apparently to avoid the more intractable social, economic, and ecological issues associated with the former . . . [this approach] virtually guaranteed that the unresolved larger questions would jeopardize the political integrity of the decision. (*Conservation Law Fnd. et al. v. Federal Hwy. Admin. et al.* 1993, 121–22)

Rather than dealing with the social, economic, and ecological issues associated with overlogging by ceasing the activity and working to repair the damage, the USFS has instead continued to log old-growth habitat, assuring the public that trees are renewable and that timber famine and species extinction can be prevented if we just throw enough money at the problem. The federal agencies have continued this trend of ostrich-like avoidance of the hard issues, preferring to delay the endgame decision to a subsequent administration—preferably of the opposing political party. This is truly the "conspiracy of optimism" (Hirt 1996).

National Forest Management Act

Like the similarities between the requirements of the ESA and NEPA, an analogy between the ESA and NFMA can be drawn, particularly the intersection between LRMPs and related consultation requirements. LRMPs "do not establish what will happen [on the ground], but only establish what may happen. Plans neither guarantee nor approve any on-the-ground activity, and no action can take place without extensive additional review and approval" (Smith 1994, 292). LRMPs, then, are like the "ideal" programmatic BiOp: they are broad, landscape-level documents that do not authorize actual timber harvest activities, instead outlining only what *may* happen.

The courts have held that LRMPs are "ongoing activities" that require reinitiation of consultation whenever there are changed circumstances; similarly, programmatic consultations themselves should require revision as more information comes to light. In *Connor v. Burford* (1988), the court explained that

> Our holding does not abrogate the agencies' duty of continued consultation since even the "comprehensive" biological opinions ordered here will rely on incomplete information as to the exact location, scope, and timing of future oil and gas activities. . . . When specific production becomes available, the agencies will be able to make a more accurate assessment of the impact of various post-leasing activities. (1458, n. 42)

In the case of the 2000 Willamette BiOp, as in the oil and gas leases at issue in *Burford*, more information became available only later, after consultation was complete. As an ongoing activity, the timber harvest permitted pursuant to the 2000 Willamette BiOp should trigger reinitiation of consultation.

A New Approach

The foregoing analysis suggests that programmatic consultation exemplified in the 2000 Willamette Province BiOp violates the ESA because it fails to adequately assess the site-specific effects of timber harvest on the northern spotted owl. The BiOp for the NWFP specifically deferred making a decision about whether the NWFP would result in extinction of the species until later, site-specific consultation was undertaken. To date, this analysis has not occurred. Instead, the FWS, USFS, and BLM obscure the actual impacts to the owl by consulting on the ambiguous nature of a provincial timber sale program.

To meet ESA requirements, federal agencies must engage in consultation at multiple scales. First, the consultation completed for the NWFP serves as a regional assessment of the effects of the implementation of an ecosystem management program that spans three states. Second, the agencies should engage in provincial consultation, much as they have in the 2000 Willamette BiOp. Finally, the FWS, USFS, and BLM should consult on individual timber sales, or, at the very least, small groups of sales in the same subwatershed. This approach would ensure that analysis occurs on all appropriate scales, much as was required in *Pacific Coast Federation of Fishermen's Associations* (1999).

In support of this approach, it is instructive to consider the two following sentiments, and how the suggested approach would alleviate many of the concerns raised in this article. Smith first notes that

> The most convincing reason for barring incremental consultation is to assure that planning options are fully considered before an agency becomes committed to a course of action. While it seems unlikely that a limited number of future actions would inadvertently foreclose planning options, it is impossible to say whether or when such a junction might be reached and a bar on any implementation of policy pending program review is prophylactic. However, ongoing projects present a finite quantity and thus do not present the same open-ended potential for evading programmatic consultation. While courts may

legitimately be concerned that indefinite incremental consultation might neglect full policy consultation, this concern should
not foreclose piecemeal consideration of ongoing actions as a
transition to policy reconsideration. (Smith 1994, 300)

Second, Patlis explains that "it is difficult to develop a meaningful analysis of the watershed—or landscape—level impacts on a
site-specific level. Furthermore, where an adequate analysis may
be undertaken, it is even more difficult to conclude that any one
site-specific project would jeopardize listed species" (Patlis 1994,
71). Indeed, the Federal Highway Administration already engages in such tiering of projects,[2] and existing case law interpreting NEPA, NFMA, and the ESA all suggest that such an
approach—so long as the ultimate environmental effects on a
listed species are discussed at some point—is warranted.

The current practice of programmatic ESA consultation for
timber harvest in the Pacific Northwest is of questionable legal
validity and is likely to have long-term deleterious effects on a
species already on the brink of extinction. While consultation on
a broad scale may avoid dealing with the "intractable social, economic, and ecological issues" identified by Cooper (1993), the
fact remains that the ESA was created with the single goal of preventing and reversing species extinction. Continuing to ignore
this fact is both unlawful and unnecessary: a tiered approach to
ESA consultation would not only give society a more informed
picture of the status of one of the Northwest's most infamous residents but also shape management decisions accordingly.

The Bush administration has already begun to streamline environmental review of projects that affect threatened and endangered species. As part of the administration's proposal to alleviate
"analysis paralysis" and address the hazardous fuels and wildfire
issues, the FWS and NMFS in October 2002 issued revised guidance on evaluating the effects of fuels reduction projects in ESA
consultation documents (68 Fed. Reg. 1,629 (January 13, 2003)). The
Services proposed two new methods of conducting consultation in
an effort to expedite approval of fuels reduction projects: "project
batching" and "programmatic consultation." Under the former
method, "the action agencies [USFS, BLM] group, or batch, a series
of similar proposed hazardous fuels treatment projects and the Ser-

vices [FWS, NMFS] will produce a single review document that is appended to the programmatic consultation" (USFWS 2002). In turn, programmatic consultation could be completed with an "appended consultation approach."

This two-stage approach first involves the initial development of a programmatic BiOp, or concurrence if no adverse effects are anticipated, that analyzes the potential effects of implementing the action agencies' hazardous fuels treatment program at the conservation and/or management unit level. The second stage involves the development of appropriate project-specific documentation that addresses the specific effects of individual treatment projects proposed under these programs. Upon completion of the project-specific review, the associated documentation is appended to the programmatic BiOp, or concurrence document. This programmatic document, together with the appended project-specific documentation, encompasses the complete consultation document for each discrete project (USFWS 2002).

While these two approaches may in fact decrease the time it takes the Services to complete consultation, there is a real risk that in an effort to save time in the consultation process, both methods will suffer from the same lack of analysis and specificity seen in the Willamette BiOp. Although the Services caution that both project batching and programmatic consultation with appended consultations require the action agencies to provide the Services with enough site-specific information to accurately assess the effect on listed species from the proposed activities, this is a requirement that is already present in the ESA and yet has been eschewed in documents like the Willamette BiOp. Moreover, it remains to be seen whether the substantive analysis undertaken via expeditious tools like project batching and programmatic consultation will result in promptly issued biological opinions that withstand judicial scrutiny.

With its numbers dwindling annually, the decision to change the federal government's consultation practices may ultimately come too late for the northern spotted owl. After the felling was complete and the Berry Patch owls became big news with the media and local residents, the H. J. Andrews Experimental Forest—a research outpost administered by the USFS and located adjacent to the Willamette National Forest—sent its best "hooter," or owl surveyor, to locate the owls and to evaluate their condition. At last, the USFS was finally concerned. After days of trying, however, the hooter was unable to locate the family. It is unknown whether the three survive.

Notes

This chapter is based on a talk given at the Forest Futures Conference at Willamette University in Salem, Oregon, on September 25, 2002.

1. See also 40 C.F.R. §§ 1508.28, 1502.20.
2. See 23 C.F.R. § 171.111(g).

12

Toward a Better Forest Future: Contracting for Critters

Richard L. Stroup

Over the past few decades, owners and managers of western forests have been called upon to manage for a new product: habitat for endangered species. The Endangered Species Act (ESA), the law that makes most of these demands, empowers government agencies to order managers to preserve specified habitat for listed species. This is an attractive option for the agencies—the Fish and Wildlife Service (FWS) and the National Marine Fisheries Service (NMFS)— because it reduces their costs. But regulations promulgated under the law have unintended side effects. For most land managers (public and private), the demands from the ESA can be onerous and costly to their other goals, such as growing timber, providing recreation, and reducing the dangers of uncontrolled forest fires. Furthermore, the ESA artificially reduces the cost to the enforcing agencies, but not to society, of some ways of protecting listed species. This means that agency decision makers are not held accountable for some important costs of their decisions.

This chapter explains how the combination of these factors is leading to unintended results that pose problems (sometimes severe problems) to the landowners and managers, while, on balance, reducing available habitat and thus harming the very mission of the ESA. The first section describes the ESA. The next section explains how good people with good intentions can bring about the problems indicated in the first section. The third section suggests some fairly simple, if not politically easy, solutions that can enhance the goals of the ESA while reducing its cost to everyone.

The Endangered Species Act

The ESA is a sweeping piece of command-and-control legislation. It provides certain species (those listed as "endangered" or "threatened") with extraordinary levels of protection from human impacts. The Supreme Court described the law as "the most comprehensive legislation for the preservation of species ever enacted by any nation" (*Tennessee Valley Authority v. Hill* 1978). The Congressional Research Service labeled the law "one of this country's most important and powerful environmental laws" (Corn 1992). Unlike other national environmental laws, which often temper their goals by requiring action only where practicable, the ESA "elevated protection of all species to one of the U.S. government's highest priorities" without considering feasibility or cost (Barker 1993).

When the ESA was enacted in 1973, it stirred relatively little debate, mostly on "issues relatively inconsequential to later developments." Saving endangered species such as the bald eagle was an uncontroversial environmental goal with broad support. The ESA was the end product of seventy years of incremental federal wildlife law. It was spawned by an extremely symbolic issue that fed public sentiment and support and was buttressed by a strong and well-organized set of activist groups and a powerful set of congressional staff and members. No one perceived any significant costs of achieving its goals. The act was seen as a low-cost, no-lose legislative situation.

Like the other major national environmental laws adopted in the late 1960s and early 1970s, the ESA was designed around a command-and-control model. The basic idea was that experts in the federal government would determine which species were threatened and endangered, then design regulations to ensure that those species' habitat was protected and enforce those regulations to make sure that public and private landowners complied.

The problem the ESA was intended to protect against, habitat destruction, is a serious one. As David Wilcove (1998) writes, "Habitat destruction and degradation are by far the leading threats to biodiversity, contributing to the endangerment of at least 88 percent of the plants and animals on the endangered species list" (277–78). Extensive action has been taken under the ESA. By 2003, 1,262 U.S. species were listed as "endangered" or "threatened," and millions of acres of public and private land were subject to restrictions on use because of the presence of listed species. Yet the success of the ESA in actually saving species is questionable. The FWS website on the ESA reveals that in the thirty years since the ESA was passed, only 35 species out of those listed have made it off the endangered and threatened species list. But of those, seven were delisted due to their extinction, six had been removed because their listing had been due to taxonomic revision, and seven others were delisted due to new information, an act amendment, or erroneous data (USFWS 2003).[1]

Problems with the Endangered Species Act

How can such a powerful piece of legislation be performing so badly, especially considering that it has a great deal of authority and substantial funding? In 1993, more than $500 million in federal dollars were spent on endangered species protection across many agencies, and the figure had been rapidly rising (Gordon et al. 1997). States also bear substantial costs, running in some cases into the tens of millions of dollars per year, per state (Gordon et al. 1997). Many times as much is spent by private sources across the nation. For example, negotiating an incidental take permit outside an expedited program available only in central Texas requires negotiations that are "typically time consuming and costly, lasting from three months to three years" (Thompson 1997, 317). In the FWS-approved creation of a "conservation bank" for red-cockaded woodpeckers (*Picoides borealis*) by International Paper in Georgia, a "credit" for a pair of woodpeckers is estimated to be worth up to $100,000, suggesting the high cost imposed on landowners by the presence of the birds ("Endangered Woodpeckers to Get Preserve," 1999).

Considering expenditures is, however, a misleading measure of the ESA's ability to commandeer resources. The power of the ESA comes not from direct governmental expenditures on endangered species preservation, but from the ESA's ability to control how landowners use their property. Yet this control is the *hidden* weakness of the ESA. Because landowners may be subject to substantial penalties (in the form of prohibitions on such activities as building, logging, and even farming), landowners and managers have a powerful incentive to make their land less attractive to the listed species they are supposed to protect (Petersen 1999, Yaffee 1982).

In western forests as elsewhere, the ESA process today most often involves FWS biologists vetoing any use of land, public or private, that is home to one or more endangered species, if they judge that the usage might endanger the listed species. (The NMFS carries out these duties with respect to fish and other marine life.) It is the agency biologists, not landowners, who decide if land can be used for logging, farming, or building (Stroup 1995). This is due, in part, to the expansive interpretation the federal government has given to prohibited activities under the ESA.[2]

This decision-making power is the root of one of the most serious structural problems with the ESA. Land managers and owners, not the government biologists with ESA authority, face the costs of the decisions to place restrictions on the use of private or other government agency land (Stroup and Shaw 2003). Government officials understand this, even if they do not appreciate its importance. "Taxpayer money spent on compensation for legally required agency actions is money not spent on protection and recovering the species needing the protection of the ESA," said the director of the FWS, Jamie Rappaport Clark, during congressional testimony in 1999. Director Clark's testimony is a clear statement of the concept of opportunity cost, if not of its importance (Clark 1999). Since the federal government is not required to compensate landowners for reducing the value of the landowners' property, its officials need not consider the value of the forbidden uses of the land. Indeed the ESA, as interpreted, forbids such considerations. "The plain intent of Congress was to halt and reverse the trend towards species extinction, whatever the cost. This is reflected not only in the stated policies of the ESA, but in literally every section of the statute" (*Tennessee Valley Authority v. Hill* 1978). The 1978 amendments to the ESA did create "an administrative exemption process that effectively reversed the Court's determination that the ESA protects species at all costs" (Doremus 1997). While this process may "solve" the problem when the cost is a multimillion-dollar federal public works project stopped by the presence of endangered species, the amendments did not significantly alter conditions for private landowners confronted with the presence of a listed species. Obtaining an exemption from the "God Squad" remains effectively out of the reach of most private individuals because of the enormous political capital required to secure a decision.

The ESA did not, however, make land free to society. The uses prevented by the ESA in the name of habitat preservation are valuable uses forgone by the landowners or managers and by the rest of society—even if the rules allow government agents to treat it as free. Rules that separate authority from the responsibility for the costs of actions taken under that authority have destructive results.

One problem is FWS biologists will allocate "too much" land to habitat protection, because where they have determined that a species must be protected, habitat protection by prohibiting other uses has no cost to them from a budget perspective. FWS officials have no reason to economize on the true cost of their efforts to others. If the costs had to be compensated from their own budget, they would no doubt seek the land and the habitat enhancement techniques that would minimize the cost to society of achieving their goals. Their efforts are land-intensive because land-use restrictions are free to them. Furthermore, they fail to take even simple steps to increase the productivity of habitat. While use of the land is "free" to them, technology is not free to them. They cannot simply order landowners to utilize habitat-enhancing measures without paying them to do so. Thus, protection of endangered species, as they pursue it, is more expensive for society than it need be—leading ultimately to too little habitat protection overall.

Raising the cost to landowners and public land managers leads to less habitat protection once those paying the costs have made all their adjustments. Both public and private landowners have had to change their management strategies to accommodate agency demands under the ESA. For instance, public managers who cannot build a hospital, use their military firing ranges, or log trees face costs from these controls. We should expect them to alter their management practices over time to minimize the likelihood of losing their ability to manage for their mission. So, for example, if controlled burning not only suits their mission but also makes the land more attractive to a listed species, FWS biologists may then prohibit land uses (e.g., logging, building a road or a hospital, practicing military maneuvers, or improving trails for recreation access) for which they were hired to manage. To avoid this, land managers may choose to reduce or eliminate controlled burning. Indeed, assuming these managers believe strongly in their primary missions—and this writer's personal experience with many bureau and program heads indicates this strongly and uniformly—we should be quite surprised if management regimes were not affected in this way.

Private landowners face problems from the ESA like those of public land managers. However, they also find it personally costly, because they have to pay the financial costs themselves. Given these costs, they probably will act similarly; but they will also make their concerns known to politicians and bureaucrats, who are reluctant to incur the ire of those affected. We observe, therefore, too much government action in individual instances where the government seizes more property rights than it needs to protect a given habitat, simultaneously with too little habitat protection overall, as the government avoids the political costs of the ESA by dragging its feet on actions such as listing species (Lieber 1997). These results clearly are dismal for both land managers and endangered species. Instead of buying as much protection as possible within the budget for endangered species, resources are uselessly squandered, destroying the value of individual landowners' properties.

One hopeful factor in the presence of any dysfunctional policy is the corresponding opportunity for important gains if the policy can be improved. Currently, the ESA offers such an opportunity. There are four categories of problems brought on by the ESA, and each can be significantly reduced or eliminated, with important gains to the critters, to the environment, and to the individuals who resent being asked to bear individually—or organizationally—a disproportionate share of the cost of a national goal. In the next section each of these categories is considered in turn, and policy changes are suggested that should produce substantial improvements in program results (Morriss and Stroup 2000).

Perverse Incentives

As currently applied the ESA gives landowners, whether private or governmental, unfortunate incentives for land-management practices. The possibly draconian penalties that landowners will experience because of having endangered species on their property leads them to change the habitat to reduce the likelihood that the listed species will be present. Landowners naturally prefer to maintain management authority. The populations affected are, in the current situation, likely to be seriously harmed by such preemptive habitat modification. Each landowner has reason to (1) find what a listed species in the area likes or needs, (2) tweak land-management practices so as to reduce the availability of that quality on owned land, and (3) inform neighbors and even lobby them to do the same, since a resident population anywhere in the area can lead to land-management controls imposed by the FWS under the ESA. Both anecdotal (Stroup 1995) and statistical evidence (Lueck and Michael 2003) support this conclusion. The penalties of the ESA give landowners an incentive to manage their land *against* the listed species. This incentive reportedly even leads some landowners, managers, and those who lease government lands to "shoot, shovel, and shut up" (Brown and Stroup 1999). As landowners' ability to destroy or block out animals increases due to increased knowledge and technology, the argument in favor of the current ESA is further eroded.

Incentives matter, and the favorable results possible from reducing negative incentives, paired with even modest positive incentives, may allow large gains for listed species while simultaneously avoiding policy "train wrecks," such as the famous destructive conflicts over the northern spotted owl (NSO) (*Strix occidentalis caurina*), where restrictions have reportedly cost more than $20 billion and thousands of Pacific Northwest (PNW) jobs (Burnet and Allen 1998).

Distorted Prices

The second problem with the ESA is inefficiency. Currently, as perceived by FWS decision makers, the prices of resources used to protect species are distorted. Land services are free to the FWS, while other resources are costly. Yet other resources more costly to the FWS could increase the habitat effectively available to a population of a listed species. Habitat could readily be improved, so that it could house many more individuals of the listed species.

If the FWS requires landowners (private or public) to provide habitat, the costs of doing so does not fall on the agency, even though the costs to society (due to restrictions on landowners) may be much higher than the costs of other attainable solutions. To view this in simplified terms, consider using two inputs, technology and land, in various combinations to produce the habitat needed to support a specific population of the listed species. This habitat can be produced using lots of land and little technology or a smaller amount of land and more technology. The cost or price of each input will help determine the least-cost combination of inputs needed to support the population in question.

Suppose that without the presence of the costly penalties provided in Section 9 of the ESA, the least-cost combination to produce the desired habitat for a specific population of red-cockaded woodpeckers on private land is $20,000 per year in renting land and $20,000 per year spent on technology such as nest boxes on trees and frequent burning of underbrush. The total cost would be $40,000 per year to maintain the habitat.

Now assume the current penalties. The FWS can restrict the use of the land so that nothing done on it would be inconsistent with bird habitat; however, the FWS does not have to pay anything. Under these conditions, few landowners would be willing to use technology to support the birds, even for a sum far exceeding $20,000, the direct cost of applying the technology. Enhancing the habitat and encouraging additional birds to live in the area would risk the loss of freedom to use any or all land owned in the vicinity. Thus, without the cooperation of the landowner in providing nest boxes, producing habitat for the same number of birds might require twenty times as much land and the total cost might be ten times as great, or $400,000. All the cost would be for land. However, the FWS would require the landowner to provide it without renting the land or providing compensation. Yet, without the use of technology such as fire and artificial nest cavities, it is possible that setting aside even this much larger acreage would not guarantee success.

While this option is far more costly to society, it is far cheaper (and thus more attractive) to the FWS. (The agency would have to monitor land-use restrictions in either case, but that cost should be small either way.) If the FWS had to pay the cost of setting the land aside, its budget would be hit with $400,000. The agency would likely switch to the $40,000 solution instead. The cost to society would be minimized. But the current distortion leads to a higher cost for whatever benefits are gained by the species that are protected. Environmental policy is harmed in at least three ways:

1. When gains from a policy are more costly, then over time less of that policy is chosen.
2. Such problems in a prominent environmental policy like endangered species protection give environmental policy in general, not just the ESA, a bad name for being inefficient—not delivering enough "bang for the buck." This leads to less demand for strong environmental policy over time.
3. Inefficient policies reduce the wealth of citizens, and poorer citizens demand less in the way of environmental

improvement. (The latter effect is, for economists, a "wealth effect" and is especially significant in influencing the demand for stronger environmental policy measures.)

Perceived Unfairness

A third problem stemming from the current application of the ESA is that of fairness. The ESA was enacted on the grounds that there was a large benefit to the general public by preventing species extinction. But if the general public gets the benefit, then why should a few specific individuals, specific landowners in this case, pay the major share? Similarly, why should one legitimate mission of the U.S. Forest Service (USFS)—logging or recreation, including motorized recreation—bear the brunt rather than the general public?

Some may respond that we all share an obligation not to destroy the wild populations owned by the public and held in trust for the public by the government. But then, an obligation not to destroy is not an obligation to feed specific populations for the public, at one's private expense. By comparison, we each have an obligation to respect the rights of homeless persons and not to harm them; but we do not have an obligation as individuals to feed such persons at personal and private expense on our own property. We may, however, instead be given by law a duty to pay taxes in support of governmentally arranged homeless shelters. Similarly the public, if it owns and benefits from endangered species, should be expected to provide for those populations when necessary, with habitat arranged at public expense.

There is a way within the ESA to introduce more fairness. The agency protecting a listed species could move from rules that exercise its claim of total veto power over any and all other land uses regardless of cost and without compensation, on land it deems important to the survival of a population of a listed species, to what all other agencies do when they seek services like habitat: they could rent, lease, or purchase land, or contract for specified improvements in a population of special interest on a given property. In that way, the general public would pay, rather than a private landowner. Furthermore, landowners quite likely would, as they have so often, be glad to cooperate at little or no cost with plans that impose little or no net cost on them. When federal, state, or local government lands are crucial, the agency could seek reassignment by the appropriate legislative bodies of those specific tracts from other agencies to their own. Elected officials, not biologists, would decide whether the transfer is in the public interest. Not only are these procedures more fair; over time, they are likely to be politically wise for the saving of species as well. Otherwise, as voters learn about the current high cost of compliance faced by some landowners due to FWS orders to forgo productive uses, they are likely to increasingly recognize that the policy is unfair. Policies considered unfair are politically vulnerable, and are apt to be politically weakened as a consequence.

Use of the ESA for Non-ESA Goals

The broad powers of the ESA have led to a fourth impact that may be effective in the short term but damaging to the goal of protecting species in the long run. That is the use of the ESA to achieve other goals.

In 1988, Andy Stahl of the Sierra Club Legal Defense Fund said, "Thank goodness the spotted owl evolved in the Pacific Northwest, for if it hadn't, we'd have to genetically engineer it" (Fitzgerald 1992). Andy Stahl was joking, but the statement was revealing. His organization was using the ESA to stop logging. The Sierra Club Legal Defense Fund was not primarily concerned about the northern spotted owl (which, it turns out, is not as threatened as most people think), but rather about keeping private companies and the federal government from logging old-growth timber in Oregon and Washington. Use of the ESA has been an effective tactic. Opponents of logging, livestock grazing, building, or the development of roads can invoke the ESA process to stop the activities they oppose. For example, anti-growth activists used the possible impact on a small bird, the California gnatcatcher (*Polioptila californica californica*), and the San Diego fairy shrimp (*Branchinecta sandiegonensis*) as reasons to set aside a half-million acres in southern California that otherwise would be used to build houses. Similarly, opponents of a high-way near San Diego argued that the potential danger to the Quino checkerspot butterfly (*Euphydryas editha quino*) should stop the highway's construction (Perkins 2003).

Achieving Success at Lower Costs

Better policies to help meet the goal of the ESA are possible—they could dramatically lower its cost to society and probably increase substantially its positive effects as well. All of this is likely to be possible at low cost, judging by the low-budget successes historically recorded (see Anderson and Leal 2001, and CEQ 1984, ch. 9). To be fully successful, the current regulations that penalize landowners for changing the habitat of endangered species should be revised. Cooperative programs that do not depend on coercion should be introduced, as indicated later in this chapter. Such cooperation would lead to creative management that will expand the carrying capacity of habitat.

Conservation Rental Contracts

One improvement would allow the FWS to enter into conservation rental contracts (CRCs) for private or governmental land that it needs to protect endangered species (Bourland and Stroup 1996). This arrangement would allow the FWS to specify management techniques or technologies that it believes will be most productive. At the same time, it would have an incentive to seek the low-cost provider of these services in the areas of concern. A variation would allow the FWS to contract with landowners and perhaps other firms or groups as well, to produce continuing survival of a listed species, or a combination of them, verified by periodic censuses, and possibly with incentive clauses that rewarded outstanding cases of success.

A problem with CRCs under the current ESA rules, however, is the one mentioned earlier. The powers of FWS biologists to veto any land use have such a chilling impact on constructive habitat enhancement, as evidenced by preemptive habitat destruction, that CRCs right now might be prohibitively expensive unless the rules were changed to emphasize some form of compensation. It will be difficult to gain the approval of environmental groups for this change, for the understandable reason that the current arrangement places species preservation goals above all others. It is a trump, and a source of pride as well as power to those who use it. But the sad fact is that it is harming species habitat as well as landowners and the economy. Removing this single power should lead to much lower cost, and more effective species recovery. Of course there are unusual situations where a species exists in only one location, which could be owned by an uncooperative individual or group. In that case, the FWS could resort to the use of eminent domain power, seizing the land and paying what a court says is fair market value. In any case, if this problem of landowner resistance and high resulting costs is solved, CRCs could potentially lead to recovery of most listed species. Even a few landowners, working enthusiastically with FWS, volunteer groups, and environmental scientists to discover and apply the best techniques for enhancing habitat for a given species, should be able to find new and less costly ways to increase populations of most listed species.

Learning from the Past

The United States has a long, if largely unknown history of successful restorations, most preceding the ESA and its negative incentives for landowners. It is appropriate to distinguish two kinds of problems with wildlife populations. One is the decline of large mammals and migratory birds, such as pronghorn antelope (*Antilocapra americana*) and white-tailed deer (*Odocoileus virginianus*), that did not threaten extinction. The other is the actual approach of extinction for a few species.

In both cases, declines were reversed through a combination of government and private actions. For example, the pronghorn antelope population had declined to 26,600 in the United States in 1924. By 1964, the U.S. population of pronghorn had increased more than thirteen times (Lueck 2000, Harrington 1981).

Many species that had actually been in danger of extinction were saved as well. The wood duck (*Aix sponsa*) and the bluebird

(*Sialia sialis*) were protected by the creation, placement, and maintenance of nesting boxes, many on private land. At the turn of the century as bison numbers were dwindling fast, efforts led by naturalist Ernest Harold Baynes formed the American Bison Society, which was instrumental in the creation of a bison refuge in Montana.

Technology

These restorations took place when far less was known about how to manage wildlife, how to trace animals in the wild, and how to breed animals for release or re-release into the wild. Today, however, much more could be done. Technology, both high- and low-tech, exists to increase the productivity of existing habitat, and research is finding more. However, with some exceptions, government protection of endangered species today relies primarily on obtaining more habitat—more land dedicated to a listed species—not on the advancement or application of know-how.

Many technologies could be applied at low cost and would go a long way to increase the likelihood of recovery for endangered species. Efforts to save the red-cockaded woodpecker illustrate how relatively simple technology can magnify available habitat. Found in the southeastern United States, these endangered birds frequent the longleaf (*Pinus palustris*) and loblolly pines (*Pinus taeda*) where there is a clear, grassy understory and little or no hardwood. They make nest cavities near the tops of trees, usually very old pines because old trees frequently have heart rot, which softens the wood and makes it easy for woodpeckers to peck out a cavity. Because people have cut down the oldest pines, cultivated the land, and suppressed fire, this woodpecker's preferred habitat has largely disappeared. Existing pines tend to be younger trees.

Carole Capeyn and David Allen discovered in the 1980s that it is possible to create an artificial cavity (with a chain saw) near the top of a tree, even a young tree, and place nest boxes inside. The boxes cost about $30 each, and some skill with a chain saw is required for installation. The boxes are being used in several places, including the Joseph W. Jones Center, a nonprofit ecological conservation institution at Ichauway, Georgia (J. Stober 2000, telephone conversation).

Captive Breeding and Genetics

Captive breeding, followed by release and reintroduction, is increasingly conducted by zoos and other private organizations. Captive breeding is a science that depends on integrating a variety of biological techniques, from artificial insemination to identification of appropriate release habitat. One success story was the restoration of the peregrine falcon (*Falco peregrinus*) by the Cornell Ornithology Center (subsequently, the project moved to Boise, Idaho, and is now known as the World Center for Birds of Prey). While there is some scientific debate over whether the released birds were "pure" enough to qualify as peregrine falcons, it is apparent that reintroduction would never have occurred without the decades-long study and experimentation by the laboratory headed by Thomas Cade. Drawing on techniques ranging from artificial insemination to traditional falconry methods of training young hawks, Cade made possible the comeback of falcons to the point where they are nesting atop skyscrapers in major cities.

Genetic studies of animals in the field are used for a variety of purposes. DNA studies can show whether specific populations are related, helping biologists determine whether a population of, say, grizzly bears (*Ursus arctos*) is genetically diverse enough to be viable through natural reproduction (Cronin 1997). Tagging, monitoring, and geographic information systems (GIS) are all available to the endangered species biologist. Radio collars are widely used to monitor reintroduced animals such as the gray wolves (*Canis lupus*) recently introduced into Yellowstone National Park. However, this tracking technology is a two-edged sword. While killing a wolf (except in unusual circumstances) could bring down the arm of the law, killing wolves that don't have radio collars (but that may be in the same pack) is not likely to lead to penalties. In the end, these technologies are used only sporadically by the federal government because the federal agencies benefit from placing the burden of protection on landowners by requiring them to provide habitat without compensation.

A Budget for the Endangered Species Act

Until the high costs to landowners are removed from the ESA, technology will not be used effectively to protect species. It may instead be used, surreptitiously or otherwise, to reduce or degrade habitat. To correct this severe flaw, the government should be required to pay when it takes away ordinary uses of land. The FWS should be put "on budget" when it comes to protecting habitat.

By compensating landowners and removing the fear of penalties, the government will encourage low-cost solutions and concentrate its funds on those populations and subspecies of animals that the American public wants to see protected. When the FWS spends its own money to buy habitat or otherwise protect species, only a small portion of the agency's expenditures go for animals such as the Stephens kangaroo rat (*Dipodomys stephensi*), the Karner blue butterfly (*Lycaeides melissa samuelis*), or the Delhi sands flower-loving fly (*Rhaphiomidas terminatus abdominalis*). Most go to the popular and attractive animals that Americans generally expect the act to protect (Coursey 1994). Yet the FWS makes landowners pay an often high burden to protect these animals on their lands. In an ideal world, it would be excellent policy to protect every population of every subspecies that faces extinction or decline. The American taxpayer, however, is not willing to pay for that protection, which would be quite costly under the current system. The ESA is a substitution of compulsion for purchases and trades. Those who are left to shoulder the burden of species preservation under this approach are too often a relatively few, mostly rural, landowners and those who lease or work in public lands, such as loggers. Putting the FWS "on budget" would result in a program for saving species that is far more productive and far more in line with the wishes of the American people than the policies operating today. There is evidence that this is the case. For example, a program in western states called "ranching for wildlife" illustrates how a different set of incentives could encourage technological innovation (Leal and Grewell 1999).

Ranching for wildlife programs, which exist in eight western states, are cooperative arrangements between landowners (often ranchers with large expanses of land) and state wildlife agencies. The programs have their origins in landowners' practice of charging hunters for access to their land—fee hunting. To increase their profits, ranchers would like greater freedom from state hunting regulations such as short seasons and tight limits on the number of animals that can be taken. Although such rules are designed to help the state agency maintain large game populations over broad regions, such "one-size-fits-all" rules can interfere with carefully managed hunts. In ranching for wildlife programs, state agencies agree to free up regulations because more freedom will give landowners incentives to invest in wildlife management, leading to more wild game in the state.

Without heavy penalties and with the freedom to use more management tools, landowners adopt new techniques. In the state of Utah (which does not even require a specific management plan for participating in the program), landowners have seeded more than 4,600 hectares (11,500 acres) in native vegetation to encourage wild game.

Deliberate efforts to manage land this way can succeed spectacularly. The Deseret Ranch in northeastern Utah, for example, had an elk (*Cervus elaphus*) herd that numbered about 350 in 1976. Today, through careful management, the herd has 2,000 animals. The experience of the White Mountain Apache Tribe in east-central Arizona also illustrates the ability to protect and enhance wildlife species when the incentive is there. In 1977, the state of Arizona was issuing 700 permits a year for elk hunting on the reservation. That year, however, the tribe took over management of hunting on the reservation. To build a mature herd, the tribe drastically reduced the number of elk licenses to twelve, increasing them gradually over the years. Today, licenses cost about $12,500 because the chance of taking a trophy elk is so great. Other animals, including black bear (*Ursus americanus*), mountain lion (*Puma concolor*), and wild turkey (*Meleagris gallopavo*), are sufficiently abundant that they too can be hunted for a price (Anderson 1999).

There is no reason why comparable management of wildlife habitat could not be used to protect endangered species. For most species, when low-cost providers are sought out and worked with, we should expect the cost to be quite low, as they have been historically for groups doing just that to help bluebirds and wood ducks. But some funding to pursue such management would be useful. In the case of hunting, the market (i.e., hunters who pay) provides the funds to carry out the objective. If preservation of endangered species is a public good, as many argue, then public funds may be appropriate. Paying landowners to supply endangered wildlife is similar to paying them to supply game animals.

There are other ways, too, to protect endangered species that do not require government funds. Numerous environmental organizations work cooperatively with landowners to ensure that they protect wildlife. One example is the Delta Waterfowl Foundation, headquartered in Deerfield, Illinois (Anderson and Leal 1997, 58–61). It has an "Adopt-a-Pothole" program that compensates farmers in the Midwestern United States and Canada for saving "potholes"—that is, the shallow depressions in their farmland that provide nesting areas for ducks and geese—from being drained for agriculture. Zoos, membership organizations like the Audubon Society, and private foundations all could be a source of funding to develop the management of endangered species.

Achieving More Effective Species Protection

The ESA, by objective measures, must be viewed as inadequate, even though it is touted as a powerful law. Until its penalties are removed, growing numbers of people will continue to reduce habitat that could, instead, be enriched to enhance species survival. New approaches will be more effective in achieving the goals of saving species. They include government contracts to "rent" land from landowners who have listed species on their property, as well as the kinds of private rental contracts that have worked well in other settings which occur when interested parties such as environmental groups pay for habitat or protection. If the FWS (and the NMFS) must pay for habitat protection this way, or procure it from other public agencies by well-considered legislative measures, landowners (including public agency land managers as well as private individuals or organizations) will be more cooperative. Such contracts can unleash creative and entrepreneurial management that encourages the adoption of new land-management techniques. The result will be an expansion of the carrying capacity of habitat and more effective species protection.

Notes

This chapter is based on a talk given at the Forest Futures Conference at Willamette University in Salem, Oregon, on September 25, 2002.

1. See also Stroup (1995). "The [ESA] program can point to few successes at least when measured against its statutory goal" (Tobin 1990). "Measured against the logical, absolute standard, the small number of domestic species officially declared recovered would suggest that the program has been of limited success in recovering species" (GAO 1988). Defenders of the ESA argue that the appropriate measure of effectiveness is not recovered species but those whose condition has improved or stabilized (Irvin 1992).

2. The definition of *taking* has proven especially troubling. Because the term includes activities that "harm" a protected species and because the U.S. Fish and Wildlife Service has defined *harm* to include harming habitat, "landclearing, timber harvest, conversion of rangeland to cropland, and other activities on private land can potentially 'take' endangered species and thus be prohibited by the ESA unless expressly authorized by a permit" (Bean 1998).

13

The Struggle
over Species Survival

Peter List

The Endangered Species Act (ESA) has been with us now for thirty years. It has been hailed as one of our country's most far-reaching and unique examples of environmental law. One reason for this is that the ESA's philosophical grounding and ethical commitments reflect our societal view that wild animal and plant species exhibit a multitude of noneconomic values and provide more than mere commercial utility in our lives (Leopold 1949, Sagoff 1988). The ESA's language explicitly expresses a national desire to temper the effects of economic development and exploitation of our environment with mechanisms that protect species and their critical habitats. It presupposes, correctly, that some species extinctions are a consequence of economic activity and are not "natural" in their character and operation. Consequently it sets us on a path to do what is needed to prevent species decline and extinction, ahead of time, despite the economic costs.

The three chapters in part III of this volume are disparate in focus with regard to the ESA, and it is difficult to identify any single thread that runs throughout their various conclusions. Clearly the authors of the chapters do not appear to disagree with the important ethical idea that nonhuman species that are threatened or endangered should be protected. The main difference is that Steven Ackers and Susan Jane Brown plow ground within the domain of existing ESA processes, while Richard Stroup poses a radical challenge to the very legal and bureaucratic framework that the ESA uses to achieve its environmental goals. In what follows, I want to spell out some of the implications for species protection that I find in the chapters and raise some questions about Stroup's proposal.

The Biological Status of the Northern Spotted Owl

The chapter by Ackers informs us about some of the crucial scientific issues that have existed in regard to northern spotted owl (NSO) (*Strix occidentalis caurina*) research. One thing we learn is that spotted owl populations in the areas covered by the Northwest Forest Plan (NWFP) have steadily declined since population studies were first begun some years ago, though scientists are still unclear whether this decline will eventually mean extinction, stabilize at some acceptable population density, or is part of a long-term, natural population fluctuation that will ultimately result in owl recovery. We also learn that scientists know very little about the owl's "extinction threshold," the point beyond which nothing can be done to prevent the owl's demise, though it has also been said that this is a difficult concept to define and quantify for any species. Other scientists have asserted that there is a lack of evidence that spotted owl populations are declining in all Pacific Northwest (PNW) habitats where they are located. In some parts of the Northwest they have stabilized, and in others the NWFP may be responsible for reducing the rate of owl decline.

Ackers reveals the uncertainty that exists about the spotted owl's status in and around the H. J. Andrews Experimental Forest near Blue River, Oregon. In this case timber harvesting has mostly ceased in "matrix" areas established by the NWFP, and no harvesting of old forests is allowed in riparian and late-successional reserves—prime spotted owl territory. However, management guidelines outside of these reserves are not as strict and pose more threats to spotted owls and their habitat. Consequently, once timber harvesting resumes, the destiny of the spotted owl may not completely synchronize with logging plans.

Given this uncertainty about the owl's exact status and about the long-run success of creating new owl habitat in matrix areas where there are young tree stands, I wonder whether it would make sense to adopt a more conservative approach to timber management under the NWFP. Until more is known about these important scientific matters, harvesting old growth outside of the reserves, even if this is only a small proportion of NWFP lands, may not be advisable. If we really are "gambling" with extinction, as Ackers states, we should not risk further losses of spotted owls for the short-term gains in timber volume that would result from more fully implementing the NWFP's timber management goals. As one prominent forest scientist and administrator included in this volume has said, the paramount concern behind the NWFP is species protection, not wood production (see Thomas, this volume). This becomes important when one asks, does the country really need this volume of wood from these forests, or could the wood be harvested from other lands, public and private, without opening up the possibility of further declines in populations of threatened species?

Consultation by Federal Resource Agencies under the ESA

Brown asks what kind of consultation, programmatic and site-specific, is required by federal resource agencies as they review timber harvest plans under the ESA and NWFP. Is the current approach to consultation of "questionable legal validity," as she concludes? The arguments Brown makes in regard to legal problems raised by the scale and scope of current consultations seem reasonable to this reader. Common sense would tell one that unless biological information about threatened and endangered species is sufficiently specific to the affected habitats in which timber harvests are being planned, and unless the effects of those harvests on the relevant species are well understood and the resulting knowledge fully utilized by the agencies in their consultations, the likelihood that harm will be done to spotted owls cannot be ruled out and thus the requirements of the ESA will not be met.

While it might be true that conducting both programmatic and site-specific consultations is sometimes time-consuming and expensive for the agencies, and thus might be difficult to bring off, I would ask why such practical considerations should trump ESA ethical commitments and legal obligations in regard to protecting threatened and endangered species. Why shouldn't the latest, the best, and the most site-specific biological information about spotted owls and their habitat be used in as thorough a manner as is feasible, in agency discussions? Finally, if current efforts being considered by the upper echelon of federal resource administrators and national politicians to "streamline" agency consultation and speed up logging succeed (see Bush 2002; USFS/USDI 2002, H. Res. 1904, 2003), vigilance will be needed to determine whether this will further jeopardize northern spotted owl survival.

The Alternative Path of Incentives: A Route around the ESA

In the third chapter of part III, Richard Stroup proposes an alternative pathway that would gut the ESA's current machinery for species protection by substituting a system of economic incentives. Stroup leaves many of the specifics of his approach vague and would need to spell out in more detail how it would operate. Thus, given that various kinds of incentive programs could be designed, what does he have in mind for landowners and land agencies, aside from conservation rental contracts? How would these programs be established, and by whom? Further, how would their operation be monitored, and what role would biological science play in the whole process? Moreover, what evidence is there that such a system would be sufficiently attractive to enough landowners to *systematically* preserve the species that need protection?

Stroup bases part of his argument on his assessment of how ineffective the ESA has been in protecting species. As he

correctly asserts, the ESA apparatus has not been very successful in delisting species or in preventing some listed species
from declining further. But to properly assess this issue, one
needs much more information than he provides. Thus he says
nothing about those species listed under the ESA whose numbers have not declined, *because of* actions taken under ESA programs. Nor does he mention the fact that there are no recovery
plans in place for some listed species and consequently that
one could hardly expect the ESA to succeed in those cases. Finally, he does not account for "habitat conservation plans"
that have been established for some landowners by the U.S.
Fish and Wildlife Service, and these plans show some promise
both for species protection and fairer cost sharing (see Hatch
et al. 2002, Clark et al. 2002).

But assume for a moment that the ESA has not been a re-
sounding success. What then are the underlying causes of this
state of affairs? Is it a result of the so-called command-and-control
approach, or is it due to other, more powerful factors beyond the
purview of federal resource agencies?

To this I would ask, how realistic is it to expect the ESA apparatus to "save" threatened and endangered species, given
the *relatively small* amount of money that is being devoted to
protecting and preserving species by federal agencies, compared to the *vast* sums that our society and economic system
spend to push species into a threatened or endangered condition? Aren't our extensive and protracted efforts to spur economic development and growth, along with other factors, such
as increasing incursions into wilder habitats for recreational
purposes and government programs that eradicate species
which threaten agriculture and other resource industries, actually posing much more of a danger to wild species and their
habitats? Given these deeply rooted economic and political circumstances, how can one expect better species protection to result from existing ESA measures alone? Examining the total
ledger might lead one to conclude that the budgets of the relevant federal resource agencies are grossly underfunded and we
are currently expecting too much of them.

Some Final Points

One difficulty for the environmental policy process is reflected in Acker's chapter. It has to do with the level of scientific certainty that exists regarding species survival. Due to the complexity of scientific issues involving ecosystems and the conservative nature of the scientific process, it can be quite difficult for researchers to provide clear enough judgments about ecosystem components to satisfy the demands of the public policy process (Lemons 1998). Given the way public environmental issues are typically resolved, this is troublesome because the burden of proving that environmental degradation is significant usually rests with those who seek to preserve ecosystems rather than with those who would use them for economic purposes. This front-loading of the issues requires that there be "reasonable certainty" about whether a species is threatened or endangered and about the causes of any threats to its viability. In contrast, one attractive feature of the ESA is that it undermines this issue formulation bias and reverses the burden of proof. Those who believe that timber harvesting in species habitat should proceed must now have convincing evidence that it will not exacerbate spotted owl decline. The ESA thus embodies something like a precautionary principle for threatened and endangered species.

Still, the question Stroup raises about fairness is an important one, and we should ask whether the economic costs of species protection ought to be shared more equitably. This is important because wild species are a public good, and the causes of species loss are not all attributable to the actions of private landowners. In various ways and in varying degrees, all consumers and users of natural resources benefit from the existence of these species and are responsible for species decline through their own consumption behavior, though that is not the whole picture from an economic perspective. Thus, are there additional methods of protecting species that more fairly impose economic costs on all those who are responsible and also reduce the economic burdens on those who can ill afford to pay?

I question whether we are faced with a simple, two-valued choice of either keeping the ESA as presently constituted or doing away with it and substituting a system of economic incentives. The alternatives are certainly richer than this, and policy makers could think more creatively about methods that supplement the ESA and promote economic equity. Moreover, economic incentives are already being used with some success in regard to other federal environmental laws, without demolishing the laws themselves, so that experience would be useful in this regard (see, for instance, Bryner 1993 and Goodstein 1999).

Eliminating the ESA would revoke the public values and social consensus that lie within the very foundations of this environmental law. It would do away with the basic philosophy that threatened and endangered species carry noneconomic values that are more important than economic ones, and that species protection should proceed regardless of the economic costs. This course would be unwise, in my judgment.

Note

My thanks to Joe Kerkvliet, Bob Anthony, and George Stankey for their help with this commentary.

IV

FOREST FUTURES AND PRESENT CHALLENGES: BEYOND THE NORTHWEST FOREST PLAN

14

Principles and Politics of Sustainable Forestry in the Pacific Northwest: Charting a New Course

John A. Kitzhaber

The future of Pacific Northwest forests rests in a common understanding and acceptance of the concept of sustainable forestry. By that I mean not just environmental and economic sustainability, but political sustainability as well. If we are willing to consider a new paradigm for the management of public forestlands, I believe we can move beyond the seemingly intractable conflict between the environmental community and the timber industry to a future of healthy, thriving forests yielding clean water, diverse habitat, and commercial wood products.

Clearly, we need a new paradigm to replace the one under which we have been operating since the late nineteenth century. On one side is the position bluntly articulated by George Coggins, a public land legal authority: "The public lands are public. They are the property of all of the people, not just those who live in their immediate vicinity. They are national assets, not local storehouses to be looted." At the other end of the spectrum is the "Sagebrush Rebellion" of the late 1970s and early 1980s, which held that all federal land was state property to do with as states pleased. The truth, and the future of sustainable forestry, lies somewhere in between these two positions. In this chapter, I will describe sustainability and offer a definition of sustainable forestry. I will focus on the key elements that must be in place to achieve sustainable forestry and apply these principles to some examples of large-scale forest management.

The Fabric of Sustainability

I define sustainability as managing the use, development, and protection of our economic, environmental, and community resources in a way and at a rate that enables people to meet their current needs without compromising the ability of future generations to do the same (Prugh et al. 2000, Daly 1996, Daly 1991). This definition requires that we recognize a larger truth—the interdependence among our economic, environmental, and community needs—and that we find a balance among these often competing values.

Imagine, if you will, three overlapping circles, one representing our economic needs, one representing our environmental needs, and one representing our social or community needs. The area where the three circles overlap is the area of sustainability— the area through which run all the elements of a good quality of life: a healthy, functioning natural environment; a strong economy with jobs and job security; and safe, secure communities where people have a sense of belonging and purpose and a commitment to each other (Executive Order No. 00-07, 2000). These elements, these threads, which together weave the fabric of sustainability, are things we hold in common. They represent a common set of desires and aspirations that add value and quality to our lives. To me this relationship lies at the heart of sustainability, and if we are to be successful in creating a truly sustainable forest management strategy, an awareness of this interdependence must constantly guide our work.

Sustainability and the Politics of Scarcity

And yet, as our social, environmental, and economic problems become more complex, our traditional governmental structures of law and regulation (and the culture of our agencies) increasingly fail to recognize this relationship and, in fact, often get in the way of it, creating conflict, polarization, and lost opportunities instead of collaboration and a sense of community and of accomplishment. Increasingly, we are viewing economic, environmental, and community needs as separate, competing entities, mutually exclusive values, if you will. Of course, this perspective undermines sustainability because it creates a politics of scarcity—a zero-sum situation in which there must always be a winner and a loser (see Ophuls and Boyan 1992, Torgerson 1999).

We can see this disturbing trend unfolding in many ways: in the challenge of accommodating growth while maintaining livable communities and in the tension between sprawl and compact development. In the West, however, nothing better illustrates the politics of scarcity than the conflict between economic activity and long-term environmental stewardship. To illustrate this point, let me offer a brief history of the forests east of the Cascades.

For hundreds of years, the forests of eastern Oregon and much of the Intermountain West were blessed with huge stands of old-growth pine covering millions of acres. For much of the last century, however, forest management policy was characterized by active fire suppression, widespread livestock grazing, the harvesting of valuable old-growth pine, and a resistance to active management by conservation groups (Quigley 1992, Mutch and Quigley 1993, Cochran and Barrett 1995, Tanaka et al. 1995). The legacy of these management practices (especially on public lands) is forests overstocked with stands of young fir and pine, the loss of older, fire-resistant trees, thousands of acres of dead and dying timber infested with insects, and a high risk of catastrophic fire (Johnson et al. 1995).

This situation has led to a significant reduction in watershed health and the destruction of habitat for sensitive species, coupled with a catastrophic decline in employment for timber-dependent communities. Yet efforts to address this widely recognized problem have been thwarted by the conflict between those who wish to harvest timber and those who wish to preserve it, and by their distrust of each other and of the federal land-management agencies themselves. Each side in the debate operates from its own deeply entrenched positions, pointing at the other as the culprit. We saw this conflict erupt during the 2002 fire season, with each side blaming the other for the vulnerable state of many of our western forests. This situation is a classic example of the black-and-white way in which the debate over the management of federal lands has historically been framed. And it offers a fitting backdrop for our discussion of sustainable forestry.

Principles of Sustainable Forestry

I believe that sustainable forest management rests on a foundation of six key building blocks, or principles: (1) establishing a single overarching policy objective that drives forest management plans; (2) reframing the debate between commercial forestry and environmental stewardship; (3) basing decisions on interdisciplinary science; (4) managing at the landscape level; (5) ensuring broad public involvement in and ownership of the management plan; and (6) redefining the relationship with our federal partners (Kitzhaber 1999a).

When I became governor of Oregon in 1995 it was apparent that the status quo in the forests of eastern Oregon was not serving anyone—not the industry, not the environment, not the rural communities. The challenge of getting beyond the gridlock depended first and foremost on finding a common policy objective that could bring the stakeholders together. And the policy objective we settled on was a healthy, functioning forest ecosystem, with an emphasis on watershed health. This first principle, a single overarching policy objective, lies at the heart of the new paradigm for forest management.

Now, given the multiple values represented by our forests—economic, environmental, recreational, and aesthetic—it is important to recognize that focusing on watershed health does not mean that we are elevating the importance of one value above another. Rather, it serves as a common denominator for all the values, and acts as a guidepost by which we can shape our management efforts in the context of the other values. We cannot provide sustainable forest products, assure clean water, and provide habitat for species unless we first have a healthy, functioning ecosystem. The three legs upon which the strategy stands—social, environmental, and economic—are all interwoven and are dependent first on a healthy, functioning forest ecosystem.

Addressing the Principles—Recent Efforts and Continuing Obstacles

In March of 1995, using forest ecosystem health as the overarching policy objective, I appointed a panel of highly respected scientists from throughout the Northwest, including faculty from Oregon State University, the University of Washington, and scientists from the private sector. They reached a remarkable consensus of opinion on what it would take to restore health to the forests of eastern Oregon. Their recommendations were subsequently embodied in a broadly supported set of eleven guiding principles (Kitzhaber 1999b).

This "11-point plan" calls for using active management to promote ecosystem health, while avoiding areas of high public controversy. This is an important point. Since there is such a high level of distrust, we need to restore confidence in the U.S. Forest Service and other federal agencies and to demonstrate that active management can be accomplished in an environmentally sensitive manner. Such active management requires restoration treatments such as understory and commercial thinning; road maintenance, closure, and obliteration; prescribed burning; noxious weed treatment; and stream rehabilitation. It also emphasizes adaptive management through monitoring (Johnson et al. 1995).

The objective of this management strategy is to improve the health of the forest ecosystem, including watershed health and habitat for forest species. At the same time, a by-product of many of the thinning treatments would be wood for local mills and value-added products to help stabilize rural communities. Thinning and prescribed burns would also reduce the risk of catastrophic fires that has increased significantly as forest health has deteriorated (Johnson et al. 1995).

Beyond providing the foundation of an overarching policy objective, this Eastside strategy has helped reframe the debate between commercial forestry and environmental stewardship, the second principle of sustainable forestry. It accomplishes this by focusing on areas of broad agreement instead of conflict, and by taking advantage of the "area of sustainability" where environmental, economic, and community needs overlap. In formulating the plan, we sought to move the debate from the question of "management versus no management" to a discussion of "how to manage" these lands. I suggest that by using good science and by focusing on reducing risk—risk to the watershed, risk to sensitive species, and risk to the local economy—we can build public and scientific support for active forest management.

This approach is based on a strong underpinning of multi-disciplinary science, the third principle of sustainable forestry. We use this science in a number of ways. On the federal lands, for example, we want to know what these systems historically were like in order to demonstrate what the watersheds need to function properly. For instance, we know that it is appropriate to mimic past fire regimes and thin forests at lower and middle elevations but not the higher elevations. Historically, higher-elevation forests burned infrequently, and when they did they did not experience low-intensity creeping fires, rather they were characterized by stand-replacing fires (Johnson et al. 1995).

Because of the importance we placed on restoring healthy, functioning watersheds, our work is also based on a commitment to management at the landscape level—the fourth principle of sustainable forestry. This principle acknowledges that the ecologic "landscape" does not stop at political boundaries, nor at those based on ownership. In fact, in June of 1999 the U.S. Forest Service approved the 1.04 million hectares (2.6-million-acre) Blue Mountain Demonstration Area, in eastern Oregon, which has allowed us to move beyond the consideration of separate, individual projects to the consideration of an entire landscape that includes federal, state, tribal, and private lands (USFS 2001).

To meet the fifth principle—ensuring broad public involvement in and ownership of the management plan—we established an Eastside Forest Health Advisory Panel, consisting of a diverse group of eastern Oregon citizens and stakeholders. This was a reflection of our recognition that just having the best science is not enough; we also needed to blend in the values of the local population if the plan is to be sustainable, especially from a political standpoint. The advisory panel worked to identify and prioritize local projects based on the plan.

In the first years, the Eastside Panel identified nearly sixty Forest Service and Bureau of Land Management projects that exemplified the 11-point plan (Governor's Eastside Forest Health Advisory Panel 2002). This offered a clear demonstration that it is possible to engage in broadly supported watershed and forest restoration work that both improves ecosystem health and provides some economic benefits to local communities. Unfortunately, the volume of marketable timber flowing from this work has been less than we hoped. Some of this was due to unrealistic expectations. Some was due to poor market conditions. But much of the problem flows from the very structure and culture of the federal land-management agencies themselves. And this brings us to the sixth principle of sustainable forestry: redefining the relationship with our federal partners.

The current federal governance structure has, in many cases, frustrated the very collaborative, community-based approaches to forest management that offer the most promise. Examples include the Applegate Partnership, the Quincy Library Group, and the Grand Canyon Forest Trust.[1] All of these efforts were built on collaboration at the local level among people working together to solve shared problems on behalf of a shared place. All enjoyed initial enthusiasm and support from the federal land-management agencies. And all have been frustrated to one degree or another by the unwillingness or inability of these same agencies to allow the collaborators to make actual decisions on the ground.

Dan Kemmis, in his recently published book *This Sovereign Land* (2001), characterizes the phenomenon as the inevitable collision between local collaborative problem solving and the "procedural republic," his term for the complex administrative processes that try to ensure that all stakeholders have equal access to federal decision makers. As Kemmis puts it:

> At the bottom of this difficulty lies the fact that the collaboration movement represents a form and philosophy of decision-making fundamentally different from the decision structure in which the land management agencies are embedded. One is an

inherently decentralized, democratic form of governing; the other is inherently centralized and hierarchical. The effort to make something like collaborative stewardship an integral part of Forest Service operations, for example, cannot really succeed unless the agency is willing to turn some actual decision-making and management authority over to the people who are doing the collaborating. (Kemmis 2001, 129–30)

Kemmis, of course, describes the extreme—or perhaps the norm as we have known it in the past. Yet we have also experienced firsthand that another reality is possible. In the Blue Mountain Demonstration Area we have many examples of how local collaboration focused toward a common objective can help overcome barriers posed by the National Environmental Policy Act (NEPA), the Endangered Species Act (ESA), consultation, contracting, and a host of community issues.

The Present Political and Ecological Context

The debate currently raging in Congress (ostensibly over the issue of forest health) is a prime example of how easily political sustainability can be sacrificed to the false hope of short-term economic gain. To fully understand what is going on in Congress, and what is really at stake, we need to first put the debate into its proper context.

At the end of the terrible fire season of 2000, six western governors (including myself) met with then-Secretary of the Interior Bruce Babbitt and Secretary of Agriculture Dan Glickman in Salt Lake City to discuss what might be done. The outline for action that emerged from that meeting was based largely on the principles of sustainable forestry developed for eastern Oregon (USFS/USDI 2000). The resulting National Fire Plan was built around a deceptively simple agreement—to focus on the one thing upon which the industry and the environmental community could agree—the need to improve forest health (USFS/USDI 2000).

At the same time, we openly acknowledged that our efforts to improve forest health would not resolve the long-standing and controversial issues of roadless areas, salvage logging, sufficiency language, or the preservation of old-growth forests. We knew that we would continue to debate these policies, but agreed to do so in other forums and to separate them from the strategy to improve forest health. In other words, we agreed to stay within the "area of sustainability" where environmental, economic, and community interests coincide.

Thus, harvest activities under the National Fire Plan would have, as their primary objective, improving forest health as opposed to commercial logging. That is, trees would be removed based not on their commercial value, but rather on the ecological needs of the forest as dictated by good multidisciplinary science. In many cases, however, the by-products of thinning activities and fuel reductions would be wood products of commercial value. Furthermore, the Fire Plan makes it clear that the forest health treatments are to be done in a way that meets federal environmental laws (USFS/USDI 2000).

From this modest beginning emerged the Ten-Year Comprehensive Strategy and Implementation Plan, which was signed May 2002 at a ceremony in Idaho by myself, several other western governors, and Secretary of the Interior Gale Norton and Secretary of Agriculture Ann Vennemun representing the Bush administration (USFS/USDI 2000). What has happened since then, while predictable, serves only to move us further away from our new vision of sustainable forestry and to reemphasize the need for a new paradigm. In August 2002 President Bush visited Oregon to review the 200,000-hectare (500,000-acre) Biscuit Fire, the largest in the nation that year. He used the occasion to announce his new Healthy Forests Initiative and to make vague references to the Northwest Forest Plan (NWFP) (Bush 2002). And while the visit certainly served the important purpose of elevating the issue of forest policy to the national level, the president's plan deviated significantly from the Western Governors' Ten-Year Strategy that the administration had publicly embraced just four months earlier.

What needs to be emphasized here is that the overarching policy objective of the forest management strategy that emerged from the meeting in Salt Lake City is not, in fact, the prevention of wildland fires. On the contrary, the objective is to improve forest ecosystem health. Wildfire is but one of many symptoms of the declining health of our forests. Other symptoms include insect infestations, the invasion of noxious weeds, overstocked stands of young pine and fir, a decline in water quality, and the loss of habitat (Quigley 1992, Mutch and Quigley 1993, Cochran and Barrett 1995, Tanaka et al. 1995). Our objective is not to treat the symptoms, but rather to treat the cause. But by addressing the primary problem—declining forest health—we will also be addressing the symptoms, including the risk of catastrophic fire.

The Bush administration, however, has put the primary focus on the symptom of wildfire rather than on the larger issue of forest health. Consequently, in order to treat this symptom as promptly as possible, the administration proposes to exempt activities aimed at reducing fuel loads from aspects of key environmental laws such as the NEPA and to severely limit public access to the courts. While the Healthy Forests Initiative did not succeed in Congress, Bush took steps to implement its provisions via strategic use of Executive Orders, effectively circumventing the legislative process (Bush 2003).

Capitalizing on the legitimate concern over wildfire to justify circumventing Congress as well as federal environmental laws will not, in the end, improve overall forest health. On the contrary, it simply moves us back to the old paradigm of forest management, repolarizes the debate, and increases the likelihood that nothing will happen. The problem with this approach is that it runs the risk of destroying the trust and the delicate consensus for action that has been so painstakingly achieved, and of undermining the local collaboration necessary to strategically invest in the health of our forest ecosystems over the long term.

Making the Northwest Forest Plan Sustainable

That fact is that the principles underlying the Ten-Year Comprehensive Strategy and Implementation Plan represent the new paradigm of sustainable forestry. What would happen, for example, if, instead of destroying trust and collaboration, we were to build upon what we have achieved so far and apply these same principles to the NWFP (Tuchmann et al. 1996)? Since its implementation in 1994, the NWFP has done a good job of protecting habitat for various sensitive species. Unfortunately, it has fallen far short of its goal of providing a stable and predictable supply of wood products (see Beuter, this volume). It is instructive to ask why. On the positive side, the NWFP adheres to two of the most important principles of sustainable forestry. First, it did an excellent job of using an interdisciplinary team of respected scientists on which to build its foundation. Second, it met the test—in fact it set the standard—for a landscape-based approach to resource management. It was almost unheard of at the time, and still constitutes the largest ecosystem planning effort in the world. On the other hand, however, the NWFP falls short in two important respects. First, it lacks a single overarching policy objective to drive the management strategy. Ecosystem restoration is not the primary goal of the plan. Instead, the planning team had a diverse set of objectives. Among these were protection of habitat for the northern spotted owl (*Strix occidentalis caurina*), protection of riparian habitat, providing a predictable and sustainable level of timber sales, meeting requirements of federal environmental laws, and improving interagency coordination (Clinton and Gore 1993, Tuchmann et al. 1996). The result was a plan, based on sound science, that became a political compromise (Yaffee 1994).

The second shortcoming stems from the lack of broad public involvement in and ownership of the management plan as it was developed. The NWFP was developed largely in a closed setting. To this day it lacks the buy-in of the affected parties, and thus does not have a constituency to come to its defense when it is challenged. Consequently, there is still a great deal of tension surrounding it. The NWFP creates this tension, on the one hand by acknowledging that any additional harvest of old-growth forests will further threaten sensitive species dependent on these forests, and on the other hand by expecting this same old-growth forest to provide 80 percent of the projected timber volume over the next twenty years (Tuchmann et al. 1996). By trying to maintain parity between multiple goals, the NWFP falls short of adequately addressing any of them and is not politically sustainable over the long run.

If, however, we were to establish forest ecosystem health as the policy objective for management activities under the NWFP, thinning across the landscape (including in Late-Successional

Reserves) could at once promote the growth of older forest habitat and increase not only the volume but, just as importantly, the predictability of the timber flowing from these forests. Having a single overarching policy objective would hold all of the stakeholders accountable. Trees would be removed based not on their commercial value, but rather on the ecological needs of the forest as dictated by good multidisciplinary science. By the same token, the environmental community could not arbitrarily set a diameter or age limit for harvest. They would be compelled, for example, to demonstrate the difference between a 20-inch-diameter tree and a 23-inch-diameter tree from the standpoint of forest ecosystem health. Both sides would be measured by the same yardstick.

Pacific Northwest Forests: Our Common Interest

For all this to occur, however, we must maintain the trust and local collaboration on which success depends. We must also be open to challenging the "procedural republic": the means by which we translate policy into meaningful action on the ground. I recognize that the stakeholders on both sides of this issue believe that they are engaged in a mighty struggle. And they are. The challenge is not to give up on the entrenched positions of one's various constituencies. The challenge is to see beyond them, to honestly recognize that both sides are clinging to a paradigm that no longer serves their interests or the interests of the broader American public.

There is no doubt but that the exploitation of public lands for private and community gain is an established part of western history. Indeed, the conservation movement in America can trace its roots to efforts in 1870 to prevent corporate interests from abusing homesteading laws, passed to help settle the frontier, in order to gain access to public lands for the extraction of natural resources. These were not sustainable land-management practices.

But it is equally true that the current procedure-bound, litigious, cumbersome, glacial process that has engulfed federal land-management agencies does not produce sustainable land-management practices either. As evidence, look at the sad state of the health of the public forests throughout the Intermountain

West. Or consider the fact that over the ten years after the listing of the Snake River Chinook (*Oncorhynchus tshawytscha*) under the ESA, there is still no recovery plan in place.

It is no secret that I do not support the kind of sufficiency language proposed by the Bush II administration. Such language would declare that activities implemented under the administration's plan would be deemed sufficient to meet the requirements of various environmental laws. These activities would, in effect, be exempt from having to meet provisions of those laws. These environmental laws serve legitimate national interests. National environmental legislation, like the ESA and the Clean Water Act (Federal Water Pollution Control Act of 1972), were enacted for a reason, and a good reason: to secure the long-term and sustainable health of the ecosystems we all share. I believe in the need for this strong framework of federal environmental laws and in having the ability to enforce them.

At the same time, however, I also believe, just as strongly, that we need to have both the wisdom and the courage to periodically reevaluate the effectiveness of our tools and the way in which we have traditionally applied them. For example, with over 1,200 species listed, the lengthy, complex, and contentious process of actually developing recovery plans under the ESA will doom many of these species to extinction long before anything happens on the ground. Likewise, the processes that guide and shackle our federal land-management agencies are leading to similar results regarding the health of our forest ecosystems, and the health of our natural resource dependent communities.

What I am suggesting is that unless we address this fundamental problem, not with our environmental laws themselves, but with the processes and procedures by which they are applied, we will never achieve our goal of sustainable forestry. Likewise, if we undermine the trust and local collaboration that makes meaningful action possible, our forest management strategy will fail the test of political sustainability. We need to get beyond this; beyond the dogma, beyond the ideology, and beyond the legal and political gridlock. And the only way we are going to do that is to do it together; to recognize that we have a common interest here. It is up to us and to us alone.

As William Jennings Bryan pointed out: "Destiny is not a matter of chance, it is a matter of choice; it is not a thing to be waited for, it is a thing to be achieved."

Notes

This chapter is based on a keynote speech given at the Forest Futures Conference at Willamette University in Salem, Oregon, on September 25, 2002.

1. For more information on these collaborative efforts, see http://watershed.org/news/sum_95/applegate.html (Applegate Partnership); www.qlg.org/ (Quincy Library Group); and www.grandcanyontrust.org/ (Grand Canyon Forest Trust).

15

Fire on the Hill: Using Ecological Disturbance Theory to Understand the Ambiguous Prospects of the Northwest Forest Plan

Joe Bowersox

Even before the ink was dry on the Forest Ecosystem Management Assessment Team's (FEMAT) blueprint for ending the "timber wars" of the Pacific Northwest (PNW), the Northwest Forest Plan (NWFP) was under attack by both environmentalists and industry representatives concerned that the Plan did too little to protect species, or did so at too great a cost to the regional economy (Yaffee 1994). From its inception, the NWFP has been a lightning rod for environmental and industry interests alike. Many of the contributors to this volume have been active participants in legislative, administrative, or judicial attempts to modify the NWFP. Such attempts, and some of their own, continue to this day. In fact, as this book goes to press, the fate of the NWFP and the direction of federal forest policy generally are unclear, as Congress considers a fundamental restructuring of federal forest management policies to address the perceived threat posed by catastrophic wildland fire to forest ecosystems and human communities.

To shed light on the avenues and prospects for change in forest policy in the Pacific Northwest and the nation, I employ a hybrid policy framework informed by traditional public policy concepts as well as insights and metaphors from forest ecology.

Using this hybrid framework exposes the constrained nature of policy action and policy choice, while also suggesting why certain actions and choices find greater acceptance.

I begin by highlighting the utility of this analytical framework with a brief illustration of the origins of the NWFP itself. I then develop an extended narrative, describing attempts by certain policy elites within the U.S. Congress to alter forest policy in the wake of the NWFP. This is followed by an analysis that imposes the framework and ecological metaphors upon the post-NWFP narrative. A short conclusion follows, drawing attention to broader issues regarding our understanding of action and context in public policy making.

Punctuated Equilibrium, Policy Disturbance, and the Role of Memory: Using the Context of the NWFP as Preliminary Illustration

If there is one constant to the policy process, it is its dynamism: policies are crafted, adopted, implemented, critiqued, revisited, and possibly amended, overridden, or rendered obsolete. Policy making is not static, but an iterative, even discursive, process (Clark 2002, Press 1994, Kingdon 2003). The nature of American pluralism assures plenty of opportunities for groups advantaged or disadvantaged under a given policy to seek responses and redress from decision makers and administrative personnel (Lowi 1969). Since its inception over 130 years ago, U.S. forest policy has been no exception—the agencies in charge of the nation's public forests have been very responsive to politicians and stakeholders (Clarke and McCool 1996, Sabatier et al. 1996). Yet, it is a truism in American public policy that radical, non-incremental change—change that fundamentally alters the premises and goals of policy—is something less common. Policy change normally occurs at the margins, as existing policies are evaluated and tweaked to address perceived shortcomings or inequities (Wildavsky 1964, Lindblom 1959). Such is the phenomenon of "muddling through" (Lindblom 1959).

Nevertheless, under certain conditions policy entrepreneurs—those actors within a policy subsystem actively seeking to reconceive policy—can initiate non-incremental change (Kingdon 2003). Baumgartner and Jones, drawing on a concept from evolution theory (punctuated equilibrium) postulate that disturbance events occurring within a policy subsystem may throw an otherwise stable subsystem into disequilibrium, setting the stage for radical policy departure (Jones et al. 1998, Baumgartner and Jones 1993). However, it is possible to carry the ecological metaphor further: disturbance events in the policy subsystem (here also called the policy landscape) can disrupt the incrementalist and linear policy pathways, creating the necessary window or "gap" in that policy landscape upon which policy entrepreneurs may opportunistically establish "pioneer" policy initiatives (Kingdon 2003).

In the early 1990s, such was clearly the case with the formation of the NWFP. As the chapters of this book indicate, the NWFP was clearly a radical, non-incremental departure from the incremental changes in forest policy that had occurred since the 1970s (see Clarke and McCool 1996, Yaffee 1994, LeMaster 1984, Taylor 1984, Twight 1983, Mazmanian and Nienaber 1979). The political and legal crises created by the demographic collapse of old-growth-dependent species like the northern spotted owl (*Strix occidentalis caurina*) and marbled murrelet (*Brachyramphus marmoratus*), combined with the political disturbance of the 1992 presidential election, created a sufficient gap in the forest policy landscape. This allowed policy entrepreneurs like Jack Ward Thomas and the newly elected Clinton administration to establish ecosystem management policies upon the charred grounds of the commodity–oriented, multiple-use paradigm that had dominated forest policy since the 1960s (see Shannon, this volume).

But just as in the physical landscape, new policy recruitment was largely determined by the legacies that lay dormant in the policy landscape. Past actions and policies have left their memory upon the landscape. For instance, certain mandates contained in earlier legislation (like the requirement to maintain biological diversity in the National Forest Management Act [NFMA] of 1976) provided the basis for the survey-and-manage requirements of the NWFP (see Thomas, Perry, this volume). But like a real forest landscape, the forest policy landscape of the Pacific Northwest—and of the nation as a whole—is not static. A policy subsystem like forest policy is just as dynamic and subject to deterministic and stochastic events as any forest ecosystem. A series of political and ecological "disturbance events," beginning shortly after the judicial approval of the NWFP (*Seattle Audubon Society v. Lyons* 1994) and peaking in the first years of the twenty-first century, suggests we are once again at a juncture that could signal major change in the federal forest policy arena.

Post-NWFP Events: A Story of Persistence

Early congressional attempts to amend or circumvent the NWFP introduced critical entrepreneurial actors and policy components that would be instrumental in more fundamental challenges later. Their actions and processes echoed the policy strategies of earlier actors, and in turn influenced future actions undertaken in the policy subsystem.

Early Disturbance and Policy Memory: The 1995 Salvage Rider

The unlikely event that signaled the start of congressional endeavors to adjust the NWFP was an emergency supplemental appropriation, providing disaster assistance and funding counterterrorist activities, passed by Congress in the wake of the 1995 Oklahoma City bombing (Gorte 1996). Recognizing that the emergency supplemental provided an excellent and nearly veto-proof vehicle for increasing harvests on federal lands, Senator Larry Craig (R–Idaho), chairman of the subcommittee on Public Lands and Forests of the Senate Energy and Natural Resources Committee, successfully attached section 2001, popularly known as the "salvage rider." Just one year after the approval of the NWFP, President Clinton signed into law the "Emergency Salvage Timber Sale Program." With the help of professional staff member Mark Rey, a former vice president of the American Forest and Paper Association and longtime veteran of the spotted owl wars (see Yaffee 1994), Senator Craig's salvage rider expressly sought higher commodity volumes. The rider revived a provision of an earlier rider, section 318 of the Fiscal Year 1990 Interior Appropriations bill. Crafted by pro-timber members of Congress in 1989, Section 318 set a Northwest timber harvest of over 9.6 billion board feet and mandated that 1 billion board feet of litigated old-growth sales be immediately released for harvest (Yaffee 1994). Many of these "318 sales" had been stopped by the courts, and the 1995 rider required replacement volume. Second, the 1995 rider went after the NWFP directly, mandating additional "Option 9" sales of green trees in order to meet the NWFP's commodity target of 1.1 billion board feet per year. Finally, the Craig/Rey rider revived another trait of the 318 strategy, by sharply constraining National Environmental Policy Act (NEPA) environmental analyses, administrative appeals, and judicial review of 318 sales, the Option 9 sales, and any "emergency salvage logging" the agency deemed necessary to remove dead, dying, diseased, and "associated green trees" (Gorte 1996).

While environmentalists' fears of massive clear-cuts of old growth and other green trees under the 1995 rider never fully materialized,[1] its legacy remains: agencies still struggle to find replacement sales to meet the harvest mandates prescribed by the rider, while the criticisms and policy components articulated within the rider still resonate. The basic mechanisms utilized by Senator Craig and Rey—NEPA exemptions, curtailment of administrative appeals, and limitation of judicial review—continue to be the solution of choice for commodity interests.

But policy entrepreneurs like Senator Craig and Rey found few gaps in the policy landscape in the mid-1990s: opponents of the NWFP and other ecosystem management plans faced a series of obstacles. President Clinton, reelected by a wide margin in 1996, vigorously utilized the veto power and administrative control to block Republican efforts at unraveling management objectives. Furthermore, as the nation prospered in the expanding economy of the late 1990s, the timber industry's predictions of tens of thousands or even hundreds of thousands of displaced workers in the PNW never materialized, as the region's economy grew at twice the national average (Yaffee 1994, Raettig 1999, Raettig and Christensen 1999). Finally, the timber industry and their allies faced an uphill battle in terms of rhetoric and public perception. In the dot-com-dominated landscape of the late 1990s, public lands management emphasized ecological, aesthetic, and recreational values highly prized by a society of increasing affluence. Big Timber seemed to be an industry and orientation increasingly out of step with the nation and its public land managers (Bengston et. al. 1999, Brown and Harris 1998).

Despite such political, economic, and ideological obstacles, Senator Craig, staff member Rey, and other congressional allies in the late 1990s continued to utilize control of congressional committees to push for policy reform amenable to greater commodity production. Senator Craig alone chaired over 100 hearings of the subcommittee on Public Lands and Forests, often on comprehensive ecosystem management plans like the NWFP and its inland cousin, the Interior Columbia Basin Ecosystem Management Plan (ICBEMP). Senator Craig used these hearings to highlight their impacts upon rural communities, to point out the plans' failure to meet projected commodity targets, and to propose legislation mandating higher harvest volumes and curtailing public participation and judicial discretion (see Rey 2000, U.S. Senate 1998). But the most significant accomplishment of Senator Craig, Rey, and others during these years was rhetorically linking reduced harvests to the ecological health of fire-adapted forest ecosystems of the interior West. In so doing, they laid the groundwork for reframing the image of forest health in a manner beneficial to extractive industry in future years by embedding these concepts and ideas in the contextual memory of the policy landscape (U.S. Senate 1998, Kingdon 2003).

Fire Science and Fire Politics

Though public attention in the early 1990s remained focused upon the lush old-growth forests west of the Cascades in the Pacific Northwest, public land managers and political officials were shifting their focus to the forests of the interior. In July of 1993 President Clinton directed federal land-management agencies to develop an ecosystem management plan for the Interior Columbia River Basin, encompassing over 25.5 million hectares (63 million acres) of federal forest and rangeland. In addition to addressing threatened and endangered species issues, the agencies were charged with returning stand conditions to within the range of historical variability. The loss of ponderosa pine (*Pinus ponderosa*) forests to insect and disease damage, competition, and stand-replacing fires was of central concern (ICBEMP 2000, Bosworth 2000).

For some time forest scientists had expressed concern regarding the ecological effects on the nation's forests of 100 years of fire suppression. No place was this more evident than in the ponderosa pine forests of the interior West, in which frequent (ten- to thirty-five-year) low-intensity fires historically played an important role in regeneration and maintenance of open stands (Romme 1982, Baker 1992, Agee 1993, Covington and Moore 1994). In addition to preventing the periodic thinning of small-diameter ponderosa pine, fire suppression also encouraged more shade-tolerant and less fire-resistant species like white fir (*Abies concolor*) and grand fir (*Abies grandis*) to encroach upon and even outcompete ponderosa pine. Currently, stand densities in much of the interior West are several orders above the range of historical variability, with consequent effects on fuel loading and susceptibility to stress and disease (Covington and Moore 1994, Hessburg et al. 1999, Landres et al. 1999, McKenzie et al. 2000; but see also Swetnam et al. 1999, Brown et al. 1999).

Fire events in the mid-1990s dramatized the predicament. Exacerbated by drought throughout the Intermountain West, 1994 and 1996 were severe wildfire years: 2.6 of 2.7 million hectares (6.4 of 6.7 million acres) burned in the 1996 season alone were in national forests (Gorte 2000, GAO 1999). Concerned with the increasing costs of fire suppression, in 1994 the Clinton administration instructed federal land-management agencies to examine their fire policies. The directives produced a series of reports mandating increased emphasis upon protecting public values (not simply private residences), and recommending a vigorous acceleration of prescribed burning and mechanical thinning to reduce fuel loads throughout the West (USFS 1995a, USFS 1995b, GAO 1998, GAO 1999, Gorte 2000). Republican members of Congress capitalized on these developments, repeatedly calling upon federal agencies and government auditors to appear before the public lands subcommittees to testify regarding fuel buildup, fire risks, and account for fire suppression efforts, efficacy, and priorities (see GAO 1998, GAO 1999, Gorte 2000). In the late 1990s, the powerful Western Governors' Association (WGA) entered the fray as well, demanding federal action to restore forest health and reduce the threat of wildfire to communities in the intermountain region (WGA 2002,[2] see Kitzhaber this volume). By 1999 most policy makers in Congress, the White House, and in the states agreed with the findings of a General Accounting Office assessment: a comprehensive strategy to address fuel loads in an ecologically sound manner was essential to reducing risk to communities and avoiding loss of vital ecosystem services (GAO 1999). Fire was an increasingly volatile agenda item.

Physical and Political Firestorms: The 2000 Fire Season

In 2000 natural and political disturbances conspired to provide an opportunity for commodity interests. Perhaps the single most important was a rather low-intensity fire in the desert Southwest. On May 4, National Park Service (NPS) personnel ignited a prescribed fire to reduce fuel loads on approximately 400 hectares (1,000 acres) of Bandelier National Park, just outside of Los Alamos, New Mexico. Within twenty-four hours the fire had escaped control of an insufficient and tired crew. In the next fifteen days, it burned some 19,000 hectares (48,000 acres) and 235 homes, and forced the evacuation of the renowned Los Alamos National Laboratory.[3] And the summer fire season hadn't even started. By summer's end, over 2.8 million hectares (7 million acres) had burned across the country. Additional reports to Congress (see GAO 2000), federal agencies (NAPA 2000), and presidential and gubernatorial calls for new management policies (see USFS/USDI 2000, WGA 2000), demonstrate the extent to which the policy agenda that year was driven by ecological events.

Though the reports to Congress and the president highlighted the importance of addressing fuel loads throughout the West, they were circumspect with regard to the ecological consequences of hazardous fuels reduction, often noting the difficulty of simultaneously returning forest stands to conditions within the historical range of natural variability, reducing risks to communities, and preserving critical ecosystem functions (see GAO 1999, GAO 2000, USFS/USDI 2000). But such circumspection was not necessarily the disposition of members of Congress.

For instance, in the wake of the Los Alamos fire, Senators Domenici and Bingaman (both of New Mexico) worked closely with Senator Craig to pass yet another appropriations rider, dubbed the "Happy Forests" bill. Happy Forests authorized more aggressive "active management" of federal forest lands throughout the West in order to reduce fuel loads. In its original form, it included expedited NEPA processes and contract provisions to allow harvest of green trees. However, after a threatened veto by President Clinton, the amendment was rewritten to simply provide funds for fuels treatment within existing management authorities and in compliance with existing environmental laws (Rey 2000, Cong. Rec. 30 June 2000: S6220, Cong. Rec. 12 July 2000: S6508–S6515). As the presidential election of 2000 loomed, in which control of both the legislative and executive branches seemed up for grabs, the revised amendment was easily adopted into law (see P.L. 106–291, 2000).

2001 and 2002: Opportunities for Non-incremental Change

For many observers it was clear that the 2000 elections posed a critical juncture for federal natural resources policy. Thus, it came as no surprise when the new administration announced its intent to reexamine numerous Clinton-era natural resources policies. The nomination and confirmation of Senator Craig's natural resources advisor, Mark Rey, as USDA undersecretary for Natural Resources and Environment, signaled the administration's commitment to reformulating federal lands policies. As undersecretary, Rey had direct responsibility for the U.S. Forest Service, and with his extensive legislative ties from his years on Senator Craig's staff, he was in an ideal position to redirect federal forest policy. But the opening months of the Bush administration were marred by controversial missteps on energy and natural resources policy and by the sudden shift of Senate control when James Jeffords (VT) left the Republican caucus to become an independent. By late summer, as a rather mild fire season drew to a close, it appeared the opportunity to fundamentally rewrite Clinton-era natural resources policies was fading (Adams 2001, Tully 2001; see also Kingdon 2003, Baumgartner and Jones 1993).

September 11, 2001, redirected the administration and the nation, giving new life to a beleaguered presidency. After action supporting the war in Afghanistan and responses to terrorism, in the spring of 2002 attention could once again return to domestic issues. Drought and fuel conditions in the West assured fire would be a major concern.

The fires of 2002 burned over 2.9 million hectares (7.2 million acres) and consumed a record $2.2 billion in suppression costs (USFS 2003a). The Bush administration and its congressional allies quickly capitalized on the public's fascination with the conflagrations to propose an overhaul of Clinton's forest management policies. In August 2002, President Bush visited Southern Oregon's 202,000 hectare (499,000-acre) Biscuit Fire to announce his "Healthy Forest Initiative," resurrecting the most controversial parts of the Happy Forests legislation from 2000 (Goldstein and Sanchez 2002, Bush 2002). The Healthy Forest Initiative proposed hazardous fuels reduction on 77 million hectares (191 million acres) of federal lands, expediting or exempting thinning and prescribed burning projects from environmental reviews, administrative appeals, and limiting judicial review. It also encouraged long-term stewardship contracting with private parties to conduct fuels reduction and thinning projects under contract provisions allowing harvest of green trees to subsidize the costs of thinning (Bush 2002). As justification for limiting environmental reviews, the Bush administration cited Forest Service studies suggesting that litigation and appeals from environmental groups significantly delayed or curtailed fuels reduction projects (USFS 2002a, USFS 2002b).[4] Congress responded with bipartisan attempts focusing on the problematic "wildland urban interface"—where forested lands and communities intersect. Negotiations broke down over the extent and scope of NEPA exemptions and limitations on public participation. The position of the Democrats was further undermined when Senate Majority Leader Tom Daschle (D-S.D.) successfully atttached language to an emergency supplemental appropriations bill implementing fuels reduction projects in the Black Hills and exempting them from further environmental analysis and judicial review (see Monoson 2002, Adams 2002).

In the wake of Republican gains in both chambers in the 2002 congressional elections, the administration and its legislative allies moved on numerous domestic issues, including forest policy (see Scally 2003). The administration gave notice that it intended to remove the "survey and manage" requirements of the NWFP, a critical component of its legality (USFS/BLM 2002). Similarly, the administration sought to relax application of NEPA environmental assessment requirements for a broad range of fuels reduction and salvage activities which could be "categorically excluded" from review (USFS/USDI 2002). It also proposed administrative and legislative fixes to eliminate or constrict administrative appeals and legal challenges (USFS 2003a). Though Undersecretary Rey stated the goal was simply to make existing environmental laws work more efficiently, some members of Congress worried the administration was making a major assault on forest policy under the guise of fire (U.S. Senate 2003a).

In spring 2003, members of Congress sympathetic to industry and loyal to the vision of Undersecretary Rey and President Bush introduced sweeping legislation designed to reduce fuel loads and increase commodity outputs. Stocked by the policy legacy of the riders and the 2000 Happy Forests bill, well fertilized by the media attention paid to the previous fire season, and basking in the bright sunlight of strong presidential support and Republican congressional control, the Healthy Forests Restoration Act (HFRA) sharply curtails environmental assessment of management activities designed to reduce fuel loads in the wildland urban interface, municipal watersheds, and surrounding backcountry. It also fully exempts from all environmental reviews and administrative appeals "insect data logging" projects of up to 400 hectares (1,000 acres) each (H.R. 1904–108th 2003) and legislates a new judicial "balance of harms" test, requiring judges to give greater deference to agency claims of risks and benefits. As this book goes to press, the HFRA had passed the House, though its fate in the Senate was less certain (see Duncan 2003).

Analysis: Metaphor and Framework

If President Bush signs the Healthy Forests Restoration Act into law, it will signal one of the most profound shifts in forest policy in the last thirty years. However, no matter what the fate of this legislation, examining its emergence—and the political resurgence of interests backing it—brings to light critical details of the contemporary environmental policy process. The policy framework and ecological analogies discussed at the beginning of this chapter help us to observe order in this otherwise chaotic process. These observations can be divided into two general categories: the role of actors as agents of policy change and the significance of the policy landscape in which they operate.

Actors: Exploiting Gaps, Defining Problems and Solutions

In a representative democracy, politics and policy making are about and by people. Individuals seeking to change or maintain particular policies mobilize their political assets—political position, economic resources, education/expertise—within a policy subsystem. Nevertheless, as policy actors they face information, time, resource, and opportunity constraints in a policy landscape that is dynamic and often ill defined and unbounded. Actors who become successful policy entrepreneurs are those who, in addition to having sufficient resources of some kind, are either able to perceive opportunities for redirecting the policy agenda as they occur, or successful at manipulating the situation so as to create an opportunity (see Zaharaidis 1999, Kingdon 2003).

Since the early days of the NWFP, Senator Craig and Undersecretary Rey have been critical policy entrepreneurs doggedly highlighting impacts upon rural communities and forest-related industries of management plans that emphasized protection of ecosystem components and processes over commodity production. In the 1990s, as chair and professional staff member of a Senate subcommittee with jurisdiction over federal forest lands, they presided over a critical locale in the policy process, which made them potential policy brokers despite White House opposition. As chair, Senator Craig had virtual control over any action of the subcommittee, and could expect consideration (if not always enthusiastic support) for his proposals by the Republican leadership in both chambers (Sinclair 2000a, Sinclair 2000b, Schiller 2000). Such positioning was critical to achieving passage of the 1995 rider to the Oklahoma City emergency supplemental appropriation. When the events of 2000 and 2002 occurred, Senator Craig and Undersecretary Rey were (once again) both in positions ideally suited to advancing their agenda.

It is one thing to be at the right place at the right time to push forward one's agenda. In one sense, that reflects the ambiguous nature of the policy process—without the window or gap, policy change may never occur (see Kingdon 2003). However, successful policy entrepreneurs have done the sufficient groundwork to assure that if the gap does appear, their understanding of the problem and their particular solution are salient (Kingdon 2003, Zaharaidis 1999). Senator Craig and Undersecretary Rey utilized the Senate subcommittee to change the tenor and framework of the policy debate over fire and forest health. While much of the scientific literature was noting the necessary role of fire in forest ecosystems (Romme 1982, Baker 1992, Agee 1993, Covington and Moore 1994, Taylor and Skinner 1998, Brown et al. 1999), Senator Craig and other members of Congress were working diligently to redefine the threat posed by fire in ecological, economic, and social terms. Thus, in the aftermath of the 2002 fire season, congressional testimony on both sides of the aisle focused almost exclusively on the negative consequences of fire in fire-adapted ecosystems. Some members of Congress were even espousing a return to a total fire suppression policy (U.S. Senate 2003b).

In addition to seizing upon sudden opportunities and reframing and redefining problems, successful policy entrepreneurs frame solutions (Zaharaidis 1999). As Kingdon (2003) notes, many solutions may be available upon the policy landscape for any given issue, but the critical role of the entrepreneur is to identify one that can find sufficient support when the policy gap arises. Selection and redefinition may not be a rational process, being influenced by time, information, and resource constraints as well as the entrepreneur's own ideological biases (Kingdon 2003, Zaharaidis 1999). In the years following the NWFP, Senator Craig, Undersecretary Rey, and other congressional allies successfully used their position and power to promote a particular suite of policy solutions. None were new: salvage sales, exemptions from environmental analyses, elimination of administrative appeals, and restrictions on judicial review had all been tried in the late 1980s. But Senator Craig, Undersecretary Rey, and their allies took literally years to reiterate the utility and logic of the solution and develop a functional coalition of interests inside and outside of Congress to advocate on their behalf. When the political and natural disturbances of 2000 and 2002 occurred, the coalition of interests, their congressional allies, and the administration were prepared and unified behind a particular course of action (see Sabatier and Jenkins-Smith 1993, Egan 2002, Bush 2002, Jalonick 2003).

The Policy Landscape: Memory, Place, and Time Matter

Actors, however, do not operate on a formless policy landscape. Rather, the policy landscape is a complex mosaic constructed by previous political, socioeconomic, and natural disturbances that have altered patterns and processes of behavior. As seen in the case of forest policy in the wake of the NWFP, the policy successes of actors like Senator Craig and Undersecretary Rey were largely constrained by their ability to adapt to and learn from the changing policy subsystem. The effects of the landscape itself on the policy process can be broken down into considerations of the past disturbances, which have imprinted "policy memory" upon the landscape, the policy legacies left behind, and the landscape's continued susceptibility to natural and human disturbances.

Prior to 1993, the forest policy landscape was a "policy monoculture," despite the effects of comprehensive planning legislation like NFMA (1976) and Federal Land Policy and Management Act (1976), and new environmental mandates imposed by the National Environmental Policy Act (1969) and Endangered Species Act (1973). These acts had tweaked the missions of the USFS and BLM, requiring more detailed resource inventories and assessments and creating new "products" like recreation and wilderness. But they did not seriously divert the agencies from maximizing commodity production in conjunction with multiple use (see Clarke and McCool 1996, Yaffee 1994, Taylor 1984).

However, this policy monoculture was characterized by a small set of inhabitants involved in a rather simple relationship of distributive politics (Lowi 1969). In the case of public forestry, members of Congress, federal agencies, and commodity interests pursued a common policy objective of "getting the cut out," under which each received tangible benefits (Clarke and McCool 1996, Twight 1983, Clawson 1983). But monocultures—even metaphorical ones like the forest policy subsystem—are susceptible to disturbance. The cascade of forest-species declines that occurred in PNW forests throughout the 1980s and 1990s—ranging from spotted owls to jumping slugs—swept across the policy landscape like a fire storm, severely disturbing the simple, effective policy relationships that had prevailed. FEMAT and the NWFP were a concerted attempt not simply to restore the previous policy landscape, but to create a much more complex and holistic policy landscape involving more actors, more numerous and more robust relationships, and interconnection with other substantive policy areas like regional economic development, education and retraining, and international trade (see Shannon, this volume).

Despite the best efforts of proponents of the new policy landscape, the memory and the legacies of the previous landscape proved quite resilient. Rural communities throughout the Northwest remained dependent upon forest industries, and found it difficult (or were unwilling) to diversify. Financial resources to assist these communities in transition were inadequate (FCR 2002, Donoghue and Haynes 2002, Harris et al. 2000, Raettig and Christensen 1999). Agency personnel who had spent their careers managing forests for timber still wished to produce volume (Brown and Harris 1999). Politicians representing timber-dependent communities still needed their support. Hence, Senator Craig, Undersecretary Rey, and other congressional allies were advantaged by the sheer influence upon the policy landscape of past patterns and processes—what lay dormant could be revived.

Finally, policy landscapes remain susceptible to disturbance, and recently established and emergent relationships are more easily disturbed than more mature and resistant ones. The old policy legacies lay dormant, advantaged by their long residence time upon the landscape. However, the NWFP and its counterparts have not put down deep roots within the forest policy subsystem. Many of the components of ecosystem management—adaptive management, conservation biology, restoration ecology, stakeholder participation, sustainable community development—have yet to mature and produce tangible results either economically or biologically. Demographic trends for spotted owls are still declining (see Ackers, this volume), even as harvest rates continue to drop (see Beuter, this volume). Consequently, the complex biological, social, economic, and political relations envisioned by ecosystem management have not generated sufficient support among actors within the policy landscape—scientists and policy advocates sympathetic to species protection and preserving biological diversity give at best lukewarm endorsements (see Perry, Brown, this volume). Hence, when physical disturbance events like severe wildland fire seasons burst onto the policy landscape, threatening the fragile relationships and processes developed under the ecosystem management rubric, few rush to their defense.

Fire, Forests, and Human Values

Understanding public policy—whether it be forestry or health care policy—is a frustrating undertaking. We see actors, institutions, behaviors, and outcomes, but as with research in the social sciences generally, the establishment of any conclusions regarding causality is difficult. Nevertheless, we know (or, more cynically, we want to believe) that human action and human will shapes (if not fully determines) the outcome. Frankly, our commitment to democracy rests upon this assumption of political efficacy of the individual will: like Kant, we have to believe that things could have been otherwise if we so desired (Kant 1965, Arendt 1989). Recently, an extended debate has occurred in the policy sciences regarding the proper methodologies and models for observing—and even predicting—political behavior (see Sabatier 1999, deLeon and Kaufmanis 2000, Dudley et al. 2000). While utilizing some theories and concepts common in public policy (i.e., incrementalism, punctuated equilibrium, policy entrepreneurs, etc.), this chapter has utilized the language and metaphors of forest ecology to frame forest policy generally and the politics of the NWFP in particular. There is indeed significant interest in contemporary political science in understanding politics through the lens of the natural sciences (see Masters 1989, Arnhart 1998, Blank and Hines 2001, Rubin 2002). This in turn comes with certain attendant risks: there is great fear that the free will and responsibility which Kant so longed to observe may completely disappear in the causal and stochastic stream of life processes (see Masters 1989, Arnhart 1998). While acknowledging that risk, I believe that the language of ecology provides robust insight into relations of not only forest ecosystems but of political institutions and processes as well.

In the preceding analysis, the concepts and metaphors of forest ecology illustrate the complex interaction between individual agents and the system within which they operate and interact. The policy subsystem—or policy landscape as referred to here—is itself a complex and dynamic entity within which agents must operate. External events occur that disturb the landscape and the agent, disrupting successional pathways—that is, providing opportunities for non-incremental change initiated by the agents themselves. Nevertheless, the landscape itself retains legacies and memories that may persist and influence those new policy pathways. In essence, change—the result of human will—may occur (Zaharaidis 1999), but it is always bounded.

In the case of national forest policy, this analysis has highlighted the context and actions of particular policy entrepreneurs in Congress and the bureaucracy. By no means should it be construed that the foregoing discussion claims that these are the *only* significant actors in forest policy, nor that the fate of the nation's forests lies solely in the hands of members of one or two congressional committees. Rather, my point has been to demonstrate the ways in which certain policy actors with significant political and social resources can manipulate and modify the policy landscape itself to achieve or approximate their desired ends. Hence, the focus is by necessity on policy elites (Dye 2001). Furthermore, it should be noted that this analysis has not addressed the substantive impacts of the policy changes being sought by those wishing to return federal forest policies to a more commodity-oriented paradigm. I have my doubts about the desirability of that approach.[5] Nevertheless, it is important to stress that we do face a forest health crisis in fire-adapted ecosystems. But it is indeed a crisis of our own making. The ecological change and "fuels build-up" throughout our federal forests is the result of explicit policies created to protect commodity values. It was those same commodity values that encouraged the removal of habitat that led to the decline of old-growth-dependent species, and thus the NWFP. So far, the policy process is not sufficiently linking the two crises. Both demonstrate that we continue to underestimate and misunderstand the complexity of forest ecosystems, and thus through actions we once deemed benign or even beneficial to the landscape (harvesting, fire suppression), we in fact have placed that landscape at risk. Thus, it may be wise to take seriously the concerns expressed by some leading forest scientists regarding our ability to "restore" ecosystems—such restoration will necessarily reflect concrete human management goals (e.g., protection of communities, commodity extraction, wildlife management) and thus may not adequately address issues of human uncertainty or the dynamism and variability of the ecosystem itself (Landres et al. 1999, Swetnam et al. 1999). We must design policies which, when we fail to grasp how the forest "really works" (and we invariably will), won't put the forest at greater risk. A little humility might do us well.

Notes

1. In 1996 the House narrowly defeated a bill sponsored by Elizabeth Furse (D–Oregon) to defund the rider, and the Clinton administration issued a directive that rider salvage sales had to minimize green tree harvest and meet certain forest health criteria for consideration as an emergency salvage harvest. Finally, the federal courts halted many

of the resurrected section 318 sales because of their impact upon the marbled murrelet, a seagoing bird dependent upon old-growth forests for nesting habitat (see Farmer 1996).

2. Although originally adopted by the WGA in 1999, Improving Forest Ecosystem Health on Federal Lands (WGA Policy Resolution 99–011) was readopted by the governors in 2002 as Policy Resolution 02–09, Improving Forest and Rangeland Ecosystem Health in the West. See WGA 2002.

3. Even as the fire consumed homes in the affluent suburbs of Los Alamos, Interior Secretary Bruce Babbitt called for an inquiry into the debacle. The political impact of the Los Alamos fire was greater than the ecological. Much of the fire was a low-intensity underburn, with only patches of high-severity canopy fire. Postfire analysis confirmed that much of the $1 billion in property damage was due to avoidable buildup of fine fuels on and around private residences. Lightly scorched trees around completely destroyed homes confirmed that much of the residential loss was due to the fire moving from structure to structure. (See Cohen 2000.)

4. A recent GAO study contradicts the Forest Service on the effects of appeals and litigation, finding 76 percent of all hazardous fuels projects were not appealed; of the remaining 24 percent that were appealed, 79 percent were completed in the required ninety-day time frame. (See GAO 2003.)

5. I remain skeptical of the ecological and economic logic of hazardous fuels reduction. The Bush administration proposals do little to assure that vital structure, composition, and processes of treated areas will be returned to the range of historical variability, and that sufficient protections will be provided for threatened and endangered species and their habitat. For the economics of hazardous fuels reduction, simply consider Gorte (2003): "At $300 per acre for treatment (the cost given to GAO by the Forest Service), it would cost $39 *billion* to treat the national forest lands [80 million acres] and $29 *billion* to treat the other [75 million acres of] federal lands [considered at risk]. At the current (FY 2002) appropriation level of $395 million annually . . . it would take 172 years to treat all these lands. The first time."

16

The Northwest Forest Plan as a Learning Process: A Call for New Institutions Bridging Science and Politics

Margaret A. Shannon

The Need for a Critical Policy Analysis

A decade ago, on April 5, 1993, a team of scientists, charged with developing a new forest management plan for the federal forests along the western side of Washington, Oregon, and Northern California, gathered in hurriedly assembled office space on the fourteenth floor of the U.S. Bank building in Portland, Oregon. These seventy scientists brought a new perspective to developing a forest management plan—scientific, risk-based, interdisciplinary, integrated, and reflexive. Never before had scientists, untethered from the constraints of managerial policies and tacit political commitments, conceptualized and developed a management plan. Never before had a management plan been developed for managing 8.2 million hectares (20.4 million acres)[1] of federal forest lands across twenty-eight administrative units[2] and three states. Powerful global, regional, and local forces tearing across this vast, diverse region had unraveled familiar relationships and accepted institutions, leading to an intractable political conflict. What these scientists—and the hundreds of others who participated along the way—brought to the task of resolving this conflict was a way of thinking emerging around the world as to how to conserve and sustainably manage forest ecosystems by building new political institutions.

Self-designated as the Forest Ecosystem Management Assessment Team, the FEMAT is notable for the enormous role that scientific networks of ideas, principles, and concepts played in crafting the basic assumptions, innovative approaches, and scientific monitoring in the Northwest Forest Plan (NWFP). Today, ten years later, many of the concepts are familiar—landscape scale, forest structure and function, adaptive management, disturbance regimes, biodiversity, sustainability. The focus of my analysis is how these scientific concepts are linked to a new set of governance principles emerging across government and nongovernment forest policy processes in the last decade.

Participatory approaches; holistic and intersectoral approaches; iterative approaches with long-term commitments; and *capacity building*—these policy principles form the foundation of the FEMAT and NWFP (USDA/USDI 1994a).[3] Unclear in 1993 was that these planning principles reflect a twenty-first-century postmodernist framework based on emergent processes and learning that fits uneasily within a twentieth-century-modernist set of political and administrative institutions built to ensure consistency and stability.[4] The challenge for future forest policy in the Pacific Northwest lies in whether the political and institutional environments can transform by embracing these new principles and moving toward emergent governance (Shannon 2002a, Shannon 2002b).

The NWFP provides a future-oriented policy framework, but will it serve as a transformative policy instrument? Answering in the affirmative depends upon the social and political capacity of the region to engage new policy questions and create new institutions. Can we build bridging institutions to better link local knowledge with science and technical information (Gunderson 1999, Shannon 2002c)? Can we create generative politics capable of creating new social values and interests by constructing new institutions (Alexander 1988, Shannon 2002a, Shannon 2002b)? What kinds of participatory processes are needed in order for multi-stakeholder groups to work effectively together on common, shared public problems (Shannon 2002a, Shannon 2002c)?

Grappling with these questions requires a critical analysis that seeks to deconstruct familiar concepts so as to reveal the interests and values implicit within them (Allmendinger 2001). I am taking a *post-normal* approach to policy analysis in this chapter by seeking to uncover the invisible exercise of power and control held in scientific concepts, organizational structures, and institutional rules. "However, in contemporary society the dominance of a utilitarian, instrumental mode of thinking about social life inherited from classical liberalism has made the articulation of critical positions not so much impossible as professionally and often politically unacceptable and, therefore, often unheard" (Sullivan 1983, 305). Notwithstanding this warning, understanding the future of the NWFP means understanding what has not yet happened as well as what might not happen due to resistance from entrenched powerful interests. To undertake a critical analysis, we need a theoretical perspective based upon self-conscious social inquiry (Fischer and Forester 1993). The next section opens a way to critically assess the origins, approaches, and policy solutions of the NWFP. I draw upon a framework of analysis—postmodernism—that can illuminate why building a new politics with new institutions is both necessary and resisted.

What Is Meant by Modern and Postmodern?

When FEMAT scientists write about their work, they focus on the scientific concepts and principles that informed their work (Franklin 1994, Johnson et al. 1999b). When critics review FEMAT, they focus largely on how the FEMAT did not involve public and interest group participation, did not defer to agency managers, and did not include some scientists in the region who expected to be involved (Johnson and Shannon 1994, Nelson 1999, Burgess and Cheek 1999). But the future lies in the question: What kinds of new institutions and political processes are needed to carry forward the ideas in the NWFP? The NWFP is a vision for a new future forest policy, not merely a corrective for past actions. To understand the nature of this vision, we need to employ a set of concepts that allow us to deconstruct the elements of the FEMAT and the NWFP. For this purpose, the concepts of modern and postmodern are useful windows through which to see the FEMAT process and NWFP differently.

What is meant by *modern*? When people started making decisions using information based upon empirical observations and developed through a scientific process linking cause with effect, the Modern Age began. In modern society the authority for making policy choices comes from one's knowledge of facts about the world that are objectively discernible (Gans 1975, 4).

> If we accept values as given and consistent, if we postulate an objective description of the world as it really is, and if we assume that the decision maker's computational powers are unlimited, then . . . we do not need to distinguish between the real world and the decision maker's perception of it: He or she perceives the world as it really is . . . we can predict the choices that will be made by a rational decision maker entirely from our knowledge of the real world and without a knowledge of the decision maker's perceptions or modes of calculation. (Simon 1986, 210–11)

These facts include not only the physical aspects of the world but also personal preferences and the expectation that individuals act based upon their objectively observable interests (e.g., if you are hungry, you will choose food before clothing). Policy choices are based upon empirical analysis; and the *analysis* provides the authority for the choice, not the person or office making it. In order for analysis to provide authority for policy choices, new forms of social organizations have evolved in which experts create information and use it to authorize their actions (Reich 1985, Shannon 1999, Shannon 1998).

Modern society is based upon the assumption that all individuals are rational actors, and their choices are consistent with their objective interests and preferences (Arrow 1963, North 1990). When choices are not in the interest of the individual, then they are considered irrational (Simon 1986). Science searches for general laws in order to predict the behavior of physical, biological, and social systems as well as individual behavior. Policy choices assume predictable relationships between interests and desired outcomes. For example, economics relies upon general laws—like supply and demand—to predict how individual choices lead to predictable collective outcomes. This form of modern society is all most of us have ever known; it seems normal to us, and we do not usually question it since it appears to us as inevitable, not based upon some flimsy assumptions.

Postmodernism provides a critical lens to understand how preferences are endogenous to policies and institutions, rather than exogenous to them. Instead of analyzing the preferences of individuals to understand the nature of their choices, postmodernists analyze the institutions and ideas that create preferences leading to some kinds of choices rather than others (Wildavsky 1987). Rather than viewing policies as a response to preexisting interests and preferences, postmodernists question what preferences are created by policies. For example, individuals might prefer fast cars with big engines; but if policies require fuel efficiency, then the social interest expressed by the institution is for conservation. Postmodernists understand policy as shaping, not just responding to interests and social values. Thus, it is not enough to examine the objective interests of individuals; one must link these interests to the institutions that shape and create them. Again, do people prefer high-fat food from fast-food restaurants, or are their preferences created by a fast-food culture? Postmodernism looks beyond the obvious and asks, why do we see the world as we do? and what power relationships are produced by our concepts and institutions?

In relation to science, postmodernism assumes that facts are constructed by the very processes used to represent them (Ankersmit 1996, Ankersmit 2001). In other words, the scientific method creates a world represented by scientific theories and concepts (Rorty 1979). This does not mean that the physical world is not there; just that what we see is a product of how we represent it to ourselves (Berger and Luckmann 1967). Language is the most obvious way in which we represent the world, and the classic example of cultural difference is that Eskimos have dozens of words for snow, since the subtle differences are central to their survival. Different languages and different theories employ different concepts to represent the world (Rorty 1983, 156).

These examples demonstrate that how we represent what we observe creates what we understand. For this reason, the postmodern reality is a multiple one composed and constructed by the very actors who inhabit it. Does this mean there is no physical reality beyond human invention? No. What it means is that our understanding of this reality is constructed through processes like scientific inquiry, experience, and tradition as we explain the nature of the world to ourselves (Laird 1993).

What Does This Mean for Forests and Forest Management?

Clearly, from a postmodernist view, the question of "what is a forest?" becomes problematic (Luoma 1999). In modernist terms, a forest can be defined as a certain set of observed elements. But in postmodernist terms, a forest is what someone thinks it is. To make this idea clearer, let me take an example familiar to the Pacific Northwest. If a forest is simply a place with trees, then the age of the trees doesn't matter—after all, if they are young, they will grow; and if they are old, they will die and young ones will follow. Okay, so we walk out into an area where only young (say less than 10 years old) trees are growing (in the Pacific Northwest they are likely over 10 feet high). By a modernist definition, this is a forest—it has trees. But what of all the people living in this region who say "no, that is not a forest!"? They are reflecting ideas consistent with postmodernism, wherein a forest is not just a set of elements, but a repository of a set of meanings. These meanings may include many species living there, big trees and little ones, a sense of time and space, and interactions among elements of the ecosystem. These meanings are not apparent in the plantation of young trees, and thus it is not a forest—it may be a collection of young trees, but not a forest. This distinction has long frustrated foresters, who reply that they simply don't understand—after all, the young trees will grow. But even when they do grow, many of the expected components of a forest remain missing—it is merely a collection of middle-aged trees (seldom do they see old age). By defining a plantation of young trees as a forest, forestry institutions exercise power over how forests can be treated by people. This is the postmodern critique of the power-producing aspect of categories.

To clarify this idea, let us take another example related to forestry: defining *ecological integrity* and *ecosystem health*. Just what elements are necessary for ecological integrity? Can a bio-physical system have integrity? A modernist answer would be to describe integrity in terms of scientific, objective, observable facts, based on the assumption that ecosystems have these characteristics and the only problem is adequate definition and proper information. A postmodernist reply would seek to inter-pret the meaning of integrity based on the reasons we would use the term to describe the ecological system. The meaning of eco-logical integrity would be found in the observer, rather than in the observed. Ecological integrity is often used to contrast ecosys-tems with significant degradation through human overuse with ecosystems that are still relatively unmodified. Ecosystem health is a term used to describe a desired state that management and policy should aim to achieve. Thus, modernism assumes these concepts simply describe physical facts, whereas postmodernists examine the underlying normative choices embodied within the concepts as a source of political power and social control. Post-modernist policy analysis seeks to uncover the power relation-ships expressed in institutions and policies. This means that postmodern policy analysis looks critically at understanding how power is expressed in policy as well as what values are cre-ated by different policy approaches (Chatterjee and Finger 1994).

Modern and postmodern describe not the actual nature of reality—both accept that there is "stuff" out there. Rather, these philosophical perspectives serve as critical lenses for policy analysis. Both are useful frameworks for understanding and analysis. The rest of this chapter will apply these frameworks to interpreting the origins, approach, and institutional context of the NWFP in order to look forward to the future challenges fac-ing forest management in the Pacific Northwest and the nation.

NWFP: A Postmodern Plan

The NWFP actually emerged not in ninety days, but over two decades as scientists, judges, managers, politicians, industrialists, interest groups, and the public wrangled over forest management practices. By the time the FEMAT was constituted in April 1993, many of the scientific and legal elements were in place and simply required assembly into a template to guide management that would meet scientifically, legally, and socially acceptable standards. The options developed by the FEMAT grew from pieces accumulated through various scientific efforts to answer the question of how to conserve the ecological systems upon which plant and animal species including old-growth trees were dependent and still utilize the vast resources of the forest for human needs. This question was not new; it was old. But because the policy system failed to respond adequately to this question, the federal courts ordered the agencies to stop all activities related to timber harvesting until they developed a scientifically credible and legally defensible conservation plan for various endangered species and old-growth forest ecosystems (Caldwell et al. 1994).

FEMAT originated from the same impulses that created the previous scientific policy analysis processes—create authority based upon credible science. But the policy problems given to the FEMAT by President Clinton could not be solved by current approaches and existing institutions (Bowersox 2002). New concepts, new policy approaches, and new institutions were needed to address the wicked problems facing forest management. Bringing together scientists from a broad diversity of disciplines began as a modernist strategy seeking to authorize new ideas and new management approaches through scientific analysis. But, the FEMAT scientists were operating within a postmodernist planning process.

The FEMAT options were new representations of the ecosystem, the landscape, the economy, and society (McGinnis 1999). For example, theories of island biogeography played a central role in several of the options. This theory represented the landscape as a series of islands that had to be connected in order to function as elements of the ecosystem. The ecosystem concept focused on the relationships among the parts, rather than viewing the parts (like trees) in isolation. The landscape perspective shifted the scale of representation in order to include spatial relationships among ecological systems, including time. The critical watershed concept represented some watersheds as having special value to the functioning of the ecosystems across the entire region. Thus, the very concepts brought by the scientists to develop the planning options in themselves represented the forest landscape in different ways with different meanings and based on different values. In this way, the FEMAT scientists served as conduits to a set of ideas.

A postmodernist perspective focuses on the new values and interests created by the ideas and their use in FEMAT. These ideas were emerging from new theories that were coalescing around the globe into new forest policy principles. Indeed, these emerging global policy principles were in opposition to the fundamental policy of timber primacy still reigning in the PNW until the courts intervened. These concepts were themselves products of new institutions that grew out of the 1992 World Conference on the Environment and Development. (Recall that President George H. Bush first introduced "ecosystem management" at this conference based upon a June 4, 1992 letter from Forest Service Chief Dale Robertson declaring this the new policy for federal forest management.)

Key Principles of the NWFP

Having looked briefly at the kinds of general policy principles emerging globally in forest policy, let us take a closer look at the articulation of these principles in the development of the NWFP. These principles are expressed by the FEMAT explicitly in the text as well as implicitly in relation to what kinds of options were developed.

Principle 1: Use an Iterative Approach with Long-Term Commitments

While appearing contradictory, this principle is the essence of adaptive management. Although the long-term goal is sustainability, meeting this goal necessitates continuous learning as proximate goals are sought with near-term means. Adaptive management takes the modernist desire for rationality and reason and applies it to reflexive learning and continuous change. Reflexive learning occurs when actions are viewed as opportunities for critical analysis. Thus, scientific information and communicative processes are used to monitor and evaluate the effectiveness of management approaches to meeting proximate goals on the path to sustainability.

Just as people respond to one another in an open, and to some extent indeterminate way, so nature responds to human interventions in sometimes surprising ways. Thus, adaptive management is not just more facts; rather it is an inquiry process in which nature is an actor. Just how nature will respond is more or less open and indeterminate depending on the scale and scope of the intervention. For this reason, monitoring protocols designed by scientists incorporate a contingent response structure (if x, then y; but if z, then w) to facilitate learning about the particularities of the situation. As context-based learning accumulates, better intervention strategies can be developed to achieve desired results, but always with the knowledge that next time the system might respond differently.

Adaptive management is the central mechanism for reflexive learning in the NWFP. However, the practice of adaptive management depends upon the degree of openness in organizations to respond structurally as well as procedurally. This organizational quality remains illusive in the federal agencies governed by the NWFP.

Principle 2: Take a Holistic Approach and Develop Integrated, Cross-Sectoral, and Multi-resource/Multi-functional Plans

The move away from functional resource planning had been growing since the passage of first the National Environmental Policy Act (NEPA) in 1969 and then the National Forest Management Act (NFMA) in 1976. At first, multi-resource plans were simply functional plans stapled together. Initial efforts to multi-resource planning problems popular in the 1970s led to an artificial compartmentalization of the resources that neglected both the relationships among them and the ecosystems giving rise to them. But it did lead to the recognition of the complexity of interactions among resources and within the ecological system. As the saying goes, ecosystems are not only more complex than we think; they are more complex than we can think. Recognition of complexity was joined by recognition of uncertainty and created a new forestry movement in the 1990s, based upon new perspectives. New forestry and new perspectives conceptualized forests as ecosystems and focused on what was left on the land, rather than what was removed.

The NWFP was by design a multi-sector plan that included the ecological, social, economic, administrative, governance, and economic policy aspects related to managing the federal forestlands *in context*. Three teams were involved with the development of the NWFP: the FEMAT focused on development of a conservation strategy and forest policy; a team of economic advisors worked on policy tools for addressing the anticipated regional economic effects of the forest plan; and a team of policy makers developed new cross-agency administrative processes to improve coordination of policy and management.

The NWFP is a virtual plan in that it creates a metaframework revising all the administrative-unit plans of the agencies within the analysis area. In other words, the NWFP exists in relation to how it is interpreted through other planning documents and processes. What the NWFP really did was to change how the federal forests are represented so that other management activities operate within a new context. This is part of what makes it a postmodern plan—it is not implemented through discrete actions, but rather through a process of re-visioning and reinterpretation. This is what is meant by *reflexive*—implementation is a process of "re-looking" at management practices so as to reframe them within a new context.

The NWFP does not simply change a few plans, it transforms planning. No longer can the elements of a forest ecosystem be analyzed independent of each other, without consideration of the large ecological context, and the social and economic relationships defining *resources*. Now the interconnected relationships of ecosystems with social systems mean that management of the parts must be taken in the context of the whole. Planning no longer leads to a plan, which is handed to a manager, who implements it. Now planning is continuous, reflexive learning (Allmendinger 2001, Committee of Scientists 1999). Will agencies that are accustomed to exercising authority through experts be capable of transforming themselves into learning organizations where authority emerges through deliberation? We will have to wait and see.

Principle 3: Use a Capacity-Building Approach That Will Create the Administrative, Scientific, Managerial, Social, and Economic Capacity to Sustainably Manage the Federal Forests

The FEMAT recognized that neither scientists nor managers knew how to manage the federal forests for long-term sustainability of all the forest values, including species dependent upon old-growth forest ecosystems. The FEMAT report included a variety of new institutions and practices designed to build the human, organizational, and technical capacity to carry out sustainable forest management in the Pacific Northwest. For example, recognizing that the region was highly diverse in its landownership patterns, administrative jurisdictions, local communities and economies, history, and culture, the FEMAT developed adaptive management areas to learn about these different contexts and to develop management approaches that fit the particular history and context of specific places. The FEMAT created ten Adaptive Management Areas (AMAs) with some capacity to experiment with different management approaches to conserving species and old growth while producing timber. The FEMAT anticipated that the AMAs would be linked into a learning institution, so that new ideas could be applied to other places once tested and evaluated. While retained by the NWFP, the key elements of funding and learning across the system of AMAs have not been supported by the agencies; thus the contribution of AMAs to learning and reflexivity has been limited.

Another mechanism for capacity building was the linking of local specialists and managers with research scientists in order to refine, site by site, standards and guidelines for protection of forest and aquatic ecosystems. The NWFP provided a set of generic standards and guides to serve as an initial baseline; but only through a communicative process based on contextual factors (history, location, uses, context factors) could place-specific policies be developed, tested, and refined. This communicative mechanism has also been limited by the lack of change in the political environment, leaving agency specialists risk-averse to potential legal challenges to any changes from the default standards and guidelines.

Administrative capacity for integrated planning and adaptive management was clearly a problem, and so new institutions for administrative coordination and cooperation were developed. A framework of communication was created that was place- and context-specific (Provincial Teams) and was linked to interagency coordinative teams (Regional Ecosystem Office). This reliance upon continuous horizontal and vertical communication was intended to develop mutual understanding and improved coordination across agencies, across scales, and among other actors (Ostroff 1999).

Improved administrative capacity was expected to lead to the ability to implement the capacity building and experimental, adaptive management features of the NWFP. Unfortunately the link between resource functions and agency structure and personnel meant that budgets fell precipitously with the NWFP. As personnel, especially experienced staff, were "surplused" in large numbers, the capacity of the agencies to carry out these challenging aspects of the NWFP was drastically reduced. We can still ask: Have the Provincial Teams provided a deliberative forum among scientists, local communities, and managers? Are the interagency coordination processes leading to deliberative processes improving understanding and coordination across agencies? These are empirical questions and will need answers if learning is to occur.

Principle 4: Take a Participatory Approach and Develop Collaborative Mechanisms for Joint and Coordinated Decision Making

While the FEMAT did not engage in face-to-face public participation in developing the report, it did rely on the two decades of public comments, legislative responses, judicial responses, and historical analysis as well as community-based social and economic data. The FEMAT resulted from strong public policy critique of federal forest management, and thus was a product of a democratic process. Because the inability of public institutions to resolve the conflicts over federal forest management gave rise to the FEMAT, it incorporated very strong participatory and collaborative approaches (Yankelovich 1991). First, management decisions would be based upon deliberation among scientists, managers, and members of the public. Second, taking a context or place-specific approach meant that understanding the place required a communicative process. Without involving local people knowledgeable of the particular aspects of the place, its history, changes over time, and events that shaped its current appearance, it would be impossible to really understand the context in order to manage effectively. Scientists are a key element of this communicative process, since they can make visible some of the invisible attributes (e.g., how chemical processes link ecosystem elements together) and processes (e.g., long-term, large-scale disturbance processes) giving a place its particular nature (Shannon 2002a).

Since federal managers do not have control over all the forces and factors affecting the resources they are responsible for managing, a collaborative process is essential. The FEMAT assumed that management would be done in multi-stakeholder teams wherein federal agencies were in partnership with each other and with other key landowners, nongovernmental organizations, community organizations, and individuals. This recognition of planning and managing in context is perhaps the greatest challenge to existing agency culture of expertise and control. Can federal agencies designed to exercise social control through technical expertise become forums for scientific and public deliberation creating the political legitimacy necessary to address contentious public issues?

A twenty-first-century government agency will need to be decentralized and innovative, organized around fluid, multi-stakeholder networks, capable of flexible regulatory responses based upon place-based contextual factors, and capable of rapid change through reflexive processes, like adaptive management

(Benveniste 1994, Kanter 1991). The social and organizational transformations embodied in the NWFP are affecting all of society, not just this one small corner of the world (Bourdieu and Coleman 1991).

In summary, these four principles are the keystones of the FEMAT analysis. While new scientific concepts formed the foundation of the options and their analysis (e.g., a landscape approach, an ecosystem approach, a reserve system), these governing principles provide a coherent framework for understanding the options as transformative agents of political and organizational change. These principles represent a shift away from a modernist approach for policy analysis (simply adding more facts) toward a postmodernist policy analysis (assembling new representations to provide the capacity for new institutions to emerge and new management approaches to evolve). The NWFP is a postmodern plan developed by a postmodern planning process, but will it lead to the kinds of political institutions that can address the complex policy issues in federal forest policy in the Pacific Northwest?

Toward Emergent Governance in Forest Policy

The most important outcome of the NWFP was the creation of a new policy environment for forests. The policy transformation from high federal timber harvest to minimal federal harvest levels happened immediately when President Clinton declared on July 1, 1993, "Option 9 shall be my forest plan."[5] The reserve system that formed the core of Option 9 went from lines on paper to reality overnight. The aquatic conservation strategy designating sizeable riparian buffers along all streams on federal lands was instantly adopted. This was an incredible achievement.[6]

But what aspects of the NWFP did not become instant reality? One way to explain why the elements listed earlier were immediately implemented is that they fit well into a modernist policy approach. The FEMAT provided scientific authority supporting the analysis in the NWFP, and thus the policy elements legitimated by scientific authority were accepted. While environmental groups and industrial associations both challenged the Plan based upon a long list of legal issues (*Seattle Audubon Society v. Lyons* 1994), the basic facts were generally accepted. Because Judge Dwyer declared the NWFP legal based upon its analytical quality, he might be interpreted as modernist. However, Dwyer's finding of legality was based on the postmodernist process elements: continuous monitoring, adaptive management, flexible policy based upon learning, and institutional change. The following excerpt from the 1994 Dwyer decision illustrates this point.

> The ROD [Record of Decision] anticipated that new information affecting forest management within the range of the northern spotted owl would arise, and it provides mechanisms by which decision makers may respond. The survey and manage requirements presume that new information will be discovered regarding the location and populations of certain species, and state that with respect to category two species "where surveys are completed, the information gathered from them should be used to establish managed sites for species."

On a broader level, the NWFP adopts an adaptive management strategy, defined as

> a continuing process of action-based planning, monitoring, researching, evaluation and adjusting with the objective of improving the implementation and achieving the goals of [the ROD]. . . . To be successful, it must have the flexibility to adapt and respond to new information. Under the concept of adaptive management, new information will be evaluated and a decision will be made whether to make adjustments or changes. (ROD at E-12)

The Plan's adaptive management approach is adequate to deal with any new information plaintiffs have identified. If circumstances warrant, the ROD gives the Forest Service and Bureau of Land Management (BLM) the flexibility to reduce or halt logging in order to comply with their statutory mandates. (See *Seattle Audubon v. Lyons*, 871 F. Supp. at 1321 ["New information may require that timber sales be ended or curtailed."]) But they are not required to conduct a new Supplemental Environmental Impact

Statement (SEIS) at this point. (See *Enos v. Marsh*, 769 F.2d 1363, 1373-74 [9th Cir. 1985]), upholding the decision not to conduct SEIS despite nearly 50 percent increase in the size of the project. If the wildlife survey requirements were abolished or substantially weakened, the outcome under NEPA might be different.

Adaptive management presumes that when management strategies are not achieving desired goals, new strategies are created. Such a management approach relies upon the flexibility of managers and organizations to incorporate new practices and new policies easily. However, bureaucratic organizations are designed to carry out routine management strategies aimed at providing consistent and predictable actions over time (Crozier 1964, Kamenka 1989). Looking at the Forest Service, for example, historically the structure of the agency reflected specialized areas of expertise and management responsibilities (e.g., timber staff, wildlife staff, recreation staff, planning staff). Each functional division operated according to accepted policies and relied upon codified management techniques. This form of organization is highly effective as long as its environment is stable and predictable (Hage and Aiken 1970).

Not surprisingly, in times of social turmoil and political demands for change, it is difficult for a bureaucracy to simply incorporate new ideas without changing its structure and personnel. When technical management approaches are strongly reflected in organizational structures, developing new approaches most likely means creating new organizational forms with new capacities and personnel. When technical knowledge located in experts is linked to the structure of an organization, strategic change in response to new information is impeded by the structure (Kaufman 1960). The Forest Service has been reorganizing itself since the 1970s, when NEPA demanded an interdisciplinary approach and NFMA required integrated management plans. However, these reorganization efforts fit easily into a modernist perspective of adding expertise and using multidisciplinary teams to create management plans. It is not surprising (but interesting) that the policy elements in the NWFP that fit existing agency capacity, culture, and expertise were adopted more readily than those that did not.

If twentieth-century public policy were to be characterized using two words, they might be *consistency* and *expertise.* Organizations and policies over this past century exhibited a strong commitment to achieving fairness procedurally, by treating individuals or situations the same (Scott 1998). Defining *sameness* led to the need for standardization and categorization—as illustrated by the concept of *forest.* Standardization meant that things were defined based upon a designated set of categories.

Time, for example, was standardized according to when the sun reached the zenith so that trains moving across the country could predict what time they would arrive at distant destinations. Railroad tracks were standardized to a specific size to facilitate transportation. Forests were standardized according to concepts like the regulated forest, where a forest area was divided into units equal to the rotation age of the entire management area. Or, to take another example, *sustained yield,* where the amount of harvest is to equal the annual growth (see Beuter, this volume). These concepts sought to stabilize the meanings of the forest so that scientific forest management could be applied by experts (foresters) without the need for political consultation. By treating all forests with these same categories, however, the other social values and interests in forests were ignored by experts. Limited public participation insulated expert decisions from adapting to changes in social values. Ignoring these values led to the public controversies over forest management continuing today.

From a postmodernist perspective, concepts are value based and explicitly serve powerful interests in society. Rather than being merely empirical facts about what existed, these concepts created the facts. Is a fully regulated forest simply a physical fact, or is it a normative idea? This is one way to understand the critiques of forest management today—a critical assessment of power and interest.

Another approach is to embrace the postmodernist understanding of difference and differentiation. Rather than a one-size fits all approach, a postmodern forest policy would look to differences in context, history, culture, values, and location to develop policies appropriate to the place (Giddens 1991). This urge toward place-based management found in forest policy today can be traced to the failure of standardized management prescriptions to adequately take into account the differences in site and location factors. Unfortunately, so far the one-size-fits-all, default standards and guidelines in the NWFP remain in place due to a lack of agency leadership and a failure to create collaborative deliberation among scientists, technical experts, managers, and the public (Shannon 2002a). Until collaborative deliberation within an open network of participants links the representative power of science with the preference formation of politics, the NWFP will remain an imposition of power rather than a liberating institution.

This relationship between global policy principles and contextualized, or place-based, forest management is a defining feature of postmodern forest policy. Figure 16.1 is a simple schematic that represents the new governance framework for forests.

Important to notice in this schematic is the lack of a tightly linked vertical delegation of political authority. Rather, this is a loosely coupled policy system coordinated through communicative processes. *Participatory approaches* refers to the necessary engagement of multi-stakeholder groups, including scientists, in a collaborative public deliberation. *Cross-sectoral policy integration* refers to the necessity of coordination of policy across sectors

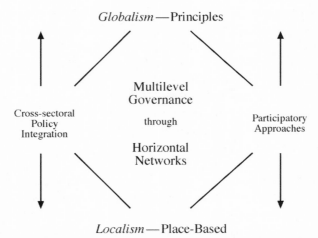

Figure 16.1. Emergent Governance: Multilevel Institutions and Participatory Processes. This new governance framework for forests is coupled by ideas and actors, rather than structures or procedures.

(forestry, transportation, human services, health, etc.) as well as within a sector (public and private forestry). *Multilevel governance* means that there are policy processes at all levels (global, national, regional, local) and across multiple sectors and types of actors. These actors are organized into *horizontal networks* at the different scales, and communicative processes (policy integration and participatory approaches) provide linkages across these networks, not top-down mandates or formal procedures. In an emergent governance framework, ideas and actors are the essential connective elements, rather than procedures or structures. The essential feature of this framework is that it is emergent—it emerges through action rather than existing as fixed structures (Calhoun 1991).[7]

Generative Politics: Building Institutions for a Sustainable Region

Innovation and change depend on our ability to invent and reinvent ideas and institutions. *Generative politics* refers to the capacity to create new meanings by inventing new ideas. Generative politics creates new social capital and new political capacity for new forms of action. Generative politics forms new social organizations based upon new values and new interests. All of this occurs through participation in political deliberation—a democratic form of political dialogue.

The capacity for generative politics arises from new institutions that lead to new social values through new social valuations. Valuation—what something is worth to an individual or a society—is a political process (Reich 1985). Valuation is not the same as price or willingness to pay, and so cannot be understood only through economic analysis. Rather, valuation is a social process of assigning value. For example, when wood is believed to be the primary value of a forest, then protecting and enhancing that value is an important social goal. When biodiversity is believed to be a primary value of a forest ecosystem, then protecting and enhancing that value is a social goal. As this example illustrates, social goals can conflict and yet be based equally strongly on social values (Minteer and Taylor 2002). When goals conflict but are equally desirable, we look to institutions to understand how these goals and values are reconciled.

Institutions are built from valuations, and thus are social solutions to problems of competing goals and values. For example, forest policy is an institution that provided a stable set of rules allocating values to forests to create a predictable environment for conservation, use, and investment. The NWFP created different institutional rules based upon different valuations. While scientists and many stakeholders expected this new institution to provide new rules for predictable behavior, this has not happened. The best example is the goal of providing a predictable harvest level of timber off the federal forest lands. The NWFP provided a set of rules under which some old-growth trees could be harvested in order to improve the quality of the forest and habitat while at the same time supporting a sustainable forest industry and forest-based communities. The NWFP created the matrix to represent forest lands available for timber production in combination with other goals related to biodiversity and ecosystem protection. To date little harvest has occurred in the matrix, due to continued political controversy over the harvest of old growth. In contrast, the designation of old-growth reserves also provided for the removal of some trees in order to enhance the quality of the old growth. In these areas, timber harvest has moved forward in part because the prioritization of social values gave clearer predictability to the limits of potential actions.

The analysis in this chapter suggests a way to understand this apparent contradiction: when institutional rules address valuation questions, then predictable action may result. However, sometimes—as in the case of the matrix—the political contest over values cannot simply be resolved through deliberation. This suggests that the problem is the need for institutional responses—but what kinds?

What Have We Learned?

First, participatory and multi-stakeholder political processes are necessary to create social valuations (Cortner and Shannon 1993,

Press 1994, Shannon 2002a, Shannon 2003a). Rather than expect a simple consensus, or agreement on a single set of values (Landy and Plotkin 1982), the desired outcome is a social valuation that creates predictable rules for future action (Reich 1985). But, this is not a computational algorithm to be applied by experts acting alone. Rather, it is a continuous process of reflexive action wherein learning based upon deliberation is the predictable process—not a single management prescription (Braun and Duguid 1991). Thus, when the problem is a need for iterative processes and adaptive management, this form of action becomes the predictable rule of the institution (Haas et al. 1993, 20).

Second, creating learning organizations and institutions means embedding the ability for change and reflection within organizational forms and institutional rules (Shannon 2003b). Lance Gunderson has called "for new institutions that actively learn and respond to their environment" (Gunderson 1999, 38). Active learning means not only receiving information but also producing new behavior based on that information. Active learning occurs at those moments when information does not conform to expectations— surprise (Gunderson 1999, 32). This reflexive process—looking inward to create new capacity—requires a responsive organizational structure (Weick 1990). Kai Lee (1993) termed this kind of learning double-loop learning, in that the goals of the organization are open to change, not just the means (single-loop learning). Typically, adaptive management is viewed as learning about the means; but in the NWFP, adaptive management means learning about the goals. For this reason, the NWFP requires an institutional environment characterized by cross-sectoral linking relationships through participatory processes and cross-scale linkages through networks of multilevel governance.

Third, the NWFP exists only through action (Van Dijk 1997). Words on paper do not make a plan. A plan is a framework for future action—it creates the future. The transformative power of the NWFP lies in its representations of a new forest, new interests, and new social values. These representations open new public questions for political dialogue.

This is the challenge given to the region by the NWFP; not answers or rigid prescriptions, but questions and open possibilities.

Will the people in the Pacific Northwest create a politics to match their glorious scenery?

Notes

This chapter is based on a talk given at the Forest Futures Conference at Williamette University in Salem, Oregon, on September 25, 2002. My thanks to Guyora Binder for long conversations about postmodernism and for sharing his unpublished manuscript, "The Aesthetic Value of Law," with me; to Norm Johnson for discussing the NWFP and helping to make this analysis accurate; and to Errol Meidinger for reviewing my first attempts with this chapter and helping to clarify the argument. Errors and weaknesses are mine, but this chapter is strengthened by the time and effort of my friends who read and thought about it.

1. Total federal acres in FEMAT analysis (acres within the range of the northern spotted owl): 24.3 million; total forested federal acres = 20.4 million. Non-federal acres within the range of the northern spotted owl: 32.7 million (source: FEMAT 1993). The 24.3 million acres breaks down as follows: Forest Service, 19.4; Bureau of Land Management, 2.7; National Park Service, 2.0; other federal, 0.2 (source: FEMAT 1993).

2. Two Forest Service Regions (5 and 6), nineteen national forests, and seven Bureau of Land Management districts are governed by the NWFP.

3. This chapter separates the FEMAT from the NWFP analytically in order to discuss the sources of ideas, nature of the process, and importance of relationships in creating the framework embodied in the FEMAT report. The NWFP represents the joint product of the FEMAT report and scientists, the agency teams that wrote the Environmental Impact Statement, the intervention of agency scientists and managers in adding components not included in the FEMAT, and the response to public comments. All of these factors are represented within the Record of Decision that is the formal statement of the NWFP, but the plan itself rests in the revisions to the administrative plans for federal administrative units.

4. These principles are common to national and international forest policy regimes. For example, they were formally adopted by a multinational policy-making body, the Ministerial Conference for the Pro-

tection of Forests in Europe (MCPFE), in its policy position on national forest programs published in April 2002.

5. As a matter of law, the NWFP did not officially revise the twenty-eight administrative unit plans until the publication of the Record of Decision on April 13, 1994.

6. I am indebted to Dr. K. Norman Johnson for reminding me of the remarkable nature of these achievements.

7. The observation from Craig Calhoun focuses on an emerging split between the everyday life of interpersonal relationships and the mode of organization and integration in large-scale complex systems. This societal trend is revealed in the decoupling of forest policy from simple responsiveness to political interests and a shift toward a policy of transformative institutions.

Conclusion: Forests Past and Forests Future—Connecting Science, Politics, and Policy

Joe Bowersox and Karen Arabas

Forests mean many things to many people. For some, forests represent the immensity, beauty, and sheer awe-inspiring grandeur of nature: to paraphrase John Muir, forests are nature's magnificent cathedrals, within which humanity may find sanctuary, reflection, and humility (Muir 1912). In this view, forests are meaningful because they are an antidote to the pace, priorities, and scale of civilization, and put us back in touch with nature and a worldview that we have forgotten. For others, forests are a vast reservoir of renewable wealth that, with proper management, can be harvested indefinitely across the generations. Like Pinchot (1947), this view may argue that this natural wealth should be managed for the greatest good, and for the greatest number. Some see forests as habitat for everything from microbes to pine martins (*Martes americana*), or as a collection of biotic and abiotic elements providing critical ecosystem services to humans and non-humans alike. Others look at a forest and see living history—the ways of their ancestors, the economic engine of change for a region, the prize over which many a political battle has been waged. To complicate matters further, these meanings are not mutually exclusive. Individuals may affirm any or all of these meanings. Thus it should not be surprising that when debates occur regarding the fate of the forests of the Pacific Northwest (PNW) or the nation generally, it appears we are at war with ourselves—for in a sense, we are.

This book is a depiction of that ongoing, internal war. Careful reading of the authors' contributions reveals that none of them fit simplistic stereotypes: most recognize several meanings of PNW forests. In one sense, that in itself reflects how complicated the issue of forest management in the PNW (and the nation) has become over the last ten years. The viewpoints of the authors also reflect the diversity and conflict of views of the public at large. Recent surveys suggest that Northwesterners care about their forests, follow the decisions made regarding those forests, and yet simultaneously possess management goals prone to evoke conflict. They wish to protect biological diversity and health of forests yet maximize timber extraction. They want to preserve old growth yet harvest second growth. Forests must support a variety of jobs, not simply those related to timber extraction. Most feel that many uses of the forest are incompatible, yet they want each to have its own place (Ribe and Silvaggio 2002, Davis et al. 2001). Trying to discern the management implications of this "have your cake and eat it too" view is a complex and daunting enterprise, for it indicates that ultimately the citizenry believes that commodity production and the maintenance of forest ecosystems are reconcilable. Hence, they demand policies reflecting that reconciliation.

The Northwest Forest Plan (NWFP) was indeed designed to do just that. What these authors appear to agree upon is that the NWFP has not and probably never will achieve its conflicting goals. But what have we learned from their interpretations of the successes and failures of the NWFP ten years after its inception that might better direct forest policy generally over the next ten years? We see several critical issues emerging. First, what ought to be the role of public forestlands, and at what scale (local vs. national) should that role be defined? Second, assuming we desire a balance between social values and ecosystem requirements, how might that balance best be achieved? Finally, given the momentum emerging toward a paradigm shift in management from the passive to active model (Thomas, Perry, Swanson, Shannon, this volume) how might institutions be organized to most effectively shepherd and coordinate forest management (Kitzhaber, Bowersox, Shannon, this volume)? We raise these questions here not in any attempt to answer them fully, but rather to further the ongoing debate and dialogue.

Defining the Role of Public Forestlands and the Scale of Decision Making

As highlighted in this volume, our overarching public forest management philosophy in the United States evolved in response to a variety of conditions experienced by settlers, and by the mid-twentieth century a commodity-driven, agricultural model dominated. In the 1960s and 1970s, in the wake of rising affluence and increasing environmental concern, federal and state governments passed a broad array of environmental laws that redirected forest management, and in turn set the stage for later policy change. Yet, such legislation has channeled (and even inhibited) efforts to improve management for forest ecosystems. The past can act as a barrier to change (see Shannon, Bowersox, this volume). Two important questions are raised here. First, what ought to be the role of public forest lands? If we were to start from scratch tomorrow, with no Multiple Use and Sustained Yield Act (MUSYA), no Endangered Species Act (ESA), no National Forest Management Act (NFMA), and no Federal Land Policy and Management Act (FLPMA), how might we reconceptualize forest management? Would we focus solely on habitat? Extractive resources? Intrinsic values? Some combination or subset of these? What sort of organizational arrangements would we create in order to implement those management objectives, and how would we construct proper incentives for managers to fulfill them? Our second question relates to the scale at which forest policy decisions should be made. We ask: should forest policy decisions reflect local, regional, national or even global values and objectives? Should we choose to redefine who has the expertise to make these decisions? Should that decision come from Congress, the executive branch, the judicial system, or the public?

Together, these two questions regarding the role of public forest lands and the scale of decision making aptly summarize present and future forest controversies. Current debates over forest health provide an excellent example of how existing decision-making processes inhibit stakeholders and decision makers from reaching consensus on the role of public forest lands. Though all parties agree on the importance of forest health, they cannot agree on its definition, its causes, and its solutions. Because the debate occurs in an adversarial arena (Congresss and the courts, for example) a strategic dualism is fostered, compelling the participants to take oversimplified positions fitting traditional stereotypes, such as commodity interests versus the environmental community. Sadly, this may prevent parties with varying, though not mutually exclusive goals and values from finding common ground.

The issue of scale of decision making is a battle that has been waged for more than 100 years, since the first federal forest reserves were established over the objections of local political and economic elites. Over the years, various initiatives have been undertaken to ameliorate the conflict—from Pinchot's desire that foresters be from the local community (Pinchot 1947) to the NWFP's creation of regional and provincial advisory committees consisting of local stakeholders as well as federal agency personnel. While some of these "bridge building" efforts have had tangible benefits (see Yaffee and Wondolleck 1997), present debates still focus on the extent to which local communities and states should have influence (if not control) over federal forest lands within their jurisdiction, and the extent to which federal judges should enforce national environmental mandates over apparent local and regional objections.

Given the implacable nature of these questions of role and scale, we are not sure that our present mandates and institutions are adequate to the task of reconciling these conflicts. In fact, the mandates and institutions are themselves the result of 100 years of political conflict over these concerns; they represent political resilience and adaptation but they certainly have not provided lasting resolution. Nevertheless, it is worthwhile to reconsider this dilemma in light of an issue raised by Bob

Pepperman Taylor (this volume) when he observed, "While the politics may look like the problem to those inside the policy system . . . from the perspective of citizens at large the politics looks more like the best solution available." This ultimately requires us to reconsider our democratic commitments and the extent to which we are willing to entrust a group of individuals (whether local or national, elected or unelected) to manage resources with the common good in mind.

An Impossible Balancing Act? Digging Deeper

Should we agree that we need a philosophy driving forest management that reconciles social values and ecosystem requirements (and research seems to indicate that most people desire such balance), how do we achieve that balance? The old commodity-driven, agricultural model of the post–World War II era made sense at a time when complex ecological relationships were not well understood (if their existence was even recognized at all), and the nation needed wood products. Over the past thirty years our appreciation for the importance of ecological complexity has increased, though certainly there is still much to learn. But despite this greater realization of the biophysical characteristics of forest ecosystems, we still are at a loss as to how we can reconcile the needs of human communities with the basic requirements of these same ecosystems.

Part of the problem is that current policy initiatives such as the Healthy Forests Restoration Act of 2003 (HFRA) and even the NWFP attempt a balance through a single lens. This monocular approach is perhaps understandable, given the context in which these initiatives were created. The primary context within which the NWFP was created was a political and legal gridlock, arising from earlier administrations' refusal to adequately address the habitat requirements of federally listed endangered species: without rewriting or repealing NEPA, ESA, NFMA, *and* the FLPMA, federal forest managers and their political counterparts would be held accountable. Hence, despite efforts to include timber values within the NWFP (i.e., the now almost legendary "promise" of a commodity volume of 1.1 billion board feet per year), it is first and foremost a species recovery plan. When conditionally approving the NWFP in 1994, Judge Dwyer was not concerned with its commodity projections, but with its biological sufficiency (*Seattle Audubon v. Lyons* 1994). Unfortunately, in light of current evidence regarding the state of species recovery under the Plan (see Ackers, this volume) and the vulnerability of the created "habitat islands" to disturbance events,[1] it is questionable whether the NWFP is succeeding even when viewed through this single lens.

The HFRA and similar policy initiatives are afflicted with a comparable myopia. These initiatives are less concerned about endangered species and habitat than with the risk of communities and commodities to fire. Hence, the HFRA attempts to reduce fire risk at the wildland-urban interface (WUI) and protect extractive resources by reducing fire's impact on the landscape through fuel removal/reduction. To some extent fuels reduction is critical to restoring more natural fire regimes (see Perry, this volume) and thus *may* improve critical habitat. However, to the extent that fuels reduction and fire suppression become the goals, rather than eventual restoration of more natural fire regimes, this approach is dangerous and ultimately self-defeating. Indeed, while many of the scientists examining restoration in fire-adapted forest ecosystems stress the problems of fuel loads and species composition outside the range of historical variability, they also note that fuels management techniques may not necessarily promote other management objectives like species protection (see Landres et al. 1999, Swetnam et al. 1999). To paraphrase the argument of one member of Congress during House floor debates of the HFRA, one way to solve the forest fire problem is to leave no tree behind: no forest, no problem. But then no habitat either (see Stark 2003).

The focus on fire and fire mitigation illustrates the contemporary conflict over our forest management priorities more clearly than do concerns over species, if simply because fire disturbances at work upon the land are stochastic, immense, and immediately visible to the public. Most of our western forests are fire-prone, with a broad range of fire return intervals (see Arabas and Bowersox, this volume). Fires become "catastrophic" and "tragic" only through the lens of human values placed at risk, whether they be private property, timber, or endangered species habitat. Should we desire truly "healthy forests" at some point in the future, we are going to have to learn to coexist with fire as it occurs in its natural spatial and temporal rhythms on the landscape—as do the species dependent upon that landscape. To this end, an approach that enhances our ability to coexist with this critical natural disturbance process rather than exacerbating it seems to make social, political, economic, and ecological sense. To illustrate, let's turn for a moment to another natural disturbance with which we must coexist: hurricanes. Though it is not a perfect analogy to fire, examining our policy and strategy regarding hurricanes provides insight into alternative strategies for living with wildfire.

Since 1900 approximately 165 hurricanes have stuck the U.S. mainland: 65 of these have been "major" hurricanes (Jarrell et al. 2001). Our strategy for coping with this natural disturbance is not based on attempts to stop or alter the disturbance itself—that would be impossible. Rather, our approach has been to reduce loss of life and economic damage by making people less vulnerable to the impacts of hurricanes: developing hurricane prediction systems, coordinating evacuation procedures, and implementing zoning restrictions.[2] Just as with hurricanes, we suggest that possibilities exist for making people less vulnerable to fire in a way that keeps fire on the landscape performing its critical ecological functions. Consider the following examples of where this has already happened on a small scale.

Over 1.3 million hectares (3.3 million acres) of Oregon forestland and some 225,000 private homes valued at over $6 billion are in the WUI. Recognizing the need to not only reduce the risk to people and property yet also require personal accountability for those who live in fire-prone ecosystems, in 1997 the Oregon legislature passed Senate Bill (SB) 360, the Oregon Forestland-Urban Interface Fire Protection Act. SB 360 requires homeowners in the WUI to take proactive measures to improve the fire resistance of their homes and reduce fine fuels near them. Without actual certification of such measures, homeowners are responsible for the first $100,000 of fire mitigation and response costs in the event of wildfire (State of Oregon 1997). To promote compliance, the State of Oregon provides small grants to homeowners and homeowner associations, and estimates compliance costs at about $300 per household (Ballou 2003, personal communication).

In addition to making individuals more aware of the ecosystem in which they live and more responsible for the choices they make in living there, other efforts are under way to protect people and improve forest health. In central Oregon on the Sister's Ranger District, a small-fuels reduction project along the Highway 20 corridor has begun. The project utilizes prescribed fire, brush removal, and noncommercial thinning to remove small-diameter trees. It includes an extensive public participation component, involving various stakeholders such as homeowners and environmental groups. While not without controversy, the project has moved forward and may serve as an example for similar collaborative projects (CEC n.d.).

The Promise and Perils of Adaptive Ecosystem Management: Implementing a New Paradigm

Such steps are necessary if we are going to give more than mere lip service to the notion of improving the health of fire-adapted ecosystems. Clearly, when compared to the previous multiple-use paradigm, the NWFP and its espousal of ecosystem management was a more comprehensive, holistic, and robust plan that recognized in theory (if not in practice) the interrelationship of management actions and ecosystem effects. In essence, it sought to close the loop. However, as several authors here have pointed out, a major shortcoming has been our failure to fully implement adaptive management in land classifications for which it was intended, especially matrix and Adaptive Management Areas (AMAs), and to a lesser extent, Late-Successional Reserves (LSRs) and Riparian Reserves (Rohlf, Mitchell et al., Shannon, this volume). Part of the problem has been our relative inexperience with taking the concept of ecosystem and adaptive management and using it in applied settings (but see Johnson et al. 1999a). Though we have the will, we don't seem to have the way.

As noted by Thomas, Perry and Rohlf (this volume), this was due in great measure to the "survey-and-manage" provisions of the NWFP, which provided additional habitat protection for sensitive species not specifically covered by the Plan. FEMAT could have drafted a plan that was essentially a single, vast, lightly managed sea of reserve lands with matrix islands available for intensive commodity production within it (see Perry 1994, 569). However, this would have caused greater political controversy. Instead, FEMAT drafted a plan with fewer reserve areas and connectivity corridors in a sea of matrix. Yet, in effect, survey-and-manage implementation has reversed the nature of the sea—leading to distrust and disappointment on the part of environmentalists and industry alike.

Several other factors have inhibited implementation of the NWFP's adaptive management provisions. One important factor is simply the lack of funds and personnel available for implementation. National forests throughout the Northwest have seen reductions in workforce on the average of over 40 percent—with some Forest Service units losing more than 60 percent of their personnel. There simply are fewer bodies available to do the planning, treatments, and monitoring necessary. Similarly, money just isn't available for experimental treatments that are not commercially viable to improve stand structures. In addition to personnel and resource constraints, most forest managers find few incentives to proceed with management activities to increase diversity in stand composition and improve, enhance, or create habitat (Stankey et al. 2003). Finally, as Rohlf points out, the "science process" occurring at the government agency level lacks transparency. The body of knowledge upon which we base much of our management decisions is research generated by government agencies that has not gone through the traditional, rigorous peer-review process that is the standard for scientific research.

Clearly, we don't have the process or structure in place to adequately implement adaptive ecosystem management (Shannon, Kitzhaber, Bowersox, Rohlf, this volume). In Shannon's emergent governance model (this volume) this is best achieved by an institution with a "responsive organizational structure," in which behaviors as well as goals will change based on new information. We are intrigued by the possibilities for generating such new information. What follows is our take on the critical elements of new information and a brief example of the process for gathering and processing that information, applicable to a range of natural resources issues, not just forests.

Like Shannon, we maintain that the scale and scope of the desired information is best defined based on linkages and communicative processes in an emergent governance framework, consisting of various stakeholders, including scientists, managers, public officials, interest groups, and community members. This could be a landscape-scale bioregional endeavor (e.g., NWFP, ICBEMP, or the Sierra Nevada Ecosystem Project), or a framework created to plan and implement a local hazardous fuels reduction project.

Such frameworks require information or research to clarify the problem, select an alternative approach, and move toward implementation. The overarching characteristics necessary for generating a more reflexive process and better outcomes are transparency and context in the information gathering or research endeavor. By *transparency* we mean the methods by which data is collected as well as the consistency, rigor, and availability of the data. *Context* implies that data must be interpreted within a framework informed by the broader ecological, social, historical, and political conditions that produced it.

Transparency and context are assured only when the research community is redefined to reach across disciplinary boundaries from the natural to the social sciences, as well as across institutional divisions among agency personnel, academic researchers, and not-for-profit groups.[3] Transparency also requires establishment and application of rigorous standards to data collection and analysis, as well as a commitment to ongoing monitoring. This includes expanding the scope of information to include past, present, and the range of future ecological, political, social, and economic conditions.

More transparent and contextualized information does not assure better decision making. Indeed, decision makers at all levels now have—due to the World Wide Web—fingertip access to a plethora of forest-related data sets and analyses, ranging from Government Accounting Office reports on fire fighting costs to satellite imagery on forest cover. While some information may (often haphazardly) find its way into the decision-making process, much goes unheeded or even unnoticed. Hence, it is imperative to improve the transfer and dissemination of information to stakeholders and decision makers, providing them appropriate opportunity for review, response, and possibly redirection of the information gathering itself.

Such an iterative, nonlinear process requires greater coordination and integration of the research and decision-making communities themselves. Additionally, each must recognize the unique and functionally necessary characteristics of the other: the research community must recognize the fiscal, social, and even political constraints of the decision-making community, along with its need for timely "useable knowledge." Similarly, the decision-making community must understand the importance of the research community's norms of thoroughness, caution, and peer review. Too often, we believe, the two communities simply dismiss each other as a world apart, unrelated and perhaps irrelevant to the other's mission. We hope that one of the lasting legacies of the NWFP may be a greater realization of the two communities' interdependence.

The future of the NWFP and of federal forest policy generally is uncertain. The beginning of the twenty-first century finds us at a critical juncture in the way that we think about, understand, and manage our forestlands. The NWFP seeks to reconcile the multiple demands that we place upon these critical ecosystems, and for good or for ill, has inspired much debate regarding how best to address these demands. Although presently we lack the organizational structure, political consensus, and financial commitment necessary to implement the Plan, or one like it, what is increasingly evident from this volume is that there will be forests in our future. How those are managed and the values they will embody depend upon our willingness to be creative, flexible, and humble.

Notes

1. Witness the impact on the Late-Successional Reserve (LSR) and spotted owl habitat in the 2002 Biscuit Fire in Southern Oregon. Thirty-two percent of the LSR was inside the burn perimeter, with more than 20 percent suffering high-canopy mortality. Over 67,000 acres of critical habitat were within the fire. The impacts upon the northern spotted owl are not yet clear (See USFS 2003b, 8, 16, 96). What is clear is that static designations of habitat may be inadequate for protecting species in ecosystems with mixed-severity or stand-replacing fire disturbance regimes.

2. Note that this strategy is not perfect and has been subject to much criticism for a variety of reasons (see Pielke 1997).

3. To some extent this is being realized in the national network of Cooperative Ecosystem Studies Units (CESUs) established by Congress in 1998. For more information see www.cesu.org/cesu/.

References

These references are followed by a list of court cases.

Aber, J., et al., 2000. "Applying Ecological Principles to the Management of the U.S. National Forests." *Issues in Ecology* 6:1–20.

Adams, R. 2001. "Bush Attack on Regulations for Arsenic, Surface Mining Has Democrats Vowing Action." *CQ Weekly*, March 24, 670.

———. 2002. "Senate to Consider Bush's Call to Thin Forests of Fire Hazards." *CQ Weekly*, September 7, 2309.

Agee, J. K. 1993. *Fire Ecology of Pacific Northwest Forests.* Washington, D.C.: Island Press.

Alcock, F. in press. "A Contrast of Assessment Failure in New England and Newfoundland." In *Global Environmental Assessments: Information, Institutions, and Influence,* ed. R. B. Mitchell, W. C. Clark, D. W. Cash, and F. Alcock. Cambridge, Mass.: MIT Press.

Alexander, J. C. 1988. *Action and Its Environments.* New York: Columbia University Press.

Allmendinger, P. 2001. *Planning in Postmodern Times.* London: Routledge Press.

Amaranthus, M. P., J. M. Trappe, L. Bednar, and D. Arthur. 1994. "Hypogeous Fungal Production in Mature Douglas-Fir Forest Fragments and Surrounding Plantations and Its Relation to Coarse Woody Debris and Animal Mycophagy." *Canadian Journal of Forest Research* 24:2157–65.

Anderson, D. R., and K. P. Burnham. 1992. "Demographic Analysis of Northern Spotted Owl Populations." In *Draft Recovery Plan for the Northern Spotted Owl*, 319–28. Portland, Ore.: U.S. Department of the Interior, Fish and Wildlife Service.

Anderson, T. L. 1999, December 19. "Truly Sustainable." *PERC Reports*, Bozeman, Mont.

Anderson, T. L., and D. R. Leal. 1997. *Enviro-capitalists: Doing Good While Doing Well*. Lanham, Md.: Rowman & Littlefield.

———. 2001. *Free Market Environmentalism*. New York: Palgrave.

Andonova, L. B. in press. "Structure and Influence of International Assessments: Lessons from Eastern Europe." In *Global Environmental Assessments: Information, Institutions, and Influence*, ed. R. B. Mitchell, W. C. Clark, D. W. Cash, and F. Alcock. Cambridge, Mass.: MIT Press.

Andrews, H. J., and R. W. Cowlin. 1940. *Forest Resources of the Douglas-Fir Region*. (Misc. Pub. 389). Washington, D.C.: USDA Forest Service.

Ankersmit, F. R. 1996. *Aesthetic Politics: Political Philosophy Beyond Fact and Value*. Stanford, Calif.: Stanford University Press.

———. 2001. *Historical Representation*. Stanford, Calif.: Stanford University Press.

Arendt, H. 1989. *Lectures on Kant's Political Philosophy*, ed. R. Beiner. Chicago: University of Chicago Press.

Arnhart, L. 1998. *Darwinian Natural Right: The Biological Ethics of Human Nature*. Albany: State University of New York Press.

Arrow, K. J. 1963. *Social Choice and Individual Values*, 2d ed. New Haven, Conn.: Yale University Press.

Baker, W. 1992. "Effects of Settlement and Fire Suppression on Landscape Structure." *Ecology* 73(5):1879–87.

Barker, R. 1993. *Saving All the Parts: Reconciling Economics and the Endangered Species Act*. Washington, D.C.: Island Press.

Barnes, B. V., D. R. Zak, S. R. Denton, and S. H. Spurr. 1998. *Forest Ecology*. New York: Wiley.

Bart, J., and E. D. Forsman. 1992. "Dependence of Northern Spotted Owls, *Strix occidentalis caurina*, on Old-Growth Forests in the Western USA." *Biological Conservation* 62:95–100.

Baumgartner, F., and B. D. Jones. 1993. *Agendas and Instability in American Politics*. Chicago: University of Chicago Press.

Bean, M. J. 1998. "The Endangered Species Act and Private Land: Four Lessons Learned from the Past Quarter Century." *Environmental Law Reporter* 28:10701–2.

Bengston, D. N., D. P. Fan, and D. N. Celarier. 1999. "A New Approach to Monitoring the Social Environment for Natural Resource Management and Policy: The Case of U.S. National Forest Benefits and Values." *Journal of Environmental Management* 56:181–93.

Benveniste, G. 1994. *The Twenty-First Century Organization: Analyzing Current Trends, Imagining the Future.* San Francisco: Jossey-Bass.

Berger, P. L., and T. Luckmann. 1967. *The Social Construction of Reality.* Garden City, N.Y.: Anchor Books, Doubleday.

Beuter, J. H. 1974. "Forest Regulation: Farewell to the Simple Formula—an Introduction." *Journal of Forestry* 72(4):212–13.

———. 1998a. *Legacy and Promise: Oregon's Forests and Wood Products Industry.* Portland: Oregon Forest Resources Institute.

———. 1998b. *Ballot Measure 64: Its Potential Impact on Oregon's Forests and Forest Economy.* Salem: Oregon Forest Industry Council (unpublished).

Beuter, J. H., K. N. Johnson, and H. L. Scheurman. 1976. *Timber for Oregon's Tomorrow: An Analysis of Reasonably Possible Occurrences.* Research Bulletin 19, Forest Research Lab. Corvallis: Oregon State University.

Biermann, F. in press. "Whose Experts? The Role of Geographic Representation in Scientific Advisory Institutions." In *Global Environmental Assessments: Information, Institutions, and Influence,* ed. R. B. Mitchell, W. C. Clark, D. W. Cash, and F. Alcock. Cambridge, Mass.: MIT Press.

Blank, R., and S. Hines. 2001. *Biology and Political Science.* New York: Routledge.

Bolsinger, C. L., and K. L. Waddell. 1993. *Area of Old-Growth Forests in California, Oregon, and Washington* (Resource Bulletin PNW-RB-197). Portland, Ore.: U.S. Forest Service Pacific Northwest Research Station.

Bond, W. J. 1994. "Keystone Species." In *Biodiversity and Ecosystem Function,* ed. E. D. Schulze and H. A. Mooney, 237–53. New York: Springer-Verlag.

Bosworth, D. 2000. Testimony before the Subcommittee on Public Lands and Forests, Committee on Energy and Natural Resources, Concerning Interior Columbia Basin Ecosystem Management Project. June 29. U.S. Senate.

Botkin, D. B. 1990. *Discordant Harmonies: A New Ecology for the 21st Century.* New York: Oxford University Press.

Botkin, D. B., and M. J. Sobel. 1975. "Stability in Time-Varying Ecosystems." *American Naturalist* 109:625–26.

Bourdieu, P., and J. S. Coleman, eds. 1991. *Social Theory for a Changing Society.* Boulder, Colo.: Westview.

Bourland, T. R., and Stroup, R. L. 1996. "Rent Payments as Incentives: Making Endangered Species Welcome on Private Lands." *Journal of Forestry* 4:18–21.

Bowersox, J. 2002. "The Legitimacy Crisis in Environmental Ethics and Politics." In *Democracy and the Claims of Nature: Critical Perspectives for a New Century,* ed. Ben A. Minteer and Bob Pepperman Taylor, 71–90. Lanham, Md.: Rowman & Littlefield.

———. in press. "People, Place." In *Oregon Government and Politics Today,* ed. R. Clucas, M. Henkels, and B. Steel. Omaha: University of Nebraska Press.

Boyce, M. S. 2002. "Reconciling the Small Population and Declining Population Paradigms." In *Population Viability Analysis,* ed. S. R. Beissinger and D. R. McCullough, 41–49. Chicago: University of Chicago Press.

Braun, J. S., and P. Duguid. 1991. "Organizational Learning and Communities-of-Practice: Toward a Unified View of Working, Learning and Innovation." *Organization Science* 2(1):40ff.

Brown, G., and C. Harris. 1998. "Professional Foresters and the Land Ethic, Revisited." *Journal of Forestry* 96:4–12.

Brown, M., and R. L. Stroup. 1999. "The Takings Debate." *Environmental Protection,* June, 59–61.

Brown, P. M., M. R. Kaufmann, and W. D. Shepperd. 1999. "Long-Term, Landscape Patterns of Past Fire Events in Montane Ponderosa Pine Forest of Central Colorado." *Landscape Ecology* 14:513–32.

Bryner, Gary. 1993. *Blue Skies, Green Politics: The Clean Air Act of 1990.* Washington, D.C.: CQ Press.

Burgess, P., and K. A. Cheek. 1999. "Policy Review on FEMAT Case Study." In *Bioregional Assessments: Science at the Crossroads of Management and Policy,* ed. K. N. Johnson, F. Swanson, M. Herring, and S. Greene. Washington, D.C.: Island Press.

Burnett, M., and C. Davis. 2002. "Getting Out the Cut: Politics and National Forest Timber Harvests, 1960–1995." *Administration and Society* 34(2):202–28.

Burnett, S., and B. Allen. 1998, August. "The Endangered Species Act: First Step toward Fixing a Costly Failure." *NCPA Brief Analysis* (No. 276), at www.ncpa.org/ba/ba276.html (accessed 11 August 2003).

Burnham, K. P., D. R. Anderson, and G. C. White. 1994. "Estimation of Vital Rates of the Northern Spotted Owl." In *Final Supplemental*

Environmental Impact Statement, on Management of Habitat for Late-Successional and Old-Growth Forest Related Species within the Range of the Northern Spotted Owl. Vol. 2 (Appendix J), 1–44. Portland, Ore.: USDA, Forest Service.

Bush, G. W. 2002. "President Announces Healthy Forests Initiative." Speech (August 22), at www.whitehouse.gov/news/releases/2002/08/20020822-3.html (accessed 11 August 2003).

———. 2003. *The Healthy Forests Initiative*, at www.whitehouse.gov/infocus/healthyforests/ (accessed 11 August 2003).

Caldwell, K. L., C. Wilkinson, and M. Shannon. 1994. "Making Ecosystem Policy: Three Decades of Change." *Journal of Forestry* 92(4):6–10.

Calhoun, C. 1991. "Indirect Relationships and Imagined Communities: Large-Scale Social Integration and the Transformation of Everyday Life." In *Social Theory for a Changing Society*, ed. P. Bourdieu and J. S. Coleman, 95–121. Boulder, Colo.: Westview.

Carey, A. B., D. R. Thysell, and B. Angus. 1999. *The Forest Ecosystem Study: Background, Rationale, Implementation, Baseline Conditions, and Silvicultural Assessment* (General Technical Report, PNW-GTR-457). Portland, Ore.: USDA Forest Service, Pacific Northwest Research Station.

Cash, D. W. 2001. "'In Order to Aid in Diffusing Useful and Practical Information . . . ': Cross-Scale Boundary Organizations and Agricultural Extension." *Science, Technology, and Human Values* 26(4):431–53.

———. in press. "Mining Water, Drying Wells: Multi-Level Assessment and Decision Making for Water Management." In *Global Environmental Assessments: Information, Institutions, and Influence*, ed. R. B. Mitchell, W. C. Clark, D. W. Cash, and F. Alcock. Cambridge, Mass.: MIT Press.

Cashore, B., and J. Lawson. in press. "Explaining Regional Differences in Global Sustainable Forestry Certification Rules: The Case of the U.S. Northeast and the Canadian Maritimes." *Canadian-American Public Policy*, The Canadian-American Center, University of Maine.

CEC (Cascade Environmental Consulting). n.d. *Highway 20 Integrated Vegetation Management Project: Environmental Assessment, Deschutes National Forest, Sisters Ranger District* (unpublished). Bend, Ore.: Cascade Environmental Consulting.

CEQ (President's Council on Environmental Quality). 1984. *Environmental Quality: 15th Annual Report of the Council on Environmental Quality* Washington, D.C.: U.S. Government Printing Office.

Certification Watch. 2002. At www.certificationwatch.org (accessed 11 August 2003).

Chatterjee, P., and M. Finger. 1994. *The Earth Brokers: Power, Politics and World Development*. London: Routledge.

Cissel, J. H., F. J. Swanson, and P. H. Weisberg. 1999. "Landscape Management Using Historical Fire Regimes: Blue River, Oregon." *Ecological Applications* 9(4):1217–31.

Clark, J. A., J. M. Hoekstra, P. D. Boersma, and P. Kareiva. 2002. "Improving U.S. Endangered Species Act Recovery Plans: Key Findings and Recommendations of the SCB Recovery Plan Project." *Conservation Biology* 16(6):1510–19.

Clarke, J. N., and D. McCool. 1996. *Staking Out the Terrain*, 2d ed. Albany: State University of New York Press.

Clark, J. R. (Director, Fish and Wildlife Service). 1999, April 14. Testimony before the House Committee on Resources, on H.R. 1142, the Landowners Equal Treatment Act (1999 WL 16946072).

Clark, T. 2002. *The Policy Process: A Practical Guide for Natural Resource Professionals*. New Haven, Conn.: Yale University Press.

Clawson, M. 1983. *The Federal Lands Revisited*. Washington, D.C.: Resources for the Future.

Clinton, W. J., and A. Gore Jr. 1993. *The Forest Conference: Transcript, April 2*. Portland, Ore.: Portland Convention Center.

Cochran, P. H., and J. W. Barrett. 1995. *Growth and Mortality of Ponderosa Pine Poles Thinned to Various Densities in the Blue Mountains of Oregon* (Research Paper PNW-RP-483). Portland, Ore.: USDA Forest Service, Pacific Northwest Research Station.

Cohen, J. 2000. "Examination of the Home Destruction in Los Alamos Associated with the Cerro Grande Fire, May, 2000." *Wildfire News and Notes* 14(30):1, 6–7.

Cohen, W. 1988. *Western Oregon Vegetation Map: Conifer Age*. Laboratory for Applications of Remote Sensing in Ecology, USDA Forest Service PNW Research Station, at www.fsl.orst.edu/larse/wov/88wov.html (accessed 11 August 2003).

Committee of Scientists. 1999. *Sustaining the People's Lands: Recommendations for the Stewardship of the National Forests and Grasslands Into the Next Century*. Washington, D.C.: U.S. Department of Agriculture.

Cong. Rec. (Congressional Record). 30 June 2000: S6220.

———. 12 July 2000: S6508–S6515.

Congalton, R. G., K. Green, and J. Teply. 1993. "Mapping Old Growth Forests on National Forests and Park Lands in the Pacific Northwest from Remotely Sensed Data." *Photogrammetric Engineering and Remote Sensing* 59:529–35.

Cooper, J. C. 1993. "Broad Programmatic, Policy and Planning Assessments under the National Environmental Policy Act and Similar Devices: A Quiet Revolution in an Approach to Environmental Considerations." *Pace Environmental Law Review* 11:89–156.

Corn, M. L. 1992, May 27. *Endangered Species Act Issues* (Congressional Research Service). Washington, D.C.: Library of Congress.

Cortner, H. J., and M. A. Shannon. 1993. "Embedding Public Participation in Its Political Context." *Journal of Forestry* 91(7):14–16.

Cote, M.-A. 1999. "Possible Impact of Forest Product Certification on the Worldwide Forest Environment." *Forestry Chronicle* 75(2):208–12.

Coursey, D. 1994. *The Revealed Demand for a Public Good: Evidence from Endangered and Threatened Species* (Harris School Working Paper Series: 94.2), at www.harrisschool.uchicago.edu/wp/94-2.html (accessed 11 August 2003).

Covington, W., and M. Moore. 1994. "Southwestern Ponderosa Forest Structure—Changes since Euro-American Settlement." *Journal of Forestry* 92(1):39–47.

Crawford, R. H., and C. Y. Li. 1997. "Nitrogen Fixation in Root-Colonized Large Woody Residue of Oregon Coastal Forests." *Forest Ecology and Management* 92:229–34.

Cronin, M. A. 1997. "Systematics, Taxonomy, and the Endangered Species Act: The Example of the California Gnatcatcher." *Wildlife Society Bulletin* 25(3):661–66.

Crozier, M. 1964. *The Bureaucratic Phenomenon.* Chicago: University of Chicago Press.

Curtis, R. O. 1997. "The Role of Extended Rotations." In *Creating a Forestry for the 21st Century*, eds. K. A. Kohm and J. F. Franklin. Washington, D.C.: Island Press.

Curtis, R. O., and D. D. Marshall. 1993. "Douglas-Fir Rotations: Time for Reappraisal?" *Western Journal of Applied Forestry* 8:81–85.

Daily, G. C. 1997. *Nature's Services: Societal Dependence on Natural Ecosystems.* Washington, D.C.: Island Press.

Daly, H. E. 1991. *Steady State Economics*, 2d ed. Washington, D.C.: Island Press.

———. 1996. *Beyond Growth: The Economics of Sustainable Development.* Boston: Beacon.

Davis, Hibbitts, and McCaig, Inc. 2001. *A Forestry Program for Oregon: Oregonians Discuss Their Opinions on Forest Management and Sustainability.* A Quantitative Research Project Prepared for Oregon Department of Forestry. Portland, Ore.: Davis, Hibbitts, and McCaig, Inc.

DeBell, D. S., R. O. Curtis, C. A. Harrington, and J. C. Tappeiner. 1997. "Shaping Stand Development through Silvicultural Practices." In *Creating a Forestry for the 21st Century*, ed. K. Kohm and J. F. Franklin, 141–49. Washington, D.C.: Island Press.

deLeon, P., and K. Kaufmanis. 2000. "Public Policy Theory: Will It Play in Peoria?" *Policy Currents* 10(4):9–12.

Detling, L. 1968. *Historical Background of the Flora of the Pacific Northwest.* (Oregon Natural History Museum Bulletin 13). Eugene: University of Oregon.

Deyrup, M. A. 1976. *The Insect Community of Dead and Dying Douglas Fir: Diptera, Coleoptera, and Neuroptera.* Ph.D. diss., University of Washington, Seattle.

Donoghue, E., and R. Haynes. 2002. *Assessing the Viability and Adaptability of Oregon Communities* (General Technical Report PNW-GTR-549). Portland, Ore.: USDA Forest Service Pacific Northwest Research Station.

Doremus, H. 1997. "Decisions under the Endangered Species Act: Why Better Science Isn't Always Better Policy." *Washington University Law Review* 75:1029–51.

Dudley, G., W. Parsons, C. Radaelli, and P. Sabatier. 2000. "Symposium: Theories of the Policy Process." *Journal of European Public Policy* 7(1):122–40.

Duncan, L. A. 2003. "House Ready to Vote on Legislation to Speed Forest Thinning Projects." *Congressional Green Sheets*, May 19.

Dye, T. R. 2001. *Top-Down Policymaking.* New York: Chatham House.

Eckley, N. in press. "From Regional to Global Information: Assessment of Persistent Organic Pollutants (POPs)." In *Global Environmental Assessments: Information, Institutions, and Influence*, ed. R. B. Mitchell, W. C. Clark, D. W. Cash, and F. Alcock. Cambridge, Mass.: MIT Press.

Egan, A. 2002. "Uniting an Independent and Isolated Workforce: The Logger Association Phenomenon in the United States." *Society and Natural Resources* 15:541–52.

Ehrlich, P. R. 1994. "Biodiversity and Ecosystem Function: Need We Know More?" In *Biodiversity and Ecosystem Function*, ed. E.-D. Schulze and H. A. Mooney, vii–xi. New York: Springer-Verlag.

Ehrlich, P. R., and A. H. Ehrlich. 1981. *Extinction: The Causes and Consequences of the Disappearance of Species.* New York: Random House.

Emerson, R. W. 1983. *Essays and Lectures*, ed. Joel Porte. New York: Library of America.

Emmingham, W. H. 2002. "Development of Ecosystem Management in the Pacific Northwest." *Plant Biosystems* 136:167–76.

"Endangered Woodpeckers to Get Preserve." 1999, February 19. *Augusta (Georgia) Chronicle*, p. C2.

Executive Order No. 00-07. 2000. *Development of a State Strategy Promoting Sustainability in Internal State Government Operations*, signed by Governor John Kitzhaber, May 2000, at www.sos.state.or.us/archives/governors/Kitzhaber/web_pages/governor/legal/execords.htm (accessed 11 August 2003).

Fahnestock, G., and J. K. Agee. 1983. "Biomass Consumption and Smoke Production from Prehistoric and Modern Forest Fires in Western Washington." *Journal of Forestry* 81:653–57.

Fahrig, L. 1999. "Forest Loss or Fragmentation: Which Has the Greater Effect on the Persistence of Forest-Dwelling Animals?" In *Forest Fragmentation: Wildlife and Management Implications*, ed. J. A. Rochelle, L. A. Lehmann, and J. Wisniewski. Boston: Brill.

Farmer, A. 1996, July 22. "The Salvage Rider—Down, but Not Out." *High Country News*, 13.

FCR (Forest Community Research). 2002. *Northwest Economic Adjustment Initiative: An Assessment*. Taylorsville, Calif.: Forest Community Research.

FEMAT (Forest Ecosystem Management Assessment Team). 1993. *Forest Ecosystem Management: An Ecological, Economic, and Social Assessment—Report of the Forest Ecosystem Management Assessment Team* (USDA Forest Service). Washington, D.C.: U.S. Government Printing Office.

Ficken, R. E. 1987. *The Forested Land: A History of Lumbering in Western Washington*. Seattle: University of Washington Press.

Filip, G., A. Kanaskie, K. Kavanagh, G. Johnson, R. Johnson, and D. Maguire. 2000. *Silviculture and Swiss Needle Cast: Research and Recommendations*. Corvallis: College of Forestry, Forest Research Laboratory, Oregon State University.

Fischer, F., and J. Forester, eds. 1993. *The Argumentative Turn in Policy Analysis and Planning*. Durham, N.C.: Duke University Press.

Fitzgerald, R. 1992. "The Great Spotted Owl War." *Reader's Digest*, November, 91–95.

Flasche, F. 1997. Presentation to the II International Forest Policy Forum, Solsona, Spain, March 12.

Forsman, E. D., S. DeStephano, M. G. Raphael, and R. J. Gutierrez, eds. 1996. *Demography of the Northern Spotted Owl* (Studies in Avian Biology, No. 17). Los Angeles: Cooper Ornithological Society.

Forsman, E. D., E. C. Meslow, and H. M. Wight. 1984. "Distribution and Biology of the Spotted Owl in Oregon." *Wildlife Monographs* 87:1–64.

Foster, D., F. Swanson, J. Aber, I. Burke, N. Brokaw, D. Tilman, and A. Knapp. 2003. "The Importance of Land-Use Legacies to Ecology and Conservation." *BioScience* 53:77–88.

Franklin, A. B. 1992. "Population Regulation in Northern Spotted Owls: Theoretical Implications for Management." In *Wildlife 2001: Populations*, ed. D. R. McCullough and R. H. Barrett, 815–27. London: Elsevier Applied Sciences.

Franklin, A. B., D. R. Anderson, E. D. Forsman, K. P. Burnham, and F. W. Wagner. 1996. "Methods for Collecting and Analyzing Demographic Data on the Northern Spotted Owl." *Studies in Avian Biology* 17:12–20.

Franklin, A. B., K. P. Burnham, G. C. White, R. G. Anthony, E. D. Forsman, C. Schwarz, J. D. Nichols, and J. Hines. 1999. *Range-Wide Status and Trends in Northern Spotted Owl Populations* (unpublished report). Fort Collins, Colo.: Colorado Cooperative Fish and Wildlife Research Unit; U.S. Geological Survey, Biological Resources Division; Dept. of Fishery and Wildlife Biology. Corvallis, Ore.: Oregon Cooperative Fish and Wildlife Research Unit; U.S. Geological Survey, Biological Resources Division; Dept. of Fish and Wildlife.

Franklin, J. F. 1993. "Preserving Biodiversity: Species, Ecosystems, or Landscapes?" *Ecological Applications* 3:202–5.

———. 1994. "Ecological Sciences: A Conceptual Basis for FEMAT." *Journal of Forestry* 92:21–23.

———. 1995. "Scientists in Wonderland: Experiences in Development of Forest Policy." Supplement to *BioScience*, pp. S74–S78.

Franklin, J. F., and C. T. Dyrness. 1988. *Natural Vegetation of Oregon and Washington.* Corvallis: Oregon State University Press.

Franklin, J. F., and R. T. T. Forman. 1987. "Creating Landscape Patterns by Forest Cutting: Ecological Consequences and Principles." *Landscape Ecology* 1:5–18.

Franklin, J. F., D. R. Berg, D. A. Thornburg, and J. C. Tappenier. 1997. "Alternative Silvicultural Approaches to Timber Harvesting: Variable Retention Harvest Systems." In *Creating a Forestry for the 21st Century*, ed. K. Kohm and J. F. Franklin, 111–39. Washington, D.C.: Island Press.

Franklin, J. F., K. Cromack Jr., W. Dennison, A. McKee, C. Maser, J. Sedell, F. Swanson, and G. Juday. 1981. *Ecological Characteristics of Old-Growth Douglas-Fir Forests.* (General Technical Report GTR-PNW-118). Portland, Ore.: USDA Forest Service.

Franz, W. 1998. *Science, Skeptics, and Non-State Actors in the Greenhouse* (Belfer Center for Science and International Affairs (BCSIA) Discussion

Paper E-98-18). Cambridge, Mass.: Environment and Natural Resources Program, Kennedy School of Government, Harvard University.

Freeman, R. 2002. "The EcoFactory: U.S. Forest Service and the Political Construction of Ecosystem Management." *Environmental History* 7(4):632–58.

Gans, H. J. 1975. "Social Science for Social Policy." In *The Use and Abuse of Social Science*, 2d ed., ed. I. L. Horowitz. New Brunswick, N.J.: Transaction Books.

GAO (General Accounting Office). 1998. *Western National Forests: Catastrophic Wildfires Threaten Resources and Communities* (GAO/T-RCED-98-273). Washington, D.C.: U.S. General Accounting Office.

———. 1999. *Western National Forests: A Cohesive Strategy Is Needed to Address Catastrophic Wildland Fire Threats* (GAO/RCED-99-65). Washington, D.C.: U.S. General Accounting Office.

———. 2000. *Fire Management: Lessons Learned from the Cerro Grande (Los Alamos) Fire* (GAO/T-RCED-00-257). Washington, D.C.: U.S. General Accounting Office.

———. 2003. *Forest Service: Information on Decisions Involving Fuels Reduction* (GAO-03-689R). Washington, D.C.: U.S. General Accounting Office.

Giddens, A. 1991. *Modernity and Self-Identity: Self and Society in the Late Modern Age*. Stanford, Calif.: Stanford University Press.

Goldstein A., and R. Sanchez. 2002, August 23. "Bush Calls for Tree Thinning," *Washington Post*, A4.

Goodman, D. M., and J. A. Trofymow. 1998. "Distribution of Ectomycorrhizas in Microhabitats in Mature and Old-Growth Stands of Douglas Fir on Southeastern Vancouver Island." *Soil Biology and Biochemistry* 30:2127–38.

Goodstein, E. 1999. *Economics and the Environment*, 2d ed. Upper Saddle River, N.J.: Prentice Hall.

Gordon, R. E. Jr., J. K. Lacy, and J. R. Streeter. 1997. "Conservation under the Endangered Species Act." *Environmental International* 23:359–400.

Gorte, R. W. 1996. *The Salvage Timber Sale Rider: Overview and Policy Issues* (Congressional Research Service Report to Congress, 96-569 ENR). Washington, D.C.: Library of Congress.

———. 2000. *Forest Fire Protection* (Congressional Research Service Report, RL30755). Washington, D.C.: Library of Congress.

———. 2003. "Policy Response." In *Humans, Fires, and Forests—Social Science Applied to Fire Management*, ed. H. J. Cortner, D. R. Field, P. Jakes, and J. D. Buthman, 59–63 (ERI Papers in Restoration Policy). Flagstaff, Ariz.: Ecological Restoration Institute.

Governor's Eastside Forest Health Advisory Panel. 2002. *Working to Restore Oregon's Eastside Forest Ecosystems and Community Health: Oregon's Experience: A Report to Governor John Kitzhaber,* at www.sos.state.or.us/archives/governors/Kitzhaber/web_pages/gol_natural.htm (accessed 11 August 2003).

Griffiths, R. P., M. E. Harmon, B. A. Caldwell, and S. E. Carpenter. 1993. "Acetylene Reduction in Conifer Logs during Early Stages of Decomposition." *Plant and Soil* 148:53–61.

Groom, M., D. B. Jensen, R. L. Knight, S. Gatewood, L. Mills, D. Boyd-Heger, L. S. Mills, and M. Soule. 1999. "Buffer Zones: Benefits and Dangers of Compatible Stewardship." In *Continental Conservation,* ed. M. E. Soule and J. Terborgh, 171–97. Washington, D.C.: Island Press.

Grove, S. J. 2002. "Saproxylic Insect Ecology and the Sustainable Management of Forests." *Annual Review of Ecology and Systematics* 33:1–23.

Gunderson, L. 1999. "Stepping Back: Assessing for Understanding in Complex Regional Systems." In *Bioregional Assessments: Science at the Crossroads of Management and Policy,* ed. K. N. Johnson, F. Swanson, M. Herring, and S. Greene, 27–40. Washington, D.C.: Island Press.

Gunderson, L. H., C. S. Holling, and S. S. Light, eds. 1995. *Barriers and Bridges to the Renewal of Ecosystems and Institutions.* New York: Columbia University Press.

Gupta, A. in press. "Information as Influence in Anticipatory Governance: The Case of Biosafety." In *Global Environmental Assessments: Information, Institutions, and Influence,* ed. R. B. Mitchell, W. C. Clark, D. W. Cash, and F. Alcock. Cambridge, Mass.: MIT Press.

Guston, D. H. 1996. "Principal-Agent Theory and the Structure of Science Policy." *Science and Public Policy* 23(4):229.

———. 1999. "Stabilizing the Boundary between Politics and Science: The Role of the Office of Technology Transfer as a Boundary Organization." *Social Studies of Science* 29(1):87–112.

Guston, D. H., et al. 2000. *Report of the Workshop on Boundary Organizations in Environmental Policy and Science.* Rutgers University, the Environmental and Occupational Health Sciences Institute at Rutgers University and UMDNJ-RWJMS, and the Global Environmental Assessment Project.

Gutiérrez, R. J. 1985. "An Overview of Recent Research on the Spotted Owl." In *Ecology and Management of the Spotted Owl in the Pacific Northwest,* ed. R. J. Gutiérrez and A. B. Carey (General Technical Report, GTR-PNW-185), 39–49. Portland, Ore.: USDA Forest Service, Pacific Northwest Research Station.

———. 1996. "Biology and Distribution of the Northern Spotted Owl." *Studies in Avian Biology* 17:2–5.

Gutiérrez, R. J., and A. B. Carey, eds. 1985. *Ecology and Management of the Spotted Owl in the Pacific Northwest* (General Technical Report, PNW-GTR-185). Portland, Ore.: USDA Forest Service, Pacific Northwest Research Station.

Haas, P. M. 1992. "Epistemic Communities and International Policy Coordination." *International Organization* 46:1–35.

Haas, P. M., R. O. Keokane, and M. A. Levy. 1993. "The Effectiveness of International Environmental Institutions." In *Institutions for the Earth: Sources of Effective International Environmental Protection*, ed. P. M. Haas, R. O. Keokane, and M.A. Levy. Cambridge, Mass.: MIT Press.

Hage, J., and M. Aiken. 1970. *Social Change in Complex Organizations.* New York: Random House.

Hammond, P. C., and J. C. Miller. 1998. "Comparison of the Biodiversity of *Lepidoptera* within Three Forested Ecosystems." *Annals of the Entomological Society of America* 91:323–28.

Hansen, A. J., T. A. Spies, F. J. Swanson, and J. L. Ohmann. 1991. "Conserving Biological Diversity in Managed Forests." *BioScience* 41:382–92.

Hanski, I. 2002. "Metapopulations of Animals in Highly Fragmented Landscapes." In *Population Viability Analysis,* ed. S. R. Beissinger and D. R. McCullough, 86–108. Chicago: University of Chicago Press.

Harmon, M. E., J. F. Franklin, F. J. Swanson, P. Sollins, S. V. Gregory, J. D. Lattin, N. H. Anderson, S. P. Cline, N. G. Aumen, J. R. Sedell, G. W. Lienkaemper, K. Cromack, and K. W. Cummins. 1986. "Ecology of Coarse Woody Debris in Temperate Ecosystems." *Advances in Ecological Research* 15:133–302.

Harrington, W. 1981. "Wildlife: Severe Decline and Partial Recovery." In *America's Renewable Resources: Historical Trends and Current Challenges,* ed. K. D. Frederick and R. A. Sedjo. Washington, D.C.: Resources for the Future.

Harris, L. D. 1984. *The Fragmented Forest.* Chicago: University of Chicago Press.

Harris, C., W. McLaughlin, G. Brown, and D. Becker. 2000. *Rural Communities in the Inland Northwest: An Assessment of Small Rural Communities in the Interior and Upper Columbia River Basins* (General Technical Report PNW-GTR-477). Portland, Ore.: USDA Forest Service Pacific Northwest Research Station.

Hatch, L., M. Uriarte, D Fink, L. Aldrich-Wolfe, R. G. Allen, C. Webb, K. Zamudio, and A. Power. 2002. "Jurisdiction over Endangered

Species' Habitat: The Impacts of People and Property on Recovery Planning." *Ecological Applications* 12(3):690–700.

Hayes, J. P., S. S. Chan, W. H. Emmingham, J. C. Tappenier, L. D. Kellog, and J. D. Bailey. 1997. "Wildlife Response to Thinning Young Forests in the Pacific Northwest." *Journal of Forestry* 95:28–33.

Hayes, J. P., and J. Hagar. 2002. "Ecology and Management of Wildlife and Their Habitats in the Oregon Coast Range." In *Forest and Stream Management in the Oregon Coast Range*, ed. S. D. Hobbs, J. P. Hayes, R. L. Johnson, G. H. Reeves, T. A. Spies, and J. C. Tappenier, 99–134. Corvallis: Oregon State University Press.

Haynes, R., ed. *An Analysis of the Timber Situation in the United States: 1952–2050.* (USDA General Technical Report PNW-GTR 560). Portland, Ore.: USDA Pacific Northwest Research Station.

Haynes, R. W., and G. E. Perez. 2001. *Northwest Forest Plan Research Synthesis* (USDA General Technical Report PNW-GTR-498). Portland, Ore.: USDA Forest Service, Pacific Northwest Research Station.

Heaton, K., and R. Donovan. 1997. "Forest Assessments." In *1996 Certification of Forest Products: Issues and Perspectives*, ed. V. Vania, M. J. Ervin, R. Z. Donovan, C. Elliott, and H. Ghotz, 54–67. Washington, D.C.: Island Press.

Hedrick, P. W., R. C. Lacy, F. W. Allendorf, and M. E. Soule. 1996. "Directions in Conservation Biology: Comments on Caughley." *Conservation Biology* 10:1312–20.

Herron, Paul. 2001. "Where There's Smoke: Wildfire Policy and Suppression in the American Southwest." In *Forests under Fire: A Century of Ecosystem Mismanagement in the Southwest*, ed. C. J. Huggard and A. R. Gomez, 181–210. Tucson: University of Arizona Press.

Hessburg, P., B. Smith, and R. B. Salter. 1999. "Detecting Change in Forest Spatial Patterns from Reference Conditions." *Ecological Applications* 9(4):1232–52.

Hirt, P. W. 1996. *A Conspiracy of Optimism: Management of the National Forests since World War Two.* Lincoln: University of Nebraska Press.

Holling, C. S. 1988. "Temperate Forest Insect Outbreaks, Tropical Deforestation, and Migratory Birds." *Memoirs of the Entomological Society of Canada* 146:21–32.

———. 1995. "What Barriers? What Bridges? In *Barriers and Bridges to Renewal of Ecosystems and Institutions*, ed. L. H. Gunderson, C. S. Holling, and S. L. Light, 3–34. New York: Columbia University Press.

Houck, O. 1997. "On the Law of Biodiversity and Ecosystem Management," *81 Minnesota Law Review* 870.

H.R. (House Resolution) 1904. 2003. The Healthy Forests Restoration Act of 2003. H. Rep. No. 108-96, 108th Cong., 1st Sess.

Hubbard, D. W. 2000. *Widow-makers and Rhododendrons.* Central Point, Ore.: Hellgate Press.

Huff, M. H. 1984. *Post-Fire Succession in the Olympic Mountains, Washington: Forest Vegetation, Fuels, and Avifauna.* Ph.D. diss., University of Washington, Seattle.

ICBEMP (Interior Columbia Basin Ecosystem Management Project). 2000. Report to the Congress on Interior Columbia Basin Ecosystem Management Project. Boise, Idaho: Interior Columbia Basin Ecosystem Management Project.

Irvin, W. R. 1992. "The Endangered Species Act: Prospects for Reauthorization." In *Transactions of the Fifty-Seventh North American Wildlife and Natural Resources Conference,* ed. R. E. McCabe, 642–44.

Jalonick, M. C. 2003. "Prevention Legislation Approved by Agriculture Panel." *CQ Today,* May 8.

Jarrell, J. D., M. Mayfield, E. N. Rappaport, and C. W. Landsea. 2001. *The Deadliest, Costliest, and Most Intense United States Hurricanes from 1900–2000 (and Other Frequently Requested Hurricane Facts),* NOAA Technical Memorandum NWS PTC-1, at www.nhc.noaa.gov/pastdec.shtml (accessed 11 August 2003).

Jasanoff, S. 1990. *The Fifth Branch: Science Advisors as Policy-Makers.* Cambridge, Mass.: Harvard University Press.

Johnson, K. N. 1997. "Science-Based Assessments of the Forests of the Pacific Northwest." In *Creating a Forestry for the 21st Century: The Science of Ecosystem Management,* ed. K. A. Kohm and J. F. Franklin, 397–409. Washington, D.C.: Island Press.

Johnson, K. N., and M. Shannon, guest eds. 1994. "Developing Forest Policy: The FEMAT Model." Special Issue, *Journal of Forestry* 92(4).

Johnson, K. N., S. Crim, K. Barber, M. Howell, and C. Cadwell. 1993. *Sustainable Harvest and Short-Term Timber Sales for Options Considered in FEMAT: Methods, Results & Implications* (unpublished). Portland, Ore.: USDA Forest Service.

Johnson, K. N., J. Agee, R. Beschta, J. Beuter, S. Gregory, L. Kellogg, W. McComb, J. Sedell, T. Scholwalter, and S. Tesch. 1995. *Forest Health and Timber Harvests on National Forest in the Blue Mountains of Oregon: A Report to Governor Kitzhaber.* Corvallis: Oregon State University.

Johnson, K. N., F. P. Swanson, M. Herring, and S. Greene, eds. 1999a. *Bioregional Assessments: Science at the Crossroads of Management and Policy.* Washington, D.C.: Island Press.

Johnson, K. N., R. Holthausen, M. A. Shannon, and J. Sedell. 1999b. "Case Study—Forest Ecosystem Management Assessment Team Assessments." In *Bioregional Assessments: Science at the Crossroads of Management and Policy*, ed. K. N. Johnson, F. P. Swanson, M. Herring, and S. Greene, 87–116. Washington, D.C.: Island Press.

Jones, B. D., F. Baumgartner, and J. True. 1998. "Policy Punctuations: U.S. Budget Authority, 1947–1995." *Journal of Politics* 60(1):1–33.

Jones, J. A., and G. E. Grant. 1996. "Peak Flow Responses to Clear-Cutting and Roads in Small and Large Basins, Western Cascades, Oregon." *Water Resources Research* 32:959–74.

Kamenka, E. 1989. *Bureaucracy: New Perspectives on the Past*. Oxford, U.K.: Blackwell.

Kant, I. 1965. *Critique of Pure Reason*, trans. Norman Kemp Smith. New York: St. Martin's.

Kanter, R. M. 1991. "The Future of Bureaucracy and Hierarchy in Organizational Theory: A Report from the Field." In *Social Theory for a Changing Society*, ed. P. Bourdieu and J. S. Coleman, 63–87. Boulder, Colo.: Westview.

Kareiva, P., and U. Wennergren. 1995. "Connecting Landscape Patterns to Ecosystem and Population Processes." *Nature* 373:299–302.

Kaufman, H. 1960. *The Forest Ranger: A Study in Administrative Behavior*. Baltimore: Johns Hopkins University Press.

Kemmis, D. 2001. *This Sovereign Land: A New Vision for Governing the West*. Washington, D.C.: Island Press.

Kingdon, J. 2003. *Agendas, Alternatives, and Public Policies*, 2d ed. New York: Longman.

Kinzig, A. P., S. W. Pacala, and D. Tilman, eds. 2001. *The Functional Consequences of Biodiversity: Empirical Progress and Theoretical Extensions* (Monographs in Population Biology, 33). Princeton, N.J.: Princeton University Press.

Kitzhaber, J. 1999a. *Speech to Society of American Foresters*, at www.sos.state.or.us/archives/governors/Kitzhaber/web_pages/governor/speeches/s990913.htm (accessed 11 August 2003).

———. (1999b). *Governor's 11-Point Strategy for Restoring Ecosystem Health in Eastern Oregon*, at www.sos.state.or.us/archives/governors/Kitzhaber/web_pages/gol_natural.htm (accessed 11 August 2003).

Klopsch, M. W. 1985. *Structure of Mature Douglas-Fir Stands in a Western Oregon Watershed and Implications for Interpretation of Disturbance History and Succession*. Unpublished master's thesis, Oregon State University, Corvallis.

Krauss, C. 2002, December 4. "On This Chick's Future a Species Could Depend." *New York Times*, p. A4.

Lach, D., P. List, B. Steel, and B. Shindler. 2003. "Advocacy and Credibility of Ecological Scientists in Resource Decision Making: A Regional Study." *BioScience* 53(2):170–78.

Laird, F. N. 1993. "Participatory Analysis, Democracy, and Technological Decision Making." *Science, Technology, & Human Values* 18(3):341–61.

Lande, R. 1988. "Demographic Models of the Northern Spotted Owl (*Strix occidentalis caurina*)." *Oecologia* 75:601–7.

Landres, P., P. Morgan, and F. Swanson. 1999. "Overview of the Use of the Natural Variability Concepts in Managing Ecological Systems." *Ecological Applications* 9(4):1179–88.

Landy, M. K., and H. A. Plotkin. 1982. "Limits of the Market Metaphor." *Society*, May–June.

Leal, D. R., and J. B. Grewell. 1999. *Hunting for Habitat: A Practical Guide to State-Landowner Partnerships*. Bozeman, Mont.: Political Economy Research Center.

Lee, J. 2003, March 2. "A Call for Softer, Greener Language." *New York Times*, p. 24.

Lee, K. 1993. *Compass and Gyroscope: Integrating Science and Politics for the Environment*. Washington, D.C.: Island Press.

Lehmkuhl, J. F., and L. F. Ruggiero. 1991. "Forest Fragmentation in the Pacific Northwest and Its Potential Effects on Wildlife." In *Wildlife and Vegetation of Unmanaged Douglas-Fir Forests*, tech. coord. L. F. Ruggiero, K. B. Aubry, A. B. Carey, and M. H. Huff (General Technical Report PNW-GTR-285), 35–46. Portland, Ore.: USDA Forest Service, Pacific Northwest Research Station.

LeMaster, D. 1984. *Decade of Change: The Remaking of Forest Service Statutory Authority during the 1970s*. Westport, Conn.: Greenwood Press.

Lemons, J. 1998. "Who Should Bear the Burdens of Risk and Proof in Changing Consumption Patterns?" In *The Business of Consumption; Environmental Ethics and the Global Economy*, ed. L. Westra and P. Werhane, 131–50. Lanham, Md.: Rowman & Littlefield.

Leopold, A. 1949. *A Sand County Almanac*. New York: Oxford University Press.

———. 1966. *A Sand County Almanac*. New York: Ballantine Books.

Lettman, G. J. 1995. *Timber Management Practices and Land Use Trends on Private Forest Land in Oregon: A Final Report to the Sixty-Eighth Oregon Legislative Assembly*. Salem, Ore.: Oregon Department of Forestry.

Li, C. Y., R. H. Crawford, and T-T. Chang. 1997. "*Frankia* in Decaying Fallen Trees Devoid of Actinorhizal Hosts and Soil." *Microbiological Research* 152:167–69.

Lieber, I. J. 1997. "Political Influences on USFWS Listing Decisions under the ESA: Time to Rethink Priorities." *Environmental Law* 27:1323.

Lindblom, C. E. 1959. "The Science of 'Muddling Through.'" *Public Administration Review* 29:79–88.

Lindenmayer, D. B., and J. F. Franklin. 2002. *Conserving Forest Biodiversity*. Washington, D.C.: Island Press.

Lint, J., B. Noon, R. Anthony, E. Forsman, M. Raphael, M. Collopy, and E. Starkey. 1999. *Northern Spotted Owl Effectiveness Monitoring Plan for the Northwest Forest Plan* (General Technical Report PNW-GTR-440). Portland, Ore.: USDA, Forest Service, Pacific Northwest Research Station.

Lippmann, W. 1985. *Drift and Mastery*. Madison: University of Wisconsin Press.

Litfin, K. T. 1994. *Ozone Discourses: Science and Politics in Global Environmental Cooperation*. New York: Columbia University Press.

Loreau, M., S. Naeem, P. Inchausti, J. Bengtsson, J. P. Grime, A. Hector, D. U. Hooper, M. A. Huston, D. Raffaelli, B. Schmid, D. Tilman, and D. A. Wardle. 2001. "Biodiversity and Ecosystem Function: Current Knowledge and Future Challenges." *Science* 294:804–8.

Lowi, T. 1969. *The End of Liberalism*. New York: Norton.

Loy, W. G., S. Allan, A. R. Buckley, and J. E. Meacham. 2001. *Atlas of Oregon*. Eugene: University of Oregon Press.

Lubchenco, J. 1998. "Entering the Century of the Environment: A New Social Contract for Science." *Science* 279:491–97.

Luecke, D. 2000. "The Law and Politics of Federal Wildlife Preservation." In *Political Environmentalism*, ed. Terry L. Anderson, 61–119. Stanford, Calif.: Hoover Institution Press.

Luecke, D., and J. A. Michael. 2003. "Preemptive Habitat Destruction under the Endangered Species Act." *Journal of Law & Economics* 46: 27–60.

Luoma, J. R. 1999. *The Hidden Forest: A Biography of an Ecosystem*. New York: Holt.

MacDonald, G. 2003. *Biogeography: Introduction to Space, Time, and Life*. New York: Wiley.

Manion, P. D. 1981. *Tree Disease Concepts*. Englewood Cliffs, N.J.: Prentice Hall.

Mapes, L. V. 2003, April 16. "Despite Protections, Spotted Owl on the Decline," *Seattle Times*, p. B1.

Marcot, B. 1997. "Biodiversity of Old Forests of the West: A Lesson from Our Elders." In *Creating a Forestry for the 21st Century*, ed. K. Kohm and J. F. Franklin, 87–106. Washington, D.C.: Island Press.

Masters, R. D. 1989. *The Nature of Politics*. New Haven, Conn.: Yale University Press.

Mater, C., V. A. Sample, and W. Price. 2002. *Certification Assessments on Public and University Lands: A Field-Based Comparative Evaluation of the*

Forest Stewardship Council (FSC) and the Sustainable Forestry Initiative (SFI). Washington, D.C.: Pinchot Institute for Conservation.

Mazmanian, D., and J. Nienaber. 1979. Can Organizations Change? Washington, D.C.: Brookings.

McComb, W. C., K. McGarigal, and R. G. Anthony. 1993. "Small Mammal and Amphibian Abundance in Streamside and Upslope Habitats of Mature Douglas-Fir Stands, Western Oregon." Northwest Science 67:7–15.

McGarigal, K., and W. C. McComb. 1992. "Streamside versus Upslope Breeding Bird Communities in the Central Oregon Coast Range." Journal of Wildlife Management 56:10–23.

McGinnis, M. V., ed. 1999. Bioregionalism. London: Routledge.

McKenzie, D., D. Peterson, and J. Agee. 2000. "Fire Frequency in the Interior Columbia River Basin: Building Regional Models from Fire History Data." Ecological Applications 10(5):1497–1516.

Meffe, G. P., D. Boersma, D. Murphy, B. Noon, H. R. Pulliam, M. Soule, and D. Waller. 1998. "Independent Scientific Review in Natural Resource Management." Conservation Biology 12:268–70.

Meridian Institute. 2001. Comparative Analysis of the Forest Stewardship Council and Sustainable Forestry Initiative Certification Programs, at www2.merid.org/comparison/ (accessed 11 August 2003).

Miller, G. S., S. R. Beissinger, H. R. Carter, B. Csuti, T. E. Hamer, and D. A. Perry. 1997. Recovery Plan for the Marbled Murrelet (Brachyramphus marmoratus) in Washington, Oregon, and California. Portland, Ore.: U.S. Fish and Wildlife Service.

Miller, G. S., S. DeStephano, K. A. Swindle, and E. C. Meslow. 1996. "Demography of Northern Spotted Owls on the H. J. Andrews Study Area in the Central Cascade Mountains, Oregon." Studies in Avian Biology 17:37–46.

Mills, T. J., and R. N. Clark. 2001. "Roles of Research Scientists in Natural Resource Decision-Making." Forest Ecology and Management 153(1–3):189–98.

Minteer, B. A., and B. Pepperman Taylor, eds. 2002. Democracy and the Claims of Nature. Lanham, Md.: Rowman & Littlefield.

Mitchell, R. B., W. C. Clark, D. W. Cash, and F. ALcock, eds. in press. Global Environmental Assessments: Information, Institutions, and Influence. Cambridge, Mass.: MIT press.

Moldenke, A. R., and J. D. Lattin. 1990. "Dispersal Characteristics of Old-Growth Soil Arthropods: The Potential for Loss of Diversity and Biological Function." Northwest Environmental Journal 6:408–9.

Molina, R., D. Pilz, J. Smith, S. Dunham, T. Dreisbach, T. O'Dell, and M. Castellano. 2001. "Conservation and Management of Forest Fungi in the Pacific Northwestern United States: An Integrated Ecosystem Approach." In *Fungal Conservation: Issues and Solutions*, ed. D. Moore, M. N. Nauta, S. E. Evans, and M. Rotheroe, 19–63. Cambridge, U.K.: Cambridge University Press.

Monoson, T. 2002. "Western Lawmakers Reach for a Deal on Wildfire Prevention Rules." *CQ Today Monitor News*, October 15.

Morrison, P. H. 1990. *Ancient Forests on the Olympic National Forest: Analysis from a Historical and Landscape Perspective*. Washington, D.C.: Wilderness Society.

Morrison, P. H., and F. J. Swanson. 1990. *Fire History and Patterns in a Cascade Range Landscape* (General Technical Report PNW-GTR-254). Portland, Ore.: U.S. Forest Service, Pacific Northwest Research Station.

Morriss, A. P., and Stroup, R. L. 2000. "Quartering Species: The 'Living Constitution,' the 'Third Amendment,' and the 'Endangered Species Act.'" *Environmental Law* 30:769–809.

Morrow, R. J. 1985. *Age Structure and Spatial Pattern of Old-Growth Ponderosa Pine in Pringle Falls Experimental Forest, Central Oregon*. M.S. thesis, Oregon State University at Corvallis.

Moser, S. C. in press. "Climate Change and Sea-Level Rise in Maine and Hawai'i: The Changing Tides of an Issue Domain." In *Global Environmental Assessments: Information, Institutions, and Influence*, ed. R. B. Mitchell, W. C. Clark, D. W. Cash, and F. Alcock. Cambridge, Mass.: MIT Press.

Muir, J. 1912. "The Yosemite." *Century*, 255–57, 260–62.

Mutch, R.W., and T. M. Quigley. 1993. *Forest Health in the Blue Mountains: A Management Strategy for Fire-Adapted Ecosystems* (General Technical Report PNW-GTR-310). Portland, Ore.: USDA Forest Service, Pacific Northwest Research Station.

NAPA (National Academy of Public Administration). 2000. *Study of the Implementation of the Federal Wildland Fire Policy: Phase I Report* (report by a panel of the National Academy of Public Administration for the U.S. Department of the Interior). Washington, D.C.: NAPA.

Neitlich, P. N., and B. McCune. 1997. "Hotspots of Epiphytic Lichen Diversity in Two Young Managed Forests." *Conservation Biology* 11:172–82.

Nelson, J. 1999. "Management Review on FEMAT Case Study." In *Bioregional Assessments: Science at the Crossroads of Management and Policy*, ed. K. N. Johnson, F. Swanson, M. Herring, and S. Greene, 121–26. Washington, D.C.: Island Press.

Niemi, E., E. Whitelaw, and A. Johnston. 1999. *The Sky Did Not Fall: The Pacific Northwest's Response to Logging Reductions.* Eugene, Ore.: ECONorthwest.

NMFS (National Marine Fisheries Service). 1998. *Biological Opinion Re: Section 7 Consultation on Actions Affecting Umpqua River Cutthroat Trout and Oregon Coast Coho Salmon Issued to Roseburg BLM District Manager* 1, 6 (November 23, 1998).

North, D. 1990. *Institutions, Institutional Change and Economic Performance.* Cambridge, U.K.: Cambridge University Press.

Noss, R. F., and A. Y. Cooperrider. 1994. *Saving Nature's Legacy.* Washington, D.C.: Island Press.

Noss, R. F., E. Dinerstein, B. Gilbert, M. Gilpin, B. J. Miller, J. Terborgh, and Steve Trombulak. 1999. "Core Areas: Where Nature Reigns." In *Continental Conservation,* ed. M. E. Soule and J. Terborgh, 99–128. Washington, D.C.: Island Press.

NRC (National Research Council). 2000. *Environmental Issues in Pacific Northwest Forest Management.* Washington, D.C.: National Academy Press.

NWI (National Wilderness Institute). 1995. "State by State Government Landownership," at www.nwi.org/Maps/LandChart.html (accessed 11 August 2003).

ODF (Oregon Department of Forestry). 1977–2001 (annual). *Oregon Timber Harvest Report.* Salem: Oregon Department of Forestry.

———. 2001. *Reforestation Accomplishment Report, 1999.* Salem, Ore., at www.odf.state.or.us/Portal/pubs/pubsdownload.asp (accessed 11 August 2003).

OFRI (Oregon Forest Resources Institute). 2002. *Oregon's Forest Protection Laws: An Illustrated Manual.* Portland: Oregon Forest Resources Institute.

Oliver, C. D., D. Adams, T. Bonnicksen, J. Bowyer, F. Cubbage, N. Sampson, S. Schlarbaum, R. Whaley, and H. Wiant. 1997. *Report on Forest Health of the United States by the Forest Health Science Panel.* Seattle: Center for International Trade in Forest Products, University of Washington.

Ophuls, W., and S. Boyan. 1992. *Ecology and the Politics of Scarcity Revisited: The Unraveling of the American Dream.* New York: Freeman.

Oregon Cooperative Fish and Wildlife Research Unit. 2002a. "The Ecology of Northern Spotted Owls (*Strix occidentalis caurina*) on the Williamette National Forest." Unpublished annual research report available from Oregon Cooperative Fish and Wildlife Research Unit, Department of Fisheries and Wildlife, Oregon State University, Corvallis, Oregon.

———. 2000b. "Demographic Characteristics of Spotted Owls (*Strix occidentalis caurina*) in the Southern Cascades." Unpublished annual research report available from Oregon Cooperative Fish and Wildlife Research Unit, Department of Fisheries and Wildlife, Oregon State University, Corvallis Oregon.

Ostroff, F. 1999. *The Horizontal Organization*. Oxford, U.K.: Oxford University Press.

Patlis, J. M. 1994. "Biodiversity Symposium: Biodiversity, Ecosystems and Species: Where Does the Endangered Species Act Fit In?" *Tulane Environmental Law Journal* 8:33–76.

Patt, A. in press. "Trust, Respect, Patience, and Sea Surface Temperatures: Useful Climate Forecasting in Zimbabwe." In *Global Environmental Assessments: Information, Institutions, and Influence*, ed. R. B. Mitchell, W. C. Clark, D. W. Cash, and F. Alcock. Cambridge, Mass.: MIT Press.

Perkins, J. 2003, February 14. "Environmental Groups Push for Misuse of the Endangered Species Act." *San Diego Union-Tribune*, p. 87.

Perry, D. A. 1988. "Landscape Patterns and Forest Pests." *Northwest Environmental Journal* 4:213–28.

———. 1994. *Forest Ecosystems*. Baltimore: Johns Hopkins University Press.

———. 1995. "Self-organizing Systems Across Scales." *Trends in Ecology and Evolution* 10:241–44.

———. 1998. "The Scientific Basis of Forestry." *Annual Review of Ecology and Systematics* 29:435–66.

Perry, D. A., M. P. Amaranthus, J. G. Borchers, S. L. Borchers, and R. Brainerd. 1989. "Bootstrapping in Ecosystems." *BioScience* 39:230–37.

Petersen, S. 1999. "Congress and Charismatic Megafauna: A Legislative History of the Endangered Species Act." *Environmental Law* 29:463–74.

Pielke, R. A. Jr. 1997. "Reframing the U.S. Hurricane Problem." *Society and Natural Resources* 10:485–99.

———. 2002. "Policy, Politics and Perspective." *Nature* 416:368.

Pinchot, G. 1947. *Breaking New Ground*. New York: Harcourt Brace.

Poage, N. 2001. *Structure and Development of Old-Growth Douglas-Fir in the Central Western Oregon*. Ph.D. diss., Oregon State University, Corvallis.

Press, D. 1994. *Democratic Dilemmas in the Age of Ecology*. Durham, N.C.: Duke University Press.

Prestemon, J., and R. Abt. 2002. "Timber Products Supply and Demand." In *Southern Forest Resource Assessment*, ed. D. N. Wear and J. G. Greis (General Technical Report GTR-SRS-053). Asheville, N.C.: U.S. Forest Service, Southern Research Station.

Prugh, T., R. Costanza, and H. E. Daly. 2000. *The Local Politics of Global Sustainability*. Washington, D.C.: Island Press.

Quigley, T. M. 1992. *Forest Health in the Blue Mountains: Social and Economic Perspectives* (General Technical Report PNW-GTR-296). Portland, Ore.: USDA Forest Service, Pacific Northwest Research Station.

Raettig, T. 1999. *Trends in Key Economic and Social Indicators for Pacific Northwest States and Counties* (General Technical Report PNW-GTR-474). Portland, Ore.: U.S. Forest Service Pacific Northwest Research Station.

Raettig, T., and H. Christensen. 1999. *Timber Harvesting, Processing, and Employment in the Northwest Economic Adjustment Initiative Region: Changes and Economic Assistance* (General Technical Report PNW-GTR-465). Portland, Ore.: U.S. Forest Service Pacific Northwest Research Station.

Reich, B. R. 1985. "Public Administration and Public Deliberation: An Interpretive Essay." *Yale Law Journal* 94:1617–41.

Rey, M. 2000, October 13. *Collaborative Stewardship: A New Environmental Ethic for the West* (S. J. Hall Lectureship in Industrial Forestry). College of Natural Resources, University of California, Berkeley, at www/cnr.berkeley.edu/forestry/lectures/hall/2000rey.html (accessed 11 August 2003).

Ribe, R., and T. Silvaggio. 2002. *National Forest Management in Timber and Spotted Owl Country; A Survey of Interested People in Western Oregon and Washington.* Eugene: Institute for a Sustainable Environment, University of Oregon.

Ripple, W. J. 1994. "Historical Spatial Patterns of Old Forests of Western Oregon." *Journal of Forestry* 92:45–49.

Robbins, W. 1988. *Hard Times in Paradise: Coos Bay, Oregon 1850–1986.* Seattle: University of Washington Press.

———. 1997. "The Social Context of Forestry: The Pacific Northwest in the Twentieth Century." In *American Forests: Nature, Culture, and Politics,* ed. Char Miller, 195–207. Lawrence: University Press of Kansas.

Romme, W. H. 1982. "Fire and Landscape Diversity of Subalpine Forests in Yellowstone National Park." *Ecological Monographs* 52:199–221.

Roosevelt, T. 1926. *Works,* vol. 12. New York: Scribner.

Rorty, R. 1979. *Philosophy and the Mirror of Nature.* Princeton, N.J.: Princeton University Press.

———. 1983. "Method and Morality." In *Social Science as Moral Inquiry,* ed. N. Haan, R. N. Bellah, P. Rabinow, and W. Sullivan. New York: Columbia University Press.

Rosenberg, K. V., and M. G. Raphael. 1986. "Effects of Forest Fragmentation on Vertebrates in Douglas-Fir Forests." In *Wildlife 2000,* ed.

J. Verner, M. L. Morrison, and C. J. Ralph, 263–72. Madison: University of Wisconsin Press.

Rubin, P. H. 2002. *Darwinian Politics: The Evolutionary Origin of Freedom.* New Brunswick, N.J.: Rutgers University Press.

Ruggiero, L. F., R. S. Holthausen, B. G. Marcot, K. B. Aubry, J. W. Thomas, and E. C. Meslow. 1988. "Ecological Dependency: The Concept and Its Implications for Research and Management." *Trans. 53rd North American Wildlife and Natural Resource Conference* 53:115–26.

Rule, L. 2000. "Enforcing Ecosystem Management under the Northwest Forest Plan: The Judicial Role." *12 Fordham Environmental Law Journal* 211.

Sabatier, P., ed. 1999. *Theories of the Policy Process.* Boulder, Colo.: Westview.

Sabatier, P., and H. C. Jenkins-Smith. 1993. *Policy Change and Learning: An Advocacy Coalition Approach.* Boulder, Colo.: Westview.

Sabatier, P., J. Loomis, and C. McCarthy. 1996. "Policy Attitudes and Decisions within the Forest Service." *Journal of Forestry* 94(1):42–46.

Sagoff, M. 1988. *The Economy of the Earth: Philosophy, Law and the Environment.* Cambridge, U.K.: Cambridge University Press.

Sarewitz, D. 1999. "Science and Environmental Policy: An Excess of Objectivity." In *Earth Matters: The Earth Sciences, Philosophy, and the Claims of Community,* ed. R. Frodeman, 79-98. Upper Saddle River, N.J.: Prentice Hall.

———. 2000. *Uncertainty in Science and Politics: Lessons from the Presidential Election,* CSPO Commentary. Washington, D.C.: Center for Science Policy and Outcomes, at www.cspo.org/resources/news/may2001.html#commentary (accessed 11 August 2003).

Scally, W. 2003. "Bush Environmental Rollbacks Attacked by Senators." *Congressional Green Sheets,* January 17.

Schiller, W. 2000. *Partners and Rivals: Representation in U.S. Senate Delegations.* Princeton, N.J.: Princeton University Press.

Scott, J. C. 1998. *Seeing Like a State: How Certain Schemes to Improve the Human Condition Have Failed.* New Haven, Conn.: Yale University Press.

Schulze, E.-D., and H. A. Mooney, eds. 1994. *Biodiversity and Ecosystem Function.* New York: Springer-Verlag.

Sedjo, R. A., A. Goetzl, and S. O. Moffat. 1998. *Sustainability of Temperate Forests.* Washington, D.C.: Resources for the Future.

Sedjo, R. A., and S. K. Swallow. 2002. "Voluntary Eco-Labeling and the Price Premium." *Land Economics* 87(2):272–84.

Sensenig, T. S. 2002. *Development, Fire History, and Current and Past Growth of Old-Growth and Young-Growth Forest Stands in the Cascade, Siskiyou, and Mid-Coast Mountains of Southwestern Oregon.* Ph.D. diss., Oregon State University, Corvallis.

Sessions, J., K. N. Johnson, and B. Greeber. 1991. *Timber for Oregon's Tomorrow: The 1989 Update* (revision). Corvallis: Forest Research Lab, Oregon State University.

Shaffer, M. L. 1981. "Minimum Population Sizes for Species Conservation." *BioScience* 31:131–34.

Shannon, M. A. 1998. "Social Organizations and Institutions." In *River Ecology and Management: Lessons from the Pacific Coastal Ecoregion*, ed. R. J. Naiman and R. E. Bilby, 529–52. New York: Springer-Verlag.

———. 1999. "Moving from the Limits and Problems of Rational Planning: Toward a Collaborative and Participatory Planning Approach." In *International Seminar on the Formulation and Implementation of National Forest Programmes*, ed. P. Glück, G. Oesten, H. Schanz, and K.-R. Volz, 30(1):131–59. Joensuu, Finland: European Forest Institute.

———. 2002a. "Understanding Collaboration: Organizational Form, Negotiation Strategy, and Pathway to Multi-level Governance." In *National Forest Programs in a National Context*, ed. O. Gislerud and I. Neven, 44:9–27. Joensuu, Finland: European Forest Institute.

———. 2002b. "Theoretical Approaches to Understanding Intersectoral Policy Integration." In *Cross Sectoral Impacts on Forests*, ed. I. Tikkanan, P. Glueck, and H. Pajouja 46:15–26. Joensuu, Finland: European Forest Institute.

———. 2002c. "Future Visions: Landscape Planning in Places That Matter." In *Landscape Futures: Social and Institutional Dimensions*, ed. J. Graham, I. Reeve, and D. Brunckhorst. Armidale, Australia: Institute for Rural Futures, University of New England (ISBN 1 86389 811 5 on CD-ROM).

———. 2003a. "Social Aspects: Roles of Actors, Participatory Processes, and New Governance Institutions." In *Cross-Sectoral Policy Impacts between Forestry and Other Sectors—Policy and Legal, Economic, Environmental Accounting and Social Aspects*, ed. Y. Dube and F. Schmithusen. Policy and Institutions Branch, Policy and Planning Division, Forestry Department. Rome, Italy: UN Food and Agriculture Organization.

———. 2003b. "The Use of Participatory Approaches, Methods and Techniques in the Elaboration of Integrated Management Plans." In *The Formulation of Integrated Management Plans for Mountain Forests*, ed. G. Buttoud, M. A. Shannon, G. Weiss, and I. Yunusova. Turin, Italy: University of Torino.

Shannon, M. A., and K. N. Johnson. 1994. "Lessons from FEMAT." *Journal of Forestry* 92:6–7.

Shannon, M. A., E. E. Meideinger, and R. N. Clark. 1996. "Science Advocacy Is Inevitable: Deal with It." Society of American Foresters annual meeting, November 11, 1996, Albuquerque, N.M.

Simon, H. 1986. "Rationality in Psychology and Economics." In *The Behavioral Foundations of Economic Theory*, ed. R. M. Hogarth and M. W. Reder, *Journal of Business* (supplement) 59:209–24.

Sinclair, B. 2000a. *Unorthodox Lawmaking: New Legislative Processes in the U.S. Congress.* Washington, D.C.: CQ Press.

——. 2000b. "Individualism, Partisanship, and Cooperation in the Senate." In *Esteemed Colleagues: Civility and Deliberation in the U.S. Senate*, ed. B. Loomis. Washington, D.C.: Brookings.

Smith, A. D. 1994. "Programmatic Consultation under the Endangered Species Act: An Anatomy of the Salmon Habitat Litigation." *Journal of Environmental Law and Litigation* 11:247–329.

Smith, J. E., R. Molina, M. M. P. Huso, and M. J. Larsen. 2000. "Occurrence of *Piloderma fallax* in Young, Rotation-Age, and Old-Growth Stands of Douglas Fir (*Pseudotsuga menziesii*) in the Cascade Range of Oregon, USA." *Canadian Journal of Botany* 7:995–1001.

Social Learning Group, ed. 2001a. *Learning to Manage Global Environmental Risks, Volume 1: A Functional Analysis of Social Responses to Climate Change, Ozone Depletion, and Acid Rain.* Cambridge, Mass.: MIT Press.

Social Learning Group, ed. 2001b. *Learning to Manage Global Environmental Risks, Volume 2: A Comparative History of Social Responses to Climate Change, Ozone Depletion, and Acid Rain.* Cambridge, Mass.: MIT Press.

Society of American Foresters. 1958. *Forestry Terminology.* Bethesda, Md.

Sohngen, B. L., and R. W. Haynes. 1994. *The "Great" Price Spike of '93: An Analysis of Lumber and Stumpage Prices in the Pacific Northwest* (Research Paper PNW-RP-476). Portland, Ore.: USDA, Forest Service, PNW Research Station.

Soule, M. E., and M. Sanjayan. 1998. "Conservation Targets: Do They Help?" *Science* 279:2060–61.

Soule, M. E., and J. Terborgh, eds. 1999. *Continental Conservation.* Washington, D.C.: Island Press.

Spies, T. A., G. H. Reeves, K. M. Burnett, W. C. McComb, K. N. Johnson, G. Grant, J. L. Ohmann, S. L. Garman, and P. Bettinger. 2002a. "Assessing the Ecological Consequences of Forest Policies in a Multi-Ownership Province in Oregon." In *Integrating Landscape Ecology into Natural Resource Management*, ed. J. Liu and W. W. Taylor, 179–207). New York: Cambridge University Press.

Spies, T. A., K. N. Johnson, R. Reeves, P. Bettinger, M. T. McGrath, R. Pabst, and K. Olson. 2002b. *An Evaluation of Tradeoffs between Wood Production and Ecological Integrity in the Oregon Coast Range*. Portland, Ore.: U.S. Forest Service, Pacific Northwest Forest and Range Experiment Station.

Stanfield, B. J., J. C. Bliss, and T. A. Spies. 2002. "Land Ownership and Landscape Structure: Spatial Analysis of 66 Oregon Coast Watersheds." *Landscape Ecology* 17:685–97.

Stankey, G. H., B. T. Bormann, C. Ryan, B. Shindler, V. Sturtevant, R. N. Clark, and C. Philpot. 2003. "Adaptive Management and the Northwest Forest Plan." *Journal of Forestry* 101(1):40–51.

Stark, F. P. 2003. *Extension of Remarks on the Health Forests Restoration Act of 2003*. Cong. Rec. 21 May 2003: E1031.

State of Oregon. 1997. Senate Bill 360, the Oregon Forestland-Urban Interface Fire Protection Act of 1997.

Steel, B., D. Lach, P. List, and B. Shindler. 2001. "The Role of Scientists in the Natural Resource Policy Process: A Comparison of Canadian and American Publics." *Journal of Environmental Systems* 28(2):135–57.

Strittholt, J. R., R. F. Noss, P. A. Frost, K. Vance-Borland, C. Carroll, and G. Hellman Jr. 1999. *A Science-Based Conservation Assessment for the Klamath-Siskiyou Region*. Corvallis, Ore.: Earth Design Consultants and the Conservation Biology Institute.

Stroup, R. L. 1995. *The Endangered Species Act: Making Innocent Species the Enemy* (PERC Policy Series PS-3). Bozeman, Mont.: Political Economy Research Center.

Stroup, R. L., and Shaw, J. S. 2003. "Technology and the Protection of Endangered Species." In *The Half-Life of Policy Rationales: How New Technology Affects Old Policy Issues*, ed. F. Foldvary and D. Klein. New York: Cato Institute/New York University Press.

Sullivan, W. 1983. "Beyond Policy Science: The Social Sciences as Moral Sciences." In *Social Science as Moral Inquiry*, ed. N. Haan, R. N. Bellah, P. Rabinow, and W. Sullivan. New York: Columbia University Press.

Swanson, F. J., J. L. Clayton, W. F. Megahan, and G. Bush. 1989. "Erosional Processes and Long-Term Site Productivity." In *Maintaining the Long-Term Productivity of Pacific Northwest Forest Ecosystems*, ed. D. A. Perry, R. Meurisse, B. Thomas, R. Miller, J. Boyle, J. Means, C. R. Perry, and R. F. Powers, 67–81. Portland, Ore.: Timber Press.

Swanson, F. J., and S. Greene. 1999. "Perspectives on Scientists and Science in Bioregional Assessments." In *Bioregional Assessments: Science at the Crossroads of Management and Policy*, ed. K. N. Johnson, F. J. Swanson, M. Herring, and S. Greene, 55–69. Washington, D.C.: Island Press.

Swetnam, T., C. Allen, and J. Betancourt. 1999. "Applied Historical Ecology: Using the Past to Manage for the Future." *Ecological Applications* 9(4):1189–1206.

Tanaka, J. A., G. L. Starr, and T. M. Quigley. 1995. *Strategies and Recommendations for Addressing Forest Health Issues in the Blue Mountains of Oregon and Washington* (General Technical Report GTR-350 94-156). Portland, Ore.: USDA Forest Service, Pacific Northwest Research Station.

Tappeiner, J. C., D. Huffman, D. Marshall, T. A. Spies, and J. D. Bailey. 1997a. "Density, Ages, and Growth Rates in Old-Growth and Young-Growth Douglas Fir in Coastal Oregon." *Canadian Journal of Forest Research* 27:638–48.

Tappeiner, J. C., D. Lavender, J. Walstad, R. O. Curtis, and D. S. DeBell. 1997b. "Silvicultural Systems and Regeneration Methods: Current Practices and New Alternatives." In *Creating a Forestry for the 21st Century*, ed. K. Kohm and J. F. Franklin, 151–64. Washington, D.C.: Island Press.

Taylor, S. 1984. *Making Bureaucracies Think.* Stanford, Calif.: Stanford University Press.

Taylor, A. H., and C. N. Skinner. 1998. "Fire History and Landscape Dynamics in a Late-Successional Reserve, Klamath Mountains, California, USA." *Forest Ecology and Management* 111:285–301.

Teensma, P. D., J. T. Rienstra, and M. A. Yeiter. 1991. *Preliminary Reconstruction and Analysis of Change in Forest Stand Age Classes of the Oregon Coast Range from 1850 to 1940* (Technical Note T/N OR-9). Portland, Ore.: USDI Bureau of Land Management.

Terborgh, J., and M. E. Soule. 1999. "Why We Need Megareserves: Large-Scale Reserve Networks and How to Design Them." In *Continental Conservation*, ed. M. E. Soule and J. Terborgh, 199–209. Washington, D.C.: Island Press.

Thomas, J. W. 1994. "FEMAT: Objectives, Processes, and Options." *Journal of Forestry* 92:12–20.

Thomas, J. W. 2000. "What Now? From a Former Chief of the Forest Service." In *A Vision for the Forest Service: Goals for its Next Century*, ed. R. A. Sedjo, 10–44. Washington, D.C.: Resources for the Future.

Thomas, J. W., E. D. Forsman, J. B. Lint, E. C. Meslow, B. R. Noon, and J. Verner. 1990. *A Conservation Strategy for the Northern Spotted Owl: A Report of the Interagency Scientific Committee to Address the Conservation of the Northern Spotted Owl.* Portland, Ore.: U.S. Department of Agriculture, Forest Service; U.S. Department of the Interior, Bureau of Land Management, Fish and Wildlife Service, National Park Service.

Thomas, J. W., M. G. Raphael, R. G. Anthony, E. D. Forsman, A. G. Gunderson, R. S. Holthausen, B. G. Marcot, G. H. Reeves, J. R. Sedell, and D. M. Solis. 1993. *Viability Assessments and Management Considerations for Species Associated with Late-Succession and Old-Growth Forests of the Pacific Northwest: The Report of the Scientific Analysis Team.* Washington, D.C.: U.S. Department of Agriculture, National Forest System, Forest Service Research.

Thompson, B. H. 1997. "The Endangered Species Act: A Case Study in Takings and Incentives." *Stanford Law Review* 49:305, 344–45.

Tobin, R. J. 1990. *The Expendable Future: U. S. Politics and the Protection of Biological Diversity.* Durham, N.C.: Duke University Press.

Torgerson, D. 1999. *The Promise of Green Politics: Environmentalism and the Public Sphere.* Durham, N.C.: Duke University Press.

Torrance, W. E. F. in press. "Science or Salience: Building an Agenda for Climate Change." In *Global Environmental Assessments: Information, Institutions, and Influence,* ed. R. B. Mitchell, W. C. Clark, D. W. Cash, and F. Alcock. Cambridge, Mass.: MIT Press.

Tuchmann, E. T., K. Connaughton, L. Freedman, and C. Moriwaki. 1996. *The Northwest Forest Plan: A Report to the President and Congress.* Portland, Ore.: USDA Forest Service, Pacific Northwest Research Station.

Tully, M. 2001. "Democrats Take the Wheel in the Senate as Talks Continue on Ground Rules." *CQ Today Monitor News,* June 6.

Turner, M. G. 1989. "Landscape Ecology: The Effect of Pattern on Process." *Annual Review of Ecology and Systematics* 20:171–97.

Twight, B. 1983. *Organizational Values and Political Power: The Forest Service versus Olympic National Park.* University Park: Pennsylvania State University Press.

USDA Forest Service. (U.S. Department of Agriculture—Forest Service). 1950–1976 (annual). Oregon Log Production. Portland, Ore.: Pacific Northwest Forest & Range Experiment Station.

USDA/USDI (U.S. Department of Agriculture—Forest Service, and U.S. Department of the Interior—Bureau of Land Management). 1994a. *Record of Decision for Amendments to Forest Service and Bureau of Land Management Planning Documents within the Range of the Northern Spotted Owl & Standards and Guidelines for Management of Habitat for Late-Successional and Old-Growth Forest Related Species within the Range of the Northern Spotted Owl.* Portland, Ore.: USDA Forest Service and USDI BLM.

———. 1994b. *Final Supplemental Environmental Impact Statement on Management of Habitat for Late-Successional and Old-Growth Forest*

Related Species within the Range of the Northern Spotted Owl. Portland, Oregon.

USDA/USDI (U.S. Department of Agriculture—Willamette National Forest; U.S. Department of the Interior—Salem District, Bureau of Land Management; and U.S. Department of the Interior—Fish and Wildlife Service). 1998. *Mid-Willamette Late-Successional Reserve Assessment.* Available in PDF format from the Willamette National Forest, 211 E. 7th Ave., Eugene, Ore. 97401.

USDI (U.S. Department of the Interior, Fish and Wildlife Service). 1990. "Endangered and Threatened Wildlife and Plants: Determination of Threatened Status for the Northern Spotted Owl." *Federal Register* 55:26114–94.

———. 1992. *Recovery Plan for the Northern Spotted Owl: Draft.* Portland, Oregon.

———. 1994, February 4. *Biological Opinion on Alternative 9* (FEIS) 47.

———. 2000, February 14. *Formal and Informal Programmatic Consultation on FY 2000 Routine Habitat Modification Projects within the Willamette Province* [1-7-00-F-155] 2–3.

USFS (U.S. Forest Service). n.d. "A Brief History of the Willamette National Forest," at www.fs.fed.us/r6/willamette/forest/history/index.html (accessed 11 August 2003).

———. 1995a. *Fire Economics Assessment Report.* Washington, D.C.: USDA Forest Service.

———. 1995b. *Course to the Future: Positioning Fire and Aviation Management.* Washington, D.C.: USDA Forest Service.

———. 2001. *Blue Mountain Demonstration Area Charter,* at www.fs.fed.us/bluemountains/docs/charter.htm (accessed 11 August, 2003).

———. 2002a, June. *The Process Predicament: How Statutory, Regulatory, and Administrative Factors Affect National Forest Management.* Washington, D.C.: U.S. Forest Service. Available online at www.fs.fed.us/projects/documents (accessed 11 August 2003).

———. 2002b, July. *Factors Affecting Timely Mechanical Fuel Treatment Decisions.* Washington, D.C.: U.S. Forest Service.

———. 2003a, February 4. *Fiscal Year 2004 President's Budget: USDA Forest Service.*

———. 2003b, January. *Biscuit Post-Fire Assessment: Rogue River and Siskiyou National Forests, Josephine and Curry Counties, Oregon,* at www.biscuitfire.com (accessed 11 August 2003).

USFS/BLM (U.S. Forest Service and Bureau of Land Management). 2002. *National Forests and Bureau of Land Management Districts within the Range* of the Northern Spotted Owl; Western Oregon and Washington, and North-western California; Removal of Survey and Manage Mitigation Measure Standards and Guidelines. Federal Register 67 No. 203 (October 21), 64601.

USFS/USDI (U.S. Forest Service and U.S. Department of the Interior). 2000, September 8. Managing the Impact of Wildfires on Communities and the Environment: A Report to the President in Response to the Wildfires of 2000. Washington, D.C.: U.S. Forest Service/U.S. Department of the Interior. Available online at www.fireplan.gov/contents/reports/?LanguageID=1 (accessed 11 August 2003).

———. 2002. "National Environmental Policy Act Documentation Needed for Fire Management Activities: Categorical Exclusions." Federal Register 67 No. 241 (December 16) 77038.

USFWS (U.S. Fish and Wildlife Service). 2002, October 11. Letter from Director FWS and Dr. William T. Hogarth, Assistant Administrator for Fisheries, National Oceanic and Atmospheric Administration to Regional Directors, Regions 1–7 and California and Nevada Operations, and Regional Administrators, NOAA Fisheries.

———. 2003. Threatened and endangered species system, at http://ecos.fws.gov/tess_public/TESSWebpageDelisted?listings=0 (accessed 11 August 2003).

USFWS/NMFS (U.S. Fish and Wildlife Service and National Marine Fisheries Service). 1998. Endangered Species Act Consultation Handbook: Procedures for Conducting Section 7 Consultations and Conferences.

U.S. Senate. 1998. Columbia Basin Ecosystem Management Plan. Joint Hearing before the Subcommittee of the Department of the Interior and Related Agencies Committee on Appropriations, United States Senate and the Subcommittee on Forests and Public Lands Management, Committee on Energy and Natural Resources, 105th Congress. S. Hrg. 105-906 (May 28). Washington, D.C.: U.S. Government Printing Office.

———. 2003a. Proposed Fiscal Year 2004 Budget Request for the Forest Service. Hearing before the Committee on Energy and Natural Resources, 108th Congress. S. Hrg. 108-7 (February 13). Washington, D.C.: U.S. Government Printing Office.

———. 2003b. Fire Preparedness toward the 2003 Fire Season. Hearing before the Energy and Natural Resources Committee, 108th Congress. Washington, D.C.: U.S. Government Printing Office.

Van Dijk, T. A. 1997. Discourse as Social Interaction. London: Sage.

VanDeveer, S. D. in press. "Assessment Information in European Politics: East and West." In Global Environmental Assessments: Information, Institutions, and Influence, ed. R. B. Mitchell, W. C. Clark, D. W. Cash, and F. Alcock. Cambridge, Mass.: MIT Press.

Wall, B. R. 1972. *Log Production in Washington and Oregon: An Historical Perspective* (Research Bulletin PNW-42). Portland, Ore.: Pacific Northwest Forest & Range Experiment Station.

Waring, R. H., and J. F. Franklin. 1979. "Evergreen Coniferous Forests of the Pacific Northwest." *Science* 204:1380–86.

Warren, D. D. 2002. *Harvest, Employment, Exports, and Prices in Pacific Northwest Forests, 1965–2000* (PNW-GTR-547). Portland, Ore.: USDA Forest Service Pacific Northwest Research Station.

Waters, J. R., K. S. McKelvey, D. L. Luoma, and C. J. Zabel. 1997. "Truffle Production in Old-Growth and Mature Fir Stands in Northeastern California." *Forest Ecology and Management* 96:155–66.

Watson, R. T., and the Core Writing Team. 2001. *Climate Change 2001: Synthesis Report, Summary for Policymakers: An Assessment of the Intergovernmental Panel on Climate Change.* Geneva, Switzerland: IPCC Secretariat.

Weatherspoon, C. P., and C. N. Skinner. 1995. "An Assessment of Factors Associated with Damage to Tree Crowns from the 1987 Wildfires in Northern California." *Forest Science* 41:430–51.

Weick, K. E. 1990. "The Nontraditional Quality of Organizational Learning." *Organization Science* 2(1).

Wells, G. 1999. *The Tillamook: A Created Forest Comes of Age.* Corvallis: Oregon State University Press.

Weyl, W. E. 1912. *The New Democracy.* New York: Macmillan.

WGA (Western Governors' Association). 2002. "Improving Forest and Rangeland Ecosystem Health in the West." WGA Policy Resolution 02–09, at www.westgov.org/wga/policy/02/index.htm (accessed 11 August 2003).

———. 2000. "Prescribed Fire on Federal Lands in the West." WGA Policy Resolution 00-029, at www.westgov.org/wga/policy/00/00029.htm (accessed 11 August 2003).

Whitlock, C. 1992. "Vegetational and Climatic History of the Pacific Northwest during the Last 20,000 Years: Implications for Understanding Present-Day Biodiversity." *Northwest Environmental Journal* 8:5–28.

Whitlock, C., and M. A. Knox. 2002. "Prehistoric Burning in the Pacific Northwest." In *Fire, Native Peoples, and the Natural Landscape,* ed. T. R. Vale, 195–231. Washington, D.C.: Island Press.

Whitlock, C., S. L. Shafer, and J. Marlon. 2003. "The Role of Climate and Vegetation Change in Shaping Past and Future Fire Regimes in the Northwestern United States and Implications for Ecosystem Management." *Forest Ecology and Management* 178:5–21.

Wiener, A. A. 1982. *The Forest Service Timber Appraisal System: A Historical Perspective, 1891–1981* (unpublished). Washington, D.C.: Timber Management Section, USDA Forest Service.

Wilcove, D. S. 1994. "Turning Conservation Goals into Tangible Results: The Case of the Spotted Owl and Old-Growth Forests." In *Large-Scale Ecology and Conservation Biology*, ed. P. J. Edwards, R. M. May, and N. R. Webb, 313–29. London: Blackwell.

———. 1998. "The Promise and the Disappointment of the Endangered Species Act." *New York University Environmental Law Journal* 6:277–78.

Wildavsky, A. 1964. *The Politics of the Budgetary Process*. Boston: Little, Brown.

———. 1987. "Choosing Preferences by Constructing Institutions: A Cultural Theory of Preference Formation." *American Political Science Review* 81(1):3–21.

Wilkinson, C. F. 1992. *Crossing the Next Meridian*. Washington, D.C.: Island Press.

Williams, M. 1992. *Americans and Their Forests: A Historical Geography*. New York: Cambridge University Press.

Wolfe, J. A. 1968. "Neogene Floristic and Vegetational History of the Pacific Northwest." *Madrono* 20:83–110.

Yaffee, S. L. 1982. *Prohibitive Policy: Implementing the Federal Endangered Species Act 57*. Cambridge, Mass.: MIT Press.

———. 1994. *The Wisdom of the Spotted Owl: Policy Lessons for a New Century*. Washington, D.C.: Island Press.

Yaffee, S. L., and J. M. Wondolleck. 1997. "Building Bridges across Agency Boundaries." In *Creating A Forestry for the 21st Century: The Science of Ecosystem Management*, eds. K. A. Kohm and J. F. Franklin, 381–396. Washington, D.C.: Island Press.

Yankelovich, D. 1991. *Coming to Public Judgment: Making Democracy Work in a Complex World*. Syracuse, N.Y.: Syracuse University Press.

Yoakum, J., and W. P. Dasmann. 1971. "Habitat Manipulation Practices." In *Wildlife Management Techniques*, ed. R. H. Giles, 173–231. Washington, D.C.: Wildlife Society.

Zaharaidis, N. 1999. "Ambiguity, Time, and Multiple Streams." In *Theories of the Policy Process*, ed. Paul Sabatier, 73–93. Boulder, Colo.: Westview.

Court Cases

City of Tenakee Springs v. Block, 778 F.2d 1402 (9th Cir. 1985).
Connor v. Burford, 848 F.2d 1441 (9th Cir. 1988).

Conservation Law Fnd. et al. v. Federal Hwy. Admin. et al., 827 F.Supp. 871, 881 (D. RI. 1993).

Daubert v. Merrill Dow Pharmaceuticals, Inc., 509 U.S. 579 (1993).

Enos v. Marsh, 769 F.2d 1363, (9th Cir. 1985).

Gifford Pinchot Task Force v. U.S. Fish and Wildlife Service, Civ. No. C00-5462-FDB (W.D. Wash.), on appeal, No. 03–35279 (9th Cir.).

Idaho Sporting Congress v. Rittenhouse, 305 F.3d 957 (9th Cir. 2002).

Inland Empire Public Lands Council v. U.S. Forest Service, 88 F.3d 754, 760 (9th Cir. 1996).

Lane County Audubon Society v. Jamison, 958 F.2d 290 (9th Cir. 1992).

North Slope Borough v. Andrus, 642 F.2d 589 (D.C. Cir. 1980).

Northern Spotted Owl v. Hodel, 716 F. Supp. 479 (W.D. Wash. 1988).

Oregon Natural Resources Council Action v. U.S. Forest Service, 59 F. Supp. 2d 1085 (W.D. Wash. 1999).

Pacific Coast Federation of Fishermen's Associations v. National Marine Fisheries Service, 71 F. Supp.2d 1063 (W.D. Wash. 1999).

Pacific Rivers Council v. Thomas, 30 F.3d 1050 (9th Cir. 1994).

Seattle Audubon Society v. Evans, 771 F. Supp. 1081 (W.D. Wash. 1991).

Seattle Audubon Society v. Lyons (1994), 871 F. Supp. 1291.

Tennessee Valley Authority v. Hill (1978). 437 U. S. 153, 180.

Thomas v. Peterson, 753 F.2d 754 (9th Cir. 1985).

Index

San Diego fairy shrimp, 205
San Francisco, development
    impact on forests, xxv
Sanjayan, M., 37
saproxylic insects, 30
Sarewitz, Daniel, 149, 150
SAT. *See* Scientific Assessment
    Team (SAT)
scarcity, politics of, 224–26
Schurz, Carl, 52
science, 145, 288; captive
    breeding, 209; as component
    of forest policy, 143;
    conservation, 44–46;
    definition, 144; forest science,
    242–44; as foundation for
    NWFP, 128, 144;
    multidisciplinary, 228, 231,
    234; and policy making, xl–xli,
    113–18, 122–26, 140–42, 143;
    and politics, 128, 144, 253; and
    postmodernism, 260–61;
    process for assessing
    consistency with NWFP
    standards, 134–38; role of, 259;
    and viable populations, 130–31
Scientific Assessment Team
    (SAT), 8–9, 11
scientific information, 146,
    147–48, 150–52
Section 7 consultations, 175;
    flowchart of formal process,
    179*f*11.2; flowchart of informal
    process, 178*f*11.1;
    programmatic basis, 176–77;
    site-specific basis, 176
Section 318 timber sales, 241,
    254–55*n*1
Sedell, James, 10
Sedjo, Roger A., xl, 68–93
seedlings, 59

SEIS. *See* Supplemental
    Environmental Impact
    Statement (SEIS)
selection harvesting, 40, 41
senescence, 29
September 11, *2001,* 246
Sessions, John, 57
SFI. *See* Sustainable Forestry
    Initiative (SFI)
Shannon, Margaret, xlii, 256–79,
    288–89
shorebirds, 32
Sierra Club, 148–49
Sierra Club Legal Defense Fund,
    205
silviculture, 41–42, 44, 50, 51
site-specific analysis, 176–77, 181,
    187–90, 216–17
Sitka spruce, xxv
small-fuels reduction project,
    287
Smith, Arthur D., 191
Snake River chinook, 235
social valuation, 275–76, 277
soil, characteristics of, xxv–xxvi
Soule, Michael E., 37
The Sovereign Land, 229–30
species: biotic interactions of,
    xxvi; cost of protection of,
    219–20; implementation
    failure, 139; security of,
    131–32; standards for, 129–34,
    135
staggered setting logging, 25–26
Stahl, Andy, 205
standardization, 273–74
standards, 141; for forest
    management and species
    protection, 129–34; science
    process for assessing, 134–38;
    of species security, 132–33

diameter of timber from, 61; federal forests, 53–54; from *1965–1999*, xxxv*f*1.1; government subsidies for, xxxiv; limited by policy decisions, 53; nonfederal forests, 54–57; Oregon, 55–58; relationship to biodiversity, 64–65; scheduling and projection models of, 67*n*2; technological innovations in, xxxii–xxxiii; under 2000 Willamette BiOp, 182–84; under NWFP, 48, 49; under sustained yield model, 52
timber yields: impact of ESA on, 5; under NWFP, 14–16, 19
topography, xxv–xxvi
tornado politics, 145, 147–48, 149–50, 152*n*1
trade, timber market, xxxi
transparency, 288, 289–90, 291*n*3
tree age classes, 65
tree maturity, 49
trophic cascading, xxvi–xxviii, xxix
Turner, John, 7

umbrella species, 30
UN Conference on Environment and Development, 72
understory growth, 40
United Nations, 72
United States, challenges to sustainable forestry, 79–81
University of Maine, 78
upslope areas, 39
urban-wildland interface areas, 20
U.S. Fish and Wildlife Service (FWS), 5, 128, 129, 174, 177;

consultation process, 177–80; and CRCs, 206–7; and fuels reduction projects, 293; and land use rulings, 198, 213*n*2; prices of resources used to protect species, 202–4; veto power of biologists in, 206–7; and Willamette Province BiOp, 182–84
U.S. Forest Service, xxxii, 24, 174, 245; allowable cut concept, 69; approval of Blue Mountain Demonstration Area, 228; case law and programmatic consultations, 184–87; effectiveness of, 272; effects of appeals and litigation, 246, 255*n*4; implementation of survey-and-manage requirements, 139; logging of old-growth habitat, 189–90; monitoring of MIS, 135; objectives of, 80; and politics, xxxvi–xxviii; preparation of BA, 177–78; preparation of BiOp, 175; request for species list, 177; Section 7 consultation, 175; standard for spotted owls and old-growth species, 132–33; timber offerings, 57. *See also* demographic studies, spotted owl; viability standard
Utah, landowner plan to encourage wild game, 211

valleys of Coast Range, xxv
valuation, 275–76
variable retention harvest system (VRHS), 40, 41
Vennemun, Anne, 231

About the Contributors

Steven H. Ackers is a faculty research assistant with the Oregon Cooperative Fish and Wildlife Research Unit in the Department of Fish and Wildlife at Oregon State University. His duties include supervising seasonal biologists, managing, analyzing, and reporting the data, participating in regional analyses of spotted owl demography, consulting with Forest Service biologists, and collecting data in the field whenever possible. Previously, Ackers supervised a field crew for the Rocky Mountain Research Station in Flagstaff, Arizona. Ackers received a Ph.D. from Northern Arizona University in 1997, his M.S. at Utah State University in 1992, and B.S. at Oregon State University in 1986.

Frank Alcock is an assistant professor of political science at the New College of Florida and a research fellow for the Institutional Dimensions of Global Environmental Change project. His research interests include global environmental politics, the relationship between science and environmental policy and the political economy of natural resource industries. He is a coauthor of a number of recent journal articles and book chapters on science-policy interactions in environmental issue areas. Alcock spent over five years at the U.S. Department of Energy as a policy analyst/economist. He has a B.A. in Economics from SUNY–Binghamton and an M.A. in international affairs from George Washington University.

Karen Arabas is associate professor of geography in the Department of Environmental and Earth Sciences at Willamette University, Salem, Oregon. Her research interests include the vegetation dynamics of forests, focusing on human disturbance, fire, climate, and insects. She conducts her research in a variety of settings including the eastern North American serpentine barrens and the kipuka (forest islands) of central Oregon. She teaches courses including biogeography, forest ecology and policy, introductory environmental science, and water resources. She holds a Ph.D. in Geography from the Pennsylvania State University, a M.A. in Environmental and Resources Policy from George Washington University, and a B.A. from Wesleyan University.

John H. Beuter has been a forester and forest economist for over forty-five years. He is a fellow of the Society of American Foresters, and will serve as SAF's president in 2004. He also serves on the World Forestry Center governing board. As owner of Umpqua-Tualatin, Inc. in Corvallis, Oregon, he consults and manages his own forests. His professional specialties include forest management, valuation, resource analysis, forest economics and policy, and education. He has been a university professor, acting assistant secretary of agriculture, and research forester. He holds B.S. and M.S. degrees from Michigan State, and a Ph.D. from Iowa State.

Joe Bowersox is associate professor of politics in the Department of Politics at Willamette University, Salem, Oregon. His research focuses on questions of political legitimacy in environmental politics, policy, and law. He teaches courses in forest ecology and policy, environmental policy making, international environmental policy, environmental ethics, and law and public policy in both the Politics Department and Willamette's environmental science program. Dr. Bowersox has been an American Political

Science Association congressional fellow. He has published articles and chapters on environmental policy and environmental theory, and is coeditor (with John Martin Gillroy) of *The Moral Austerity of Environmental Decisionmaking* (Duke 2002).

Susan Jane Brown is the executive director of the Gifford Pinchot Task Force, a grassroots forest protection and advocacy organization in Vancouver, Washington. Susan Jane graduated from the Northwestern School of Law of Lewis and Clark College with a Juris Doctorate and the Certificate in Environmental and Natural Resources Law, and is an active member of the Washington State Bar. Since 1997, she has worked on the Gifford Pinchot National Forest (GPNF) in southwest Washington monitoring and litigating timber sales on the GPNF. Susan Jane is also actively involved in forest monitoring and litigation on national forests in eastern Oregon. Additionally, she is past editor of *Environmental Law.*

David W. Cash is a research associate at the Belfer Center for Science and International Affairs and lecturer in Environmental Science and Public Policy at Harvard University. He studies the interaction of science and the negotiation and development of environmental policy in a range of issues including climate change, biodiversity conservation and food security. His current work explores how to effectively build and maintain research, assessments and decision support systems for addressing issues of sustainability across multiple levels. He has specific interests in how information and decision-making systems can best support the management of cross-scale environmental risks. He has published articles in *Science, Technology, and Human Values,* and in *Global Environmental Change.*

William C. Clark is the Harvey Brooks Professor of International Science, Public Policy and Human Development at Harvard University's John F. Kennedy School of Government. Trained as an ecologist, his research focuses on the interactions of environment, development and security concerns in international affairs. Clark serves on the scientific advisory committees for the Science and

Technology for Sustainability Initiative, and the International Human Dimensions Programme on Global Environmental Change. He is coeditor of *The Earth Transformed by Human Action* (1990) and *Environment* magazine. Clark is a member of the U.S. National Academy of Sciences, and a recipient of the MacArthur Prize, the Humboldt Prize, and the Kennedy School's Carballo Award for excellence in teaching.

John A. Kitzhaber was born in Colfax, Washington, in 1947. He received a bachelor's degree from Dartmouth College and a medical degree from the University of Oregon Medical School. He practiced emergency medicine in Roseburg, Oregon, for thirteen years. His political career includes service in the Oregon House of Representatives (1979–1981) and the Oregon State Senate (1981–1993). In 1994 Kitzhaber was elected governor of Oregon, serving until 2003. Kitzhaber's political career has been marked by active leadership in the areas of public education, community development, and environmental stewardship.

Peter List is professor emeritus of philosophy at Oregon State University (OSU), where for many years he has been chair of the Philosophy Department, teaching courses on environmental ethics, contemporary ethics, sustainable forestry, and history of classical western philosophy. He is particularly interested in the application of systems of environmental ethics to land management, especially the land ethic of Aldo Leopold, and is editor of *Environmental Ethics and Forestry: A Reader* (2000). He is part of the sustainable forestry curriculum group at OSU and member of a social research group that most recently published an article in *Bioscience* on attitudes about advocacy and credibility of environmental scientists in natural resource management.

Ronald B. Mitchell is an associate professor of political science at the University of Oregon. His 1994 book, *Intentional Oil Pollution at Sea: Environmental Policy and Treaty Compliance*, received the International Studies 1995 Sprout Award for best book on international environmental politics. He has published in *International Organization, International Studies Quarterly, Global Gover-*

nance, and other journals, and he has contributed chapters to numerous edited volumes. He is a member of the National Research Council's Committee on Human Dimensions of Global Change and the editorial boards of *International Organization, Journal of Environment and Development,* and *Global Environmental Politics.*

David A. Perry is professor (emeritus) of ecosystem studies at the Oregon State University, an affiliate professor at the University of Hawaii (Hilo), and a Science Curriculum Specialist in the Center for Disability Learning, the University of Hawai'i (Manoa). He is also a program director at Malama Kukui Cultural Learning Center in Kohala, Hawaii. Perry received an M.S. degree in physics and a Ph.D. in ecology from Montana State University (1974). His research interests include the structure and function of ecosystems and landscapes, the role of biodiversity in ecosystem processes, interactions among ecological scales, sustainable ecosystem management, restoration ecology, and culturally responsive science education.

Roger A. Pielke Jr. joined the faculty of the University of Colorado in 2001 and is an associate professor in the environmental studies program and a fellow of the Cooperative Institute for Research in the Environmental Sciences (CIRES). At CIRES Roger serves as the director of the Center for Science and Technology Policy Research. He also serves as the director of graduate studies for the University's graduate program in environmental studies. Roger's current areas of interest include understanding the relations of science and politics, use and value of prediction in decision making, and policy education for scientists.

Daniel J. Rohlf is an associate professor at Lewis and Clark Law School. In addition, he serves as director of the Pacific Environmental Advocacy Center (PEAC), the law school's environmental law clinic. His teaching and scholarship center on management and conservation of biological diversity and the intersection of law and science. Rohlf has published and lectured widely on the Endangered Species Act. His caseload at PEAC also focuses primarily on endangered species issues, including extensive work on issues involving restoration of salmonids in the Columbia River Basin. Professor Rohlf earned his B.A. in geology from Colorado College and his J.D. from Stanford.

Roger A. Sedjo is a senior fellow and the director of the Forest Economics and Policy Program at Resources for the Future (RFF), a Washington-based policy research organization. He has written on forestry and environmental issues, having authored or edited fourteen books related to forestry, natural resources, and the environment. He was a member of the Secretary of Agriculture's Committee of Scientists, and has been a consultant to a wide array of organizations including The World Bank, the Global Environmental Facility, U.S. Agency for International Development, Harvard Institute for International Development, and others. Sedjo earned his B.A. and M.S. degrees at the University of Illinois, and a Ph.D. at the University of Washington.

Margaret A. Shannon is an associate professor in the University at Buffalo Law School, where she is the director for the environmental law concentration and coordinator of the Baldy Center Working Group on Environmental Stewardship. She is a *professor in honor* at the University of Freiburg Faculty of Forestry in Freiburg in Breisgau. Her research focuses on how the emergence of a participatory approach to developing natural resource policy that engages people and organizations in substantive, creative roles rather than reactive and passive roles is reforming environmental governance at all levels. She received her B.A. degree from the University of Montana, and M.S. and Ph.D. degrees in Wildland Resource Science from the University of California at Berkeley.

Richard L. Stroup is a senior associate with PERC in Bozeman, Montana and professor of economics at Montana State University. His Ph.D. is from the University of Washington. From 1982 to 1984, he directed the Office of Policy Analysis at the U.S. Department of the Interior. Mr. Stroup publishes and speaks widely on the economics of natural resource and environmental issues.

He recently published *Eco-nomics: What Everyone Should Know about Economics and the Environment,* and is coauthor with James D. Gwartney, Russell S. Sobel, and David Macpherson of a leading college economics textbook, *Economics Private and Public Choice,* now in its tenth edition.

Frederick J. Swanson is a geologist and ecosystem scientist with the U.S. Forest Service, Pacific Northwest Research Station, and Professor (courtesy) in the Departments of Forest Science and Geoscience, Oregon State University. He has studied the interactions of physical processes with forest and stream ecosystems. With the USFS he has developed landscape management plans based in part on the historic wildfire regime. He has also participated in the Forest Ecosystem Management Assessment Team, which developed the framework for the Northwest Forest Plan, and has been a codeveloper of the conference and resulting book, "Bioregional Assessments: Science at the Crossroads of Management and Policy."

Bob Pepperman Taylor is professor of political science and dean of the John Dewey Honors Program at the University of Vermont. He is also the author of *Our Limits Transgressed: Environmental Political Thought in America, America's Bachelor Uncle: Henry Thoreau and American Polity,* and coeditor (with Ben Minteer) of *Democracy and the Claims of Nature: Critical Perspectives for a New Century.*

Jack Ward Thomas is the Boone and Crockett Professor of Wildlife Conservation at the University of Montana (Missoula). His career as a research wildlife biologist began in 1957. While working for the Forest Service from 1966 until 1993, he was leader of the Interagency Scientific Committee to Address Conservation of the Spotted Owl, the Scientific Assessment Team, and was appointed leader for the Forest Ecosystem Management Assessment Team (FEMAT) by the president of the United States in early 1993. In 1993, Dr. Thomas was appointed chief of the U.S. Forest Service, serving through 1996. Dr. Thomas has authored over 500 research and management publications.